Post-Continental Philosophy

TRANSVERSALS
NEW DIRECTIONS IN PHILOSOPHY

SERIES EDITOR
Keith Ansell Pearson, University of Warwick

CONSULTANT EDITORS
Eric Alliez, Richard Beardsworth, Howard Caygill, Gary Genosko, Elisabeth Grosz, Michael Hardt, Diane Morgan, John Mullarkey, Paul Patton, Stanley Shostak, Isabelle Stengers, James Williams, David Wood.

Transversals explores the most exciting collisions within contemporary thought, as philosophy encounters nature, materiality, time, technology, science, culture, politics, art and everyday life. The series aims to present work which is both theoretically innovative and challenging, while retaining a commitment to rigour and clarity and to the power and precision of thought.

Philosophy in the Age of Science and Capital	Gregory Dale Adamson
Intensive Science and Virtual Philosophy	Manuel DeLanda
Félix Guattari: An Aberrant Introduction	Gary Genosko
Political Physics: Deleuze, Derrida and the Body Politic	John Protevi
The Idea of Pure Critique	Iain Mackenzie
Abstract Sex: Philosophy, Bio-technology and the Mutations of Desire	Luciana Parisi
Post-Continental Philosophy: An Outline	John Mullarkey
Philosophies of Nature after Schelling	Iain Hamilton Grant

POST-CONTINENTAL PHILOSOPHY

AN OUTLINE

JOHN MULLARKEY

continuum

Continuum International Publishing Group
The Tower Building, 11 York Road, London, SE1 7NX
80 Maiden Lane, Suite 704, New York, NY 10038
www.continuumbooks.com

© John Mullarkey 2006

All rights reserved. No part of this publication may be reproduced
or transmitted in any form or by any means, electronic or mechanical, including
photocopying, recording, or any information storage or retrieval system,
without prior permission in writing from the publishers.

John Mullarkey has asserted his right under the Copyright, Designs and Patents
Act, 1988, to be identified as Author of this work

British Library Cataloguing-in-Publication Data
A catalogue record for this book is available from the British Library.

ISBN: ISBN 0-8264-6462-9 (HB) ISBN 0-8264-6461-0 (PB)

Library of Congress Cataloging-in-Publication Data
A catalog record for this book is available from the Library of Congress.

Typeset by Fakenham Photosetting Ltd
Printed and bound in Great Britain by MPG Books Ltd, Bodmin, Cornwall

To Laura and the two James,
James I and James II

Contents

Acknowledgements

I would like to express my appreciation to all those who have helped in the growth of this book over the last six years, who have either listened to its ideas or read through its arguments, always responding with generosity each time: Keith Ansell Pearson, Andrew Atkin, Miriam Baldwin, Stella Baraklianou (for teaching me about Lacan and much else), Miguel Beistegui, Ray Brassier, James Burton, Justin Clemens, Claire Colebrook, Robin Durie, Pete Gunter, Peter Hallward (for helping me track down Badiou's latest texts), Wahida Khandker, Maria Lakka (for her infinite defence of the virtual), Paul-Antoine Miquel, David Morris, Christopher Norris, Brian O'Conner, Anna Powell, John Protevi, Mark Richardson, Naomi Salaman, Ole-Martin Skilleås, Brian Smith, Dan Smith and Frédéric Worms (a true Bergsonian in every sense). I'd also like to thank all those who made up the various audiences at talks in Bergen, Cardiff, Cork, Dublin, Dundee, Durham, Edinburgh, Goldsmiths London, Manchester, Nice, Sunderland, and Warwick, whether they asked any questions or were simply dumbfounded: they also serve who only sit and wait for deferred enlightenment. In addition, those at Continuum Press who have helped this project along – especially Tristan Palmer who guided its inception and Sarah Douglas who patiently saw it through its last days and gave me access to the English proofs of *Being and Event* – deserve a huge amount of credit. Tim Clark's copy-editing and John Sargant's proofreading improved it greatly.

A special indebtedness is to those whose academic support has also been mixed with friendship during some difficult times. Duane Davis in particular allowed me to test these ideas on an unsuspecting audience at the University of North Carolina at Asheville in 2005 with marvellous results (as well as the discovery of how good Scottish whisky and Leonard Cohen's music can be). In the summer of 2003, Len Lawlor invited me to give a talk at the *Collegium Phaenomenologicum* in Umbria at a crucial stage of development: the encouragement I received there reassured me that I wasn't going completely mad. A similar mix of collegial support and friendship has always come from Barbara Muriel Kennedy at Staffordshire University. And, of course, my colleagues at both Sunderland and Dundee Universities have also shared the burden, no matter how vicariously: James Williams, Rachel Jones, Tim Chappell, Lily Forrester, Roger Young, David Over, Angela Smith, and especially Susan Mandala deserve all my gratitude and all your pity.

Further thanks must go to two people who were willing to share their time and work with me in a way that fundamentally helped the project: Alan Hook at Design, Technology and ICT, in the Institute of Education, Manchester, for his genius at turning my ideas about diagrams into three-dimensional reality, and Professor Alain Badiou for his generosity in allowing me early access to his *Logiques des mondes*.

Finally, I would like to mention the warm friendship I've received over the last few years from Beth Lord and Julie Bradford, without which things would have been much harder. Even more, however, is my indefinite debt to Laura Cull, whose constant supply of coffee, biscuits, intellectual companionship, and love have kept me alive for the last year. I dedicate this book to her, and also to the two best men that I know, my father James Mullarkey, and his grandson, my son, James Dallavalle Mullarkey.

Earlier versions of some of the material from Chapter 1 appeared in 'Deleuze and Materialism: One or Several Matters?', in *A Deleuzian Century?*, edited by Ian Buchanan, Duke University Press, 1999, pp. 59–83, and 'Forget the Virtual: Bergson, Actualism, and the Refraction of Reality', in *Continental Philosophy Review*, vol. 37 (2005), pp. 469–493. I gratefully acknowledge the permissions granted to use this material.

Introduction: 1988, Outlines of a Philosophical Event

This book may well have been written too early. It is not about something, or some idea, that has actually occurred as yet, an objective event. It is about something that is unfolding, an event in the making. The 'Post-' in 'Post-Continental' is not an accurate description of what is, but a prescription for what could be, an intervention into the contemporary reception of European thought in the Anglophone world. All the same, it is not completely subjective either: it has its roots or 'site' in the thoughts of four philosophers – Gilles Deleuze, Alain Badiou, Michel Henry and François Laruelle – who each represent a real change in the intellectual current, one that both retains and abandons parts of what previously went under the rubric of 'Continental philosophy'. Put simply, this change amounts to an embrace of absolute immanence over transcendence, the tendency of previous Franco-German thought being to make immanence supervene on transcendence. The book makes this hypothesis while also introducing the reader to some of the most interesting philosophy written over the last two decades by a set of thinkers who, with the exception of Deleuze, are only now becoming known outside of France. In addition to this, it looks at the very idea of philosophical immanence and its connection with metaphysics, while offering in conclusion a theory concerning the expression of thought within the regime of immanence. Whether any or all of this warrants the name of 'Post-Continental' or some other title is irrelevant: the primary wager being made is that an event is unfolding in philosophical thought and that we are presently witnessing its formative outlines.

Philosophically speaking, of course, there is no such thing as 'Continental philosophy' at all – this is both a sham geo-cultural distinction and a category error. There is not one philosophical theme that is exclusive to the European Continent, nor any outside the Continent that is confined to 'Anglo-American' philosophy. The mention of Continental philosophy also brings to mind its other ill-coined associate, 'Analytic philosophy'; but no methodological barrier exists between the two traditions either. In fact, it is extremely difficult to make any distinction stand up under historical, methodological, or philosophical scrutiny. That it continues to be used, and continues to have at least some intuitive appeal, however, must surely indicate some basis, if not in fact then at least in perception. There clearly is a division between departments, books (and book publishers), journals, conferences and personnel. But it is a question of names and representations. How philosophers see things. Proof? A Google search of the Internet (the nearest we have to God's eye view today) returns the following results: 'Žižek and Deleuze' (60 entries); 'Wittgenstein and Frege' (244 entries); 'Žižek and Frege' (no entries). Does this mean that Frege has nothing to say to Žižek? Not at all. Does this mean that language must be studied Janus-faced, once through the Lacanian Symbolic, once again through Logical Analysis, and that the findings from the two are totally incommensurate? Even less so.

It only means that there is a difference operating here between the actual and the virtual. The presence or absence of a host of actual properties, philosophical and non-philosophical, has been cited as a decisive causal factor in the origin and maintenance of the current partition in our discipline, some of them rather obvious, some less so. Among the more obvious we have national character, political history, geographical proximity, institutional procedure, the language barrier, methodology, or different philosophical interests; among the more subtle candidates are a difference in style or mood, different philosophical lineages (most often spawned by Frege and Husserl), the supposed fact that Analytic thought is uniquely objectivist, individualist and scientistic, or the supposed fact that Continental thought is uniquely subjectivist, collectivist and historicist. But most commentators agree, nevertheless, that this segregation neither fully succeeds nor fully fails to map clearly onto any geographical, historical, methodological, or philosophical difference.[1] These factors are, at best, *tendencies* or *tropisms* – directions more or less followed by both (after all, a Google search on 'Wittgenstein and Deleuze' does result in 12 references!). The difference, then, is virtual: it is precisely about the perceived differences between philosophies, in other words, a certain self-awareness or group-consciousness, that, misplaced or not, has actually engendered the difference between Continental and Analytic philosophy. It is at best a self-fulfilling prophecy. Or, to put it another way, the Analytic–Continental distinction is philosophically erroneous but metaphilosophically accurate: it has less to do with what philosophers think about when they philosophise than *where* they philosophise, with *whom* they talk about it, and *what* they say about it to each other.

This book, therefore, is an attempt at another kind of self-fulfilling prophecy. It concerns a new relationship between the perception of Continental philosophy and immanence. It examines the shift in European thought over the last twenty years through the work of four central figures, Deleuze, Henry, Badiou and Laruelle. Though they follow seemingly different methodologies and agendas, each insists upon the need for a return to the category of immanence if philosophy is to have any future at all. Rejecting both the phenomenological tradition of transcendence (of Consciousness, the Ego, Being, or Alterity), as well as the post-structuralist valorisation of Language, they instead take the immanent categories of biology (Deleuze), mathematics (Badiou), affectivity (Henry), and science (Laruelle) as focal points for a renewal of philosophy. Consequently, Continental philosophy is taken in a new direction that engages with naturalism with a refreshingly critical and non-reductive approach to the sciences of life, set theory, embodiment and knowledge. Taken together, these strategies amount to a rekindled faith in the possibility of philosophy as a worldly and materialist thinking.

Or that, at least, is what the book should be about: a clear periodisable movement in thought from bad old transcendence to good new immanence. Let me explain. Philosophers, like most others no doubt, like to feel that they are relevant, that they have a role in the world. And certainly, the interest in Deleuze and growing interest in Badiou, for instance, is partly related to their positive engagement with both the sciences and radical politics, something less obvious in Heidegger or Derrida, for instance. It is reassuring to see philosophy thinking with Leibniz *and* embryology *and* political resistance movements, or Plato *and* set theory *and* militant insurgency. Even where Michel Henry gains some renown through a connection with radical theology, he does so through a new thinking about the body and emotion first and foremost. Philosophy has seemingly come back down to earth from the inconsequential heavens of transcendence. Immanence means relevance, even when that relevance comes through the abstractions of mathematics (Badiou) or epistemology (Laruelle). As David Papineau puts it, 'nearly everybody nowadays wants to be a "naturalist"'.[2] And everybody wants their ontology to be a *political* ontology too. But things are never so simple, alas.

The borrowed name of 'Post-Continental philosophy' will suggest to many a new turning, or perhaps a passing. In its original coinage by the Analytic philosopher Kevin Mulligan, it did indeed indicate a demise: in the event of Analytic philosophy's mounting supremacy, European and especially French thought will be seen as a passing phase that will increasingly give more and more ground to its habitual opponent, or so the argument goes.[3] Additionally, it is claimed that as the appreciation of the traditional philosophical virtues of clarity, consistency, argument, and respect for truth and science come back ever more into vogue, so the obscurity, mysticism and anti-scientism of French thought will inevitably lose its attraction. Evidently, 'Post-Continental' is invoked here in a reactionary assessment, a fantasy that the day is coming when we can dance on the grave of European thought. The controversies surrounding Sokal and Bricmont, for instance, would be another reflection of this kind of polemic, though one that I do not tackle here.[4] Let there be no misunderstanding, however: the figures treated here have no less rigour, consistency, or argument in their work than the best practitioners in any other philosophical tradition. I defend this title of 'Post-Continental philosophy' on wholly other grounds, as both an assessment of the current transitional state in which Continental thought finds itself with respect to its theorisation of science in particular and immanence in general, as well as a caution against thinking that such an engagement could ever be a straightforward evolution.

Deleuze, of course, would perfectly fit the description of a thinker animated by ideas from both the history of philosophy and the natural sciences, especially biology. Badiou too emphasises science as the special condition of philosophical thought (alongside three others – love, politics and art), because it is mathematics alone that is ontological, and so mediates our ontological understanding of all reality. Yet it is exactly here where the problem emerges, for it concerns precisely the *level* at which each of these philosophers pitch their new concrete philosophies.

Badiou's scientific thought, for example, is wholly at odds with Deleuze's biologism. Biology is just not scientific enough for Badiou, and Deleuze's use of Life for philosophy is no more than a new crypto-transcendentalism for Badiou. Turning to Michel Henry only compounds the problem. Henry's notion of pure affectivity in *The Essence of Manifestation* and subsequent works builds on what he calls 'material phenomenology'. It is a form of radical empiricism that traces the 'secret essence of our Being' back to our immanence within 'Life'. Any alliance with Deleuze would be premature, however, for Henry's idea of Life transforms classical phenomenology into an immanent performance of the Divine. Such theological aspirations hold nothing in common with either Deleuze's vitalist ideas or Badiou's *more geometrico*. Finally, we have Laruelle, whose writings over the last fifteen years have accused each and every one of the other philosophers of immanence we're studying of being insufficiently radical because they still intermix their thoughts illegitimately with transcendent categories. The turn to science in Post-Continental thought, then, is hardly one in concert and seems at times to be more akin to a scattering of philosophy in four different directions.

Clearly, these four do have something in common. As is often the case with new movements, though, it is partly to do with what they reject as much as anything else. Be it the plane of immanence in Deleuze, the immanent phenomenology of Henry (one without intentionality), the immanent non-philosophy of Laruelle, or finally the immanent sets of Badiou (where infinity is actualised), it is the rejection of transcendence (of Intentionality, of Being, of Language, of the Other) that is paramount in each of them. So the challenge now is to navigate the different theories of immanence found in these figures in the light of the fact that they each carve up reality into an inside *with no outside* in such *different* ways, be it through the categories of mathematics, biology, theory of knowledge, or a radicalised form of phenomenology. It can no longer be the argument that these thinkers *together* embody a coherent approach to naturalism in their respective positions, but rather that they all radicalise our understanding of immanence and transcendence in order to rethink naturalism and science in philosophical terms, and therewith, the science and value of philosophy itself.

Alternatively, what they do also reject is, as Badiou puts it, a type of French philosophy working 'under the gaudy veneer of ostentatious importation'.[5] It is noteworthy that all four figures differ from earlier generations by acknowledging rather than rejecting their own philosophical heritage: Descartes for Badiou, Maine de Biran for Henry, Ravaisson for Laruelle, and Bergson for Deleuze. Each of these earlier French philosophers, especially those so inappropriately labelled as 'spiritualist' (Maine de Biran, Ravaisson and Bergson), were themselves never aghast at philosophising on the topics of science, matter, biology, or nature, but were, all the same, never scientistic or uncritical in their naturalism.[6] Given the Post-Continental philosophers' willingness to re-embrace this intellectual legacy, their presence will also be felt in these pages. By contrast, what *is* rejected by the Post-Continental position is the importation that determined French thought for the sixty years between the 1930s and 1980s. In other words, they reject

4

Phenomenology, or at least Heidegger's phenomenology; but this rejection may provide another clue as to how to combine their thoughts. As the title of Eric Alliez's review of contemporary French philosophy denotes, the *Impossibility of Phenomenology* has become the question marking philosophy in France since the late 1980s.[7] Certainly, it was true that phenomenology had been 'the single most important force driving French philosophy' up until that time, and it is equally true that Heidegger in particular formed 'the horizon of contemporary French philosophy' for a good deal of that period.[8]

This has all changed in the last fifteen years. Phenomenology has either transformed itself into something completely unrecognisable as phenomenology (what Dominique Janicaud labels its 'theological turn'), or it has been entirely sidelined by the huge French interest in the anti-phenomenologies of Deleuze and Badiou. Significantly, the Heideggerian position that linked the 'end of philosophy' to the triumph of science now causes special concern. Science, on this view, only studied the regional, the *ontisch*, it did not think the fundamental; rather, it merely enframed, controlled and predicted its *Objekt*. The additional Heideggerian idea that metaphysical philosophy is not destroyed by this science but actually completed by it, that it finds its true *telos* in science because that is where its (fallen) essence lies, is regarded as naïve by most in these contemporary groupings.[9] Not that any of the Post-Continental thinkers indulge in the kind of reductive scientism that was the real target of Heidegger's censure. In each case, theirs is an *ecstatic* naturalism that restores value to levels of existence that are irreducible to classical physics; Badiou's sur-rational mathematics, Deleuze's profligate biologism, Laruelle's scientific democracy and Henry's bodily affectivity, all testify to this.

Of course, *Being and Time* was ambiguous in its views on science, which are discernible there mostly by implication of what Heidegger means by *Fundamentalontologie*: does this imply a relation to 'ultimate reality', 'sole reality' or just a 'prior reality'? Undoubtedly, though, explicit statements of anti-science are to be found in his later writings, where science is depicted busying itself only with 'theorising the regulation of the possible planning and arrangement of human labor'.[10] Admittedly, Heidegger does even there give extensive time to reflecting on the essence of science, on the meaning of the Earth and of nature. But it remains clear that, firstly, the best form of reflection on these topics is either through philosophical thinking, poetry, or some amalgam of the two, and, secondly, that that reflection additionally uncovers the status of science to be a merely regional form of enquiry. These positions are now regarded as untenable: as Badiou says, philosophy must no longer be sutured to the poem.

However, notwithstanding the status of Heidegger, phenomenology as a whole need not be the incurable case it seems to be for the new naturalism. Len Lawlor, for instance, has described two possible fates for Continental thought: Deleuze's redemptive naturalism and Merleau-Ponty's post-phenomenological thought.[11] Both turn to ontology to escape the subjectivism of classical phenomenology and both invoke a form of naturalism at the core of that ontology. But, where Deleuze's metaphysics results in a new-found epistemology of the creation of concepts,

Merleau-Ponty's ends in religion, according to Lawlor. Faith or Knowledge. With regard to this theological turn, the trajectory towards the work of Henry is again evident, but it is arguable that with Merleau-Ponty the material remainder is still palpable. Renaud Barbaras' understanding of Merleau-Ponty as a figure at the limit of phenomenology completes the reformulation: Merleau-Ponty transforms phenomenology into cosmology, but not by going beyond experience; his cosmology is always of the visible world.[12] And it is not just work on Merleau-Ponty's naturalism that marks a turn in current phenomenological thinking: the perceived need to naturalise phenomenology *in toto*, Husserl included, is equally evident in the studies of Francisco Varela, Dan Zahavi and Natalie Depraz, for instance.

Nonetheless, for Badiou, Deleuze and Laruelle in particular, the errancy of French philosophy lay in following phenomenology too closely and establishing *so* great a respect for philosophy as an autonomous resource for *Wesensschau* or *Seinsdenken* that it forgot how to engage in an open manner with such matters as the relationship between mathematics and thought, culture and biology, or human and non-human animals. But now that that dream of rigorous transcendental thought is over (as even Husserl, belatedly, realised), the investigation into its own conditions can recommence. Merleau-Ponty could be accommodated in this enterprise, especially with regard to his call for philosophy to engage with the non-philosophy of literature, painting, music and psychoanalysis. Yet he was never a pure philosopher of immanence as are the four figures studied here: Merleau-Ponty stayed with what he called 'the paradox of transcendence and immanence', whereas we are more interested in the paradoxes that ensue from having four different types of *pure* or *absolute* immanence alone.[13]

Perhaps even more important than the relationship with science, however, is the question post-Heideggerian thought raised over the existence of philosophy itself. The essence of philosophy here was to call its own being into question as an autonomous discipline, as seen in Derrida's thesis that the death of philosophy is the one question 'capable of founding the community ... of those who are still called philosophers'.[14] In his post-structuralist twist on Heidegger's *Destruktion* of metaphysics, Derrida adds that it is impossible to escape this history of metaphysics from within philosophical thought, and this is no less true of Heideggerian ontology than it is of any other thinking. We can never stand outside philosophy (that is, metaphysics) *conceptually*. This is due to the fact that philosophy is a kind of language system, namely the complete set of philosophical strategies or 'philosophemes' utilised by philosophers, and it is impossible to *think* ourselves free from and outside of that system. The 'system' of philosophical *writing* puts a limit on the supposed freedoms of philosophical *logos*. We are woken from the dreams of philosophy by the dawn of Language.

Against this delimitation of the powers of philosophy at the hands of language, the possibility and even necessity of renewing philosophy conceptually is a common objective for all four philosophers of immanence.[15] Derrida, at least in his earlier work, delimits philosophy by enframing it within a reified set of finite structural possibilities that are already historically exhausted and that consequently condemn it to endless repetition. The problem is that Derrida can say what is finite and so what is impossible only because he has already defined what is possible. Therewith, however, he has actually reinstated a transcendental point of view (on possibility itself) in his supposed out-manoeuvring of (transcendental) philosophy or metaphysics. Language, and writing in particular, takes on a new transcendental function in demarcating philosophy.[16] As Badiou writes: 'the certainty of the "end of metaphysics" proceeds within the metaphysical element of certainty'.[17] Nevertheless, there is more to be said about impossibility in Derrida's later work, as we will see.

Immanence is everywhere, but its meaning is completely open: that is our problem. 'Existing or remaining within'; being 'inherent'; being restricted entirely to some 'inside'; existing and acting 'within the physical world': these lexical definitions of immanence play out in all four of our philosophies of immanence in both literal and figurative ways. Most often, though, the equivocity of immanence is linked to the question of ontological monism: if there is nothing 'beyond' the world, no 'arrière-monde', then there can be no duality, no two-worlds view. There is only Life, Affect, or Number at the base of things, even though this reality will appear in places as non-life, unfeeling, and innumerate (in every sense of these terms). Dualism is the enemy. There is no necessary connection between immanence and monism, of course, for one could hypothesise a materialist (monist) philosophy and yet retain interior and exterior variables within it. Indeed, inside and outside might be constituted by, for example, representation or biological homeostasis (as in the work of Fred Dretske and Daniel Dennett). But this is thinking of monism and immanence *non-ontologically*. Ontologically speaking, for materialist systems, there is no fundamentally different *kind* of being (substance, process, or property) outside the system, and indeed both representation and biology here would be of the same ultimate stuff as matter. As philosophical naturalists, both Dretske and Dennett would have to agree that there is nothing outside nature – no *arrière-monde*. They may posit different things in their philosophies – minds, contents of minds, mindless things – but there is 'ultimately' or 'fundamentally' only one stuff, matter. Hence, they are ontological monists, though the link between that and the consequences for thinking about immanence (that there is ultimately no 'outside') might be harder for them to see. But for Continental philosophies of immanence, monism is always ontological; it concerns *kinds* of things, even when what it says is that the only kind of thing there is is physical process, or affectivity, or sets, or the Real.

The connection between immanence, monism and qualities (kinds of things) will be paramount in our research into the different kinds of immanence posited by Deleuze, Henry, Badiou and Laruelle. If 'nature' is one of our most overdetermined concepts, then so is immanence. Consequently, the virtues of immanence – the recourse to empirical evidence and the denial of supernatural explanations – are themselves open to multiple readings. Alternatively, Deleuze himself often presents immanence as the 'vertigo of philosophy', linking it to a proliferation that is more an ontological

7

ungrounding than an epistemic abyss.[18] In our own study, however, by examining the incompatible knowledges generated by these four figures, the abyss of understanding between them will itself be given a materialistic interpretation.

Part of this material vertigo is connected with an ongoing theme throughout the work ahead, that of process. All four thinkers of immanence are, in one form or another, process philosophers: process truth (for Badiou); process vitalism (for Deleuze); process theoretics (for Laruelle); process phenomenology (for Henry). In each case there is a focus on how immanence relates to change – the immanent change of truth procedures for Badiou, in material flows on the plane of immanence for Deleuze, on philosophical mutation as such for Laruelle, or in Life as it phenomenalises itself immanently for Henry. And here we come to what is perhaps the fundamental distinction between these thinkers, for while three of them adopt a similar approach to process (namely an Actualist one); one of them begs to differ. Badiou, Henry and Laruelle are all Actualists, but Deleuze alone believes that process needs the virtual to condition it. On the Actualist line of thinking, there is only one way in which to understand how process can be conditioned, and that is immanently within the pertinent ontological realm, to wit, auto-affectivity for Henry, the paradoxes of quantity for Badiou, and thinking according to the Real for Laruelle. But Deleuze posits his plane of pure immanence as a virtual *reality* positioned 'below' another world, that of actual, molar realities. It is the actual that is subordinate to the virtual. Despite thinking of immanence in almost the purest terms possible, despite being a monist who regards being as univocal, he still proposes a two-world ontology when explaining these ideas.

Resolving Deleuze's peculiar strategy will involve looking at the relationship between the different levels where each of the other philosophers position their own, actual and immanent realities. In a sense, where each of the three Actualists differ from Deleuze's Virtualism also points to where they differ from each other: for Badiou regards (Henry's) affectivity as the virtual to his actual, Henry regards (Badiou's) mathematics as the virtual to his actual, and Laruelle regards all three as one or other form of virtualisation of the one actual for him, the Real. The reason why the virtual–actual dyad is so important, therefore, is because it is *projective* (in both the optical and geometrical sense): one always regards as virtual what the *other* philosophy of immanence posits as actual. Like the ghosts in the film *The Others* (Alejandro Amenábar, 2001), one thinks of one's own reality as actual and that of others as virtual or ghostly; they are one's outside, one's projected transcendence. Hence, the virtual–actual dichotomy is more informative than the transcendence–immanence distinction because, ultimately, it is not about 'inside' and 'outside' at all (which are too porous and relative to be enlightening distinctions), but about the *creation of this distinction* in different modalities of projection. These modalities are found in the utterly different *kinds* of immanence posited by Badiou, Deleuze, Henry, or Laruelle, where what would be an outside for one, would be an inside for another. In other words, the virtual is the name given by each of the philosophers of immanence, save for Deleuze, to what they project as an illusory transcendence retained in other philosophies.[19]

And this is the huge irony for any comparative study of this movement of thought. Transcendence is the mark of Continental thought that these thinkers each hope to surpass. But the immanence they use to pass over it comes as a mixed blessing. It is not just that equivocation over the meaning of immanence divides the Post-Continental movement and so conquers it before it has even really begun; the problem is much deeper than that. It is that these thinkers each encounter a limit of thought when they posit a philosophy of absolute immanence, for how can they commend *any* thought and reprove any other, *if there is no outside for them?* How is illusion, error, or misrepresentation possible if there is no representation at all? How is the illusion of transcendence, or the other's virtuality even generated? How can one *say* that there is no outside without also thinking within the element of transcendental certainty (the outside) again? In the end, Post-Continental philosophy gives rise to a problem of discourse, of the possibility of epistemic norms and even political values within a naturalistic thinking that must be travailed if we are not to repeat the same philosophemes that Derrida's work highlighted so well. How can a philosophy of immanence critique its outside? Must it only describe everything it sees, or can it not also prescribe what is exemplary for it? If it is to be critical rather than just descriptive, then on what new set of values will its 'judgements' be based and how will these values be established? There is a response to these questions, though, and it will come through the topic of discourse itself, or rather through a naturalised form of discourse.

And here we return to Derrida's notion of impossibility. For his own thought never stood still and (as we will see later) shifted from undermining the possibility of experience in his early work to suggesting the experience of impossibility in its later phase. That later thinking was also marked by political, ethical and even religious themes in his writing about aporias, but it also gives us a hint as to how writing (about) aporias may be possible within a regime of philosophical immanence. In his own work entitled *Aporias*, Derrida tell us that the term's philosophical use comes to us from Aristotle's *Physics IV* and concerns the problematics of time.[20] But it also concerns the issue of regress, Aristotle taking the view in the *Categories* that any relation (like time) must have distinct *relata* lest there be an infinite regress. The *relata* need to be distinct if their relation is to be defined. And here is where we can begin to see a way out of our entanglement in immanence. It is the contention of this book that the regress, aporia, or 'vertigo' of immanence can never be undone, indeed, it can never even be said, strictly speaking. Rather, we show it by *unwriting* it. Indeed, Deleuze has a theory of abstraction that would provide the key to how a discourse of immanence might be possible – namely the theory of the diagram or philosophical drawing. The diagram can do metaphilosophical work as a moving outline that takes both a transcendent view (*representing* immanence) while also remaining immanent: it does this by diagrammatising itself – it reiterates itself as a drawing that is perpetually re-drawn, and so materialises its own aporia. The relationship between immanence and transcendence *within* philosophies of immanence is also one *between* them (how they project a virtuality onto the actuality of others); and this reiteration within and without is best captured spatially, that is, diagrammatically, rather than chronologically, genea-logically, or (in the traditional sense of the term) conceptually. It is noteworthy that Giorgio Agamben concludes his own essay on 'Absolute Immanence' with a diagram mapping the history of modern philosophy, and that in it he places Heidegger at the centre, at the heart of a chiasm between transcendence and immanence, like a spider.[21] In a fundamental sense, this book is both an expansion and distortion of that diagram (see Figure 1).

It is no coincidence that the diagram is a central theme not only in Deleuze but also Badiou and parts of Henry and Laruelle. It gives us the resource to provide a hermeneutics that is not representational but physical, a material hermeneutics of diagrammatic lines, planes, circles, and triangles (where 'interpretation' becomes physical interaction, axial projection). This doesn't operate by playing figures off

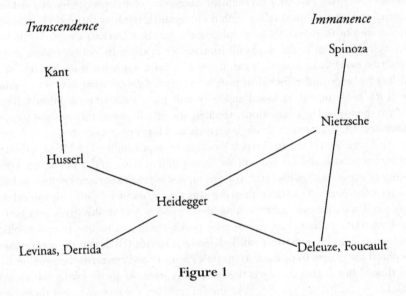

Figure 1

against each other or by synthesising them: the parallels and non-parallels between Deleuze, Badiou, Henry, and Laruelle are not transcendent representations but diagrammatic interventions. Any homologies that would allow them to be labelled under the category 'Post-Continental', therefore, can only be in outline rather than pretending to be the complete, filled-out, truth.

Consequently, this book can only be an outline as well, figuratively so at first, but by the final chapter literally so too (that is, at its end it will replace letters with figures). It is a sketch, though one as detailed as any depiction of a new regime of immanence can be, once the aporias of philosophising about pure immanence have been thought through rigorously. The book also wagers on an event in the making, an event in outline. It places a four-way bet on these thinkers as the best possible chance of renewal within Continental philosophy.[22] The site for that event was Paris 1988, and is connected with texts originally published in French by all four of these philosophers in that year – Deleuze's *Le Pli*, Badiou's *L'Être et l'événement*, Henry's *Voir l'invisible*, and Laruelle's discussion with Derrida on the possibility of a science of philosophy in *La Décision Philosophique No.5*. The reason for choosing these texts will become clearer through the course of the book, but, in essence, they each crystallise the transformation their work aspired to bring to previous (Continental) thought: Deleuze's final, sole-authored monograph fully materialises the infinite in every sphere of reality, both molar and molecular; Badiou's own 'great book' finally overcomes the duality of subjectivity and truth; Henry's analysis of Kandinsky shows the way to bring a materialised phenomenology back into the world; and Laruelle's exasperated dialogue with Derrida marks the moment when deconstruction came full circle to thematise itself as 'occasioned by the Real' rather than converting itself into a theology in phenomenology's wake. This is not to say that the history of Continental philosophy has been broken into two clear periods, but that a particular set of philosophical processes have intersected at a specific point to create a new tendency. I believe that the processes occurring in and around the 'moment' of 'Paris 1988' collectively deserve the name of 'event' in as much as it was then that a number of philosophers initiated an attempt at the seemingly impossible. In different and sometimes mutually contradictory ways, each endeavoured to incorporate tokens of transcendence (Molarity, Subjectivity, Truth, Appearance, Being, and even Philosophy itself) within a regime of absolute immanence (science, naturalism, and/or materialism) without simply eliminating them in the name of their assumed opposite.[23]

In sum, the news this nascent event brings is effectively the following: not only was the report of Continental philosophy's death at the hands of self-inflicted *aporia*, obscurantism and anti-scientism an exaggeration, but a recent change has taken place that will allow it to regenerate and renew itself with unexpected consequences for both philosophy and its relationship with science, materialism and naturalistic discourse.[24] This book is an investigation of these consequences, ongoing even as I write, and an outline of the origins of that event itself.

CHAPTER 1

Deleuze and the Travails of Virtual Immanence

> There is only one form of thought, it's the same thing: one can only
> think in a monistic or pluralistic manner. The only enemy is two.
> Monism and pluralism: it's the same thing. ... Wherever we leave
> the domain of multiplicities, we once again fall into dualisms, i.e.,
> into the domain of non-thought, we leave the domain of thought as
> process.[1]

THE DOUBLE LIFE OF GILLES DELEUZE

Amongst twenty or so alternatives, another title for this book might have been
After Deleuze. This would have reflected both the pivotal place of Deleuze as a
Continental philosopher who nonetheless remained apart from many of that
tradition's dominant themes, as well as the fact that the two figures we'll subsequently study follow one facet of his work in separation from the rest. In this,
they render Deleuzian thought even more consistent than Deleuze could, but at
immense costs. Deleuze himself seems utterly inconsistent. He is a vitalist and a
materialist. He is a process philosopher who thinks of repetition as creative. He is
a naturalist who still retains a transcendent plane of reality in his thought. Across
numerous works, he tries to unite the most opposed terms with bizarre concepts
– desiring-machines, infinite folds, atoms of womanhood, intensive quantities. But
while the anomalous make-up of his thinking operates at various levels, none is so
clearly dichotomous as is his naturalism, so it is here that I have decided to begin.
The crux of the issue is that there are distinct vocabularies we can use when introducing his peculiar brand of naturalism, only a selection from which comprise, on
the one hand, quantity, abstract machines, time-images, Senses and Ideas; and, on
the other hand, quality, vitalism, movement-images, forces, and affects. Nature as
thought-machine and nature as vital-feeling. Admittedly, these languages cannot be
consistently opposed according to a simple principle of, say, objective–real versus
subjective–appearance because they have features that respectively lie outside of
those two categories. But there are certain significant overlaps too. Certainly, we
shouldn't oppose *any* such list quite like this, for in Deleuze's philosophy dualisms
are often opposed and deposed in the name of an ontological monism, with a
neologistic vocabulary intended to reconcile not only subject and object, interior

and exterior, but also any other similar hierarchical or oppositional structures. It is said that, despite belonging to the school of difference, Deleuze is a philosopher of both difference *and* repetition, both the many *and* the one, and that his thought can only be understood through the primacy of the 'both/and' conjunction.[2] And it will become obvious in this chapter that in fact Deleuze does indeed run (at least) two vocabularies together in his work, most often with the aim of merging them through a higher synthesis (dubbed 'inclusive disjunction'). However, the probity of this operation is not always evident. The argument, for now, will be that it is not the merger *qua* conceptual product that counts, but the coalescence *qua* process that makes Deleuze's philosophical practice properly naturalistic given his view that nature *is* process.

The six most pertinent dyads with respect to this process-naturalism are immanence/transcendence, molecular/molar, virtual/actual, past/present, infinite/finite, and difference/repetition, each of which we will tackle in these pages. Rather than being rigidly dyadic, though, we will discover that they amount to tendencies in that they are processes themselves. Moreover, because they are immanent to the processes they 'describe', they are also meta-processes. This research will allow us thereafter to address the manner in which two other philosophers of immanence, Badiou and Henry, share so much of Deleuze's thinking, though at the expense of taking only one of its tendencies and extending it *ad infinitum*. The former emphasises quantity, the Idea and the abstract (or '*mathesis*'); the latter looks to quality, Life and affectivity ('*pathos*'). Neither, significantly, share Deleuze's 'Virtualism', for Badiou takes the abstract Idea and makes it actual, while Henry takes vital affect and makes it actual. In sum, Badiou and Henry take Deleuze to his respective limits in quantity (the pure multiple) and quality (pure difference as affectivity). Hence, the stark contrast Badiou and Henry set when compared with each other: for Badiou, only mathematics (and definitely not affect) concerns being as such; for Henry, affect alone exists, mathematics is unreal. It should be no surprise, therefore, that how such a radical opposition arises between two philosophies of immanence and actuality is best tackled first by looking at the more subtle and complex thought of Deleuze, who has always striven to think feeling and abstraction *together*, albeit with varied levels of success.

Though the virtual–actual pairing will eventually emerge as central to thinking about duality and conjunction in general for Deleuze (and beyond), and central also to Badiou's rejection of Deleuze's brand of naturalism, we will begin with the two pairings that are respectively more general and more concrete than that of the virtual–actual, namely transcendence/immanence and the molar/molecular.

IMMANENCE AND NATURALISM

'When immanence is no longer immanent to something other than itself it is possible to speak of a plane of immanence. Such a plane is, perhaps, a radical empiricism'.[3] There is no 'perhaps' about it. Such an 'absolutization of immanence' as this must lead to a new form of empiricism, because it is no longer about the experiences of a pre-constituted subject (myself or an Other), but those experiences that fissure my subjectivity. Deleuze stands in relation to the phenomenology of experience (be it through a philosophy of the Ego, of Consciousness, of the Flesh, or the Other) where Hegel stood in relation to Kant: whilst Hegel radicalised Kantian reason via dialectical contradiction, Deleuze radicalised phenomenology's overly anthropocentric assignment of experience via a radical novelty that transcends *any* categories of perception.[4] The transcendental cannot be 'induced' or 'traced' from the ordinary empirical forms of common sense. The being of the transcendentally sensible is that which can only and involuntarily be sensed. It is a shock to normal thought and sensibility. In fact, Deleuze proposes to reinstate a doctrine of the faculties – of thought, of memory and of sensibility – each with their own exclusive transcendental object.[5] Experience, then, being immanent to itself and not to an individualised subject, *is thereby transcendent*. One does not ask how the subject gains its experience but how experience gives us a subject.[6]

At its heart, Deleuzian empiricism is paradigmatically metaphysical or transcendental, not as a foundation for all possible knowledge, but in the sense of generating the necessary conditions for our everyday 'actual' experiences. This makes of it a 'higher', 'superior', 'radical', or 'transcendental' empiricism whose conditions are themselves neither general nor abstract, but concrete, singular and empirical. This absolutism of non-relational immanence stems from Deleuze's work on David Hume. The irreducible dualism between terms and relations – the 'externality of relations' – really amounts to the definition of empiricism being forwarded by Hume. The non-empiricist is he or she who derives relations (experience) from the nature of terms (such as subjects), while the empiricist sees relations as themselves non-relational, as transcendent or pure. But, at this early stage at least of Deleuze's thought (his monograph on Hume was his first such work), 'pure' here does not mean incorporeal: 'Hume's entire philosophy (in fact, empiricism in general)', Deleuze affirms, 'is a kind of "physicalism".' The conditions for experience are themselves experiences (without relation to a subject, and certainly not to God) that are of an 'exclusively physical and empirical nature'.[7] So, by adopting the position that runs immanence and transcendence together by making immanence absolute, Deleuzian empiricism converges with materialism, finding in purely physical matter the conditions that generate the self such that experience no longer needs a host in a (non-material) subject.

In only a short distance, then, we have seen Deleuze's naturalism initiate two mergers, that of immanence and transcendence, and that of experience and matter (empiricism and physicalism). But in the first case this was only methodological and terminological (turning on the transcendence of immanence over transcendence): we will have to wait for later works like *A Thousand Plateaus* and *The Fold* for the merger of immanence and transcendence to be materialised in the language of dermatology, geological strata, and so on. In the second case (the merger of experience and matter), the attempt remains assertoric: we have yet to see at all how a *materialised experience* might make sense as a genuine *rapprochement* between mind and matter. How Deleuze subsequently attempts this is worth studying closely.

MATERIALISM AND PHILOSOPHY

From the start, Deleuze's work must be read as a search for a naturalism that promotes the material rather than reduces mind (which would be, in any case, less an undoing of the bifurcation than a complete neglect of one half of it). But whereas phenomenology pursued a similar objective, it concerned itself primarily with the *formal* aspects of the world (as appearance *to a select audience*, as object 'for' consciousness). Deleuze's materialism works on the content of the world, its interiority: the flows, speeds and intensities of matter. On the one side, phenomenology's idealisation of material form (appearance), on the other, the vitalisation of material content (in one phrasing, a 'semiotizing' of the physical that is also a 'physicalizing' of meaning).[8]

Deleuze's philosophical heroes all reflect this same cross-categorical or 'transversal' thinking (that he legitimates, as we will see, by claiming for it a non-categorical, non-judgemental position, and so making it purely descriptive in the naturalistic sense): for the Stoics, for instance, qualities, virtues and ideas are bodies too, shaped by incorporeal events on their surfaces, that is, by intensities, problems, and simulacra, all of which have their own 'quasi-causal' efficacy. The *lekton*, for example, is *both* word and thing or rather what is between the two. Leibnizian monads, Spinozist modes, Nietzschean forces, Bergsonian creativity – all these thinkers and their 'philosophical personae' gather in this same in-between place subtending the derivative and artificial bifurcation of subject and object, mind and body, man and nature, and, indeed, of philosophical theory and practice too. As Badiou puts it, Deleuze wants a 'philosophy "of" nature' understood as a *'description in thought of the life of the world,* such that the life thus described might include, as one of its living gestures, the description'.[9] So even philosophy itself, through the notion of creativity (it creates concepts as the world creates itself), can also be incorporated into the world as bodily *event.* In Deleuze's last joint publication with Guattari, *What is Philosophy?*, concepts are materialised through the agency of the incorporeal event which runs over the surface of bodies like the configurations of a machine.[10] But even before that, in *The Logic of Sense,* meaning in general (philosophical or otherwise) was understood as corporeal surface effects best illustrated by the physical language used, or rather lived, by schizophrenics where word and object are no longer dissociable:

> In ... [the] primary order of schizophrenia, the only duality left is that between actions and passions of the body. Language is both at once, being entirely reabsorbed into the gaping depth. There is no longer anything to prevent propositions from falling back onto bodies and from mingling their sonorous elements with the body's olfactory, gustatory, or digestive affects.[11]

The speech-act is one further aspect of this material process, an incorporeal event that affects different bodies. But *every* utterance is performative for Deleuze (including his own): the basic unit of communication is the *order-word* that contains an implicit presupposition which, by ensuring that it 'goes *without* saying', is clearly *doing* something instead. Deleuze insists, then, on the materiality of language and resists the identification of 'body' and 'material' with the all-too-easily decon-structed category of 'objectivity' that facilitates so much post-modern linguistic idealism. As he puts it in *Proust and Signs*: 'The biologists would be right, if they knew that bodies in themselves are already a language. The linguists would be right if they knew that language is always the language of bodies.'[12]

But as we will see, such immanent philosophical reflexivity is a double-edged sword for the purely descriptive (naturalistic and immanent) thought that Deleuze hopes to achieve. The reason for this concerns the type of materialism Deleuze uses to embody (his) ideas. At first glance, Deleuze seems unquestionably materi-alist in outlook, even physicalist, citing as he does the Stoic's belief that physics is at the heart of philosophy.[13] Beyond the arguments themselves, his language is full of physical imagery: points and lines, surfaces, strata, machinic and biological processes. Almost the entire sociological dimension of *A Thousand Plateaus*, for instance, revolves around a distinction between nomadic and sedentary society which itself turns on a dualism of smooth space and striated space. And, moreover, none of these physical images is intended as metaphors so much as subtle points about the nature of material reality.

Many believe that Deleuzian materialism stems from his work on Spinoza, which advances a *mechanistic* and so reductive materialism of efficient causality. Yet a host of different notions of matter and materialism – reductive and non-reductive – are current across the breadth of Deleuze's philosophy. His unique approach consists in what he confusingly calls 'universal machinism', a strategy that he tries to distance from mechanism, however – it takes up material elements as processes to preserve them in larger composites called, again misleadingly, 'abstract machines'. The notion of an abstract machine is a device by which to capture surface, large-scale entities as parts of even larger material processes. But the key word here is 'abstract' and not 'machine'. Deleuze's constant complaint against philosophers is that their thought is not abstract enough, that it pitches its level of abstraction too low and consequently forfeits the virtues of abstraction. That which is more abstract is that which incorporates a larger, that is, multiple, sample, considering not only human but also animal, inorganic and other inhuman becomings.[14] An abstract machine, then, operates at levels that 'capture' human and non-human movements alike in its material processes. Sometimes the machinic is defined simply as a 'synthesis of heterogeneities', though just what the nature is of these captures or syntheses, if they are non-mechanistic, remains to be seen.[15]

Because Deleuzian abstraction is more open, it is also more creative and its philosophy is more conceptually productive. In other words, a philosophy of immanence like this is an abstract machine too. A philosophy can be abstract, in its mode of operating, no less than a body can. Characteristically for a process philosophy such as this, then, the answer to the question of what his philosophy *is*, can only be found by reformulating the question properly: what does it *do*, what is its *function*, what does it *create*?

CREATING NEW VOCABULARIES

Rosi Braidotti sums up Deleuze's naturalistic aspiration as a 'materialist, high-tech brand of vitalism'.[16] Once again, the yoking together of opposed terms is evident: materialism is normally the opposite of vitalism. But this is to remain at the level of content. Another approach, as we have intimated, is to ask what Deleuze's naturalism is doing, and the answer to that is already reflexive enough: its doing is its *creating*. If his philosophy is theatrical (as Foucault famously said), its theatrics and dramatisation rest on its performativity, on what it embodies. And this embodiment is creation, the constant creation of new concepts, of new vocabularies, ones that will, in their transversality across categories, subtend and subvert old dichotomies. The new vocabulary is also a *neu-tral* vocabulary, an in-between. Indeed, its newness, its continual renewal (each text enacting a novel set of concepts to replace those of the previous text), is what allows it to break out of the mesh of bivalent 'either/or' logic: materialist *and* vitalist, not materialist *or* vitalist. Disparate concepts are brought together to perform anew an inclusive disjunction ('or' = 'and') that allows us, for a moment, to think the new *neutrally*, and so to think what lies beneath and beyond the old dualities. Naturalism becomes neutralism. Such neutral vocabularies have been forwarded before (Spinoza's 'substance', James' 'experience', Bergson's 'images', Russell's 'neutrals', Strawson's 'persons'), but rarely have such vocabularies resisted, upon further inquiry, being repositioned in the old net of either subject or object, mind or body, culture or nature. The hypothesis I'm entertaining here is that Deleuze's neutral terms keep renewing themselves in order to resist – by movement – such reallocation: constant neologisms or alloys uncontaminated by association with other previous usage, at least for a while. But again, this is not because his thought *re*-presents the new as content (which is impossible), but because it performs it as philosophical creation. At the mere level of content, any significance new word-combinations like 'desiring-machine' might have, what motivates their choice over other terms in the first place, may well also infect them with allegiances to one side or the other, to mind or matter. What counts is not so much the words as the formal hyphen (real or implied) bringing them together, the momentary in-between of words performed in philosophical creation. The hyphen is a diagram outlining the kind of process at issue by fusing together the falsely dissociated products of the process.

The list of such performative novelty in Deleuze is extensive: the Idea beyond the one and the many, 'images' which are neither mind nor matter, 'foldings' showing 'an affinity of matter with life and organisms', the 'assemblage' or 'phylum' deducted from the flow of 'matter-movement' both artificial and natural, a 'technological vitalism', 'Sense' with 'one side [turned] toward things and one side toward propositions', the 'aliquid', 'event', 'extra-Being', and so on. Even 'body' itself is defined as 'anything; it can be an animal, a body of sounds, a mind or an idea; it can be a linguistic corpus, a social body, a collectivity'. Some of these terms, like 'Idea', 'Sense', or 'image', are more unilateral to begin with, and so perhaps less useful long-term on account of this. But *while in use*, Deleuze's employment of physical or mathematical imagery on the one side, and psychological and vital language on the other, is neither reductive nor merely metaphorical but, he writes, simultaneously 'universal physics, universal psychology and universal sociology'.[17]

But it is his aforementioned 'universal machinism' from the two volumes of *Capitalism and Schizophrenia* which is the most renowned, and also the most conflationary of the new languages. 'Everything is a machine', we are told, 'producing-machines, desiring-machines everywhere'.[18] The *Anti-Oedipus* is most famous for positing a realm of desiring-machines which are nothing but configurations or assemblages of non-intentional desire. The book opens with the description of an organ-machine 'plugged into an energy-source machine: the one produces a flow that the other interrupts. The breast is a machine that produces milk, and the mouth a machine coupled to it.' At the most general level and overarching these concrete instances of universal machinism are the abstract machines, which embody 'the aspect or moment at which nothing but *functions* and *matters* remain'. Hence, a certain functionalism seems to reign in this machinic variety of materialism. At the molecular level of these machines (which must not be confused with mechanical machines of the molar variety, Deleuze tells us), 'use, functioning, production, and formation are one and the same process'.[19]

But Deleuze is careful to remind us that these machines are neither mechanical nor technical: 'Mechanics is a system of closer and closer connections between dependent terms. The machine by contrast is a [non-contiguous] "proximity" grouping between independent and heterogeneous terms'. Machinic is a neutral term. Oddly, though, the writing-machines found in one work, *Kafka,* for example, do evoke a great deal of mechanical imagery – gears, motor parts, cogs, piston rods and the engineers who maintain them. And in other texts too, machines with 'tractable gears' that need to be 'greased' can be encountered. What price, then, the centrality of Deleuze's machinism, when even he can cash it out in the one-sided language of mechanics?[20] Hence, the usefulness of such machinic language *alone* is probably limited: it cannot resist contagion from cognate terms, and so must, one might argue, eventually be replaced or at least supplemented.[21] But this is precisely what Deleuze keeps doing.

Alongside the physical and spatial imagery of the machine in Deleuze, runs a host of organic and vitalistic images too: eggs, rhizomes, becoming-animal, vegetal cinema versus animal cinema, and so on. 'Everything I've written is vitalistic', he announced in 1988. Like Nietzsche and Bergson before him, and Michel Henry alongside him, 'Life' is often written with a capital 'L' to accentuate the difference between this metaphysical category and any mere living organism whose health can actually be disturbed when in the grip of a Life too great for it to embody

18

adequately. In fact, his philosophy of immanence is Life, according to Deleuze's last writings: 'Pure immanence is A LIFE, and nothing else. It is not immanence to life, but the immanence which is in nothing is itself a life. A life is the immanence of immanence, absolute immanence: it is sheer power, utter beatitude.'[22] But the disjunction with machinic materialism is not exclusive, given that the *Ur-text* of machinism, the *Anti-Oedipus*, was also the first to take upon itself the task of overcoming the impasse of vitalism and mechanism. Mechanism alone is said to invoke a structural unity to explain the organism's functioning, vitalism alone an individual unity which renders the organism autonomous and subordinates any mechanisms connected to it: but both unities are spurious, concludes Deleuze, as they are merely phenomenal aggregates. Mechanism and vitalism, therefore, are equally inadequate as they fail to understand the nature of desire and its role in machinic production. In the end:

> It becomes immaterial whether one says that machines are organs, or organs, machines. The two definitions are exact equivalents: man as a 'vertebro-machinate mammal', or as an 'aphidian parasite of machines'... In a word, the real difference is not between the living and the machine, vitalism and mechanism, but between two states of the machine that are two states of the living as well.[23]

Life and matter are now just states of something else, according to Deleuze: but rather than ever explain precisely what this third element is (beyond calling it both a machine and alive), Deleuze most often continues only to *rename* it with new languages fusing biological and physical terms.

But this not to say that no rationale is available, that all we can do is describe Deleuze's performative philosophy with minimal explanation beyond the notion of creativity performing the real (itself understood as immanent creation). Another type of explanation hinges on the question of Deleuze's internalism, that is, his continuing use of *intensive* physicalist terms like affect, *conatus*, force, implication, virtuality and *spatium*. Most of these belong to a set of dyads (intensive–extensive, implication–explication, virtual–actual, *spatium–extensio*), where the first element is deemed the properly physical component, while the second is a poor shadow of the same reflected in a merely empirical state of affairs. Now such selectivity is surely an odd way of going about one's naturalism or one's empiricism, and it appears to transgress a principle of Deleuze's own philosophy of immanence: that everything is *included* – 'univocity' – that being is said in the same way of every different thing. Univocity, elucidated through unequal conceptual pairings, leads to equivocity.[24]

Significantly, it is the one basic dyad of external and internal which underlies all the other pairs mentioned above. Yet it was Hume's empiricism which clearly taught Deleuze at the very start of his career that 'the given is not in space; the space is in the given. ... Extension, therefore, is only the quality of certain perceptions'.[25] Like Leibniz and Berkeley before him, Hume dissolves the notion of extension, and with that, the opposition between inside and outside. Deleuze repeats this basic tenet at numerous points: the 'exterior and interior are relative', he writes, 'the inside and the outside, the container and the contained, no longer have a precise limit', or '[t]he internal and the external, depth and height, have biological value only through this topological surface of contact. Thus, even biologically, it is necessary to understand that "the deepest is the skin".'[26] But such a deconstruction, wrought by his own hand, of one of philosophy's classic dualisms, fails to stop Deleuze from continuing to invoke internalist logic in his thought of *immanence*. In other words, it *excludes* (as mere skin, as superficial) notions of form, 'molarity', and 'actuality', by giving them derivative status in what was meant to be a non-hierarchical system. The two crucial couplings that commit this transgression are those of the molar–molecular and the virtual–actual.

THE MOLAR AND THE MOLECULAR

Deleuze uses the terminological dyad 'molar–molecular' to express a relation between two strata, the one called molecular most often appearing to have the upper hand as the microscopic material realm to which molar phenomena – subjectivity, identity, form – are reduced. What drives the implication of interior/exterior relations within the molar–molecular dichotomy (the molecular seems to be *contained in* the molar) could be read in terms of scale and dimension. Yet this distinction, Deleuze says, has nothing to do with scale: 'The molar and the molecular are not distinguished by size, scale, or dimension, but by the nature of the system of reference envisioned'.[27] By this 'system of reference' Deleuze means a particular mode of composition, organization, or consistency amongst the *same* elements – *how* they are seen or taken up: *as* nomadic, polyvocal, rhizomatic, transversal, smooth, processual, intensive and indivisible on the one molecular side; *as* sedentary, bi-univocal, arborescent, linear, striated, static, extensive and divisible on the other molar side. A concern for us, therefore, will be whether the molar and molecular belong to our apprehension of the elements or to how they relate to each other (crudely, whether they are subjective or objective), or, finally, to some domain in between subject and object enframed by this 'system of reference'. Deleuze himself insists that there is no dualism implied here, for the two types of organization are always intermixed in any concrete manifestation (though, of course, a *de facto* combination of two elements does not preclude the possibility of a *de jure* dualism).

Yet despite such assertions, Deleuze tends to use language suggestive of scale: majority, major, massive, big, mass, collective, whole, global, macro-, super-, over- and molar itself on the one hand; or partial objects, part organs, larval selves, minority, minor, local, part, component, small, miniaturization, sub-, micro- and molecular itself on the other. Sometimes the molar is equated with statistical accumulations with reference also made to 'large scale', 'large number,' and 'large aggregates'. That the molar and the molecular have been taken to imply a difference in scale is not surprising, then, nor the consequent implication of micro-materialism.[28]

And there is another interpretation that, when put alongside the implications of scale (whether acknowledged or not), tempts many to view Deleuze's analyses as reductionist ones, to wit, that there is also an *ontological* hierarchy between molarity and molecularity, that the molar is unreal, and everything genuinely *is* molecular. Any perceived molarity must be an illusion or imposition to be dismantled or reduced. Certainly, Deleuze's trenchant attacks in the *Anti-Oedipus* on self, family and state as molar representations that tyrannize and stifle our individual 'becomings' might lead one in that direction. But in work within and subsequent to that book, Deleuze most often posits a multiplicity of tyrannies, human and non-human, organic and inorganic, molar and molecular. There are micro-fascists no less than there are macro-fascists.[29] Things do change especially between the *Anti-Oedipus* and *A Thousand Plateaus*, when molar order no longer tends to be viewed as all-bad and molecular disorder as all-good.[30] Likewise, not all deterritorialisa-tions are good, or indeed, are independent of their opposites: territorialisations, deterritorialisations and reterritorialisations are always complementary, relative and intertwined rather than opposed as previously.[31] Even such molar forms as the face – so radically demonised as late as *A Thousand Plateaus* – can be rehabilitated in *Cinema 1* by recourse to a (cinematic) expressionism which allows it to participate 'in the non-organic life of things'. *Cinema 1* also reworks our perception by making it multiple, molar *and* molecular: gaseous and liquid perceptions, 'a more delicate and vaster perception', are added to solid, molar perception rather than replacing it with the imperceptible (as *A Thousand Plateaus* directs).[32]

The aspect of molar representation most consistently rejected by Deleuze is its singular and anthropocentric form handed down through the tradition from Kant onwards. Indeed, the impression that Deleuze would rather dissolve molar beings into anonymous molecular flows brought him much early criticism from feminist philosophers. When he wrote that what he termed a molar entity was, 'for example, the woman as defined by her form, endowed with organs and functions and assigned as a subject', and that he would prefer the idea of 'becoming-woman' whereby these molar women would seemingly disperse into imperceptible atoms, there followed a good deal of controversy.[33] This began with Luce Irigaray's reproach to the Deleuzian emphasis on the machinic and the consequent loss of the organic self. This was a type of male response to female bodily form that 'has long been familiar to women'.[34] Elizabeth Grosz echoed this sentiment. By invoking 'the notion of "becoming-woman" in place of a concept of "being women"', she writes, 'Deleuze and Guattari participate in the subordination, or possibly even the obliteration, of women's struggles for autonomy, identity, and self-determination, an erasure of a certain, very concrete and real set of political struggles ...'.[35]

Admittedly, Deleuze was generous enough to say that he would categorically allow women their 'molar politics', but that nonetheless their real goal should be to 'become-woman in order that the man also becomes- or can become-woman'.[36] This has allowed some of his readers to make peace with his molecularism and even to re-appropriate it for feminism.[37] But this encounter with feminist philosophy only highlights a more general problem with the reception of Deleuze's work which too often mistakes its categories for those of more orthodox theorists. This can be seen in the context of the present issue when we look again at what Deleuze calls the 'atoms of womanhood' that would comprise any becoming-woman. Such a notion is a clear cross-category concept mixing a molecular process (atoms) with molar, phenomenal behaviour (womanhood). But such examples can be found everywhere in Deleuze's work: the idea of a bird, for instance, is not found in its genus or species, but, he says, in 'the composition of its postures, colors, and songs'. Most significant here is Deleuze's treatment of the brain. Much of the inspiration for his work on cinema (but also on concepts and even on philosophy itself) looks to a microbiology of the brain in place of the more customary use of psychoanalysis, linguistics, or (increasingly) cognitive science. Crucially, however, this use of the brain is never reductive. Deleuze sees cinema as an endeavour at the molar level to shock the brain into forming new synapses, connections and pathways.[38] His treatment of the brain in *What is Philosophy?* goes even further:

> If the mental objects of philosophy, art, and science (that is to say, vital ideas) have a place, it will be in the deepest of the synaptic fissures, in the hiatuses, intervals, and meantimes of a nonobjectifiable brain. . . . [A]ccording to phenom-enology, thought depends on man's relations with the world . . . but this ascent of phenomenology beyond the brain toward a Being in the world . . . hardly gets us out of the sphere of opinions. . . . Will the turning point not be elsewhere, in the place where the brain is 'subject', where it becomes subject?[39]

Here we see Deleuze's enterprise in its true colours as an attempted escape from the traditional philosophical impasse of a singular and irreducible human life-world opposed to the anonymous and lifeless realm of pure matter in motion. His own categories of molar and molecular attempt to signify more than that. Mental objects do have a place, in the brain, but not reductively, it is in the non-objectified brain – the brain as subject.

One of Deleuze's last works, *The Fold*, a crucial work in our eyes, also has critical resources for thinking about molar forms within a naturalistic yet non-reductive perspective. To retain molar unity, or (in a Leibnizian framework) the substantial unity of any cluster of monads possessing a dominant monad, Deleuze finds a material correlate by which to render the dominant organic form into physi-calist terms: he writes of a '*vinculum*' or membrane that 'works as a sort of grid filtering the monads that it receives as terms'. Unity is in the skin. This filtering mechanism is sufficient to ground the unity of the organism as a molar whole on account of its own peculiar *surface* structure. For this *vinculum* is not any usual type of fold, but an infinite fold or torsion of the world that exteriorises or unfolds, as a wall, surface, or membrane, its own interior folding of the world; in short, it is a fractal surface, limited yet infinite. Such an infinite surface can more than cater for a molar entity without recourse to a reductive molecular substrate. Indeed, mechanism is now chastised 'for not being mechanical enough, for not being adequately machined', that is, for not being 'infinitely machined'.[40] In Deleuze's book on Foucault, subjectification was described as an inside constituted from a folding of the outside; in *The Fold*, all molar forms are presented as monadological foldings.

The first special feature of the fold, therefore, is that it enfolds the outside and the inside, reconciling them through a harmonics of space rather than by any direct efficient action between two substances or within one substance. So while the Deleuzian language of molecularity and molarity is retained even in this book (via the monads and their aggregate forms), its basis in a strictly dichotomous logic of inside and outside has been made redundant. The second contribution of the fold is that it allows Deleuze the means, at last, to do full justice to the phenomenality of the molar stratum – of architecture, fabrics and draperies, as well as the dermal surfaces of the body – while maintaining a materialist discourse. As a topological concept, the fold is a complication of surfaces that offsets any temptation to step beyond the wholly immanent plane. It is a baroque conception of matter that inflates it, not to a universal machinism so much as a universal texturology.[41]

But, one might ask, isn't the implication of the infinite (*vinculum*) into the material already begging the question, enfolding a value-term into the value-free, such that the superfold of the *vinculum* is not a true neutral? (One can allow, as we will see, the infinite to carry a whole host of other subject-sided meanings.) Likewise, resonation, harmonics, or waves have object-sided, physicalist meanings that lose their purchase when placed too long in a category for understanding vital phenomena. Or is it that the very enfolding, the *process* of re-seeing matter as mindful and infinite through Deleuze's philosophical creation of an actual new vocabulary – a process-performative description – is itself the only kind of neutrality possible: the neutrality that is always created anew?[42] This is our under-lying approach to Deleuzian naturalism, and it is to this question that we will return.

Interestingly, molar and molecular can be seen not as two ways (one right, the other wrong) of taking up elements, but also as two *tendencies* of the elements themselves. But the emphasis here is on tendency as a movement. Even molarity, which seems to embody stasis or merely quantitative movement, is a process too, 'a making-the-same'. This is now the distinction, Deleuze says, 'between matter and life, or rather, since there is only one matter, between two states, two tendencies of atomic matter...'.[43] Ultimately, it is a difference between types of multiplicity:

> On the one hand, multiplicities that are extensive, divisible, and molar; unifiable, totalizable, organizable; conscious or preconscious – and on the other hand, libidinal, unconscious, molecular, intensive multiplicities composed of particles that do not divide without changing in nature ...[44]

But again, Deleuze insists that this is not a new dualism and that the two types are always intermixed in the same assemblage: the types of multiplicity 'coexist, inter-penetrate, and change places'. But, as always, *de facto* combinations do not preclude *de jure* dualities. Perhaps 'strata are … simultaneously molecular and molar', as Deleuze maintains, but there remains a duality amongst them — now phrased a 'system of reference', now a 'tendency' or type of 'multiplicity' — that remains to be unpacked.[45] One idea is that the one (the molecular) is contained *in* the other (the molar), but what is fundamental, or rather ontological, in this is the idea that the one (the molar) comes *out of* the other (the molecular): that the molecular *actualises* the molar out of its own *virtuality*. Deleuze does now materialise molar phenomena in a genuinely *non-reductive* manner. Phenomena are materialised but not eliminated in favour of molecular substitutes. Subsequent tensions in Deleuze still arise, however, from the retention of a hierarchy of ontological levels — virtual and actual — underlying the molar and molecular.

ACTUAL AND VIRTUAL

In a central passage from *Difference and Repetition*, Deleuze marks out an 'internal multiplicity' as alone capable of thinking beyond the loose dialectic of the one and the many. This internal power belongs to 'the Idea', which he also defines as 'a structure'. Apart from thus betraying *Difference and Repetition* as at once Deleuze's most Structuralist as well as Platonist work, it also introduces us to Deleuzian ontology par excellence, which is one of 'the virtual and its actualisation'. Interiority is not so fundamental, for the Idea is a 'differential *relation*' that must be 'actualised in diverse spatio-temporal relationships, at the same time as its *elements* are actually incarnated in a variety of *terms* and forms'.[46] The Idea is virtual — and from its higher ontological status, spatio-temporal bodies, terms, or forms are derived by actualisation.

Slavoj Žižek describes Deleuze as 'the philosopher of the Virtual'.[47] But while such a scheme of virtual and actual may make sense as an ontology — indeed, it has been likened to Heidegger's ontology of 'bringing forth', 'sending' and 'unconcealment' — does it make sense within the specific field of Deleuzian naturalism? To be precise, can such a two-world ontology hold within a philosophy of immanence and a radical empiricism?[48] Hasn't reality been split in two again? Miguel de Beistegui exposes this well when writing that Deleuzian ontology is based on a 'distinction in being between the actual, or the empirical (and the science it enables), and the virtual or transcendental horizon (which philosophy brings out) from which the former unfolds'.[49] We've come a long way, it seems, from a superior, immanent empiricism. Experience has been hierarchised, spatio-temporal relationships and their terms suddenly being rendered less than really empirical. Indeed, what does 'really' mean here? If the 'essential in univocity' is that being is said in a single and same sense *of* all its individuating differences, then it is indeed 'equal' for all, even where there is still, *on other grounds*, 'hierarchy and distribution in univocal being'.[50] But the grounds we are on currently are ontological, are of being and reality, and so there should be no hierarchical distinction that would sunder immanence apart.[51]

Another philosopher of immanence, Michel Henry, is adamant that 'to want "to bring to light" the foundation of experience is the ultimate ontological absurdity'.[52] Actualisation makes no sense within immanence. Some Deleuzians themselves have urged caution with respect to the category of the virtual. James Williams in particular sets up a number of pertinent questions:

> Despite Deleuze's claims to an ontology of immanence, the use of two concepts with respect to reality, virtual and actual, and the refusal to conflate the two, raises traditional questions with respect to dualism. These split into problems of interaction and problems of unity. How do the virtual and the actual interact? How do they maintain their distinction, if they do interact? Is not interaction the place to define a higher unity that denies the priority of the initial distinction?[53]

The background to Deleuze's periodic invocation and use of the virtual are myriad, just one claimed motivation being to provide an alternative ontology to Heidegger's, or one historical source being Gilbert Simonden's concept of a dynamic background that replaces form with potentiality. Analogues in Spinozist substance or Platonic Forms can also be found. Recent works by Deleuzians such as Keith Ansell Pearson, Manuel DeLanda and Brian Massumi have gone a long way in making sense of this concept of immanent, intensive, difference by illustrating it with and applying it to ideas in biology, physics and psychology.[54] As such, it has become an '-ism' in certain quarters of recent Deleuze-studies: namely, Virtualism, which accounts for the ontology behind Deleuze's philosophy of immanence.[55] But the vital source of this notion, both in its genesis and function, belongs to the foremost member of the school of French spiritualist philosophy and the master of much of Deleuze's thought: Henri Bergson.

More than any other single influence, it was Bergson who gave Deleuze his model for thinking about empiricism, about time and movement, about the method of problematics, about the image of thought, about immanence, multiplicity, vitalism, affectivity and the virtual. Indeed, it was Bergson who first employed the terms 'virtual' and 'actual' philosophically in his *Matter and Memory* of 1896. But more importantly, a short survey of Bergson's use of the term will enlighten us as to how he can make such an apparently anti-empirical notion tally with a philosophy of immanence, and so also how we should position it in Deleuze's own complex thought. For Deleuze himself 'the virtual is opposed not to the real but to the actual. *The virtual is fully real in so far as it is virtual*'. The actual is normally aligned with a lesser realm (the One, the possible, the molar, the spatial, the phenomenological, the psychological, and so on), while the virtual alone has privileged access to reality, that is, to ontology (as the pure difference subtending our actual world). Indeed, while 'purely actual objects do not exist', the virtual has no such restrictions placed upon it.[56] But if the virtual is given its ascendancy at the expense of the actual, the former alone being real, we are left with numerous problems, the ones for Deleuze having already been spelt out.

Nonetheless, this bias is also found in many readings of Bergson too, as his thought becomes refracted through a Deleuzian Virtualism. Keith Ansell Pearson, for example, sees a fundamental advance in Bergson's shift from actual psychology to virtual ontology in his analysis of memory in *Matter and Memory*.[57] What can appear to be an equitable treatment of the actual and the virtual more often than not conceals a one-sided prioritisation by implication. Hence, Ansell Pearson is careful when writing of the 'actualization of the virtual' to note that 'the virtual is only real in so far as it is actualized'.[58] This accent on the movement of actualisation only partially conceals the fact that the actual forms thus created are ontologically dependent on a ground that is not their own. They *emerge* (according to a principle of differentiation) from the virtual. Likewise, James Williams begins impartially enough, arguing, after Deleuze, for the '"reciprocal determination" between the virtual and the actual' and for the 'inseparability of the two concepts', before returning to a general thrust that remains anti-Actualist, 'actual objects' being disassociated from 'the processes that bring us about' such that our maxim should be '*leave all actual things behind (forget everything)*'.[59] Such anti-Actualism could never stand within the immanent ontologies of Henry, Badiou and Laruelle: so how could it be made to work in Deleuze? An answer may arise if we look to Bergson's use of the virtual as an emergent form, an optical artefact that has resonance for Deleuze's difficulties in reconciling it with a radical empiricism.

In Bergson's work, the virtual is best regarded as an optical and psychological concept derived from actual processes. Though some early texts – like *Matter and Memory* – can lead one to think of the virtual as an absolute, later texts, especially in the period between 1910 and 1922, take a more Actualist approach pointing in a direction beyond the virtual. Looking at these later texts, it is possible to see a dimension in Bergson's thought emerge whereby the virtual is grounded by a play of actualities: the virtual for Bergson becomes a well-founded perspectival (optical) and psychological phenomenon – an emergent product formed through the refractive interplay between a multiplicity of actual entities (including spatial and temporal continuities *and* discontinuities, identities *and* differences, quantities *and* qualities). Being 'well-founded' here means that the virtual, while a function of the actual and an emergent product, has real effects on the actual rather than being merely epiphenomenal, which is certainly more value than the Deleuzians offer the actual, given their view that phenomenology must be epiphenomenology.[60]

Admittedly, it could be suggested that all that is really involved here is a name-change: like some inverted colour spectrum argument, we might simply swap the terms 'virtual' and 'actual' in all that Bergson or Deleuze write on the topic and end up with the same philosophical results. But the stakes are larger than that, simply because the abstract language of virtual and actual are linked to more concrete cognate terms that cannot be so easily swapped, while also being rooted in metaphysical thoughts with different emphases. One real consequence of this for Deleuze would be a loosening up of some of his own strict dualisms: one we've already reviewed as no longer so rigorous – that of the molar and the molecular – and others we will review below: that of *Chronos* and *Aion*, of the finite and the infinite, and of difference and repetition.

TIME AND MEMORY, BERGSON AND DELEUZE

Of all the dualisms set up by the virtual, the one most pertinent to Deleuze's appropriation of Bergson is in terms of past and present, and therewith, of pure memory and *durée*.[61] The virtual as pure memory is characterised in *Matter and Memory* as the persistence of the past, as the ongoing existence of the past after its passing, and as the realm out of which new presents emerge.[62] Whereas an occurrent recollection *actualises* the past, the underlying pure memory *is* this past. Yet this position is difficult to countenance without also negating the reality of time as genuine novelty (a characterisation much more in tune with Bergson's first work, *Time and Free Will*), given that *actual*, new presents seem to be *ontologically* prefigured within the virtual, persisting past. And the same problem endures with Deleuze: setting up the virtual as what conditions the actual (even if it were via differentiation) appears to set the latter off as ontologically redundant, an illegitimate outside for a philosophy aiming for no inside/outside thinking at all.[63] There will, of course, be the retort that asks what conditions this movement of time, where its potential lies, where it is synthesised, or how it is constituted, if not through the past. For instance, how is the past made from the present, how is the latter made *to pass*? *Difference and Repetition* talks of the paradox of the present as the need for a time in which to constitute or synthesise time (as the succession of past, present and future): '*there must be another time in which the first synthesis of time can occur*'.[64] And this time cannot be time as succession: it is empty, the time of eternity. Pure pastness. Ultimately, the virtual *Aion*. Were it to be another actual, processual time, we would be returned to the initial question of how and where it was constituted, how did it flow? So it must be time in name only.

The implication is that the survival of the past is required in order to make the present pass. But what if the whole question of 'support' is wrong? What if the 'support' for time was always *itself*, was simply a set of other times nested within each other? The regress would not be a logical paradox or aporia whose solution requires us to stand outside time in a virtual eternity: we could embrace the regress and naturalise it in universal, enduring matter. And Bergson's theory of the *planes* of *durée* does just that: time is a stratified system of temporal rhythms running at different rates, each a condensation of other temporal rhythms.[65] The pulsations of one actual time subsumes within itself those of other actualities in a nested order of ever more contractile *durées*. Time is not one unilinear, actual, succession, but a tiered range of different actual rhythms. The regress is not only benign, but a real cosmological system of non-quantifiable scales.[66] If *durée* is fundamental change (as Bergson argues throughout his work), then it needs no other support, be it physical (in substance), ontological (in the virtual), or even logical (the virtual as the sufficient reason for change, the *why* of this passing). Actuality is a creativity neither *ex nihilo* nor *ex potentia*: it is its own ground, auto-sufficient. The *passage* of time (or movement) comes from itself at every level.

In fact, the Deleuzian theory of the virtual, of the persistence of the past, could be made compatible with its antecedents in Bergsonian vitalism, when the latter is predicated on actual becoming and affect, and the former is read through a *virtual* ontology. That is to say, the actual and the virtual are, if not actually identical, at least *virtually* so. I'm making painful play here on the word 'virtual', alas, but this is necessary. Bergson was always very careful in his choice of terminology,[67] and we must not forget the sense of the virtual as an optical image that only *approximates* the real: the 'virtual is only virtual'.[68] Within this optical context, the virtual operates through an economy of reflection: virtual images are images that are formed in a location (whether in a plane mirror or otherwise) where light does not actually reach; it only appears to an observer *as if* the light were coming from this position. Virtuality concerns reflection and the mirroring of the unreal as real. It belongs, therefore, to a bivalent dialectic of appearance and reality. (It is not without some irony for the Deleuzian reading that the origins of the virtual as an image are representationalist and so, by its own lights, transcendental.) 'The virtual' exists *only* virtually within a virtual ontology, and by that I mean that it is a performative concept, it is produced from our point of view or frame of reference as an 'image' (another crucial term for Bergson): one can *virtualise* without anything existing other than what *we call* and *see as* 'the virtual'. It is a frame or system of reference for 'seeing as', for taking up the actual world.

For Deleuze as for Bergson there are, of course, differences between actual perspectives, between our mundane and our extreme experiences, between the perception of a neurotic and the 'enlarged' perception of a schizophrenic (or artist or mystic), between, in other words, a transcendental, shocking or radical empiricism and routine perception.[69] And again, of course, it is the difference between these types of perception – ones that are richer, transgressive, or liminal, and ones that remain simple, narrow, or predictable – that leads us to think of the virtual as a fringe around our actual (and often spatialised) experience. But thinking of the virtual in this substantive manner is incorrect (at least for Bergson), for his later works reveal it as a well-founded artefact derived from and performed within our optical situation, that is, a situation of multiple, stratified actualities with multiple interfering perspectives on each other. The planes of *durée*, these rhythms of time, are also actualities interconnecting and condensing each other. It is not that there is one type of actual perception with the virtual existing beyond and around it (as a reservoir or 'cloud' of difference), but rather that there are always already numerous different forms of actualities that *virtualise* their mutual differences such that a lowest common denominator is abstracted or spatialised – termed disparagingly 'the actual' or 'the perception of *the* present' or simply 'presence' – whilst those differences are consigned to a halo surrounding or 'encircling' that single actuality and called 'the virtual' or 'pure memory', depending on one's choice of terminology.[70]

If the first discovery of Bergsonism in *Time and FreeWill* is that there is no single present, no simultaneity (time endures in multiple forms), then *there is no single past either*: there is simply what each of us *calls our past* from the frame of reference of a (changing, that is, multiple) present: a mutating wake perpetually recreated behind us. Now this core tenet of Bergsonism – that there is no simple present and so no such thing as simple presence – is most often taken by Virtualists as a licence to crown the virtual as absolutely sovereign, even though Bergson's deconstruction of presence is rendered through a multiplication of presents rather than their dissolution in the past. In much of Bergson's work, from *Time and Free Will*, first published in 1889, to 'The Perception of Change' in 1911 (where these issues are directly addressed), it is *durée* as a whole, as a continuity of change and a multiplicity of rhythms, that constitutes novelty, not one dimension of time, the past (or the 'past in general'), in isolation from the others (as though they did not really exist, singly or multiply).[71] The continuity of *durée* is not between different temporal states, present and past; in fact, it is not a continuity *with* anything at all that might be regarded either as the basis of novelty for Virtualists, or its undoing, for anti-Bergsonians like Bachelard (who confuse continuity with homogeneity).[72] Continuity, like novelty, is an 'in-itself', an irruption. Heterogeneous continuity – Bergson's proper name for *durée* – is a continuity of change, not of any-thing, but only of itself – *auto-poesis*. There is creation at all points along the continuum and it is precisely this that makes it a continuity: each point is *similarly* new in some way.[73]

So Bergson has already deconstructed presence (singular) without removing the idea of a (plural) present *tout court*. Contrary to this lenience towards and recognition of the (multiplicity of the) present or actual advocated here, most often Virtualists tend to take the present as a monological straw man for their arguments in favour of the virtual past. Even Leonard Lawlor, one of the best readers of Deleuze and Bergson, writes that Bergsonian perception 'is identical to a consciousness enlarged beyond the present and thus it is not really a perception of matter but a *memory* of matter'.[74] 'Beyond the present'. But where is that, if Bergson has already so muddied the waters of presence as to make the past (be it an 'immemorial memory' or a 'past that was never present') equally untenable? *Any* kind of ontological conditioning like this of process still reduces the integrity of change, irrespective of it being based on a relation of indeterminacy, or non-mechanistic differentiation, or resonance, or emergence, or harmonics.[75] It reduces the being of change to something else with which it must have a magical relationship of dependence *and* separation. Process is non-relational, that is, it is unrelated to anything (save itself). To relate it to anything other than process is thereby to reduce it. Brian Massumi makes the miscalculation even clearer: 'the problem', he writes, 'is that if a body were all and only in the present, it would be all and only what it is. Nothing is all and only what it is.' But for a rigorous process metaphysics, such as Massumi wants to pursue, there is no simple present, no simple 'here and now', as he also puts it. He asks the question again of how a body can change. His answer is that to change it must find the resources 'already within itself'. So far so good. But then he dubs these resources 'its *potential*'. And this potential exists outside of the body's present. Yet Massumi himself admits that every present 'is by nature a smudged becoming, not a point-state'.[76] So the presence/present of the body is already *multiform*, already flow, already change ('smudged'), *all by itself – change doesn't need a container* (be it dubbed its resource, essence, potential, substance, structure, form, past, virtual, principle, logic, or whatever else). Change is, which is really and properly to say, *change becomes*: there are only types of change in perpetual becoming. There is only the 'being of becoming', as Whitehead's principle of process would put it.[77] Presence has been exploded by Bergson, but only within its own immanent terms by multiplying itself.

This divergence of view can be illustrated with two diagrams, one Virtualist, the other Actualist. Bergson's diagram of the Inverted Cone is the one to which Virtualists most often refer (see Figure 2). For Deleuze, the apex of the cone S represents the only possible present, the single point of insertion in our actual representation of the world P. Above it, is the one virtual plane of immanence, AB, hovering above its actualisation. But if we view it thus, then everything in the diagram but the base of the cone is set outside of immanence, the base consequently becoming a relational domain, a plane *exterior to* something else (but to what – an illusion?). In the light of everything else Bergson writes, however, the whole cone ABS must be reflected through the plane P to fashion another, upright cone, representing but one broader, multifarious actual present, with S symbolising only the ideal image of the most impoverished actual form of present (see Figure 3). In other words, we must project the inverted cone via an axial symmetry using the plane P as our axis. Thus, in parallel with the planes of virtual reality on the subject-side AB, A'B', A"B", we now have, not the one plane of the actual world P, but as many planes, P', P", and so on along the length of the upright cone, as there are different types of actuality.[78]

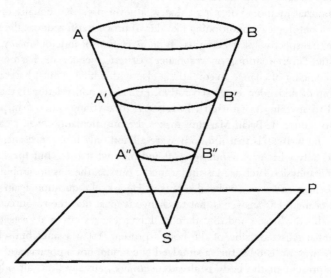

Figure 2

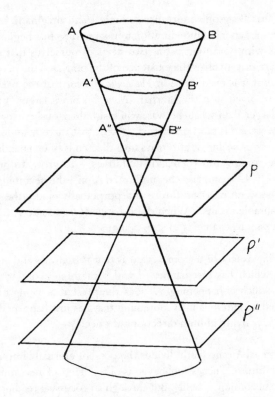

Figure 3

Returning to Deleuze now, we can begin to see how a pragmatic and processual use of the virtual itself (rather than an ontologically foundational one) can be reintegrated into his thought and how it can consequently reconfigure its thinking of immanence. For Deleuze, time is multiplicity rather than passage – *Aion* over *Chronos*: be it the 'original time' of his *Proust and Signs* (seen in either the involuntary image of eternity or the actual eternity affirmed in art), the 'crystal-image' of time in *Cinema 2*, the 'pure and empty form of time' (*Aion*) in *Difference and Repetition*, or the third synthesis of the Nietzschean eternal return, time is one metaphysical element heavily mediated by Deleuze's theory of the virtual.[79] A de-temporalisation of time. And yet, as Guattari observed separately, the plane of immanence does not affirm the coherence of a being but of a *process*.[80] And Deleuze himself writes: 'I've tried in all my books to discover the nature of events; it's a philosophical concept, the only one capable of ousting the verb "to be".'[81] So how do we reconcile these two images of time – as actual process and as what virtually conditions process?

Admittedly, Deleuze's eternalism partly comes from Spinoza, whose notion of substance has arguably more purchase on the ontological nature of the virtual in

Deleuze than has Bergson's more psychological and pragmatic implementation: 'Eternity is neither an indefinite duration nor something that begins after duration, but it coexists with duration, just as two parts of ourselves that differ in nature coexist, the part that involves the existence of the body and the part that expresses its essence.'[82] But it is even more in *The Logic of Sense* that the paradoxical nature of passage is resolved into the eternal. 'Alice becomes larger' means both that she becomes larger than what she was, while simultaneously being what becomes smaller than what she is now. An eluded present that thereby undoes self-identity. If becoming undoes be-ing, it also plays into the hands of eternal difference (*Aion*) and against be-coming too (*Chronos*). Infinitives – to grow, to grow red, to be cut, to become tall – comprise the 'unlimited Aion': the becoming that infinitely divides itself between past and future and perpetually eludes the present: incorporeal, unlocalisable events.[83] When did it happen? *It* (a static entity) could never *happen* (a process): to change is to stop being:

> The agonizing aspect of the pure event is that it is always and at the same time something which has just happened and something about to happen; never something which is happening. ... it is the present as being of reason which is subdivided *ad infinitum* into something that has just happened or is going to happen, always flying in both directions at once.[84]

The event's eternal Aionic truth divides the present eternally into proximate past and imminent future. Succession never is. The being of becoming is ironically undone by the becoming of being. But through a processual reading of the virtual, not as ground (or even groundless ground) but as itself created, there is no need for the prioritisation of *Aion* (time as the virtual *eternal*), for we can survive with the infinite series of *Chronos* (times as *actual* succession), embedding each other *indefinitely*. The elision and elusion of the present – its 'flying' away *ad infinitum* – does not make of it an illusion but a multitude. The subdivisions are not merely speculative, but real, full, self-constituting actualities. The regress is a token of real becoming, but of different types, where logic meets the real in an actual flight. There are *beings* of becoming because there is no becoming of being (virtual or otherwise). We don't need an eternity to contain other times: time is always full of *presents* plural. The paradox of the present presumes a singular present, but multiple types of actual present would obviate the need for a pre-condition or, conversely, the appearance of paradox when a pre-condition is absent.

BEYOND VIRTUALISM: THE INFINITE AND THE INDEFINITE

Just how these different actual presents are created and known to be created without reduction to *determined* actualities remains a problem. But the beginnings of an answer lie in the notion of the infinitive that we saw Deleuze attach to the event. Indeed, the related fall-out from relativising the virtual (to the actual) is a relativism concerning all infinites and absolutes in Deleuze. It is one that doesn't thereby reduce them to nothing because they cannot be *known*, but relates them to their genesis in *affectivity*: their emergence is a *felt* actuality.

Having argued that the molar/molecular distinction is actually relative and not absolute for Deleuze, and that a two-world ontology of actual and virtual is untenable for a philosophy of immanence such as this, then what can we now say of the myriad other absolute or infinite terms in his thought? Entities at their 'nth power', empty time, the eternal, chaos ('the milieu of all milieus'), 'absolute deterritorialization' (carrying the movements of 'relative deterritorialization to infinity'), singularity, nonstratified matter (where 'intensity $= 0$'), pure difference, the pure event, pure becoming, and the infinite itself, are all, in their own fashion, virtual absolutes.[85] Any such purity as these embody, automatically sets up a dyad of pure and impure, wherein the one is predicated of the other, if only by a relation of differentiation, mutation, or resonance, rather than just causal interaction. Hence, what repeats is difference, or it is the infinite that is in the finite, or the virtual that is actualised. So we arrive again at a duality inscribed within immanence – a judgement between pure and impure – one instance of the duality that 'runs throughout Deleuze's entire work', according to Badiou.[86] Purity carries within itself an *ideal* that is unadulterated by actual, empirical forms: extreme experiences alone give us access to it. Hence we have an inverse judgementalism, the schizo's experiences being judged more real than the paranoiac's, the latter somehow falling outside of reality into mere appearance or (in an attempt to get beyond epistemological terms) some analogue implying a lesser reality. A secular theology. The issue of judgement and the virtual will return again when we investigate whether Deleuze's naturalism is descriptive or prescriptive.

The most philosophically entrenched of these absolutes or purities, however, is that of the infinite. Classically, philosophers have treated the finite/infinite divide through three broad approaches: mathematically, metaphysically, or ethically. Of the philosophers examined here, the first two of these approaches are represented by Badiou, who juxtaposes finite and infinite conceptually with the mathematical notion of the transfinite, and Henry, who reconciles them metaphysically with the idea of auto-affection (the infinite Life affecting itself as finite living). The third way in contemporary thought is fairly unique to Emmanuel Levinas, who tackles the divide ethically through the affect of infinite responsibility before the face of the finite Other.

So where does Deleuze stand, the secret of whose philosophy, according to Laruelle, is the 'language of the infinite'?[87] Typical of what we have so far seen, he can take any one of these approaches depending on the context, resolving finite and infinite mathematically with the infinitesimal calculus at one time, metaphysically through movement-affect at another (infinite substance expressing itself as finite mode, for example), or even ethically as infinite, joyful creation at a third. Significantly, Deleuze is more often than not interested in the infinite as an embodied process: hence, the talk of infinite speeds or infinite mechanism in his studies of Spinoza and Leibniz, as well as his own theories of chaos, the plane of immanence, or mathematical infinitesimals. All the same, though, despite its embodiment, his is always a *virtual* infinite contrasted with an actual finite. As Actualists, on the other hand, Badiou and Henry allow the infinite an actual existence as set and affect respectively. We will not rehearse the problems with their sectarian thought yet, nor restate the dilemma for Deleuze of a virtual infinite and its inability to interact with an actual finite. But the (Bergsonian) seeds of a solution can be found for Deleuze, some of them already evident in the latter's own work.

The usual alternative to the three ways to the infinite offered above is the one offered by classical empiricism, which treats the infinite as a subjective creation (via the negation of finitude) rather than as materially and/or experientially real (be it metaphysical, mathematical, or ethical). In contrast to both positions, however, is the Bergsonian one, which tries to bypass this duality altogether through the idea of *indefinite* creation. The infinite is not pure or absolute, subjective or objective, at all, but part of a process, that of indefinite creation. This Bergsonian approach stands outside the three by bringing in this second-order term, the 'indefinite', which is both mathematical and metaphysical and yet also describes the movement between these *types* of reconciliation, and so also allows for its own surpassed actuality, that is, its own subsequent part as a type in another movement. Bergsonism always allows for a *generation of types*, of orders, a movement of movements.

Like Henry and Badiou, Bergson accepts neither a *potential* infinite, nor an actual *finite*. But, beyond metaphysics (of being, God, or the virtual), ethics (responsibility) or mathematics (the transfinite), the actual infinite for Bergson is understood as indefinite, as ongoing, as creation, as more-making.[88] The infinite is wholly indeterminate as *indefinite*. The classical infinite, by contrast, would be the substantialisation and ontologisation of the indefinite. The indefinite captures best the processual moment at issue: to say that *x* is infinite is to *decide* its being; to say that it is indefinite is to *leave it open*, to let it be beyond the finite or infinite as states or things. It is a *poesis*, a generation, but not a *potential*, which would only refer it once more to something beyond itself (what Hegel would call an improper infinite). It is actual, a 'generation' *of itself*, auto-poetic and autocatalytic. Finite and infinite are not reconciled through dialectical negation, but through an inherent and irreducible *layering*: the constant creation of types of finitude by 'regress' (so-called). The in-de-finite's own triple grammatical form is not a double negation but points to a perpetual, spiralling generation of different kinds of finitude by other levels of finitude, of actuals by actuals.[89] This makes sense from the intuitionist position that Bergson adopts; as Michael Dummett says: intuitionists admit only infinities that are 'in process of generation'.[90] But 'process' here doesn't equal potential or virtual, but the *actual*, indefinite (ongoing) creation of other actualities.

In other words, instead of a *virtual* infinite, we're offered the auto-poetic proliferation of actualities. In place of even a groundless ground comes an 'indefinite' and 'universal ungrounding' (as Deleuze himself puts it), that is, the discovery of a ground behind every other ground.[91] Not one plane of immanence but many, each with their own respective, but always relative, outsides. Not one abstract machine, but many assemblages stratifying each other, not one molecular level and one molar level, but many that are both, depending on relative non-quantifiable scales.[92]

Deleuze comes close to this indefinite generation of the actual with the paradox of the 'infinite proliferation of sense' in *The Logic of Sense*: 'I never state the sense of what I am saying. But on the other hand, I can always take the sense of what I say as the object of another proposition whose sense, in turn, I cannot state.' Now this 'paradox of regress' concerns different orders of meaning referring to themselves, and so can be related to Russell's paradox, but whether Russell's typological solution is acceptable to Deleuze is unclear. Rather than being a confusion between superior and inferior types of denotation, Deleuze emphasises an *alternation* between names used once in a denotative function and then in a sense-expressive function (this sense serving as the denotation of the other name). We go from term to relation to term. So we actually have a heterogeneity of two *series*, 'each of which is constituted by terms of the same type'.[93] The paradoxical name

circulates without end in both series and, for this reason, assures their communication. It is a two-sided entity, equally present in the signifying and the
signified series. ... It guarantees, therefore, the convergence [or 'resonation']
of the two series which it traverses, but precisely on the condition that it makes
them endlessly diverge.[94]

It would seem that Deleuze would render Russell's logical solution into a metaphysical one. But, of course, it would be Leibniz who would aid this best (Leibniz being an influence on Russell too), through a *perceptual and cosmological* proliferation of macrocosm and microcosm rather than a *semiological* one of the proliferation of sense – a proliferation of terms and relations/differentials.[95] Therewith, the propagation of series can be wrenched from its conceptualist (and Virtualist) basis and placed into something closer to a real (Leibnizian) cosmology. What can appear as a series of Spinozian *names* in Deleuze's work itself – 'schizo-analysis, micro-politics, pragmatics, diagrammatism, rhizomatics, cartography' – may become a series of actual monads or strata within the world. The paradox of regress is affirmed, not as an *aporia* for the real, but as the means by which the real propagates itself and in which his own philosophical practice partakes through an endless series of reconfigurations.

JUDGING (WITH) THE VIRTUAL

Qua *indefinite*, though, such a proliferation of strata could never exhaust its creativity and would, perhaps, be always already too determined by any one metaphysical system. According to Henry's version of the indefinite, for instance, only a non-determined *affective* growth comes close to the meaning of the indefinite in all its indeterminate unworldly being (and for him, this will be the self-feeling of divine Life). This point allows us to complete our critique of the virtual by facing up to a major metaphilosophical censure placed against the actual by Deleuzians. Keith Ansell Pearson, for example, has argued that the actual on its own cannot be univocal because in that case the actual would have to be '*already constituted*'.[96] Being *constituted* implies having an unconstituted ground, or rules of individuation, or categories of judgement, such that an ontological hierarchy, with an inside and an outside, is installed. As a consequence, radical immanence is broken, and univocity is not true, that is, being is not said in the same way of all being. But here's the rub: who says that actual beings must be constitu*ted*? Perhaps their constitution is ongoing (*indefinite*) and lies in a becoming with no outside governance or ground, no explanation of *passage* ('that which makes them pass'). This becoming is necessarily *reflexive* and *affective* – a becoming of becoming that cannot be known, only felt. Indeed, Virtualism itself sets up a judgement between the actual and the virtual (that may not constitute the actual but nonetheless grounds it), whereas Actualism is more monological and thus more immanent.

Virtualism judges *against* judgement (of the State, the Family, God) and so must set up a *ground that disallows* those who say some things are real and others unreal, those who refuse to believe in this world.[97] It combats the judgement that 'prevents the emergence of any new mode of existence', and as such is a form of resistance that 'implies no judgment'.[98] It says instead that the only *unreal* thing is whatever legitimates the statement 'some things are real and others unreal'. But this is also a form of relativism that must subvert or proliferate itself like every other relativism, that is, in reflexive terms (how does its own judgement ground itself – how are the errors or illusions of (other) judgements possible?). And so, Deleuze's proliferation of sense (a paradox of regress through self-reference, only read as a cosmological stratification rather than just a logical regression) can actually get us out of this problem by sequencing a set of perpetually growing actualities rather than any constituted ones requiring constitution. The regress becomes progress. The actual, in other words, is already virtual, so to speak, if you look at it carefully. The looking, as affect, is what counts. It is easy to miss. The crucial issue of affect, of careful looking, of whether the molar/molecular or virtual/actual is a matter of perception or reality or both (Deleuze's 'system of reference'), will be the focus for the rest of our analysis. In other words, we will be looking at the work of philosophical description and prescription, of facts and values in Deleuzian naturalism.

ON THE ACTUAL: NATURALISM AND DESCRIPTIVISM, TRUTHS AND NORMS

So far, we have focused on the problems raised for Deleuze's philosophy of immanence by its insistence (quite unique within such a philosophical approach) on a virtual–actual dimension to reality. As a theory of emergence (that nonetheless says that it is not a theory of emanation), of how less profound realities emerge from deeper ones, it contextualises the related duality of the molar–molecular:

if the molar's condition of possibility is contained *within* the molecular (often quite literally as a scalar containment) this is on the grounds of certain conditions of *emergence* following the aleatory rules of actualisation from the virtual.[99] Containment and emergence are problematic for any philosophy of immanence, and the Actualism of Henry and Badiou attempts to circumvent the problem by making appearance either illusory (phenomenology is not about the fact of emergence for Henry but its manner, its how, its self-relation) or at least non-ontological (phenomenology is not a matter of being). In more general philosophical terms, Actualism follows the view that there are no (hidden) forces, no potencies, potentials, ground or substrate to the real, no possibles awaiting actualisation, no ontological hinterworld, no absolute unconscious, no realm of anomalous identity, no pure 'Being' (be it 'as such', 'ambiguous' or 'wild'). And also that there is no virtual. In the *specific* Deleuzian context tackled here, we've seen that this means that the actual is always already actualised somewhere, within some frame or 'system' of reference. It is a form of radical ontological anti-reductionism.

In one way, Actualism can be seen as simply a radicalisation of what Deleuze himself says of desire and consciousness, namely that they *create* their object.[100] It is simply a corollary of this that perception creates memory (in both the mundane and profound sense), and so also that the actual creates the virtual. An orthodox retort might answer that the virtual is the name of the 'system' that allows creation, the condition for any production of objects by desire, perception, or even consciousness. But what if the system, the condition, is not given and can never be given, even in principle (as a principle), because it is always mutating? It is not a virtual system but an actual changing frame. What if even this changing itself mutates, so that it too cannot be named, nor left unnamed, but must always be renamed? The renaming would simply be its 'non-givenness', a given without givenness.[101] It might be pursued in various ways, some of them already discussed as Deleuze's perpetually evolving vocabulary, his actual, performative, philosophy, but also in ways that might not look like naming or even philosophy at all. But all of them, as we will see in Chapters 4 and 5, would be actual.

Actualism also rests more easily with the requirements of a philosophy of immanence because it leaves nothing out (because there is no outside) or because it leaves everything as it is. But it also tallies best with univocity, that there are no ontological hierarchies, certainly no ontological difference between pure being as such and mere empirical beings. Together, these facets underline a major requirement for any robust naturalism: that of describing rather than prescribing, and so having done with all judgement. Such descriptivism has a long history in naturalistic thought, going as far back as the Stoics and coming up through Hume's psychology, Nietzsche's *amor fati* and eternal return, and Wittgenstein's strong descriptivism (where philosophy does indeed 'leave everything as it is').[102]

It is most disconcerting, however, when this elimination of norms is turned back on philosophy itself. Take Humean associationism, for instance. If *every* string of ideas is simply a natural process of coalescence according to the mechanical principles of association, then this is also true of Hume's whole philosophy. It too is just a force of nature, a string of ideas linked by mental gravity. But then we must ask how Hume's string of ideas gets the insight into psychological reality that it purportedly has. Why are they superior to Descartes'? Naturalism and (epistemic) norms make poor bedfellows. If 'right' and 'wrong' in epistemological matters are wholly inappropriate, what is the provenance of this very notion of inappropriateness? Must it not re-admit the possibility of a transcendent viewpoint from which to judge right from wrong, true from false?

Likewise, if we are each of us a desiring-machine running blindly under the illusion of its own self-conscious volition, and if our language does not *represent* the real but orders, shapes and creates it (as Deleuze would have us think), then according to which values should we prefer the thoughts of Deleuze over those of, say, Gottlöb Frege? *How* did *he* get it right? And what does 'right' mean here? What is missing here is a rigorous theory of error in Deleuze, a lack that runs right through to the specifics of his thought. Why, for instance, are there privileged examples of Deleuzian theory in *particular* forms of literature, music and cinema? Why, say, should certain films best typify Deleuze's philosophy of cinema? If we are being given an ontology of cinema, that is, one that accounts for all film as such, then *any* film should do. How can a philosopher making a transcendent claim about film (saying that 'all films are *x, y,* or *z*') have favourites at all (that quite conveniently show this trait explicitly)? If *all films are like this,* wouldn't it prove the case better to use less convenient examples?[103] To take another instance (though not an exemplary one), at one point in *A Thousand Plateaus* Deleuze extols the synthesizer in its function of producing 'super-linear' music and thereby, supposedly, in manifesting the true nature of musical reality as a 'rhizome'.[104] Yet if music is fundamentally rhizomatic, then so is the output of the classical orchestra and the penny flute. Where is the virtue in a synthesizer? Is it because it is explicit or actual in its exemplification of Deleuzian thought?

Within the context of Deleuze's machinism, one tenable answer to the question of 'why this and not that' is, naturally, 'machinic values'. The epistemic category of truth by correspondence is obviously inappropriate to machinism on account of its position of transcendence. But an immanent and machinic analogue of a coherence theory of truth could be supplied by the image of a well-oiled and efficient machine, one that maximises the work it produces compared to the amount of energy it expends. Deleuze's philosophy might be approved because it is more friendly to the environment than most others (it *creates* more light than heat). It maximises its knowledge output with a minimum input of presupposition. 'Consistency' equals coherence. But how its knowledge-claims could be verified without begging the question would be another difficulty. And, moreover, one might still ask why efficiency (or coherence) should be valued at all? What's wrong with inefficient machines and sloppy philosophy?

We could play this game for ever. One way out is by reference to Deleuze's constructivism, his *creation* of philosophy. Rhizome-reality, and with it, Deleuze's world-view, comes to pass with the creation of the synthesizer and whatever other realities (such as the time-image in cinema, say) comprise it. So it is not that the exemplaries correspond, represent, or illustrate reality best, for in immanence, there is no outside to allow such transcendent copying (nor the judgement of the accuracy of the facsimile). At the metaphilosophical level, the *value* of a philosophy rests in its creativity: philosophy is not about solving problems (by discovering the answers 'out there', outside), but stating them 'properly', that is, responding to *new* experiences with conceptual *creativity*. But that response is not a co-respondence so much as a resonance, a vibration through thought of the experience.

This issue of descriptivism and naturalism brings us to the question of norms and values. In his *Nietzsche and Philosophy*, Deleuze goes to great lengths to de-normatise power into energy and will to power into force. And yet power-politics still underlie the philosophical energetics in this and later works. There remains an *ethics* of force quite alien to the normally materialist discourse in this work, a contrast between active and reactive force that many commentators have found problematical. To quote Deleuze: 'reactive force is . . . [that] which separates active force from what it can do. . . . And, analogously, active force is . . . force which goes to the limit of what it can do . . .'.[105] Out of this ethics of force Deleuze formulates a 'paralogism of *ressentiment*' or

> the fiction of a force separated from what it can do. . . . [R]eactive forces 'project' an abstract and neutralised image of force; such a force separated from its effects will be *blameworthy* if it acts, *deserving*, on the contrary, if it does not. . . . Although force is not separated from its manifestation, the manifestation is turned into an effect which is referred to the force as if it were a distinct and separated cause. . . . [F]orce, which has been divided in this way, is projected into a substrate, into a subject which is free to manifest it or not. . . . [T]he force thus neutralised is moralised.[106]

Significantly, the separation of a force from what it can do is Deleuze's definition of slave morality. But the problem with all this is that the moralisation of force actually *does* succeed in separating it from what it can do, according to Deleuze's own account. The very 'fiction' of the repressibility of force truly does help to repress force. But surely, it is a fallacy of retrospection to talk of forces not doing what they can, could, or even ought do? 'Can do' means overcoming any possible obstacle, hence, if something didn't do it, it couldn't do it. Talk of forces that should not do what they can do is, of course, moralistic, but so too is talk of them being *allowed* to do what they can: if they can do it, it is because they do do it; if they can't, it is because they don't.[107] 'Can do' is derived from doing, as a virtual from the actual. To think otherwise is to have the virtual – as a potential or capacity that *ought* to be actualised – reappear in normative guise. The Virtualist says: 'become what you are'. The Actualist replies: 'you are what you become'.[108] The former makes process a property of being, the latter gives the primacy to process. Of course, Deleuze is not alone in utilizing this type of language: talk of potential forces or energies, natures, dispositions and powers, is perfectly respectable in science. But Deleuze is supposedly a Humean empiricist espousing the radical *externality* of relations: the future is completely open and undetermined; hence, capacity, potentiality, and so on, are only retrospective illusions of the present reality projected into futures already past (a point Bergson also makes, as Deleuze knows).

Vincent Descombes has chastised Deleuze for this, for 'measuring *that which is* according to the standard of *that which is not*, but *which ought to be*'.[109] That is the reason why ethics has always been a problem for Deleuze: given his naturalistic premise, why *should* we be creative? Why is change, creativity, novelty, process, or becoming to be commended? Surely not from the simple dogmatic assertion of the value of freedom allied to these terms? If, on the other hand, creativity is a value just because the universe itself is in process, then we are deriving an 'ought' from an 'is' as well as making a transcendental judgement contravening the principle of immanence. We are left wondering both why a fact about the universe must be our value too, as well as how such a value was possible in the first place. In the sphere of immanent thought, epistemic norms (*how* I should believe this) merge into ethical ones (*why* I should believe this).

But perhaps Descombes is missing the point. When looking at Spinoza, for instance, Deleuze writes in a similar fashion that '*a body always goes as far as it can, in passion as in action;* and what it can do is its right'. It is our right, he adds, to fulfil our bodily potential simply because it is possible not to do so; we can easily be 'cut off, in a way, from our essence or our degree of power, cut off from what we can do.' The art of avoiding such inhibitions to our power constitutes the ethical aspect of Spinoza's naturalism which, far from falling foul of any fallacy by deriving an 'ought' from an 'is', understands the body, power, and Nature in general as a site of *simultaneously physical and ethico-political forces*. The examination of the relative compatibility of bodies amounts to a Spinozist physics which is simultaneously the cornerstone of his ethics as well. One's *natural rights* (emphasis on both terms) are defined by one's *conatus*.[110]

As Todd May puts it, difference for Deleuze is 'both ethical and metaphysical, and in most cases the ethical and the metaphysical are entwined'; indeed, his naturalism may pursue the end of effacing any distinction between metaphysics and ethics.[111] This is purportedly because Vitalism is simultaneously a metaphysical and ethical position: 'Life, for Gilles Deleuze, is the fundamental political category.'[112] Ethics comes from ethology to make of Deleuze a political ontologist. But how can what is ubiquitous and a matter of course – Life – be a value, and spawn a politics? The natural (life) may already, *actually*, be value-laden, but how can the natural determine how I should behave, what should be released or uninhibited, what rights I have? These latter determinations do not follow from an *actuality* but from a claimed potentiality, a virtuality. Even an expanded notion of Life cannot resolve this, as Badiou states: 'Life makes the multiplicity of evaluations possible, but is itself impossible to evaluate.'[113] Likewise, when Deleuze writes that ethics only makes sense if it is possible to become 'worthy of what happens to us, and thus to will and release the event', it remains an open question why the event should *deserve* our worthiness and how any such worth is possible. Alternatively, even if the living, event-ful universe already has certain vital values irreducibly folded into its very texture, there remains a *meta-ethical* gap between that fact and the altogether different idea that *we* ought therefore to pursue those values or be worthy of them (presuming that we are free so to do or be). Before we can justify Deleuze's principle that 'politics precedes being' or create a 'political physics', we will have to go further still in our transvaluation of value.[114] And to do this we will need a theory of affectivity that wears its normativity 'on its sleeve', so to speak; that is, a Deleuzian concept – affect – but one operating in actual rather than virtual mode.

THE AFFECTIVE BACKGROUND TO DIFFERENCE AND REPETITION

The Deleuzian who has done the most research of late on the theory of affect is Brian Massumi in his book *Parables of the Virtual*. But, in as much as this work is faithful to Deleuze's line of thinking, it reproduces some of the tensions within that thought, especially as regards naturalism and Virtualism. Massumi's aim is subtly naturalistic, with the endeavour to show that nature and culture feed back on each other because they belong on 'a *nature–culture continuum*'. To facilitate this he follows Bergson even more closely than Deleuze by showing how movement and sensation are intrinsically linked: 'When I think of my body and ask what it does to earn that name, two things stand out. It *moves*. It *feels*. In fact, it does both at the same time. It moves as it feels, and it feels itself moving.' Process is identified with affectivity. Movement with feeling. Massumi is, however, wholly opposed to the Idealist, Platonist reading of the virtual: intensity is equated with affect (different from emotion), not Idea.[115]

But while Massumi claims to be following a rigorously naturalistic and processual view, his Virtualism counteracts this at various points: 'In motion', he writes, 'a body is in an immediate, unfolding relation to its own nonpresent potential to vary'. Virtualised affect is given an absolute purity (it is non-intentional, non-linguistic – all these being features of mere, actual emotion). We get a 'transitional immediacy of a real relation – that of a body to its own *indeterminacy*'. But such talk of 'relation', or the 'charge of indeterminacy *carried* by a body', returns us to a subject–predicate view of movement and so to a substance-metaphysics, with a virtual charge, potential, or indeterminacy underlying the actual (body).[116] In a non-virtual process metaphysics, movement needs no carriage and the body is not underpinned by a virtual power to move: the actual body *is* already a movement, and this movement is only of other actual movements, and so on, all the way down, or up.

In this manner, Massumi continues to veer towards and away from a consistent process-view throughout his text, saying at one point that 'movement, in process, cannot be determinately indexed to anything outside of itself', only then to add problematically that 'it has withdrawn into an all-encompassing relation with what it will be. It is in becoming, absorbed in occupying its field of potential.' The catchword is 'potential', which is defined as 'the immanence of a thing to its still indeterminate variation'. But Massumi is partly aware of his dilemma, wondering to himself at one point to what extent the virtual is exhausted by a notion of potential. However, he does not make the leap to seeing that the virtual itself can be resolved not by simply affirming 'the ultimate paradox of the dynamic unity of movement and sensation', but by dissolving it (and its paradox) in an interplay of actualities and their relation to each other.[117]

All the same, Massumi does face the problem of how such Virtualism compromises Deleuze's empiricism. Here is how he negotiates that compromise:

> Although the realm of intensity that Deleuze's philosophy strives to conceptualize is transcendental in the sense that it is not directly accessible to experience, it is not transcendent, it is not exactly outside experience either.[118]

The transcendental is immanent to experience, like the other side of a coin. The 'empirical world' of the actual somehow falls short of the real experience of the event. The event is 'superempirical', being both substanceless and durationless in its purity. In fact, a new moralism appears in this Virtualist language, whereby affect is said to 'contaminate' 'empirical space through language'. Intensity, the virtual, then, is quasi-experiential: 'not exactly outside' experience but not fully within it either. So far, so fuzzy.[119]

But it is his own central concept of affectivity that may save the day for Massumi, both in terms of maintaining a consistent empiricism and naturalism (that would no longer need to yank in notions of the 'superempirical') as well as a genuine process metaphysics (with no unearthly virtual sustaining change). The key to this would be in seeing affect, the lived body, or sensed movement, as wholly *worldly and actual*. Of course, the affect in question here is not intrinsically subjective but an 'impersonal affect', 'the connecting thread of experience. It is the invisible glue that holds the world together. In event.'[120] The World is made Affect. Such being the case, the earlier problem of deriving values from facts slides away because the world is given immanent value by *being* affective: basically, there are no facts, there are only values. This would at least appease the Aristotelians, Spinozists, Humeans, Utilitarians, Bergsonians and Heideggerians who all, in one way or another, would see an affective basis to ethics as sufficient, whether that basis is predicated ultimately on happiness (*eudaimonia*), joy, pleasure, or care (*Sorge*).

The question then becomes one concerning the nature of this affective world: is it virtual or actual? For a start, it is clearly processual, a composition of events, singular novelties and excess to situations.[121] Most significantly, even the 'objects' making up this world are allowed an actual complexity:

> When we speak of 'an' object or thing, what we are referring to is a complex interweaving of attributes and contents as subsumed under a nominal identity (a name). 'An' object subsumes a multiplicity that evolves situationally. Every object is an evolving differential: a snow-balling, an open-ended variation of itself.[122]

Evidently, Massumi is a nominalist: everything is new. But here the progress halts, for we have already seen that Massumi habitually insists on thinking that such self-variation will ultimately need an index beyond itself, to a virtual potential, and so on. The new, the variation, or the event, always needs the virtual. However, in coming close to the end of our treatment of Deleuze, the final question concerning radical novelty or pure difference itself must be addressed. Here is another of these purities, another virtual absolute, but it is one that is crucial to any process thought, Virtualist *or* Actualist. What is significant, however, is that the actual – as *affectivity* – can be seen to underlie pure difference (or radical novelty) *and* pure repetition. To see this we must compare Deleuze again with his primary source in French thought, that is, with Bergson.

Of the two fundamental ways of reading the world – thinking difference from the standpoint of resemblance and identity, or thinking resemblance and identity as the 'product of a deep disparity' – Deleuze decides in favour of the latter. Difference is the noumenal; repetition, resemblance and identity merely phenomenal: 'resemblance subsists, but it is produced as the external effect. . .'.[123] For Bergson, though, matters are more complicated. Despite being a process philosopher, pure novelty is not affirmed, but rather a thinking of affect that is supposedly between the one and the many is offered in its place. Deleuze, we saw, placed the *Idea* in this position of being beyond the one and the many, in a quite Virtualist move. But the Idea was still differential. By contrast, Bergson places feeling where Deleuze locates the Idea. According to Bergson, there are bodily, affective categories underpinning our mental, cognitive categories of the one and the many, these last, when inflated into doctrines, leading to conceptualism and nominalism respectively. The problem with both the philosophy of the singular and of the general, of pure difference and pure repetition (or nominalism and conceptualism), is that they both always start with the 'fact' that we perceive individual objects. Nominalism composes the genus (which is only a name for it) by enumeration of such objects; conceptualism disengages it from them by analysis. But for Bergson, the clear perception of individual objects, and with that the conception of genera, is a product of late development. What strikes us *first* is a 'background of generality or of resemblance' that is 'experienced as forces' rather than individuals and genera.[124] For Bergson, singularity and generality, difference and repetition, are *produced* perspectivally and affectively, that is, they are *felt* creations. Only in this way can we see how the one and the many might be reconciled, through an indefinite actual bodily recognition, a creative affect, rather than a clearly defined object or principle.

Of course, difference and novelty are linked to *creation*, and by prioritising a creativity (affective or otherwise), surely Bergson himself is setting forth a new ground of *difference*? After all, doesn't *Matter and Memory* itself begin with a plurality of images that are not created but *given*? Pluralism seems to reign over monism. But this is only an impression. The images in the first chapter of *Matter and Memory* are also *affects* (as Massumi's work reiterates), but they are affects of *identity and alterity* (a point Massumi leaves out): Bergson shows how quickly we must *feel* that there *must be* others beyond me (a plurality of others), because *only I can feel* myself moving. So this plurality (of self and others), *in its own actuality,* has its basis in affect – we can only *feel* it. Affect is both personal and social (impersonal), singular and plural, indeed, it is at the core of the *creation* of self and other, of the one and the multiple. I discover myself and others through movement and sensation. So it is both meta-plural and meta-singular, being a creation of (types of) both.[125] In sum, what we are given is not a philosophy of difference *simpliciter* but one of movement and the (affective) creation of types of difference and types of identity.

WORLD AS AFFECT

Massumi reads the affective world as 'a world capable of surprise', of a mismatch with our expectations, and in response to the hypothetical question, 'a surprise to who?' he asserts that 'ultimately, the question is not "Whose?" Whose mistake, whose mismatch, whose truth? The question is "of what?" Answer: *the world's.* Altogether and openly.'[126] This is a lovely vision, but it remains to be asked whether seeing the world as affect does succeed in going beyond the subject–object dichotomy with a truly neutral vocabulary. Hasn't the ease of this answer come from already transforming the world from a 'what' into a 'who'? Where has the rationale for enfolding affectivity into the world come from, beyond simply *saying* (with Bergson, Deleuze, or Massumi) that there exists an affective layer enfolded into the world (be it at an actual or virtual level)? In Bergson's case, we could still wonder whether the role played by affect in the origin of genera is not simply a deferral of the problem rather than a true resolution of it. Admittedly, Bergson claims that he is not 'only throwing the problem further back' because bodily recognition is not of a 'psychological nature'. It works in virtue of the 'purely physical law' that objective similarities exist in nature.[127] But Bergson's defence raises the question of how such a *physical* background could serve as a background for generalisations that *are* of a *psychological* nature. If it serves as a background, then it must be related. Any such relation (causal or otherwise), however, would surely necessitate some psychological component to the background and return us consequently to the possibility that Bergson has only thrown 'the problem further back'. Is the background a genuinely neutral term, or does it secrete about itself something of the mental, some kind of *homunculus*? Can the material world have the power of a background as Bergson, Deleuze and Massumi all say it can (in their own ways), without being subjectivised? When we saw earlier how Deleuze described the brain as a subject, had he actually gone beyond a phenomenology of perception or simply miniaturised it in a *homunculus*? World as Affect or World as Affect*ed*? The issue of the relationship with the background is just another way of posing the mind–body problem. It is also the virtual–actual problem. Do they interact? If so, how? Will they need a third, mediating term? If not, then why are they two? Why is there not only the virtual?

We have been seeking a way to reconcile Deleuze's normative philosophy of creation with a descriptive naturalism: one means might have been to see how *affectivity*, seen as part of the world, might then act as a non-subjective carrier for *value* (we are commended to create because it is joyful to create in a world of joyful creation). But we failed to see how such affects could get into the world without already subjectivising it. The neutral vocabulary was still missed. Two responses to this can be pursued: either keep searching for this elusive language, or opt out of the enterprise altogether and take one side only, subject or object. Laruelle's programme of non-philosophy represents the search for a language adequate to a thinking of immanence without any transcendence whatsoever creeping back in. To this end, rather than continually inventing new terminological dyads as Deleuze does, it attempts to transform the grammar of language altogether by eradicating subject–object syntax. The problems that come with this strategy will be explored later.

The philosophies of immanence of Henry and Badiou belong to the second strategy, albeit in very different ways: objective science (mathematics alone is ontology) or subjective affect. But they can also be related to each other via the *reductios* their works inadvertently perform on the twin tendencies within Deleuze – towards an objective Idealism (the world as mathematical calculus) on the one hand, or towards a subjectivising patheticism (the world as affect) on the other.[128] Placed in their own more extreme settings, each has its merits, a shared one being that Badiou's mathematicism and Henry's patheticism both rest on an Actualist basis: the immanence they endorse leaves nothing outside of itself: set theory is all-encompassing, it alone concerns what *is*; or ontology is phenomenology understood as a process of phenomenalisation or auto-affection, the non-affective world (intentional object) is unreal. Neither have a two-worlds view (virtual–actual) when it comes to ontology: what you see is what you get, there is no *ontological* status to emergence (though Badiou does have a non-ontological theory of appearance and Henry does have a non-ontological theory of objectivity).[129]

But what Badiou and Henry respectively see is very different from each other, such that they are completely blind to the features of the other's world. The ties of visibility and invisibility between their models of actual immanence will be our ultimate concern, but for now, we will attempt to exhaust the model that pushes the virtues of affectivity to their limit: Henry. A realisation of the molar, or indeed the supermolar (God or Life), will be one product of this research. But so also will be the centrality of affect to a descriptive naturalism that leaves everything as it is. In Henry's hands, naturalism concerns an acceptance or radical passivity within the process of immanent auto-affection (because *we are all in* Life's substance of self-affect).

Turned back to Deleuze, the point would be that the *tree can be a rhizome and the rhizome can be a tree*, it depends on *how* you look at it (or what feeling you bring to it). How it appears is partly due to us and affective regard; what Deleuze rather matter-of-factly refers to as a 'system of reference', cannot be so wholly de-subjectivised (there are *homunculi* and micro-fascists everywhere). But Deleuze knew this already in part – 'trees have rhizome lines, and the rhizome points of arborescence'.[130] Extending the idea beyond its remit, it is possible to look again at all the Deleuzian dyads, not just to intertwine their terms (as Deleuze does here) but render their difference indefinite: the time-image can also become a movement-image (the irrational cut has come to be used for wholly rational, expressive ends in much commercial cinema); the 'organised' body is already a disorganised, extended 'cyborg' (just by breathing, just by wearing spectacles); some families, states and churches can just be as rhizomatic or arboreal as some packs, nomads and heretics; the very same artwork, architecture, or artefact can be *both* smooth *and* striated.

The point is that the disjunctions cannot be exclusive, for even the smooth and the non-linear, say, can be striated and linear *within a frame of reference that sees them so and thus makes them so*.[131] These dyads are made up of virtual terms whose mutual exclusivity is merely virtual (in the fullest sense of that term). It is not that 'in actuality' they are mixed, but that there *could never be* an actual example (of a film, of a type of music, of a body, of a *polis*, or even of a philosophy) that typifies one or the other in a pure, exemplary fashion – nothing we (or any being) could experience, even in our wildest dreams of a superior empiricism. This is not to determine the nature of experience other than to say that it is impure, perspectival, or enframed. Deleuze's inclusive disjunction disallows even his own pure dualities. His own principle for the 'rhizome' – 'either ... or ... or' – is metaphilosophically performed through the numerous lists, namings, and re-namings circulating through his actual philosophy. And this is performed in actuality as an indefinite and impure series, a regress of names.

A philosophical theory is a practice that interferes with the world: it doesn't just look at the world but changes, and is changed by, the world it looks at.[132] In terms of 'content', Deleuze will always have a core of ineliminable Virtualism in his work (especially in *Difference and Repetition*), though it co-exists alongside the actual, especially in the more concrete works co-authored with Félix Guattari. What is more important to us is the metaphilosophical form of Deleuzianism, its performativity as, in his own words, a 'perpetual heterogeneity' or even a 'heterogenesis' *in actu*, that is, a philosophical system that is not just changing itself, but one that is creating difference.[133]

In his own philosophy of immanence, this performative aspect is close to what Henry says, only in an affected manner that elaborates what could be described as a purified version of Deleuze. The differential *or* self-identical nature of any world-element pertains to a *subjective* frame of reference. It does so non-relativistically, however, because our affective regard is set between thresholds that are not of our making: they belong to a Life that encompasses both subject and object. Affect, therefore, while being re-connected to the subject (contra Deleuze), still does not *represent* the world: it enters us into the 'object' (as it enters us). It is mereological. Moreover, actual affect is vital for change, and differentials can only be felt *as* simple states. *But the felt simplicity precisely is the making or condensing of the differential-state from the differands, the relation from the relata.* We never affectively inhabit the differential *as* differential nor the molecular-states *as* molecular. We feel it at our own, simple, molar level – this simplicity just *is* the capturing or synthesising that brings the relata together *as* a feeling and an object. Even if Henry read little of Deleuze, his own ideas do overlap greatly with the vitalist and pathetic elements of his work, though only by differing greatly as regards the dimension of the molecular, the subjective and the abstract. We will also see Henry emphasise the radical passivity of philosophy itself to the highest, infinite levels of what we might describe as the 'supermolar' subject. The immanent divine. Such infinitism, however, will bring problems of its own.

CHAPTER 2

Henry and the Affects of Actual Immanence

> There is no mystery, because *there aren't two realities whose corre-*
> *spondence would be a problem, but one alone, a sole living force that we*
> *experience in us under the form of this pathos that acts to express itself* ...[1]

ANOTHER FORM OF IMMANENCE

One way of seeing the situation we've contrived thus far is in terms of what is thinkable. For Deleuze, there is a need for a two-world view, of actual and virtual, if process, change, or the new is to be thinkable at all. A principle of sufficient reason demands that there be an 'implicit' or virtual domain to make the present pass: for there to be change, there must be a principle of change.[2] No less than there has to be a logic of sense or of sensation, process too needs at least *some* kind of conceptual or logical support. This is not the same kind of support as a substance metaphysics warrants, to be sure, for at issue here is what allows us to think *change* rather than a *thing* that is changing. But the kinship between the thing and a logic that supports change is noteworthy in as much as, in each case, the alternative is unthinkable: process without substance or concept is unsustainable. Hence, Deleuze argues that change needs virtuality (be it metaphysical, logical, or both).[3] Badiou will amplify this rationality of the new further, even while basing it on what transgresses the normal laws of mathematics (the event as 'trans-being'). This chapter, however, will examine a philosopher who sees change, understood as Life, as wholly actual and yet not untenable. This is because the 'living force' of the quotation above is grasped through *pathos* rather than thought; we experience it affectively. In his late work, *On Touching: Jean-Luc Nancy*, Derrida characterised French philosophy as a 'metaphysics of touch' stretching from Descartes through Ravaisson to Nancy.[4] But perhaps no philosopher, French or otherwise, has made affectivity so central to his thought as Michel Henry. Henry sees process as 'self-constituting' because it is auto-affective: it fulfils its own manifestation in feeling itself, that is, it is auto-donational, 'that which gives and that which is given', and what is given is 'the flux in person, in its own reality'.[5]

To begin with a slight simplification, Henry can be seen as a process phenom-enologist who posits a wholly immanent (and affective) process where 'classical' phenomenologists (Husserl, Heidegger, Merleau-Ponty) posit a partly transcendent entity – Ego, Being, Flesh.[6] To do this, Henry looks to the constitution of phenomenality, that is, to the *process* by which what *appear to be* 'phenomena' (plural noun) are actually phenomenalised (verb).[7] This phenomenalisation has a double aspect, on the one hand being composed of self-affecting affects, on the other, having a theological dimension – *'God and I are one in process'*. But this is a thoroughly immanent divine, because the divine is also a vital process: 'this movement of coming into itself that is never separated from itself is life's own temporality, its radically immanent, inex-static, and *pathētik* temporality.' Life, understood as 'phenomenologically actual life', is process, a ceaseless happening that never 'is' in the substantive sense of the word.[8]

But the task for such a process phenomenology is both to comprehend reality *as well as* to comprehend the self-comprehension of this comprehension. It is a metaphilosophical task. How do we think process? For Henry, the answer is that we think it affectively through the body, through economy, through the unconscious, and through aesthetics. In each of his studies of Maine de Biran, Marx, Freud, or Kandinsky, an invisible, non-thetic, but not inaccessible process will be proposed: *the self-relation of affection*. The invisible is not 'enigmatic', perpetually escaping us or withdrawing from us. It is certainly not 'beyond the visible', and certainly not 'transcendent' over it. Henry wants an end to all 'going beyond' in contemporary thought. But going beyond the going beyond only brings us back to where we are – here and now. The invisible is here, in the actual: this strange formulation is not intended to be perversely paradoxical, it is simply the only way, according to Henry, to understand being as affectivity. Consequently, as he puts it himself, 'no situation is more repugnant' to Life than that 'of an afterworld'.[9]

Where Deleuze shifted his understanding of desire in the *Anti-Oedipus* away from pathos and towards the abstract (the desiring-machines become abstract machines), Henry locates immanence within a hugely extended view of the affective.[10] For both, affect means *'experiment'* in the French sense of the word (combining the empiricist meaning of active 'trial' and 'research' with the English sense of passive experience), but Henry's experimentation is one concentrated on pathos, in particular, the feeling of life as an ordeal. We will see, though, that this is an ordeal that involves joy as well as suffering.[11]

Such an inhumane focus on pain will not be to our contemporary taste for pleasure and *jouissance*, but experience, for Henry, is not particularly human in the normative sense. In its essence, it is closer to the experience of the Nietzschean animal, or of the child, a 'pure abyssal experience'. Far from representing a world, or an Other as different, there is a 'coincidence with a motion in it, with a force' such that the subject–object duality is no longer primary. Subject and object are two abstract moments in a structure that Henry calls 'presence'. Such presence is not representation, however, it is not a 'presence to' someone, for that already inscribes a virtual duality within affect.[12] It is a *felt* presence – an immediacy of affect (though one, we will see, with internal complexity – it is not pure). Thus far, his account is surprisingly Deleuzian. Nonetheless, by concentrating on *pathos* as the means for overcoming subject and object, Henry shows himself to be as non-Deleuzian as he is Deleuzian.

Henry's notion of affect is part of a larger scheme – namely that of Life as it enjoys its own affective existence. *Our* feelings are actually *Life's* own self-affection. Our own 'living present' is an 'arche-donation' from Life itself. Life is variable, but '*in such a fashion, however, that across its variations it never ceases to be Life*'. It is the same experience of itself that never ceases to test itself. Every new impression is a 'modalisation' of this self-experiencing. When one realises that Henry is as strongly influenced by Spinoza as is Deleuze, one will also realise the origin of this line of thought. The three concepts: of immanence (there is nothing real outside of life), affect (life is self-affection), and Life itself are all interconnected.[13] But again, Henry is not Deleuze. They read Spinoza in very different ways. Spinoza's double name for reality, '*Deus sive Natura*', is split and taken in separate directions by Henry and Deleuze respectively. Where Henry forwards an immanent theism, Deleuze follows an immanent naturalism.

This difference could be reduced to the basic fact that Deleuze is a naturalistic thinker and Henry is a phenomenologist. But that move would be too straight-forward. Henry is indeed a phenomenologist, but one of the strangest hue, for he claims to be radicalising phenomenology by *materialising* it. According to Henry, phenomenology is materialised in his work by being based on immanent, embodied affectivity rather than transcendent, specular structures of consciousness (with or without a world). More importantly still, such a procedure gets rid of the key notion of *intentionality*, which for most theorists is the cornerstone of phenomenology – be it in its original Husserlian guise, Heidegger's *In-der-welt-sein*, Merleau-Ponty's bodily *être-au-monde*, Levinas' ethical responsibility, or Derrida's *différance* (to take just five variations). Without intentionality, Henry, for most, is barely recognisable as a descendent of Husserl's thought. And yet, we must not take Henry's self-definition against Husserl uncritically, for such is the formal variability of immanence between Henry and Husserl that the meaning of 'inside' or 'outside', both literal and figurative, is multiplied and mobilised in their respective versions of phenomenology.

In fact, for Henry, the rationale for a distinction between transcendent and immanent is itself interior to an (erroneous) 'transcendent ontological milieu of the horizon'. In other (less technical) terms, Husserlian phenomenology is charac-terised as seeing the meaning of the finite phenomenon *refer* to an infinite horizon of potential phenomena (such that the real object transcends any one perception of it with an infinite richness of future profiles or *Abschattung*). In other words, the horizon is a kind of phenomenological virtual lying beyond the actual. Henry argues that, from the point of view of such a transcendental phenomenology, the distinction between transcendent horizon (or virtual) and immanent object (or actual) *is wholly contingent* and non-essential. Any 'given' profile can swap places with another in the horizon, so much so that the horizon itself loses its own specificity as anything other than an infinite collection of future profiles. The infinity of profiles (the horizon, the virtual) is *never given* a positive ontological characteristic — it is simply an in-finite, a negation of the actual: transcendence itself is non-transcendent.[14]

The phenomenological 'horizon' can also be understood temporally as the horizon of succession — past, present and future (Husserl's protention and retention) — but this too needs its own non-negative constitution, according to Henry. And for him, such a positive constitution can only be found by under-standing time as self-positing, that is, as self-affective process. The time of succession (what Deleuze called *Chronos*) succeeds *only in time* by affecting itself, by its own *internal* complication: there is no need for an outside abstract eternity when self-affection is already self-sufficient. External *passage* rests on affective *process*, which is self-positing. To translate this back into the Deleuzian problematic, *Chronos* transcends itself, it provides its own *Aion*, its own virtual, simply by being self-related. It makes more of itself, or 'surpasses' itself, *immanently*.[15]

Indeed, according to Henry, Husserl plays with different and incompatible forms of immanence and transcendence in order to stabilise phenomenalisation into an object and a subject, thus missing its radicalism. The transcendence suspended by the *epoché* is only of one, special variety, namely the 'empirical world', with the 'psychical ego [*moi*] inscribed within it'. An outside, albeit empty, world as such remains — one that Henry emphasises as specular, as a 'view'. The idea of immanence concomitant to this empty but still present outsideness becomes that which is not the empirical world but which aims at it emptily. This is a mitigated, half-immanence, *not immanent enough*. Henry wants to take this outside world back inside, only as concrete and moving, and not as an abstract and eternal essence: 'because understanding is affective, what it understands is also affective, namely, the world itself and its horizon. ... It is the world itself, this external and "real" world of things and objects which is affective and must be understood as such.'[16] Through the course of these revisions of phenomenology, what comes across most clearly is Henry's Actualism alongside his own version of finitism (though we will see his own variant of infinitism rise up later in place of the horizon). The actual, as all-embracing immanence, can do its own work of self-constitution, and it does it through the concept of auto-affection.

In sum, the phenomenological virtual is unnecessary. As we embellish these ideas in this chapter, we will see what Henry's version of phenomenology has to offer a philosophy of immanence and whether its affective Actualism can overcome the problems we encountered in Deleuze's implementation of pure immanence. Does it genuinely succeed in moving beyond subject and object, inside and outside, without simply eliminating one in favour of the other?

ACTUALISM/VIRTUALISM

But there is a good deal more to be said about virtuality in Henry's work. The virtual, the horizon, is not unreal for Henry. It is not a nothingness, but the 'shadow' of affectivity, 'its dream, its projection into the element of transcendent being'. If there is a plane of immanence, it is not conceptual, but a living, breathing being. The status of such a plane is neither foundational nor ultimate, for it is dynamic, interior and pathetic – indeed, the plane *itself is also an element*. Such a paradox – that the plane can be both ground and element – is resolved due to its 'phenomenological duplicity': that Life is the ground of affection while also affecting itself, Life is both whole and part.[17] In his book, *The Genealogy of Psychoanalysis*, Henry sees two senses to the virtual. The first designates a 'fabulous place' invented to guard the 'maintenance and consistency of what held itself exposed in the site opened by ek-stasis': in other words, what grounds the possibility of passage or process.[18] But there is another sense, not only to the virtual but also the actual, worth quoting in full:

> For life, the terms *actuality*, *virtuality*, and *potentiality* have another sense: actuality designates the self-affection in which potentiality is actual, the reality of possibility consubstantial to all power and identical to its essence. What is actual is not what arrives for a moment in the precondition of the ob-stant, but more essentially, *whatever enters that condition*, what persists and remains in itself, in its infrangible self-attachment: the untiring accomplishment of life.[19]

Life undoes the two-world, double-reality of actual and virtual: the virtual is always actualised in life's self-accomplishment. Or rather, there is always already and ever an actuality, with its virtual shadow thrown back as a 'projection' or 'dream'. Immanence demands it. Passage is not about actualisation but its opposite: '*light, power, force, and every actual form of energy never arrive. But it is precisely this impossibility of ever arriving in ek-static light that makes them possible as such, as power, as force, as actual, efficacious forms of energy.*'[20] Any argument is misplaced that underpins the diversity of actual forms with a 'mysterious terminus situated behind them' in some kind of 'absolute' of foundation, whether it be Spinoza's Substance, Malebranche's God, Kant's conditions of possibility, or contemporary psychology's cognitive-behaviour.[21] Everyday actual and diverse experience is its own ground. On the contrary, actualisation, or what Henry also calls 'genesis', *presupposes* the very dichotomy it tries to dissolve.[22] As we will learn, that dichotomy, of subject and object, is founded on reflexive affect, on a self-*relation* rather than a self-*other* relation.

And so, against the Virtualism of substance and mode, of power and capacity, Henry thinks it impossible to say to the essence 'become what you are', because there is nothing lacking to it – it is already actual. Accordingly, because we cannot *commend* life to be or do 'such and such' neither can we *judge* it for not being or doing such and such. It has no meaning, no intention. It cannot be 'judged or condemned', for, as absolutely immanent, life cannot perceive itself. It cannot represent itself to itself. And it cannot mean anything to itself. Contrary to Deleuze's project of a political physics, Life for Henry is beyond every power, be it of the State or as resistance to the State, though this is not what makes it absolute. Rather, being beyond power *is* what the absolute simply is in terms of its internal structure.[23]

A THEOLOGICAL TURN?

The equation of metaphysics with 'onto-theology' was once an accepted term of abuse for anyone working in the post-Heideggerian tradition, but recently it has been put to a new, positive use. The 'new phenomenology' of the so-called 'theological turn' takes the old metaphysics of presence (as enframing, as control, as simple presence) out of purportedly conservative theology while also reforming presence as donation and metaphysics as creative. Yet, compared to the various other candidates for overcoming metaphysics (Heidegger's ontology, Levinas' ethics, Derrida's grammatology, Marion's theology), Henry's thought – at once naturalistic (affect as vital and embodied) and non-naturalistic (affect as divine inspiration) – is still a strange specimen. If his work is part of the 'turn' in France, its account of divine auto-affection is, nevertheless, one based on self-generation; a Life that is engendered and engendering at the same time, and hence as immanent a form of theological phenomenology as can be imagined. *Deus est Natura*.

Certainly, one result of the theological shift within French phenomenology has been the re-admission of an (aggrandised) sentience in place of Heidegger's removal of consciousness in favour of being: Descartes' passionate *Sum* is not just a cognitive consciousness, but a feeling, sensing one too. To say that 'I see that I am certain' is a type of thought-sensing and *not* merely 'thinking that I see' in the sceptical sense: 'thinking that I see is sensing that I see'. Sensing is a type of thinking, a 'primal sensing'.[24] Additionally, while Henry may remark that 'all thought is essentially religious', he also describes faith as a 'hyperknowing' rather than any unknowing.[25] The trajectory of French phenomenology towards theology might be deemed inevitable in terms of French philosophy's institutional relations with religion as well as Heidegger's *Kehre*, without which, it is said, 'there would be no theological turn'.[26] But Henry, the first of these divine thinkers, remains Spinozist throughout and materialistic to excess. His is a heterodox thought of God, a radical empiricism rather than a 'radical orthodoxy', whose world is not that of the experimental sciences but a strange reality of affective processes and vital experiences. It does not focus on the phenomenology of the phenomena, on the given or donation (*données*) as a gift from a transcendent God (as Marion does), but on *our* inhuman experience of already being divine, on our immanent affec-tivity. Life, and our lives, are a divine experiment, a Godly ordeal. 'Life is more than man.'[27]

In a similar vein, the alterity of the Other is non-essential for Henry, as each of us is embedded in an overarching experiment that subsumes both self and other: 'the transcendental birth of the ego pertains to the other just as much as to me'. Affectivity is not in the external world: when lovers wish to embrace, to have pleasure, *who* wants them to touch? The answer is not a 'who' outside at all, but a who that is a what: the *sensation* of the other, *its* life inside both subjects. In reality I experience the pleasure of the other as this pleasure 'experiences itself'. When a drive becomes desire, the 'desire is without an object'. Hence, it wanders across the world like a phantom, it ties itself to images. It never finds pleasure *in* another as such, but only by being co-present to it.[28] The other, the neighbour, is just another me, 'an *alter ego*', when understood as an inhuman (divine) auto-affection, an experiment in feeling. The counterfactual, 'if I were you', only makes sense in terms of the *new test or trial* that the other's life embodies (literally) – this is the true alterity, but it is another aspect of the divine, it is not its substance. In Henry, Levinas' alterity meets Bergsonian cosmology. That is, cosmological life just *is* a passion, pain, joy and suffering – a 'pathos-with' subtending self and other.[29]

RADICALISING PHENOMENOLOGY

Indeed, perhaps Henry's prioritisation of affectivity should be seen as only pushing phenomenology to its true destiny. Having thought of perception as already worldly rather than as an access to the world (Merleau-Ponty), while at the same time distancing this world from that of any reductive scientism (Husserl), Henry places both existential action and epistemology (Merleau-Ponty's and Husserl's respective versions of phenomenology) within affectivity. He does this because existential action and epistemology are already *too* or *wrongly* enworlded for him, given his desire to remove *any* subject–object dualism. Henry claims to have created a purely immanent phenomenology, that is, one without the concept of intentionality. This had to be done because, from his perspective, an intentional phenomenology will always remain transcendental phenomenology. This amounts to ridding phenomenology of its cornerstone, the 'of' in 'consciousness of', that makes consciousness representational. The notion of 'being conscious of' must instead (says Henry) be repositioned in the internal, immanent aspect of the *cogitatio*, namely, its reflexive relationality or its ability to 'relate itself to itself'.[30] In Deleuze's *Cinema 1*, for instance, Husserl was marginalised precisely for making consciousness intentional in this way (consciousness is *of* an object) rather than processual and material (consciousness *is* its object). Deleuze also rails against other phenomenologists (like Merleau-Ponty and Levinas) for always retaining some kind of 'structure-Other' that would condition the entire perceptual field.[31] But in Henry, there is no intentionality, there is no structure–Other, and there is no transcendence, no external world whatsoever:

> *If the world phenomenologizes itself in the original revelation immanent to the act of imagination, it is because consciousness of world is effective only upon the foundation in it of a consciousness to which the world does not belong.* Consciousness of world is also always a consciousness without world.[32]

Phenomenology remains for Henry, of course, the 'principal movement of our time'. For it to survive, though, it must not merely be enlarged or revised, but '*radicalised*'. If it is to be the 'fundamental discipline of knowledge', it must no longer concern itself with 'phenomena but the mode of their givenness, their phenomenality, not that which appears, but the appearing'. Other sciences study specific phenomena, whereas phenomenology studies 'what allows a phenomenon to be a phenomenon'. Different words can fit this phenomenality, like manifestation, showing, unveiling, revelation, or even truth. Still, a tenet of phenomenology from the start is that being is appearing: 'I carry this precedence of phenomenology over ontology one step further by saying that it is only if the appearing appears in itself and as such that something ... can in turn appear, can show itself to us.' For Henry, consequently, we must clarify what appearing is, that is, the pure phenomenological matter in which phenomenality phenomenalises itself. As his key work, *The Essence of Manifestation*, puts it: 'to be affected by itself, to affect itself, is to constitute itself as auto-affection'.[33] 'Manifestation', originally a Hegelian term, is the essence of being – being must appear; but in Henry's hands, it does so in actual, processual, affectivity.[34] Process phenomenology. By contrast, classical phenomenology misses out on its own *metatheoretical* status as a reflexive process, a 'how' or manner of understanding, and Henry is here trying to put to flight any specular substrate (datum, ego, view ...) that would hypostasise this process. Phenomenology is oblivious to its own *how* by thinking of itself as an objective method transcending and observing its datum, and so failing to see itself as part of the phenomenon, the 'method' as immanent to its world.[35]

More radically still, the matter can be formulated as the question of whether phenomenology was ever possible at all – how can we acquire a pure view of the *cogitatio* when operating by necessity within the confines of the *cogito*? This question is not new: it was the motivation behind Heidegger's ontologisation of phenomenology as well as the constant criticism of structuralists and post-structuralists alike. But Henry's answer to it is extreme in its novel simplicity. Phenomenology is only possible through a primitive, immanent reflexivity: it is living itself which carries within it a primitive knowledge of living – each property of the lived originally carries with it an 'initial knowledge' of that which it is – and it is this that phenomenology clarifies. In fact, this knowledge is one and the same as phenomenology's ability to be immanently reflexive: 'the phenomenological method is the auto-clarification of the transcendental life of absolute subjectivity under the form of its auto-objectification'.[36] This 'auto-clarification' of the life of absolute subjectivity is the *logos* of phenomenology. To radicalise phenomenology we must not only look at 'pure phenomenality', but at the *way*, the *how*, in which phenomenality is originally phenomenalised, the 'substance' 'the stuff', the 'pure phenomenological materiality'. Phenomenology need not lose itself in being. Rather, it must be materialised by making its 'method' match its 'object' such that there is no distinction between the two. Its discourse *is* its world. Being, as Life, was always phenomenological: a reflexive, immanent, material affectivity.

Some commentators have argued that Henry is an inherently non-relational thinker, but this misses his meaning: *qua* non-intentional, his thought is indeed non-relational.[37] But *qua* affectivity, it is relational, only relational to itself and not to otherness. Henry's reflexivity is not conceptual, it is not reflective, it does not represent otherness. Reflexivity is immanently relational but transcendentally non-relational. It is auto-affective. There is a link here between the phenomeno-logical reduction and (ir)reducibility. Henry conflates Husserl's *eidetic* reduction to the phenomenological one, and in so doing keeps as irreducible the appearing itself, which, for Henry, means that which cannot appear as essence, as *eidos*. The process that allows things to appear is invisible – *it can only be felt*. Yet auto-affection is not a new idea in phenomenology: it has been invoked as the basis of its scientific rigour as well as, when subverted, its deconstruction. How Henry's specific understanding of auto-affection might resist both assimilation and critique by its precedents remains to be seen. But we can begin this research by measuring the radicality of Henry against the three classical instances of phenomenology with which he is most often connected, Husserl's, Heidegger's and Merleau-Ponty's. Doing so will elucidate the three fronts on which Henry makes his stand: a new materialism, a new pluralism and a new philosophy of incarnation.

CONTRA HUSSERL: A NEW MATERIALISM

According to Henry's account, the problem with Husserlian phenomenology is that it over-emphasises the noetic, mentalist side of phenomena, how the matter or '*hylē*' given to mind is enlivened and synthesised by noesis. Henry goes in the opposite direction. He emphasises layers of ever more primitive and fundamental givenness, or materiality, behind the multiple syntheses: a givenness or matter that is actually made up of embodied affect. Indeed, the duality of matter and form (*morphē*) belong to a theory of ecstatic consciousness and a Greek metaphysics that Henry wishes to avoid. Henry's material is nothing like the *hylē* of hylomorphism. On the one hand, it radicalises matter as it radicalises phenomenology, accounting for *hylē*'s pure givenness as auto-donation, an immanent donation. On the other hand, *hylē* is not a blind content – a nonstratified or zero-intensity matter – but an impressional material that prefigures the mode of its own supposed 'actualisation' to the noeses. *Hylē* determines how *morphē* 'constitutes' it in the modalities of perception, imagination, memory, and so on. Consequently, in considering the object in its individual and singular being, it is *hylē* which is more important. *Morphē* only appears secondarily when we consider the 'objective condition' of the object. Only to transcendence, to reflection, is the '*impressionelle*' a mere 'content, an effect, a datum', a 'flux of "sensations"', incapable of creating meaning autono-mously.[38] There is no zero-intensity or void (to use the language of Deleuze and Badiou) but only reiterated lamina of auto-morphic matter.

In rethinking *hylē* as self-grounding layers of ever more primordial matters with no *null-point*, Henry attacks the whole hylomorphic edifice of philosophy even more than Deleuze, and in so doing undoes the irredeemable duality of *hylē* and intentionality inherent in classical phenomenology (as Henry sees it).[39] It is a confusion to think of matter as the matter *of* an impression, a content for the inten-tional act – rather it is the impressionality of impression, or the affectivity of affect, that matters. But Henry's ever-more-primordial deductions of affect are also ever more *reflexive*, that is, they are quasi-logical *types of* affect, or, to be precise, of auto-affection, self-affecting affect. These levels or types are non-hierarchical, though. Henry rejects the idea of varying forms of existence that might be axiologically, metaphysically, or ontologically differentiated: affectivity isn't a virtual reservoir, but a myriad of different actualities. In contrast to Bergson, Heidegger, Scheler, or Deleuze, there are not certain feelings which are 'fundamental' and others vulgar, some that are 'superficial' and others 'profound', some merely actual, others virtual, such that the one may be contrasted with or opposed to the other.[40] They are all actual. It is as if each feeling is a monad, or a self, but a self which is itself internally structured as reflexive self-feeling.[41]

This quasi-logical reflexivity, however, is *simultaneously* psychological *and* metaphysical. Life is ultimately reflexive because all reflexivity has its source in life. Appearance, as appearance, is a process (though not an objectively temporal one), a 'movement without movement'.[42] The onto-logical is internally structured in terms of reflexive selves: it is a monadology, only one that works mostly 'upwards' rather than 'downwards' – theo-logical beatific souls being more in evidence than any micro-logical larval selves. Though Henry has a theory of stratified matter-affect, its downward multiplication towards the ever more primordial simultaneously reveals a large-scale 'supermolar' Life rather than a molecularity of non-human lives. Henry is performing a delicate balancing act between his theologism and his materialism that often breaks down. We will tackle this question in more depth towards the end of this chapter.

Returning to Husserl, when Henry reflects on his methodology in the *Idea of Phenomenology* of 1907, he claims that, while the *cogitatio* is indeed given, as Husserl thinks, its mode of givenness, the giving, cannot be seen. Our affective life (which is our only life) is invisible. Husserl confuses the 'seeing' (*le voir*) and its 'seen' or 'view' (*vu*). Consequently, the true immanence and singularity of *cogitatio* is 'lost' in the name of de-psychologising philosophy. Henry puts this failing down to Husserl's quest for scientific status, for essences, for 'eideticism'.[43] In fact, Husserl's search for a pure, presuppositionless phenomenology makes an interesting contrast with Henry's ever-more primordial methodology if the two are placed in the context of Derrida's critique of Husserlian phenomenology. Derrida claimed to have shown that a 'trace' lies within Husserl's 'living present', this metaphysical present of auto-affection (especially of the subject's voice) being eroded by a temporal flux that distances the subject from itself indefinitely.[44] In his own undoing of Husserl and radicalisation of phenomenology, Henry finds instead a living and felt present that may well be immune to Derrida's critique simply on account of its proclaimed *processual* nature. Presence must not be understood as an eternal (virtual) essence, but the essence of appearing *qua* actual process. Because intentionality once again figured so largely in Husserl's analysis of time, he overlooked the immanent and abyssal structure of auto-affection. For Henry, the auto-affection of time rests on auto-affection in general – it is just one instance of a universal pattern. Henry doesn't see time itself as protention and retention, but as a felt presence that must be internally complicated *in order* to be present.[45] It is not complicated, however, by an abyss of temporal modes *undoing* self-presence, but by the nature of presence as reiterative affect that, as self-complicating, *is consequently present*. Affect is auto-affect – relational indeed, but to itself. Felt presence is never simple but composite; its feeling, however, is simple in as much as it is *a* process of *composing* affects at any one time, of relating affects to itself. The feeling just is this confluence, this aggregating of the many to the one. The aporetic structure of auto-affection is not its ruin but its very nature as internally self-differentiated.

Henry can consequently be seen as a strange kind of sceptic, asking a version of the question, 'how do you know that you know?' that goes, '*how* is the given given'? The answer is through an infinite self-relating affectivity – the singularities of affect experienced as Life endures itself multiply. So Henry takes the *aporia* of temporal auto-affection and twists it around as the positive reflexivity of affect; the logical *aporia* becomes virtuous when *materialised*. The regress is only fatal when left reflective/transcendental, given that the transcendent tries to outdo time while the material/immanent can embody temporal regression infinitely as a complex reality rather than a logical flaw. Analytic regress leads only to a deeper 'material element'.[46] The deferral, be it of meaning, presence, or self, is not the loss of something in a logical void but its realisation as affective layers: an actual indefinite *growth* of affectivity that is Life's own self-creation and self-relation. Life is a 'self-movement', 'the relation that itself generates its own "terms"'.[47]

CONTRA HEIDEGGER: A NEW ONTOLOGICAL PLURALISM

Recall that Henry's abiding criticism of Husserl was that he always fails to show *how* intentionality shows itself and so how phenomenology was possible. One answer to this might simply say that it shows itself to another kind of intentionality poised upon it, but then, according to Henry, we would suffer an irredeemable and 'endless regression'. Alternatively, perhaps there is another mode of revelation where regression is not a logical vice and consequently less problematical. Where Husserlian phenomenology comes unstuck on the question of its own possibility is precisely where Heidegger, as we mentioned, offers an ontological solution. For Henry, however, the ontological response is still inadequate because it remains neutral or indifferent as regards the different phenomena's modes of appearing (a criticism Derrida would particularise around the issue of *Geschlecht*). This indifference is due to the fact (or *is* the fact) that the generality of ontology (monistic being *as such*) cannot create specificity: it cannot confer existence on anything in real existence; it 'unveils, uncovers, "opens", but does not create' (as Heidegger concedes, according to Henry). Why, for instance, does Heidegger start his analysis with the one phenomenon of *Dasein*? That Heidegger must start with the ontic is methodologically sound given the ontological relation of finitude to being, but why choose to begin with the existential analysis of (human) *Dasein* rather than any other phenomenon? Why is its analysis singular and privileged? The only answer stems from Heidegger's understanding of 'phenomenon' itself as *logos*, with which *Dasein* stands in the special relationship of questioning and unconcealing. But this is still excessively worldly from Henry's perspective. Heidegger's reading of phenomenon as *logos*, as the making-seen of truth, rests too much on Greek vision, despite his own unease with the primacy of seeing and *theōria* in

Aristotle. Speaking of phenomena in the Greek sense at all, that is, as general seeing, and seeing in general, reduces phenomenality to the speech and thought of *Dasein*.[48] Instead, affective Life is the only adequate starting point for Henry. Life overtakes being:

> What we must steadfastly rule out of the analysis of life — at least if we want to grasp life as coming forth in itself and, moreover, to understand the manner in which it does so — is the concept of being. ... Life 'is' not. Rather, it occurs and does not cease occurring. This incessant coming of life is its eternal coming forth in itself, a process without end, a constant movement.[49]

Admittedly, the ontologisation of phenomenology bequeathed to the tradition by Heidegger is one simple way of going beyond the ontological dualism that each of the philosophers of immanence we are studying strive for (being is linked to the appearance of the world). Oddly, though, Henry's approach can be seen as a retreat from this, in as much as his concept of being is realigned with affectivity rather than with the world (affects are not about one's 'Being in the world' — they are only 'about' themselves). And yet, this is not solipsism. Rather, we can also see Henry's radicalisation of phenomenology as a *mediation* of Heideggerian ontology on a par with Thomas Nagel's notion of what it is *like* to be something.[50] 'To be' becomes what it is *like* to be. How things seem — the small ball of the sun above me, the convergence of the sides of the road ahead of me — is an absolute *hic* for Henry, the ipseity of the subjective. But this subjectivity can never be seen because there is no distance in it, no '*écart*' into which a look could insert itself. What it is like to be me can never be seen because it is never away from me and out in the world — it is not a phenomenon in the Greek sense.[51]

But to say that affective Life — how things feel — is not reducible to ontological monism (being), is not to say that it is the object of biology either; because 'life is at the heart of being' this 'original phenomenalisation' is what makes it be. Life is not a *region* of ontology — it is not delimited in as much as 'all possible reality, that of Nature or of the cosmos, that of Others, that of the Absolute and thus of God himself only receives its effectivity from being situated in Life'.[52] Hence, 'what it is to be like' is not an epistemological issue (and therefore not a standardly solipsistic one either). Affect is ontological, or rather, it overtakes Heidegger's attempt at an ontological monism. It is not a question of what *other thing is like* this thing; rather, it concerns what it is to be (like) *x*, a theory of its *affective* identity, not its ontological/categorial similarity. Henry's 'hypersubjectivity' must not be read as an affirmation of the *contents* of subjectivity (views, ideas, and so on) but of the fact that there is something it is like to be a subject — that there exists a subjective frame of reference, right or wrong. It is an ontological pluralism founded on the singularity of affects rather than a monism founded on the univocity of being.

Hence, Henry can survive the Humean attack on subjective substance because, unlike Husserl (allegedly), the incorrigibility of subjective access to 'private' mental states lies not in a universal epistemic essence but in an affect — that of appearance itself – which is ontological rather than epistemological.[53] Understanding affect as immanent manifestation distances it from all notions of access to (or unveiling of) being, because, as with Deleuzian Life, it is not immanent *to* anything but itself.

Of course, this primacy of affectivity leaves Henry with what some philosophers refer to as the 'hard problem' – the fact that what I *feel* as affects are also called, from a 'neutral' frame of reference, (my) hormones, chemicals, and so on. The problem of *qualia*, of qualities, is central for a good deal of philosophy: it lies at the heart of the philosophy of mind (the mind–body problem), ethics (suffering), and the philosophy of language (indexicals). Being less abstract than the metaphysical problem of 'the one and the many', it is also a problem *we experience*, that strikes us in the flesh, born with an anomalous perception that some might even identify with the origin of philosophy itself. The problem is also the object, internalised in a philosophy of immanence because it is *felt* firstly and reflected on secondly. *Upon reflection*, the problem leads to the *aporia* of quality, heralded in Daniel Dennett's 'heterophenomenology' (that renders *qualia* illusory), the Structuralist reduction of auto-affection within Language, the post-structuralist dissemination of meaning, or Deleuze's molecularisation of molar forms. But, as felt, the 'regress' within quality is part of the phenomenon *qua* process. *Qualia* are not fixed essences but moving ones, self-relating ones, generative of self-differentiation: their deferral is always to another level of affect.

What pluralises Henry's ontology, therefore, is its emphasis on affectivity. The abstract univocity of being is replaced by multiple singularities – of 'what-it-is-like-to-be'. The 'how' of phenomenalisation *as a process* (*how* things appear) is central to this singularity of affects. It is vital for Henry throughout all his works: the 'how' emphasises context (tone, setting, and so on), of course, but even more so the inexhaustibility, ineliminability and irreducibility of affect. We are always left with affect after every reduction as an inexhaustible remainder; *the context is the 'how' which is the affect.* Every appearance has a manner of appearance, which itself must not be seen as content but contextualised again as another *manner* of that appearance, and so on, creating a tiered structure of reflexive affects. But again, this inexhaustible 'manner' or how or type does not lead to *aporia*, but precisely to the reality of auto-affection. The eternal remainder of affect is akin to the Cartesian *cogito* – what cannot be reduced, by any scepticism, or any reductionism. But it is a *cogito* of affect and not of concept. Henry treats the *how* question, not as a demand for logical premises or empirical causes, but as an ontological mannerism.

CONTRA MERLEAU-PONTY: A NEW INCARNATION

Of all the classical phenomenologists, one might expect the French instance of Merleau-Ponty's phenomenology of the pre-objective body to be one Henry could embrace, and yet here too, he feels it should be radicalised even further. Merleau-Ponty's turn to the Husserlian *Lebenswelt* puts too much stress on *Welt* and not enough on *Leben*: his portrayal of phenomenology as 'the determination to bring the world to light as it is before any falling back on ourselves has occurred' is anathema to Henry. Even though Merleau-Ponty attempts to counter the 'prejudice of the world' in both naïve empiricism and idealism, it still haunts his own ideas, such as the 'phenomenal field' wherein consciousness is 'nothing other than the dialectic of milieu and action', or the notion of the body as a 'schema' or 'diagram' of the logic of the world. There is still far too much *ek-stase* for Henry's taste[54] – Merleau-Ponty's categories of life and bodily intentionality remain still too infected with transcendence, 'falling back into the dualism of this and that' with a spiritualisation of the body that constitutes a 'mysterious incarnation'. It is this mystery that is the crucial error. What Merleau-Ponty counts as an essential ambiguity is, for Henry, the effect of a confusion over immanence and the fact that the foundation for exteriority (or transcendence) is exterior to itself – that is, it lies in immanence: 'It is immanence which feeds the confusions which obscurity arouses in thought.' But Merleau-Ponty believes that immanence is really an ontic category and no more – hence the confusion.[55]

Ultimately, Henry is arguing against all philosophies of the mysterious, the ambiguous and the virtual, while at the same time arguing for his own philosophy of what is hidden (from sight, from transcendence). Hidden, yes, but not in any way ambiguous: this is affectivity. The *aporia* for Husserl was that the intentionality that makes everything seen couldn't itself be seen. Yet the same can be said for the body that is *reduced* to an intentional body – how is it itself intended? Below the intentional body, Henry says that there must be immanent reflexive affect: 'Flesh is … the pure phenomenological matter of every genuine (i.e. radically immanent) auto-affection …'.[56]

No less than with Henry's estimation of Husserl and Heidegger, we should be wary of taking his appraisal of Merleau-Ponty at face value, especially as regards his approach to immanence, which was not so ontical across all his works. The whole point of auto-affection, the reversibility of touching and touched, or the chiasm that intertwines subject and world in one flesh, is that it intermixes immanence with transcendence. What is certain, though, is that keeping immanence and transcendence in tension like this (somewhat as Deleuze does too with the virtual and the actual), is not a virtue in Henry's eyes. Bodily intentionality is a hybrid, botched concept for him – an impurity. Yet Merleau-Ponty looks *to* intentionality as a coexistence supported by the pre-objective body, rather than as a site of separation and negativity to be avoided. However, the difficulty with such a position is that, as one commentator has said (similarly to Henry), the notions of intentionality and corporeal pre-objectivity are contradictory.[57] Intentionality allows for at least some kind of gap between subject and object such that the one can at least be either 'of' or 'for' the other and that, furthermore, facilitates the reflection needed for phenomenological analysis. At a minimum, the gap is syntactical. But to posit a pre-objective body is to close any possible gap; such a bodily intentionality would be a fusion, a coincidence, even though this is exactly what Merleau-Ponty wants to avoid.

Consequently, avoiding the ambiguities and tensions latent in Merleau-Ponty's depiction of the 'concentrated darkness of my bodily organs', Henry bases his own philosophy of the body on the work of the second French spiritualist we'll encounter, Pierre Maine de Biran.[58] In his approach, the body is wholly activated through the subjective 'I can'. None of it is left in the world (that would then only receive subjectivity – as the 'body subject' or the 'flesh' – mysteriously). Even Merleau-Ponty's category of the invisible is still forwarded as an 'invisible of this world' rather than Henry's absolute invisible: the invisibility of affect. The 'I can' is radically subjective and radically immanent, denuded completely of any possibility of being a 'constituted body'.[59] And this 'I can', the affectivisation of the body (and indeed, of all matter), goes all the way through to 'immaterial' thought itself, the 'I think'. The *cogito* is firstly a felt certainty because there is a *pathos* to all thought. Biran's *idée force* is rendered into force–affect, the 'primordial couple' in Henry's 'non-Greek' phenomenology. But Henry is insistent that this *idée force* has nothing to do with any impersonal power, *élan*, praxis, will to power, or dynamic unconscious. Despite being non-representational, it is a kind of *knowing* all the same. 'I think' = 'I can', and 'I can' is an affective, knowing movement: 'to say that *the most profound* intentionality of the life of the ego is movement is to say that the world which is *originally* given to us is precisely this world of the body ...'. That which I feel is also that which I see or I hear, because movement is immanent to the exercise of each of the senses.[60] Henry's proposal, then, amounts to a materialisation of the idea after Biran rather than an intentionalisation of the body after Merleau-Ponty.[61] Ideas are not disembodied states of mind – mere orientations – they are forces that passively and actively interact with other forces. There is no outside, but only these '*idées forces*' interacting with each other. And yet this is not an idealism – the view that there are only *immaterial* ideas – but a materialism beyond the duality of matter and mind, of bodily affects intertwining with each other, moving in and out of each other.

One way to elucidate this concept is with a cinematic example and a question. In the first *Matrix* film (Wachowski Brothers, 1999), we learn from one of the protagonists that the initial version of the computer system (the 'Matrix'), designed to keep humanity permanently lulled in a dream-world, failed catastrophically. It failed because it provided a perfect dream of joy and comfort that none of the sleeping bodies could believe in – people kept waking up when they realised it was a dream. Hence, the second, successful version of the Matrix introduced pain and suffering into the dream. It seemed that humans enjoy misery, they like to suffer in order to believe that what they are experiencing is real. But is this the whole answer? Was it only that the initial input was simply the wrong type of 'experience machine' with too much happiness and not enough suffering? Or was it that there was no *feedback* between each mind and the program (the program, after all, renders each human mind wholly passive)? From Henry's perspective, as forces, our thoughts are both active and passive in direct action upon each other, there is both active joy *and* passive suffering. It was the interactive nature of experience, of *idées forces* that was missing from the Matrix. Our thoughts are *embodied*. Our minds are not empty vessels waiting to be filled with experience, they are dispositions to act and be acted upon that are felt movements.

Of course, the retort could always ask whether there could not be an *idea of* such *idées forces* (that the Matrix could create and we passively imbibe)? Indeed, we could get into a regress here, with every form of embodied consciousness displaced and replaced by a disembodied (purely informational) idea *of* this embodied consciousness being pumped into the mind by the Matrix. But Henry can also carnalise this very *regress*: in terms of his argument, any mere 'idea of' will not *feel* right (and so be believed or accepted by the brain) unless it has the right feeling – which must precisely be the right mix of passive 'input' and active response. In Henry's terms, in fact, no 'idea of' or representation, *understood as pure passivity on our part*, could ever get off the ground because every idea (even those that claim to be 'of' something, to have an object, to be intentional) is an affectivity *at another level*. Hence, Henry's definition of affect is Life's auto-affection, as feeling feeling itself at another level. In other words, the very idea of the Matrix is unsustainable, for if it works it is only by falling back into a real interaction, a real world.

We can look at the matter in another way. In his analysis of the film, Slavoj Žižek asks why there is just one and not as many Matrices as there are enslaved bodies, each providing a personalised dream for each subjected mind?[62] Henry's answer would be that we must all share the one Matrix dream-world in order to get the right degree of interaction, and so feedback from others, the proper spontaneity of many wills operating on each other. If the joy and suffering is real, if it is to be believed, then it must be directly affective in order to have the correct level of spontaneity in interaction with alterity. This degree of spontaneity is more than mere computer generated randomness. It is a felt recognition of otherness, a style of becoming that other philosophers have called 'alteration', where alterity is understood as the similar becoming other.[63] This is not a transcendental 'Other' that Henry could never allow in his philosophy of immanence, but a shifting generation of felt alterity that *still* belongs to the *one* affective domain (Life), albeit one that fluctuates in its tonality. And only real others – not images of others – can generate the right feel of alterity. Only Life can generate the mix of serendipity and chance in life that feels right (a mix that is itself anomalous). But then, if *our* mutual and collective desire (for joy and suffering) *controls* the images of others and ourselves in the Matrix, in what sense is the Matrix not *ours* all along anyway? In what sense are we really enslaved? On this view, there is no Central Processing Unit controlling the interaction – there is only us. In other words, our interaction, even at the level of thoughts (which have their own pathos, their own *quale*), requires a conjoined effort and actually destroys the outside–inside dichotomy that sustains the appearance and reality distinction motivating the plot of *The Matrix*. What is real is effort, force, life, with no outside. Immanence is actual affectivity. In this respect, Henry's philosophy of immanence reincorporates phenomena (such as *qualia*) in a manner Deleuze, for instance, could never allow. What Deleuze would condemn as molar actualities (social structures, felt qualities, organised bodies), Henry's all-encompassing immanent Life must take up non-judgementally and embody at a supermolar level.

STRUCTURE OR AFFECT?

Of course, in simple terms, Structuralism also aimed for a kind of descriptive naturalism in its approach to the real (like Deleuze and Henry). Contrary to Henry, however, it took the transcendental route, looking for deep structures beneath phenomena. I mention Structuralism in particular here because, despite the differences, one might still ask why, as a *how*, as a 'form of form', Henry's auto-affection is not the same as the structures of Structuralism as such.[64] Just as a structure remains identical irrespective of content, so too affect for Henry seems impervious to the world which is its content. Affect is deep in this sense. Yet, in as much as his work does point to a form of structuralism, we should add that structures *are* affects for Henry. Affects are both structured and forceful precisely because structures are affects *first of all*. The form of a structure (meta-form) is not an originally asubjective and abstract one: it is grounded in embodied affectivity as the only thing that can *structure* (verb) the world. It is structure (noun) that derives from affect, not the other way around.

Admittedly, some like Dominique Janicaud have argued that the internal structure of immanence is not a structure at all: 'pure autoreference ... is not a structure: it is a tautological interiority'.[65] But this is to miss the point on account of an inappropriately abstract notion of structure. In other words, to seek the universal and abstract internal structure of affectivity is a mistaken approach to Henry because, for him, *all* structures are affects already and so the internal structure is affective too, that is, it is self-affecting. In short, Henry gives us an Actualism of affect over a Virtualism of structures: 'the word *structure* means nothing else. It means the how of phenomenality's mode of self-phenomenalisation identical to the how of its actualization.'[66] Crucially, though, this structured affectivity is not hierarchical: affectivity isn't a virtual reservoir subtending and guaranteeing the reality of the real, but a myriad of different actualities.

THE INELIMINABLE AFFECT

> Once a man is alive, he experiences feelings, and this not by reason of circumstances in which he might be placed, not by reason of his psycho-physical, characteriological or hereditary structure, not by reason of everything which apparently constitutes the particularity of his life, but upon the foundation of the essence of life in him ...[67]

Take an affect such as sadness. How do we explain it? If you respond to the question 'why are you so sad?' with some fact about the world, you are missing the affect altogether (according to Henry). If you respond with some fact about yourself (via Freud or chemical physiology, for example), you are still missing the affect. Anyone who has suffered a phobia will understand Henry's depiction of affect as essentially unworldly, non-informational and self-related (self understood here to mean another level of auto-affective structure again). Phobias are not essentially about the world (of snakes, spiders, airplanes, and so on), but about themselves, or rather their self *qua* affect. All fears start as phobias, so to speak, and only become rational (or measured), through a gradual process of virtualisation – that is, by means of a refraction through a worldly image. If this seems counter-intuitive, just think how common it is for 'us', in our post-Freudian world, to tell the supposed neurotic that his or her fear of the spider or snake is not actually about the spider or snake, but really about 'mommy' (spider = vagina) or 'daddy' (snake = penis). Or, if you do believe that spiders and snakes pose a real threat, think of how you would respond to the *aulophobe*: lest we be called naïve, most of us would be sceptical about taking this fear seriously as a response to the real danger of flutes (perhaps preferring to think of Freudian clichés instead). But then, it is always possible to escalate this hermeneutics of suspicion even further, as Deleuze and Guattari do, for example. For them, the family romance of Freudian symbolism is already too naïve. The arachnophobe or ophidiophobe, simultaneously fascinated and frightened by spiders or snakes, is not ultimately concerned with mommy and daddy. Rather, their ambivalence is a becoming-animal, a becoming-spider or becoming-snake. Or we could take the Nietzschean explanatory route, or the Jungian one, and so on.

Henry simply short-circuits this process; the affect is neither *about* anything else or *doing* anything else outside of itself. It is not about the world, be it in terms of representation or becoming. It is 'about' itself. This is true of the essence of every affect, not just the extreme ones (which only make explicit what is implicit in the rest). In Henry's own words, 'suffering alone allows us to know what suffering is ...'. There is no divide within suffering to allow us to insert a view that would reveal its supposed object. We can never see our suffering, anguish, or joy. Despair, for instance, is fundamentally indifferent to the circumstances surrounding it:

> Despair is not capable of acting on itself, on its own feeling, which ultimately appears in its absolute independence with regard to every condition foreign to its own nature. ... The same remarks hold for happiness, which does not depend for its existence on the alternating of its joys and pains, namely, on that which the event brings to us, but rather rests on itself with so much force that nothing which apparently seems opposed to it, not even the adversity or the caprice of fortune, is capable of changing its serene tonality.[68]

The different things that we might construe as determining our feelings – the objects of the world, or our present interpretation of that world, our project or self-narrative – far from being able to determine our sovereign affective existence, are identical to it and result from it: 'Egoistic, altruistic, moral, religious, aesthetic feelings do not differ because they *refer to* the ego, to someone else, to moral value, to God, or to a work of art; they differ in themselves, in their irreducible and peculiar phenomenological contents ...'. The differences between our various feelings is actually a difference within the unity of life such as takes place with the ceaseless *passage* from one modality of life to another.[69] Crucially, variability does not establish reducibility. The plurality of affects must not be made relative to some non-affective, transcendental element, but kept absolute as the immanent becoming of affect at other levels: auto-affection, the feeling of Life feeling itself. The variable histories of our emotional lives, far from having a non-affective cause or substrate (chemical or conceptual), are a form of affect on another plane, a point from which they are seen or virtualised as seemingly external, when in fact they are part of an internal structure. It is not that there are *homunculi* all the way down, but that there is affectivity *all the way up* (within a reflexive divinity). Not a society of minds, but of lives. Even the most pioneering work in the philosophy of mind, such as Antonio Damasio's *The Feeling of What Happens*, while putting affectivity at the heart of consciousness, still does not go far enough for Henry. As with Merleau-Ponty, a trace of transcendence always remains to blur the conception, whereas an absolutely immanent approach, in complete rigour, has no trace of the outside.[70]

Henry's theory, therefore, is one of pure monadic Actualism. There is no virtual element, no Freudian unconscious, no underlying cause conditioning our 'mental states' that is not itself also affective. Another example: you tell someone, 'I feel terribly guilty about *x*' and they respond to you, 'don't worry, it was really nothing'. And it *was* really nothing. So you then suppose instead that the real issue is that you feel guilty about *everything in life* because ... and now perhaps some Freudian explanation kicks in. Causal accounts of emotion like this point to a variability of affect correlated to variable personal histories. But there is never a perfect cause and effect correspondence (only at best a probability).[71] Indeed, Henry can be read as simply extending the Humean view that sees every causal explanation, even physical ones, as only a deferral of our ignorance. The same deferral is also to be found in any explanation resting on manner, form, or *how*: 'the French nationalisation of its car industry was a success because *they did it differently* from the British'; 'when I argue, I'm not being hostile because *I use a different tone* from you' and so on. The next hypothetical link in the chain for each of these *hows* would be another *how*, either acting as an alleged ultimate cause, or leading to a regress of further *hows* until arriving at the fundamental *how* – a grounding affect. To put it in Structuralist terms, a chain of signification can clearly show the meaning of each word gliding into the other within a seemingly infinite network. Semiologically, when one investigates the manner in which a word is used ('how does Derrida use the word "trace"?', for instance), one can respond by saying how the word is connected with other words, a process that, in principle, can continue *ad infinitum* (trace is connected to 'absence', 'memory', 'spectres', and these are each connected to other terms, and so on). However, this is not true of affectivity. If one understands the *how* of an utterance to mean the affect with which it is employed, then the chain will eventually come to a terminus in a fundamental affect. For Aristotle, for example, the end of the regress comes with happiness, because the affect of happiness always brings any chain to a close: being *eudaimon* is the highest end and needs no further explanation. To ask why we 'want' to be *eudaimon* is non-sensical, as the question embeds a tautology – 'why would we be happy with what makes us happy?' Of course, 'man is in love with his desires', as the saying goes, and sometimes the last thing we want is to get what we want; but these quasi-tautologies are only apparent, for there is a 'meta-desire' or 'meta-joy' at stake in each of them. If I *want* to be miserable, to be punished, or to suffer (say, for ethical, religious, or masochistic reasons), it is because these affects are embedded in another meta-affect that links them to a chain directed towards another end or meta-telos (that is ethical, religious, or masochistic in nature). There is no genuine ambivalence (contradictory feelings that thereby need a non-affective explanation), but always only different kinds of affect in a tiered, reflexive structure. Auto-affection is not tautological, but a theory of types. And nor is *akrasia* an insoluble paradox either; like its near-neighbour, ambivalence, it simply reflects the inner structure of affectivity as complex. So, *pace* Aristotle, Henry always internalises rather than terminates any regress in layers of further, circulating reflexivities or types of reflexivity, understood all the while as the self-relation of affect.

In his work *The Genealogy of Psychoanalysis*, Henry places strong emphasis on Freud's 1915 paper 'The Unconscious' for its positioning of affect beyond the conscious–unconscious dyad. Henry takes this as his starting point for a critique of psychoanalysis. The invisible, the non-seen, is not an unconsciousness, or the negation of phenomenality, but a first phenomenalisation – life itself in its pathos. There is repetition in our psychodynamics because Life is repetition; not because *we* re-present, but because Life repeats itself through us.[72] Consequently, there is no real unconscious, no virtual, repressed hinterworld, but always and ever actual affect:

> For in repression, whereas the *representation* bound to affect is pushed back into the unconscious, the affect is not suppressed but *qualitatively modified*, becoming some other tonality. ... Repression, therefore, does not signify any disappearance of affect or its phenomenality but only a modulation into another affect ...[73]

Accordingly, there is no non-affective 'rationality' overseeing our emotional lives, censoring our more unacceptable affects and admitting the less disturbing ones, but only ever one affect replacing and subsuming another. As every thought is already pathetic for Henry, 'rationality' is simply an honorific term for certain dominating and socially reinforced affects.

Analysing a feeling, even according to Husserl's phenomenological method, modifies it and gives the feeling another tonality due to the intervention of the objectifying gaze. Or rather, the analysis *is* the appearance of a new and real feeling.[74] Hence, analyses of affects are not *of* or *about* other affects (or states of affairs) *without also being a new affect*. You can neither divide nor join affects together without changing them qualitatively. That you cannot reductively analyse them is *de rigueur* for holistic theorists, but for Henry they do not 'emerge' in an ek-static manner from abstract, non-affective complex relations either – they are their own actuality. As Wittgenstein wrote in the *Tractatus*: 'the world of the happy man is a different one from that of the unhappy man'.[75] What is 'produced' is a new affect, or, to be precise, the 'new' affect is already another level of affect that harmonises other affects (a relation that will always appear to itself as cognitive, that is, as *about* other affects). This is what Henry refers to as an 'edificatory integration' in another 'higher' life. *Emergence is really uptake*, and so novelty is actually uptake too.[76] *Qua* affect, then, *force* is what is found between the actualities, or rather, it is what actualities do to each other. Better still, the actualities *are* this doing.

AFFECTS AND PROCESSES

Henry's process phenomenology of affectivity is highly unorthodox: as far away from classical phenomenology as it is from theology. Its emphasis on the category difference between form and content, though, can be criticised on a number of fronts. Henry wants to take affects out of the world by saying that the affectivity of affect is not worldly. But isn't this difference between phenomena and phenomenalisation only the equivalent of saying that, while oranges seem to be fruit, the *fruitiness* of oranges is not fruit, and so oranges are really not fruit? No – this would be a hasty conclusion. Henry's sometimes strange-sounding arguments will only come across as bizarre if we forget that they are about processes. To call an affect any-*thing* is to reduce its process to that state and miss its essence as an appear-ing. However, Henry doesn't want to use an abstract notion of process to be the saviour of appearances, for this would be just another reduction (that '*x*' is really '*x*-ing'); he wants the appearance *qua* actual manifestation to be as it is, or rather, to be what it is *like* to be, how it actually feels. Henry is trying to negotiate an anti-reductionism (read as an 'anti-transcendentalism') in as thoroughgoing or hyperbolic a fashion as possible; but perhaps, given its limit-value, it is also a limited strategy, as we will see.

Here is an example of what Henry seems to be doing: take movement. From his point of view, moving from one place to another brings with it some affect; it is the differential that is felt. The places or states between which we move and grow are indeed virtual, conceptual and abstract, while the movement is actual, felt and real. The state or place itself, once we 'arrive' there, is never felt – in this sense we are always journeying. There are only journeys and no arrivals, or rather, any arrival is a matter of feelings of other micro-journeys. Yet, having said all this (that we never feel the state, that the feeling is a differential made up of other micro-affects, and so on) we must add the following vital *proviso*: the feeling itself is *felt as* a state. It only appears to 'representational thought' (one affect *overseeing* another) as a differential. As Wittgenstein also wrote, 'it is remarkable that in everyday life we never have the feeling that the phenomenon is getting away from us, that appearances are continually flowing, but only when we philosophize'.[77] We never *feel* the differential, we only see or *reflect* it. The affect that understands a piece of music or a sentence, for instance, is indeed a concentration and a presencing of a plurality, but it is *felt as* one, as an actual singular affect. This created unity can be reduced by reflection to a plurality (as Derrida does to Husserl's auto-affection), but only by adopting a frame of reference that pretends to be *absolutely* transcendental rather than being just one level amongst others. Each present – a journey, a melody, a sentence – is an affect, a mood, that can 'coincide' with a day, an hour, or 12.6 seconds on a clock, as well as coexisting in the one subject with other presents of shorter or longer duration. Any one subject-present simply *is* the integration or 'capture' of other presents (or larval selves, as Deleuze might say).

But what Deleuze would not say is that *that* identity (that is, that capture) is itself subject to integration within another, 'higher' subject, which Henry would call the divine Life. For instance, when Henry writes about Christian art, the figures in works like the 'Stations of the Cross' are not stationary bodies at all. They are figures that *pose* as abstracted qualities belonging to a divine Life – of pardon, joy, love, purification, the gift, faith, certitude, fear, doubt, envy, cruelty, suffering, or adoration. They are living *tableaux* that are not alive in virtue of being organised-in-themselves, but because their organisation, as a movement, is *for* a larger phenomenological body. Rather than dismember the body into partial-objects, Henry integrates its molar postures into a wider, processual affectivity.[78] Though both do their best to decentre the anthropomorphic subject, Deleuze decomposes it looking down to the Nietzschean earth; Henry integrates it looking up to the divine skies.

We can take language acquisition as another example to illustrate this difference. Learning a language is a kind of movement: the transition to the new condition (having intermediate or advanced German, for instance) is never felt – at the level of feeling – I simply find myself afresh in a new state. Of course, I can reflect on my progress, remember when I was a beginner in German, and feel pride in the difference between that level and the one I am at now (one of Hume's 'indirect passions'). But what it is actually *like* to speak German, at any level, is a state all its own. This must not be confused with what it *is* to speak German – uttering German words with facility – for that is a neutral, ontological characterisation that must not be allowed to reduce what it is *like* to speak it. In fact, for Henry, it works entirely the other way around. *My facility, and my pride, are indeed intertwined with the actual affect, but only because they are (aspects of) the affect's auto-relation.* That Hume could analyse the affect into natural and conventional parts would beg the question for Henry. It is the actual *affect of pride* that erroneously 'sees' itself as an overview between two states, when, in fact, it is simply the singular affect that integrates or folds two other singular affects into itself (namely, what it is like to feel inadequate at German and what it is like to speak it well). Indeed, self-relation precisely is the conjoining or integration of other affective states. We never step out of the affective realm to *see* what is happening non-affectively. We only have certain affects that set themselves up as overviews; but their reflection, their seeing, is itself an affective integration, a capture, and nothing more. Affect is the affective integration of affects – an upward spiralling process of auto-relation. It is also a refraction rather than a reflection, a powerful material absorption rather than a specular distanciation.

Affects are as much like points, therefore, as they are like passages. But this is not to concede everything to some kind of mathematical punctalism or 'misplaced concreteness' (at least not yet). The *puncta* in question are felt, and are much closer to Roland Barthes' use of '*punctum*' – the shocking point in an image, the pathetic suffering of thought – than mathematical points on a line. They are monads of experience held together, or integrated, by other, dominant experiences. The integration is the passage, felt as a point. For there is no affect without passage, and conversely, no passage without affect – even if what is passed over are affects whose own self-identity appear to reflection as abyssal.[79]

Nevertheless, this same Actualism now spells a problem for Henry's *own* thinking of affect as a phenomenalisation process. Here is the problem: how is his philosophy possible, how is it achieved *as a type of representation*? For example, it is said that actual felt states, on and to reflection, appear as composite, that is, as the differential between two states (there and here, past and present), but that they are *taken up as* simple. But when we say that the affect *appears as* a differential and yet *is felt as* a simple state, what is the status of this first appearance? Why is it unreal? And *how* is it judged unreal? Moreover, is this to say that there really are no discrete affects at all (that will be integrated) because such a multitude is formed by the virtualisation of the subject's inner world into a space *partes extra partes*, or what Henry calls its projection into the milieu of exteriority? If there (really) are no such states, then what is integration 'really' doing? Or again: we said above that there are certain affects that '*set themselves up* as overviews' but that their so-called seeing is itself an affective integration of other affects and nothing more. But how and why does this 'set-up' proceed: is it affective or reflective? If the answer is that it is an affective process, then it is real; if it is a reflective one, then it is unreal. The problem here is that much of what these real affective processes do relies on other, unreal reflective processes that are actually other kinds of feelings, namely, feelings that feel that they are seeings. Seeing is needed for feeling, at least minimally as an illusion. This is not the situation Henry would wish for.

Some answers to these puzzles might come from thinking beyond the real–illusion dichotomy (which, ironically, is as prevalent in phenomenology as it is almost everywhere else in philosophy) and turning instead to the model of Spinoza's substance, attribute and mode. Seeing would be a mode of feeling (substance). It would be an appearance; but it would not be wholly false, simply inadequate. There remains one issue to raise, however, that relates directly to the distinction between seeing and feeling but that cannot be so readily circumvented by reference to Spinoza. The question concerns what Henry's philosophy *is*. When it says that *x* is *y*, what are we to make of this equation: is it a seeing or is it a feeling? To put it another way, in a philosophy of affect, one would imagine that representational identifications must come second to affective identifications – but how can that be so? If the philosophy is *true*, surely what it identifies must come first in the order of things, even though it is a representational identification. I see that it is true. I think that it is true. But if seeing and thinking are actually pathetic, does this amount to saying that I *feel* that it is true? Are all Henry's arguments, deductions and illustrations operative at the level of affect?

In one respect, the answer must be yes, for, *ex hypothesi*, there is no other way for Henry. And yet, as we saw with Deleuze's own machinic philosophy, this position is difficult to justify if justification itself is immanent to the thought. In Henry's case, justification would be a matter of feeling. In a sense, then, it is always already justified, but so too is every other philosophical position. So why should we prefer Henry's thought? For Deleuze, the quest was for a machinic norm; for Henry it would be for an affective norm. The problem here, though, is that affects are already normative, so in a philosophy of ubiquitous affect, we are still left wondering how to decide which philosophy to choose. Perhaps there is a hierarchy of affects in Henry after all? But even so, why should *we feel* that his philosophy is privy to the highest amongst them? The answer to this last question cannot be a non-affective reason (they do not exist for Henry), but nor can it be an affect (however that might be produced), for that would just beg another question about that affect in turn. Henry's philosophy of spiralling affect seems to be itself now spiralling out of control. In the opening of *Phénoménologie Matérielle*, he said that his task was to comprehend reality *as well as* the self-comprehension of this comprehension, and so to answer the crucial question: 'how is a philosophy of affectivity possible?'[80] The fundamental issue, then, is not whether Henry has answered his own question, but whether he ever could.

TRUTH AS AFFECT: NATURALISM, PASSIVISM, DESCRIPTIVISM

If thought itself is affective and immanent, not a correspondence with reality but as one with it (it contains no gaps), then each thought is neither true nor false: each is a law and norm unto itself. Such an intimacy makes truth redundant, for if everything is true, nothing is true. The concept of intentionality, on the other hand, by putting a gap between mind and world, does allow one to confine to 'error', 'prejudice', 'illusion' or 'falsity' – philosophies different from one's own. No less than we saw for Deleuze, what is lacking in Henry is a theory of error, of *doxa*: how can he reject the thoughts of other philosophers, and from where comes the gap for such a judgement?

To be fair, Henry actually embraces the problem, at one level at least. Truth is indeed a mereological rather than a referential phenomenon (affect is *part of* reality): 'because the life of truth is the very life of consciousness, consciousness is at no moment separated from the truth. *Truth is not transcendent to consciousness*'. Both the unity and disunity of thought and reality, knowledge and its object, are *unreal* even when the former unity is true knowledge and the latter disunity is false knowledge. Knowledge – true or false – is always unreal; feeling alone is real, such that 'the task of philosophy is in no way the accumulation of truths'.[81] Truth, then, is redundant, or at least, it is immanent. That means that it is indeed its own standard (as Spinoza thought) but it is a standard of feeling first and foremost.

And so we return to the issue of norms: we asked in the last chapter why we should prefer the thoughts of Deleuze over Frege. *How* did he get it right, and what is the meaning of 'rightness' in the context of a philosophy of immanence? In a thoroughgoing immanence, one can only describe rather than prescribe. Wasn't this the hallmark of Hume's own rigorous naturalism – that the price of being true to reality was not to pretend to judge which parts of reality to exclude, or even to pretend to judge that there are such parts? In his analysis of the theological turn, Dominique Janicaud had voiced worries over the confounding of the empirical and the ideal in much of the new phenomenology (including Henry's).[82] Too much emphasis was now being placed on a quest for the essences of phenomenality rather than on *descriptions* of phenomena; Husserl's 'principle of principles', the *epoché*, no longer being observed. Metaphysics, or onto-theology, was taking over from phenomenology.

But this is to neglect the level and manner in which both description and metaphysics are operating, at least in Henry. Phenomenological description can indeed claim to be a rigorous (argumentative) methodology, but it need not do so by disavowing any metaphysical insights. Contrary to the commonplace distinction between revisionary and descriptive metaphysics, Henry's descriptivism is at one and the same time a metaphysical reformulation born through the radical passivity that comes by adopting the 'merely' descriptive stance. The Marxian claim that philosophers only interpret the world does not hold *within* an immanent thought, for every interpretation *must* also be a change in the world, the most active change being the most passive (least judgemental) interpretation. The pathos of thought is such that its passivity, its passion, is precisely its action. Passive, descriptive and non-judgemental thought is active, passionate and changing thought. Passivity empowers. If metaphysics was also revisionary (or 'speculative' in Whitehead's terms) and not just descriptive, then it would revolutionise the world through its descriptions, through its spectacle. Letting be – *Gelassenheit* – transforms and interferes, *but it does not judge*.

As we stated earlier, going beyond the going beyond (judgementalism) brings us back to the (or *a*) here and now. Each of the plurality of felt presents, *qua* their own actuality, are different in kind, and are as such superlatives. Each must be accepted *indifferently*: 'To those *thoughts* of life, however, and although they all come from it, life remains indifferent.'[83] This is more than Nietzsche's *amor fati*, at least as Deleuze interprets it through *Aion*, eternal return, or univocity. It is not about the unchanging being of becoming, but about changing through passivity. There is an internal experience that can neither be obtained nor lost; remember that 'to want "to bring to light" the foundation is the ultimate ontological absurdity'.[84] Henry is adamant that 'absolute knowledge' does exist, but it is 'not the privilege of the moment. It is rather the very milieu of existence, the very essence of life.' There is no authentic *punctum*. In the tradition of Spinozist naturalism, Henry claims that truth is 'tragic' in as much as it signifies 'the inauguration of an absolute world from which nothing can be taken away, to which nothing can be added, where without detour, without lie, things are what they are'.[85] To have done with judgement is to accord with Wittgensteinian descriptivism – what 'leaves everything as it is'. But where Wittgenstein seeks conceptual therapy in order to have done with metaphysics, Henry seeks a perceptual-affective therapy that reforms metaphysics and world together. The reflexive (immanent) nature of dispensing with judgement just *is* a metaphysical (essential) judgement (judging not to judge), and so a part of a metaphysics – but one that is both revisionary *and* descriptive. This may appear paradoxical, in that the therapy (the change) is achieved by not wanting to change. Yet it is not a paradox, for it is about the affect of desire – and its illusory, virtual, artefacts – immanent to the problem.

AFFECTS OR CONCEPTS?

The idea of being 'in itself' is often found in Henry and seems to be vital for his thinking of the concept as an affect which has an interiority, an immanence. The concept is a feeling that is only understood when it is felt for itself, in itself, along the lines of Spinoza's adequate ideas (an idea that is in itself, in so far as anything can be – *quatenus in se est*).[86] The idea is materialised as force, and even as alive. So error – 'false or illusory feelings' – is rendered in this approach as 'badly understood feelings'.[87] This is a thoroughgoing ontologisation of content, that, by making it affective, and so immanent, reflexively twists around on itself to re-enfold what appears to be an outside back within the inside. Twisting free of (transcendental) metaphysics turns out to be a more literal task than we might have imagined – turning the world outside-in. It is a kind of deconstruction, only on the basis of re-sentimentalising a de-sentimentalised thought.

But now the question we raised in the last section re-emerges in full force: *how* is Henry's own philosophy achieved – is it performed conceptually or affectively? It is said that Emmanuel Levinas, spurred on by Derrida's criticisms, moved from philosophising about ethics to performing his philosophy *ethically* in his later, rhetorically richer texts.[88] Hasn't Henry himself the same task to accomplish? Must he not somehow put his own philosophical gaze in abeyance through his writing? But how does one write *affectively* – is it done through rhetoric, through argument, or through description (to mention but three possibilities)? Or perhaps this is a false problem if all writing is *already* affective, only some instances more adequately so than others (whatever 'adequacy' might mean here).[89] The problem for Henry is that writing is a form of making visible, a reflection that thereby distorts its object. By his own lights, thought does not have at its disposal 'the fundamental ontological dimension to which feeling belongs' for the very reason that 'it is reflection', and reflection is 'responsible for the disappearance or vanishing of feeling'.[90] To think affect is to falsify it, or rather, to make it virtual, to reflect it, rather than feel it. No less than phenomenology missed its own 'how', then, might we still ask whether Henry has failed to see his own thought as part of the phenomenon, immanent to itself? Near the conclusion of Henry's *The Essence of Manifestation*, however, he brings up the idea of an 'edificatory integration' wherein 'Being coheres with itself and the force of this integration'. He continues thus:

There exist two specific and fundamental modes in conformity with which the manifestation of what is takes place and is manifested. In the first of these modes, Being manifests itself to the outside, it makes itself unreal in the world, it is its light and the pure milieu of visibility wherein all things are visible, where a being manifests itself. . . .

In the second of these modes, in feeling, Being arises and reveals itself in itself, integrates itself with self and experiences itself, in suffering and in the enjoyment of self, and the profusion of its interior and living Being.[91]

What thought pulls asunder through virtualisation – a splitting of being into affect and the image of affect – can be reintegrated through a different order of affective manifestation. Which words would manifest such an edification? The only answer seems to be, for Henry, the divine word. In the wholly adequate thought of immanence, Henry's thought would also be discovering, or embodying, a position more akin to a de-rationalised Spinoza – by *becoming* the word of God. Henry asks a cognate question concerning justification precisely in the context of reading religious texts: 'What word will tell us', he asks, that 'the scriptures are the word of God?' Henry's answer to this seemingly circular question is that 'there is another Word' differing from all human communication, having no signifier–signified structure, no referent, and no proper utterer. There is always a Word spoken before being because it is that which grants being.[92] This quasi-religious and seemingly poetico-Heideggerian turn in his thought has its implicit roots, however, in speech-act theory, in the word as a performance and as a *how*. The circular question is resolved by splitting the affectivity of language into types. All words are affective, but they are layered around each other differently: some are set on high. So, it turns out, there is a hierarchy of affect in Henry, with joy and suffering taking on the role of foundation. And in addition, the performativity of language also allows us the possibility of philosophical words enacting an affect that might more or less approximate to these foundations.[93] Where the search for a machinic norm for Deleuze foundered on the problem of integrating value into a political physics, for Henry, having never left the realm of subjective value, the aim of finding an affective norm was easier from the start: it was simply a matter of founding this hierarchy of affect rather than finding a truly neutral integration. Henry's success is won only through philosophical partisanship, however, rather than a genuine resolution of the dilemma.

Nonetheless, returning this use of the speech-act to Henry's own texts, we might now investigate whether *his* words are adequately resonant; how or even whether their materiality enjoins us in the fundamental affects of joy and suffering. The problem in pursuing such an investigation, though, concerns the *specificity* of response. It is not a matter of which emotions his words might stir up in us (this is not the problem at all), but *that* each of us will respond to his words so differently. Such subjective responses could never be *adequately* treated here in the pretence of a universal context, once and for all, for each and every reader. On Henry's own terms, the adequacy of his words would be impossible to treat *thematically* because such a treatment would be reflective and so inadequate. For now, then, in the absence of any special rhetorical devices of our own, we will restrict ourselves to examining some of the *inadequacies* of Henry's thought, especially as regards what he excludes from his philosophy. These will be both general exclusions, such as alterity or the excluded *per se*, as well as more specific ones, such as that of a worldly thinking, that of science in particular. The rest of this chapter, therefore, will amount to a criticism of Henry's position until that time when we can find a way of showing the adequacy or inadequacy of his thought that somehow avoids the Scylla of distortive representation and the Charybdis of a counterfeit patheticism.

FROM AFFECT BACK TO THE WORLD: KANDINSKY AND MARX

Mannerism is a hallmark of Henry's process phenomenology; the movements he is concerned with are those of phenomenalisation – *how* the appearing of the phenomena is experienced. But if one asks how there can be an experience of *a* 'how', then Henry will refer this universality, these genera, to a higher type of experience, both more original and abstract. Ultimately, these foundational affects are the experience of God. One obvious respect in which Dominique Janicaud is right as regards the lack of structure in Henry's notion of affectivity concerns the place of God. Henry's God is another unstructured purity, his own virtual point. When Life is understood in a non-biological fashion as the infinite divine shrouding every feeling, a certain purity is established that would seem to negate the details of each affect as singular and real. One symptom of this has been Henry's rejection of the world as both virtual and, oddly, as that which can reflexively contaminate the reality of affect. The virtual at times seems to be a real cosmic force for Henry. It proceeds like the original Energy of immanent life, but it is the inversion of this energy, a re-direction, a re-flexion that is another form of reflexivity. In fact, Henry never thought that the virtual or 'view' was *absolutely nothing*; it was only unreal, a minimal reality, or in other words, virtual. The 'transcendental illusion' is not 'totally illusory', he says, because it carries 'a portion of "reality" and "truth"'. It is part of Life's own 'dissimulation'. The exterior is what is 'ideal', 'to-come and un-real,' but (contra Sartre) it is not nothing. As François Roustang asserts when writing on Henry, 'the unreal world of representation is thus an indispensable adjunct to reality. The illusion must protect the truth.'[94] And, in fact, *at times* it does seem as if Henry is not claiming that everything can be completely reduced to affect – concepts, intentional desires, and so on – but that affect, or auto-affection is the condition for anything. Yet if this is so, then there may be a (relative) outside after all – a fuller reality to the virtual or transcendent image.

Indeed, given the obvious fact that Henry's pure immanence needs *more structure* to give it some genuine explanatory power, it may be that the virtual – as an outside – could provide just the level of granularity required. Henry's real adversary would then be a certain *way* of seeing the world as such, namely as what is *visible to all, what is universal or transcendent*, rather than just what populates the exterior *per se*. The *how* of a seeing would be at fault, not seeing *simpliciter*; 'seeing as', not being (or non-being). The *making visible* to all, the forcing out of invisible and *immanent* life into a transcendent world of specular control, this is what is essentially 'barbarous' for Henry.[95] The most detailed exploration of a new, edificatory form of vision and worldliness comes in Henry's analyses of Kandinsky and Marx, where a rationale can also be found for his marginalisation of the virtual. Here, at last, Henry presents an Actualist kind of vision summed up in the apparently paradoxical name of his study of Kandinsky, '*Voir l'invisible*'. And this work in particular, we believe, is pivotal in making sense of Henry's challenge to philosophy.

To begin with his treatment of Kandinsky, Henry makes it clear from the start that it is not the world per se but *how* it proceeds that is at issue: 'the invisible does not designate a dimension of unreality or illusion, some fantastical other world, but exactly the opposite'. Kandinsky's peculiar form of abstraction embodies an 'abstract content' of 'invisible life in its tireless coming into itself', a 'radical subjectivity where there is neither light nor world'. It doesn't come from a 'weakness of the object'. Nor is it a subtraction from the plenitude of the world, but an uptake of point, line and plane in their purely qualitative form, shorn of any quantities whatsoever. This is why Henry claims that the world that figurative art tries to depict and the one that Kandinsky works with are not at all the same. The former is 'Galilean' and 'exterior'. The world in Kandinsky's abstract art is quite different, one where sensible qualities are integral, qualities that are sonorous tonalities, modes of life. Such art is non-referential in its picturality. To quote again: '*this original, subjective, dynamic, impressional, and pathetic nature, is the true nature which is the essence of life, it is the cosmos*'. But we must not be too literal about the figure either. For instance, Christian art may seem figural, and yet it too abstracts, according to Henry; as we saw earlier, it is about pardon, joy, love, purification, the gift, faith, suffering and adoration. These depictions are affective poses, living *qualia* without reference to a subject – 'hypersubjectivities', excess subjectivities – rather than subtractions taken from a static world. In fact, Henry proposes that great painting is always 'abstract', that is, non-mimetic of any exteriority, because 'the world that it paints is a cosmos whose unity takes root in the pathos of our invisible life …'. So the envisioned world is redeemed as a form of abstract process, but only by equating the abstract with life and affect.[96] The subtractive abstract, the quantitative abstract, *Badiou's* abstract, is the dead letter of mathematical inscription and nothing else.

The naturalisation of the aesthetic (seen already in Deleuzian cinema theory and also evident in Badiou, as we'll see) takes on new shape in Henry's hands. The (aesthetic) affect is both subjective and objective, or rather, it is tending to objectivity via a hypersubjectivity – a reflexive affect that is only external or transcendent relative to the subject that endures it, that is affected by it. But this is also a processual affect beyond intentionality – an aesthetic event, tying subject and object together under the higher category of Life feeling itself. Is it possible that the worldly movements of Kandinsky, as affective yet not visible, might approach the molecular and cerebral forces of Deleuze in his analysis of cinema, for example? No. Microphysical analysis only makes new objects appear, says Henry, whereas Kandinsky's abstract art creates a totally different form of knowledge, 'a knowledge without an object'.[97] There is no regard that *projects* a meaning or value onto an object, for there is no regard, meaning, or object at all, given that the relation of life to colour, line, point and plane is life itself. This abstract art does not represent or *express* anything either – neither world, force, affect, or life. It is a *way* of life. And against Deleuze once more, Henry's conception of affectivity is the *presupposition* of force and not its *effect*, it is *pathos* that founds any 'force' that painting embodies. We *feel* the actual over the virtual, the state over the differential.

Henry's turn to Marx also exposes a new form of processual world, this time the process of action in living labour and praxis. As he says near the end of his study, 'Marx's thought places us before the profound question: What is life?' In Marx's approach, concepts like the individual, subjectivity, life and reality all take on a new, vital and concrete aspect. For Henry, Marx's work fundamentally espouses a theory of praxis. This is a common enough assertion, of course, but it is rare for it to be given such a detailed analysis as Henry provides here. With praxis, Henry understands Marx to provide an account of the activity of the individual human person in a social context. Economics, the ideality of the State, or labour-time are all barbarous alienations of living labour – mere 'abstractions' (now understood as wholly virtual rather than processual): *'Labor in general, regardless of the way in which it is performed – whether it be the realization of one subjective potentiality or whether it imply a synthesis of these potentialities – is in itself and of its essence subjective.'* It is living labour alone, he writes, 'that creates surplus-value'. The possibility of economic exchange, for instance, rests on the substitution of abstract labour for this living labour. The central notion of labour-time, therefore, is no more than a theoretical construct; it is 'actual labor' alone that supports genuine value. Only the actual creates. And this is Henry's ultimate conclusion regarding the significance of Marx, to wit, that he discovered that 'labor *in itself as such* does not exist'. What he recognises instead is 'a wide range of concrete, subjective, individual, specific and qualitatively different labors' that 'refuse to submit to a common unit of measurement'.[98]

In total, the fundamental revision made by Henry to his earlier stance (in texts like *The Essence of Manifestation*, for example) allows the Marxian analyses an ontological status: the world they invoke is real.[99] This is no *unreal* outside, but an outside turned inside by living, concrete and actual processes. Where Henry seemed to retreat into the subject to found a value away from the world, he now makes the subject at one with the world through both its living labour as well as its art.[100] To invoke a comparable but still very different philosophy of Marx: where Deleuze sees *abstract* capital as the schizo-flow of desire, Henry sees *concrete* labour as the active flow of affect. The social in socialism is an *'abstract and irreal'* form, as compared to 'the *actual becoming of the social substance'*, which is identical to the becoming of actual, individual lives. In other words, the relation of the social to the individuals who compose it is immanent rather than transcendent.[101] In Deleuzian terms, the molar (individual) is immanent to the molecular (mass). And this inversion is even more significant than we might think at first.

THE BERKELEYAN PROBLEM: GODS, DEMI-GODS, AND SUPERMOLES

There is a passage in *A Thousand Plateaus* that tells of the 'giant molecule':

> He [Conan Doyle] explained that the Earth – the Deterritorialized, the Glacial, the giant Molecule – is a body without organs ... [whose strata] consist of giving form to matters, of imprisoning intensities or locking singularities into systems of resonance and redundancy, of producing upon the earth molecules large and small and organizing them into molar aggregates.[102]

It is often said that Deleuze writes as if from the point of view of the Earth on itself, not as a molar whole, but a giant molecule.[103] Given that Henry takes Spinoza's naturalism in the alternative, divine direction, in this light we could read his God as the greatest mole of them all. The supermole. But, why, for either Deleuze or Henry, must there be one, infinite entity – molar *or* molecular? Why can't there be stratification all the way down *and* all the way up? After all, in the previous chapter we saw how the Deleuzian virtual could be actualised, and how molarity and molecularity are only relative. Bergson makes a related point that is telling in this regard: 'in the eyes of a god looking down from above, the whole would appear indivisible'.[104] This indivisible whole, this mole, only needs the eyes of 'a god', not God. The equivalent of stratifying Deleuze's virtual in Henry's thought, then, would be to molecularise his HyperLife – to add even more internal detail to his immanence by pluralising God. This would result in there being many demi-gods around us rather than just the fundamental One above us.

There are a number of motivations for this extension of his pluralism beyond simply reinforcing a parallel with Deleuze. Firstly, there is the problem of idealism. Like every good phenomenologist before him (and no doubt every one after him), Henry strives to distance his position from idealism, be it subjective or transcendental in form. Though it is Fichte's egological idealism of I = I that is more commonly linked to Henry, his thought also bears considerable comparison to that of Berkeley.[105] In particular, his own *esse est senti* seems perilously close to Berkeley's *esse est percipi-percipere*. What is relevant about this proximity here is that Henry's phenomenology also shares two problems with that of Berkeley's idealism that stem from their respective incorporations of God into philosophy. In each case, the incorporation supports a desire for the infinite, but, no less than we saw with the infinite in Deleuze, it remains unwarranted for Henry's immanent thinking. Why must there be an infinite? Henry writes: 'our finite life is only comprehensible on the basis of the infinite life in which it is given to it*self*.'[106] But is this infinite life separate from the process of giving itself to itself, a process that Henry has *all the time* shown to be progressive, processual and *indefinite* (not infinite)? By Henry's own measure, the answer is no. God just is this indefinite self-affecting process. The question, then, is whether phenomena need simply a *more* powerful being to explain the appearance of reality (what Berkeley would call the illusion of the world's independent order), or something *infinitely* more powerful.

The immediate justification for the infinitist option would be that it provides a replacement for classical phenomenological transcendence (when a perceived object overflows any one perception of it). Of course, the later Husserl also introduced a transcendental Ego, but even in this work there are still the infinite aspects of the object-ive that require Henry to find an equivalent in terms of immanent affect. That equivalent, for Henry, is infinite Life or God. The order and coherence of the phenomenon is dependent upon an original essence rather than vice versa. The logic, structure and correlations we find in the world are grounded on a dissociation from this original essence, which is just another name for infinite Life or God.[107] This reasoning is analogous to Berkeley's motive for replacing Locke's mysterious substance with God's infinite perceptual power. Berkeley concedes that the great bulk of my perceptions are clearly independent of *my* mind and will. From where, then, does this independence, stability and order stem? These ordered ideas are in themselves passive; their order must therefore be produced by something other than an idea, yet not by matter/substance (which has no existence). Hence, it must be produced by a mind, though a mind hugely more powerful than my own. But the more powerful quickly becomes an infinite power because Berkeley wants to avoid a regress. God wills my ideas of sense as I will my own ideas of imagination.

It is affective power that supports the world in Henry's case, but whether it also needs to be infinite remains a moot point. A *greater* Life would suffice to embed each of our living affects. A *greatest* Life as already actual and infinite, by contrast, would seem to go against the grain of Henry's vitalism of perpetual growth and self-surpassing. And in Henry, moreover, we have already seen how he can accommodate regress by realising it in ever-deeper strata of matter-affect. Accordingly, must not affect be stratified *indefinitely* as a vitalist and processual thought like Henry's would seem to imply? God would not be the actual infinite, after Aristotle, but would manifest 'itself' indefinitely as a living process. Indeed, it would *be* this manifestation. Infinity would then be of layers, of reflexivities; not a mono-theism, but a poly-theism – the pluralisation of Life. Ironically, it would be the infinite actuality of God that is now virtual: what seems to lie behind and support the ongoing *growth* of divinity, a hypostasised infinite behind the actuality of the indefinite.[108] No less than Henry's case for re-admitting molar forms as immanent affects, so a case must also be made for the molecularisation of God's immanence, for an immanent God is an element of itself, that is, a relative God, a demi-god.

But this is only the first parallel with Berkeleyan idealism. For Berkeley, another problem arises concerning whether I know that God is infinite on account of my knowledge of my own finitude, or whether it is really the other way around: that I know that I am finite because of my idea of God as infinite? If the latter, then who is to say that my idea of myself as finite actually arises from my ideas of *others* less finite than myself but still not infinite like God? There might be demi-gods around me and against whom my finitude is measured. This leads us to the second problem for Henry. The presence of myself to myself is assured in the philosophies of both

Henry and Berkeley, but this presence is assured on account of God being the only other assured presence in their systems, not as an epistemic guarantor (following Descartes), but, being good empiricists, through perception (Berkeley's worldly coherence) and feeling (Henry's auto-affectivity). In both cases, my own finite and God's infinite self-presence stand or fall together. But the price in both cases is that *Other Minds* then become problematic – how are they supported metaphysically; why are they logically necessary; and are they even necessary at all?

Henry had already asked himself if his 'phenomenology of the invisible' lacked genuine intersubjectivity and any relation with the other. We saw earlier that Henry's tendency is to dissolve alterity in an overarching Life. No less than the 'outer' world merely *correlates* with our 'internal' emotions as their reflection in a mirror, there are the lives of others with which we are merely 'co-present', but by which we are not directly touched.[109] The 'co-', the 'pathos-with' is all that we feel – not the other or world *as different*. Life is indifferent to alterity. It is non-relational. Yet, combining the two problems together – of Other Minds and the Infinite (which are really the two sides of the problem of substance for process thought) – provides us with a solution to both. *The other minds required may well be the very demi-gods we need.* They can be the very support we seek, affective and perceptual, to provide the world with fine-grained detail. If there were plural gods – naturalised gods (in a naturalised metaphysics) – then we could have both *theos* and its correlated world of molecules and other minds. The molecules are other minds. In the words of Whitehead: 'each monadic creature is a mode of the process of "feeling" the world, of housing the world in one unit of complex feeling'.[110] Henry meets Process Theology. And the moles are demi-gods or supermoles. And, in fact, with his vitalist conception of life and body, Henry has already gone quite some distance in creating a detheologised theology. We should note that Spinoza's naturalism was read disjunctively by some as an atheism, just as his theism was read by others as an acosmism. But no less than for Henry (and perhaps even Deleuze), *Deus sive Natura* is an inclusive disjunction. Henry's is a monotheism that must devolve into a kind of polytheism or even animism in order for it to have a world at all – that is, feelings going through the process of externalising themselves (and internalising other feelings).

All of this, then, is to make a plea to Henry to acknowledge explicitly the granularity within immanence that his studies actually support in practice, in their performance. 'Life is more than man.' But the 'more than' need not be a transcendent God. Instead, it is the living, social body (Marx) or the living cosmos (Kandinsky). To re-make the world, and therewith also give greater detail to the reality of singular affects, is exactly what Henry does in his studies of Marx and Kandinsky. How, otherwise, can we salvage him from some of his own hasty claims, such as the following?

> If the pain were really in the place of the organic body where it is situated, we could withdraw from it as the sea withdraws from the beach, we could leave it there in front of us, innocuous and taken note of by us as by a foreign spectator,

by a universal Spirit. The pain would be 'true' as Lachelier understands it. Let us speak of it in a strict sense: *the pain would be transcendent.*[111]

Sensation rests on affectivity for Henry, as it is really through auto-affection that sensation affects us – it is not sensation which is external 'input', for sensation is self-affection.[112] Pain, for instance, can be referred to a part of the body. The painfulness itself, however, when phenomenologically reduced, reveals itself only to itself and not to a part/place/object. If there is a second sense to sensation *as external* – as it so appears – then it too, precisely *as sensed, that is, as affected*, is real. 'Illusions of transcendence' are real as immanent affect, but not as content. Or rather, their content is their form of appearing, which is immanent: '*this is precisely in what affectivity consists, i.e., the radical immanence of the content as identical to its form, to affectivity itself.*'[113]

We could continue the analysis of sensation in the following manner: 'sensation is never simple. It is always doubled by the feeling of having a feeling. It is self-referential. This is not necessarily the same as "self-reflexive".' It is more a 'self-complication' or 'resonation'. These other terms, familiar to us by now, are not those of Henry, however. They are those of the Deleuzian, Brian Massumi. He then goes on to write:

> Movement remains continuous. It remains in continuity with itself across its multiplication. This complex self-continuity is a putting into relation of the movement with itself; self-relation. The self-relation is immediate – in and of itself, only its own event – even though it requires distance to occur.[114]

Again, we are seeing more evidence here of the proximity between Henry and Deleuze. But note the interpolation of 'distance' in Massumi's reading. Auto-affectivity is also a distancing, and this because it also consumes other feelings in a spatial field: 'feelings have a way of folding into each other, mutually intensifying, all in unquantifiable ways apt to unfold again in action, often unpredictably. Qualitative difference: immediately the issue is change. Felt and unforeseen.'[115] Folding is a spatio-material metaphor, but it also embodies and enworlds what would otherwise be Henry's improbably immaterial theory of affect. Resonance is another material metaphor, and it captures the correlations of (seemingly) internal and external phenomena without reducing the one to the other, either in terms of cause and effect or even pure identity.

For here is the rub: contrary to Henry's depiction of the impossibility of a transcendent pain, *people can in fact withdraw from their own pain* (this is empirically exhibited through meditative practice, for instance). Pain too is localised, but it is not any less affective by being so because its locality is not an inert space so much as a *molecular* affect. Pain can be other to me, an other mind within my mind, a molecular mind. While Deleuze is himself sometimes too swift to reject the molar self in favour of larval selves, we might also say that Henry too quickly appropriates all affective phenomena to just one Self (embedded in infinite Life), thereby forgetting all the levels of difference beyond our own finitude. What is for most readers of Henry either a meaningless paradox or a tautology – that life affects itself – can be resolved, like any paradox, into *levels* of self-affection.[116] The living affects itself as another *actual* level of the living, and so on, all the way up (supermoles) and all the way down (molecular affectivity), precisely through its ability to create indefinitely – to grow. This is how it makes more of itself, or is autocatalytic. This is how it is truly internally structured – by making its inside myriad.

But perhaps that which is most other to me, that which transcends or overgrows the subject and all its qualities most, is not biology, or neurology, or even physics: it is mathematics. As mathematics is the science of the most abstract quantities possible, so it is the science *par excellence* of the outside for Henry. The coherence of mathematics – both internally within itself as sheer productive convention and also externally with the world as applied theory – fosters an outside that seems recalcitrant to any affectivist internalisation (unless, of course, mathematics too is affective). There are, indeed, constructivist approaches to explaining the fecundity of mathematics (intuitionism being the most famous), but they are epistemic and/or representational in form, and rarely, if ever, immanent and affective. Alain Badiou's mathematicism is one approach that is immanentist, but it rejects any possibility of construction, epistemic or affective. In the next chapter we will examine the manner in which his thought takes Deleuze's philosophy of immanence – and the problematics it inspires – in a very different direction from what we've seen, albeit one that matches Henry's step for step. In so doing, we will see Badiou act as Henry's virtual other, providing the necessary supplement for his excessively pathetic approach, while also, in aggregate, fashioning an outline that would make the *writing* of both his own and Henry's philosophies possible.

Clearly, Henry's work must be taken seriously in any rehabilitation of the role of affect in philosophy, and his philosophy of immanent affect does get around some of the problems we encountered for Deleuze and descriptivism in the last chapter. Even so, a philosophy of pure immanent affectivity remains moribund as regards its own theorisation.[117] *It is impossible to write about Henry's philosophy, at least if we keep to the letter of his ideas.* Our eventual objective, however, must be to discover a way of deviating from the letter of Henry's philosophy. To do this, though, firstly entails an excursion into the philosophy of Badiou that, by offering at its core mathematical symbols rather than letters, quantities rather than qualities, is fixed at the opposite pole of philosophical thought to the one occupied by Henry.

CHAPTER 3

Alain Badiou: The Universal Quantifier

> That quantity, the fetish of objectivity, is in fact evasive,
> and particularly dependent on procedures in which
> the being of the subject's effect resides,
> can be demonstrated in a spectacular manner ...[1]

THE RETURN OF PHILOSOPHY

For Henry, the ultimate virtual, the apotheosis of the outside, was mathematics. Yet, whereas Henry renounced the 'Galilean' world that writes the book of nature in the language of mathematics, Alain Badiou's seemingly more worldly philosophy is not mundane in any ordinary sense either. It is first and foremost a philosophy of the infinite. It rejects all poetic (Greco-Heideggerian) ontologies of nature.[2] Raging against the secularisation of the infinite within Continental philosophies of presence, finitude and mortality, Badiou wishes to restore all of the infinite's untainted purity and unnatural emptiness. The immanence Badiou works with rejects the finitude of our qualitative experiences in favour of a mathematical infinite founded on pure quantity.[3] The worlds of qualitative belonging, of dwelling within the world, of bodily incarnation, must be made spartan: Badiou subtracts every quality from such worlds in search of their pure immeasure, the paradox of quantitative infinities. Contra both Deleuze and Henry, then, there is no room for empiricism, radical or otherwise.

Badiou's book of nature — his naturalism — is indeed written in mathematics, but it is written this way *throughout* his work, and plays to a kind of Platonist metaphysics that never veers into biology, physics, or psychology.[4] His heroes are, in fact, Lacan, Descartes, Galileo and, behind them all, Plato, 'whose vector ... is none other than mathematicism'. Nevertheless, it is a radical mathematicism that attracts Badiou. No less than the new physics and new biology that were an inspiration for Deleuze, it is the new mathematics of set theory that interests him — creating unpredictable, unimaginable quantities, and new infinities that transform our previous modes of thinking. Number is not just quantity or measure: it is not 'an object, nor an objectivity. It is a gesture in being.'[5] Hence, Peter Hallward is right to say that 'no philosopher could be further from Henry's vitalist theology than Badiou', though such distance, as we will see, will be more a matter of topological relation than quantifiable space.[6]

The first aspect of this distance concerns the locus of truth. For Henry, it resides in a hypersubjective performative affectivity, a feeling beyond activity and passivity. For Badiou, truth is actively generated *with* the subject and not *by* any kind of subject. Truth and subjectivity are co-engendered through the 'event', which must be understood conceptually, that is, through reason. His reconfiguration of truth as the event of radical, subjective (though universalisable) commitment in either politics, science, art, or love simultaneously reveals what he describes as the four conditions of a rehabilitated philosophy itself. Like Deleuze, Badiou has never rejoiced at the supposed end of metaphysics. Though there are no philosophical events *per se*, philosophy is not therewith an exhausted set of philosophemes: it gains a genuine role and impetus from being 'seized' by and thinking through the truth-events produced by its four conditions. Badiou still has faith in the project of modernity and the powers of thought, only these powers need to be extended: we need more modernity, hypermodernity, not postmodernity.

Philosophy, in this redemptive paradigm, no longer has a direct relationship with what used to be called 'first philosophy' or ontological metaphysics, however. The study of being as such (ontology) is now the proper object of a science, mathematical set theory to be precise.[7] For Badiou, to speak about being *as such* means to speak about the multiple, the universal, the generic:

> 'As such' means that what is presented in the ontological situation is the multiple without any other predicate than its multiplicity. Ontology, insofar as it exists, must necessarily be the science of the multiple qua multiple. [8]

For Badiou, this science of the multiple qua multiple must be set theory, because it is the theory of the multiple in the purest sense, which, through its axioms and theorems, articulates all that can be said about pure multiples. Its discourse is the least constrained by the need to articulate the qualities of particular beings. It does not talk about which *quality* makes this thing what it is – *qualis*, 'of what type are you (singular)?', but about pure quantity – *quantus*, 'how many of you (plural) are there?' If Heidegger 'requalified' philosophy by abandoning Platonic reason for pre-Socratic poetry, now this same *Seinsdenken* must be dequalified, not by rejecting the poetic *tout court*, but by refusing to reduce – or '*suture*' – philosophy to poetry. Heidegger was still 'enslaved' to the essence of metaphysics that saw being as a gift and an opening – a 'poetic' ontology, haunted by Presence and lost origin. To this, Badiou will oppose a 'radically subtractive dimension of being' with a mathematical writing marked by 'dis-qualification and unpresentation'.[9]

Yet this distinction between quantity and quality is too static: Badiou is interested rather in the process by which *a* quantity becomes *this* quantity, through 'belonging to' or being 'included in' a particular *set*. Group membership as a *process*, that is, the collectivisation of individuals and all the paradoxes that come with this collectivisation, carves being at its true joints (to use the Platonic image).

They do this while also showing us (through the paradoxes of pure quantity, that is, of set theory) how being is exceeded by those things which *are not* (beings), namely, events.[10] Quantity, size, or 'cardinality' has its own set of paradoxes that are generative: they create genuine, unpredictable novelties or events.

Evidently, this type of philosophy will be at odds with the transcendent thought of classical Continental phenomenology (Heidegger, Sartre, Merleau-Ponty) as well as with Henry's immanent phenomenology that sets so much store by the notion of quality, what things are like. But what Badiou rejects in philosophy must not be allowed to overshadow what he affirms. His new association of (the multiplicity of) being with mathematics can be seen to free philosophy to pursue an immanent line of thought. Indeed, it is said that his thought is 'insatiable' in its pursuit of philosophical material.[11] He does not preach an anti-philosophy but a conditional one or 'ante-philosophy': philosophy as conditioned by an outside (rather than one finalised by history). Philosophy's four conditions in the non-philosophical realms of science, politics, art and erotic love expose it to a radical 'desacralization'. Its condition of possibility becomes plural, namely the local truths of these multiple domains – only one of which, mathematical science, being ontological. Because (Badiou's) philosophy is conditioned by an outside, it is empirical rather than deductive – it depends on encounters with heterogeneity in its four conditioning fields.[12] Philosophy's task is to subtract the truths from these fields, not as meaning (hermeneutics) or in more formal modes of language (linguistic positivism), but through 'seizure'. They are these four and no more, moreover, because only love, art, politics and science can give rise to purely disinterested (universal) ideas that can inspire pure subjective conviction.[13] We are seized by these truths, understood as 'intensities of existence', that is, as the *affects* of joy (from science), enthusiasm (from politics), happiness (from love) and pleasure (from art).

Despite this re-admission of affect by Badiou – an intensity rather than an extensity – affectivity will be the main point of divergence between Badiou and Henry in our analysis, a highly problematic one in fact. The issue of Virtualism, on the other hand, will be a peculiar point of convergence. For in spite of embracing the actual immanence of mathematics, there remain a host of virtual concepts operating in and around Badiou's philosophy (no less than affectivity and the divine operated in Henry); those of thought, being, the void, the event, and chance, being the most important. Moreover, as we set out the rest of Badiou's complex thought in more detail, other even more unusual mappings will appear, especially as regards the structural similarities between the process of belonging to a set and the process of auto-affection.[14] In this chapter we will focus on Badiou's 'great book', *Being and Event*; only in Chapter 5, however, with the sequel to *Being and Event* before us, the *Logiques des mondes*, will the implications of this isomorphism become clear.

BACK TO ONTOLOGY: PRELIMINARIES

Badiou is clearly looking for a new foundational style, as he himself admits, and follows therefore in the French tradition of Descartes. But where mathematical technique informed the Cartesian method of deduction from first principles, now it is the substance of mathematics itself, as set theory, that will supply Badiou with his ontology, making of his own work what Etienne Balibar describes as a 'meta-mathematics'. When the delirium of post-structuralism has died down, ontology is possible again: being is back, but it is the multiple-being of the situation, stripped bare of its all too deconstructable predicates: '*ontology attributes no other property to multiples than existence*, because any "property" is itself a multiple'.[15] Ontology has always been what concerns being as such, irrespective of any quality. But Badiou is eager to point out that this is precisely what concerns mathematics as well: at its foundation, all it deals with is the fact that there are beings that can be added, subtracted, divided and so on. *What* the beings are is irrelevant; that *they* – plural – are is central. In other words, the only thing that all beings have in common, their lowest common denominator so to speak, is that they exist as multiple, that they are not alone. Ironically, then, the *one* thing true of all is that there is not one thing but many, and that there is no category that captures everything other than this meta-category ('that there is no category that captures everything'). Pluralism is the not-so-secret secret of being as such. There is no-One, and every apparent 'one' is a contingent projection that subsumes the many into a 'One'. Every apparently self-identical substance is actually a 'situation', and situations themselves are always *deeply* multiple: they are composed of multiplicities that are themselves multiples of multiples. And, finally, it is mathematics that presents the truth 'of' these situations (as deeply multiple). This last point is critical: mathematics does not *represent* truth (that is why the 'of' is in scare quotes), rather, its inscriptions *perform and enact* it.

The issue of just what Badiou's equation of mathematics with ontology entails is a central question for this chapter: is it a causal, methodological, or essential relation? If set-theoretical mathematics *is* ontology, what is the meaning of this 'is' (a question we've already asked of Henry's strange equations)? On the one hand, Badiou explicitly says that he is not declaring that 'being is mathematical'.[16] His is a thesis about discourse and the identity of these two discourses – mathematics and ontology. Plato and Descartes were wrong if they thought that the world was built from 'mathematical objectivities'. But then, on the other hand, *why* is ontology – the science of being as such – the *same* as mathematics for Badiou? Why not poetry, why not physics? Is it because being as such is precisely the pure quantities that the discourse of mathematics examines? Why else does Badiou himself say in his most mathematical text, *Number and Numbers*, published shortly after *Being and Event*, that 'number is a gesture in being'? This explains why it is not surprising that Oliver Feltham, the translator of *Being and Event*, should himself assert that set theory is an ontology of immanence because it retains 'being *within* its inscriptions' and because it '*enacts* what it speaks of'. What attracts Badiou to mathematics is its *conventional* nature – mathematics has an 'absolute' grasp on its object because it invents it, its object is immanent to it. But saying that the object of mathematics is immanent to it actually entails, firstly, that its object is not objective, and secondly, that 'invention' is no mere subjective construction:

mathematics enacts being in its inscription. Badiou is not Kantian in any way and there is no portion of being that is left unknowable in principle. It is the process and performance of mathematics that exhausts and enacts its object – being as such – but not as an 'objectivity' so much as the continual co-invention of discourse and object of discourse together. Such immanence does not identify being with any particular mathematical discourse, however (before the howls of Transcendental Phenomenology become audible), because it is an immanence of infinities strewn across its 'historical becoming'. That set theory is *currently* the most adequate discourse of being is *Badiou's* assertion, but it is a falsifiable hypothesis and not a necessary deduction.[17] Where the ambiguity remains is in Badiou's intermittently twofold use of the notion of mathematical discourse as representational (therewith leaving being outside of its knowing) and performative (thereby identifying being with mathematics as such), an ambiguity that we will also see later in his use of the term 'truth'.

If the relation between mathematics and ontology is an essential one (as seems to be the case), the question remains as to whether the relation *really is* exhaustive, leaving nothing of being for philosophy to engage with. If being as such is defined in a way that only set theory can be identified with it, then of course this equation will be true, but only by definition, that is, only circularly (if one defined being as a transcendental Gift then theology might well be its proper discourse). And though there are acknowledged and necessary circles in Badiou's thought, this isn't one of them. Badiou himself asserts that the proper way to relate philosophy to mathematics is for the former to allow the latter its autonomy by letting itself be challenged by it: no longer can philosophy adjudicate, categorise, or classify the truths of mathematics. Mathematics must force a violent intervention into the complacencies of philosophy: it is the muse that provides truths for philosophy to co-ordinate with the other truths of art, politics and love within a common and egalitarian space of 'Truth' – a practice Badiou dubs 'compossibilising'. Philosophy is outside of being. Such modesty aside, the question of Badiou's meta-mathematics, or what he himself calls his 'meta-ontology', will be vital for us: what is the ontological status of his own pronouncements (categorisations, classifications) about ontology above and beyond its declaration that ontology equals mathematics.[18] What are these reflections on the truths of mathematics that comprise his philosophy? Has he not *created* in his work the very place for philosophy that he claimed was a no-place?

Badiou would beg to differ. In the preface to the English translation of *Being and Event*, he writes that 'I use mathematics and accord it a fundamental role', before adding that 'I also use, to the same extent, the resources of the poem ...'. Badiou again cautions us that he is not saying being *is* mathematical but that 'mathematics ... pronounces what is expressible of being qua being'. *Being and Event* claims to be neither epistemology nor a philosophy of mathematics: mathematics is cited, he says, to 'let its ontological essence become manifest'.[19] And Badiou knows that this Hegelian term – manifestation – also belongs to the radical phenomenology of Michel Henry.[20] He asserts that his philosophy does that rare thing of looking to both the matheme and the poem, not wishing to be sutured to either. It is said that 'disaster' ensues whenever philosophy is sutured to just one of its conditions (the poem in Heideggerian thought, science in analytic philosophy), and so Badiou's work must 'remain mobile by circulating between a plurality of its conditions and its own history'. Philosophy needs to be *de-sutured*, meaning, on the one hand, that it no longer takes the truths of art, love, politics or science for its own and, on the other hand, that it compossibilises their various truths together rather than counting only one of them as valid. And yet, it is indisputable that 'the subsequent predominance of the scientific condition of set theory' is there for all to see in Badiou's work. His subtractive approach to poetry, love and politics is itself mathematical.[21]

Love, for example, is analysed as an original two-ness that dissolves the illusion of love as initially two ones that subsequently fuse into one two.[22] This mathematicism is made even more sustainable by Badiou's position that 'love is a thought', a view that absolutely mirrors Henry's claim that 'thought is affective'.[23] So is Badiou a reductive 'socio-mathematician'? Certainly, mathematics is central: he describes how philosophy began in Greece because it was there that the matheme first interrupted the 'mytheme'.[24] But whether or not Badiou does accord both the matheme and the poem the same philosophical extent is a moot point, for, as we heard, the inscriptions of mathematics (its discourse) are also said to be the actuality of its object – being qua being – such that *nothing else could do this job*. Hence, *the* key event for Badiou's work remains Cantor's set theory and its subsequent axiomatisation.[25] Set theory is the ubiquitous beneath, the roots of the tree of philosophical conditioning.

Two points can be made here, the first concerning *any* mathematicism (and not just Badiou's). According to Badiou (and following Descartes), philosophers informed by mathematics realise the universality of truth by using a transparent language. In contrast with Heidegger's linguistic exoticism, for instance, the language of mathematics is highly transmissible, as should be any philosophy properly informed by it (one doesn't have to be fluent in German to know the meaning of the question of being).[26] And yet, mathematics is said by Badiou to be able to express what *normal* language cannot (the paradoxes of excessive quantity in an event, for instance).[27] So, where does this place the thesis of transmissibility, if, in principle, only the mathematician can express or embody (in mathematical symbols) the strangeness of the event? Must we all become mathematicians? If the answer is in the affirmative, as it seems to be, then this is no less elitist than having to become fluent in German to know the meaning of the question of being.

The problem is this: can we speak of the being of things *philosophically*, or can we only comment on that being (as 'meta-ontologists') *after* the mathematical work is done? Must philosophy only compossibilise others' truths (the artist's, the scientist's, the lover's, the political militant's), by taking their word as given? But what good is such a role over, say, some kind of Rortian commentary on the sciences, save for the promise of constructing a space wherein the truths of non-philosophy may be aligned? At times, Badiou can indeed write like a Rortian on the relation of philosophy to non-philosophy: 'In *L'Être et l'événement* the same thing occurs. There is a philosophical discussion between set theory as a mathematical creation and set theory as an ontological thinking. Science doesn't organize that discussion. This is the reason why philosophy is necessary.'[28]

I raise this issue now, before launching into discussions of mathematics and philosophy, in part because I write this chapter as a philosopher and not as a mathematician. Admittedly, this is a matter of degree – I'm not being essentialist about disciplinary boundaries – but I will not pretend that reading a number of books on mathematics or the philosophy of mathematics, or even doing a degree in mathematics would enable me to *assess* the mathematical side of Badiou's genius.[29] I say this neither out of self-effacement nor defensiveness, but because *it is precisely the philosophical point of this chapter*.[30] To write philosophy is a hybrid activity, of course: because it is intrinsically parasitic on other knowledges, to do philosophy is to be a jack-of-all-trades and master of none. On some topics, one can be more or less knowledgeable: one can write in an informed manner on biology, psychology, sociology, or whatever. But mathematics is not just a different subject, nor just a different methodology – it is also a different language. Anyone can, 'in principle', attempt to learn it (but anyone can, in principle, attempt to learn German): but if I wrote this commentary in mathematical symbols (a very large 'if', and one not without significance), only a few could read it, namely those expert enough to be able to call themselves mathematicians. But this is a book for those interested in philosophy: it has its own identity – related to other interests to be sure, but still located in a region with a recognisable landscape.

So, can one write on Badiou philosophically or not? If the study of mathematics is the 'obligation' of 'we' philosophers, as Badiou declares (in loyalty to Plato), can a study of a philosophy 'ignore' its mathematics and still be philosophical?[31] This is the question, that, as the reader might have already guessed, I'll answer in the affirmative: we *can* do philosophy un-sutured to mathematics. But doing so actually renders Badiou's own philosophy and its mathematicism problematical. In respect of the inscriptions used for expression, the issue is whether Badiou's philosophy can account for its own status as both 'meta-ontology' and as philosophy.[32] In the end, I believe that it does have the resources to do exactly this, but not until a good deal of labour has been expended on the very notion of inscription and expression.

Second point: as a (special) kind of naturalism, mathematicism is both the best and the worst of candidates. Best, because what it lacks in crude materiality (which would otherwise make of it a 'hard' science), it makes up for in rigour. Whether that rigour is or is not cashed out in *applied* mathematics is of no concern to Badiou, for it is the rigour of mathematics (its certainty and universality) that appeals to him rather than its verification through other empirical knowledges. Indeed, mathematical formalism is an ideal because it is putatively empty: as soon as it is filled in (applied), it is no longer mathematics but affect – the content that fleshes it out is always felt/intuited. But, as mentioned above, mathematics can also be regarded as a non-naturalistic science because of its conventional nature; its certainties arrive by *fiat*, that is, through axioms. These axioms do earn their keep, so to speak, in terms of their explanatory power (in the realm of mathematical problems), but one might always suspect that such power is won through question begging, that is, that the axioms explain what they do in a circular, purely definitional manner (just as an example – of course the Cantorian approach can resolve Zeno's paradoxes, *because* Cantor views the additivity of infinite divisions differently from Zeno). [33]

However, while the conventionality of mathematics is a weakness for some, for Badiou this conventionality is ontologised, or at least given the grandeur of what is for him non-ontological *par excellence*, the *event*: it is what makes conventionality doubly important, both as being (rigour) and evental non-being (creative novelty). One should consequently note how *Cartesian* the apodeicity of convention is: it is auto-justifying *because* it is axiomatic. Of course, this vouches against its objectivity, yet Badiou wants an event that is neither objective nor subjective, but, as historical, beyond both these poles. I raise this second point here because the convention of philosophy (including Badiou's), its enactment, its eventfulness, can also be seen as *processual*: so one other question to tackle will be whether such a conventional process as the making of philosophy lies on the side of ontology (being) or non-ontology (event), or whether the being of the event is also the event (process) of being. The conclusion we will be forced to make will take this third, processual line on philosophy (its being *is* its becoming) because it will be the only way to establish the possibility of writing metaphilosophy (as Badiou does): hence, the answer to the second problem also resolves the first – the 'meta' of Badiou's philosophy is a mutability of expression that attempts to move beyond subject and object.

ACTUAL ONTOLOGY

Enough of these preliminaries: what does *Being and Event* have to say in detail about ontology? Badiou summarises the book into four points, the second two of which concern truth and subjectivity (which we will leave until the proper time). But the first two points (half the significance of the entire work in other words), both concern *situations*, which he describes firstly as 'pure indifferent multiplicities', and secondly as having no power to deliver truths (for only an event, or rupture within a situation, can do that). Situations, then, are central. Situations simply *are*, and their being is akin to the ontology that stands over the ontic in Heidegger: that is, there are situations and there is the being of the situation. [34] This difference concerns counting, for when counted, the being of a situation is transformed from *being* essentially multiple to *appearing as* one. But this 'count-as-one', as it is called, is not performed by a transcendent agent, whether it be Man, God, History, or Language – it is part of a primordial duality between the *how* and the *what*: 'what *presents* itself is essentially multiple; *what* presents itself is essentially one'. [35] Of the two, Badiou argues that it is the presenting that is fundamental, and that the presenting is essentially multiple. The 'one' is *only* the product of an operation, a count-as-one. Hence, the one *is not* (has no pure being), but only concerns appearance. For now in Badiou's thought, appearance is separated off from being – though this will not always be the case.[36]

Badiou summarises his position as a 'wager' (and wagers are not without significance for Badiou) in the following manner:

> I will maintain, and it is the wager of this book, that *ontology is a situation*. I will have to resolve the two major difficulties ensuing from this option – that of the presentation within which being qua being can be rationally spoken of and that of the count-as-one – rather than making them vanish in the promise of an exception. If I succeed in this task, I will refute, point by point, the consequences of what I will name, from here on, the ontologies of presence – for presence is the exact contrary of presentation.[37]

Not presence, but presentation, that is what a situation consists in: 'there cannot be *a* presentation *of* being because being occurs in every presentation – and this is why it does not present *itself*. From this apparently anti-phenomenological point (against presence), Badiou concludes that the ontological situation is '*the presentation of presentation*', which, despite other differences, echoes Henry's radicalised phenomenology in its equal emphasis on manner.[38]

Here a crucial turning point in the analysis occurs. The inherently multiple structure of a situation is reduced to one by counting. Badiou calls this state of unity the 'state of the situation', a name whose metaphorical affinity with politics Badiou openly avows. With this, Badiou can summon a distinction concerning the *way* in which the multiplicity resides within a situation: when it is counted as one, it 'belongs' to a situation and is 'consistent'. But remember that a multiple is always a 'multiple of multiples' (monism 'is not').[39] So when *a* multiple is counted, so too, inadvertently so to speak, are the sub-multiples of that multiple. In as much, then, as those sub-multiples reside within the situation without actually being represented (to the state) as belonging to it, they are said to be 'included' in it. They are present in the state but not represented. They are included but do not belong. Or at least for now that is, for everything *may* change when an event occurs. An event concerns a situation whose internal multiplicities are no longer aligned according to their usual states of presentation or representation: something has ruptured, and the multiplicity becomes 'inconsistent' (from the point of view of the state counting it as one, trying to make it consistent). Indeed, their evental being (as non-being) makes itself felt. The event is what is both an element of the situation and the situation itself. It no longer accords to either what belongs or is included, but now does something seemingly impossible (from the point of view of the state): paradoxically, it self-belongs.

Why the need for this impossibility? Because the event can only be novel, that is, can only truly transform the situation, by both belonging to the situation and being itself *that which is to become of the situation* and so that which re-presents it anew and in full. The paradox is of being the situation in full (representing it anew) and being a part of it (coming out of it, but not by any recognisable rule – that is precisely why it is a real *change*). Ultimately, this 'impossibility' is nothing less than the unthinkability of change itself, whereby something becomes something else through becoming, that is, by being both itself and what it is not. To substance metaphysics this will always seem paradoxical. To process thought, it is axiomatic. Here we see Badiou's dualism of being and event find its decisive rationale: Nature doesn't allow the paradox of a self-belonging. Nature is Sartrean – homogeneous and with no holes in it: it is an *ensoi* heavy with the plenitude of being. Events, by contrast, are un-natural in this sense; history is made up of punctures within situations built upon (or near the edge of) a void, the exact void that allows change to occur, that is, for a situation to be negated, to be made abnormal.

So far, I've spoken about ontology and tried to keep my language, if not colloquial, at least philosophical. But the provenance of many of these ideas is set-theoretical mathematics, and at this point, a minimum of exposition (but not assessment) is both appropriate and unavoidable. Set theory is *the* theory of multiplicity for Badiou. It does not try to define a multiple, for to do so would be to introduce a property, identity, or unity under the name of some predicate. There is, Badiou boasts, 'no defined concept of the multiple to be encountered anywhere' in either set theory or in his thought based on it. And because there is no definition of *a* multiple beyond simply being multiple, neither is there a definition of set – it is simply the property of belonging. Here's the description of such set-membership from *Being and Event*: 'the totality of the elements of a multiplicity can be thought without contradiction as "being together", such that their collection in "*a* thing" is possible, I name it a *consistent multiplicity* or a *set*'. A set is simply a oneness, a consistency of belonging *generated by the elements themselves* thought of in terms of their membership.[40]

Indeed, such a position on the extent of a set's components from the 'bottom up' (what is called the 'extensional' approach) is deemed less problematic than one that works from a definition through intuition or language, for the latter 'top down' approaches historically led to paradox and impasse (though the extensional approach does not altogether get rid of paradox either).[41] The extensional, bottom up approach is simply less problematic in that it pays dividends in the development of set theory (avoiding intractable paradox, supporting the production of new theorems). The stance is still however, an assumption, a choice. But this is the axiomatic position – which in crude terms is a certain number of guiding ideas invoked *ab initio* to get things running. In fact, the axiomatisation of set theory has been momentous for all of mathematics because it not only created a foundation for a rational (consistent) thought of sets, but also for the 'entire lexicon of mathematics'. Set theory thus remained the foundation of mathematics for much of the twentieth century. This rise of set theory is no less significant for philosophy either, Badiou claims, because the ideas contained in its axioms – belonging, difference, inclusion, dissemination, the language/existence couple, and substitution — are sufficient to provide all the material needed for an ontology.[42]

We should note straight away, moreover, that the ontology built upon sets is Actualist. This simply follows from Badiou's view of mathematics itself as

Actualist: its inscriptions en-act their objects here and now rather than symbolically referring to something outside of them. Indeed, even the infinite is actualised as the transfinite sets of Cantor. But there is also a philosophical lineage to Badiou's position. He follows Descartes in emphasising the actual infinite over the potential infinite, because 'deep down', he admits, he is Cartesian (another reason for seeing Badiou as a very French philosopher).[43] The actual is the active, the activity of reason: 'I uphold that the forms of the multiple are ... always actual and that the virtual does not exist.'[44] Badiou's ontological Actualism entails that every object and thus every appearing 'is determined by its [actual] ontological position'.[45] As he writes in respect of the death of God (another virtual): '*tout est ici*'. The truth and novelty of love, for instance, is immanent and actual, a 'non-rapport', non-relational. There is no virtual (Deleuzian or otherwise), or, as Badiou puts it, the virtual is an 'inverted transcendence', an '*ignorantiae asylum*'. For his philosophy of transmissible rationality, there can be no inaccessible transcendence, and it will therefore strive to dissolve any alterity, possibility, potentiality, secrecy, ambiguity, responsibility and deferral, just as Plato once had, given that it was Plato's genius to think 'virtuality as actuality'.[46]

And yet, though Badiou's Actualist position does bear comparison with that of Henry, Henry takes an intuitionist and psychological approach (in the phenomenological sense): actuals are affective and only take a mathematical (or geometrical) form through exteriorisation. Badiou, on the contrary, sees Actualism as a rejection of intuition understood as a non-conceptual access to the unthinkable.[47] Nonetheless, Badiou's Actualism, as we'll see, veers at times towards a Virtualism of thought – infinite mathematical thought is, in principle (or virtually), the universal mark of humanity and our incomparable worth. Badiou's attraction to set theory, we should always note, is on account of its wholly abstract, pure and empty formalism, involving no particular qualities. Concepts without intuitions may be empty, but that emptiness, that void, is what allows no particular thing to be privileged, and so for every particular thing to be affirmed equally, universally. The politics of set theory (against privilege, for universality) is as important as its mathematical abstractness, but, ironically, what allows it to work is a virtual: the spark of infinite rationality that (virtually) makes mathematicians of us all (all of us humans that is). Badiou openly refers to a 'Noumenal Humanity' that is intrinsically connected to his characterisation of a real event.[48] But there is more to the virtual and the actual than just the link between Badiou's ontology and his politics, for the every same association between the virtual and value can be found in Deleuze.

BADIOU–DELEUZE

For Badiou, the perpetual 'cross of metaphysics' has been the choice between the animal and the number, the organic and the mathematical. Unlike Badiou, of course, Deleuze chooses 'without hesitation' for the animal.[49] The merits and de-merits of Badiou's reading of Deleuze in *The Clamor of Being* have exercised many on both the Deleuzian and Badiouian sides of the argument, and it is not my purpose to enter into that overwrought debate here. Clearly, there are elements of Badiou's Platonist reading of Deleuze that correspond with his ideas (some of which Badiou rejects, some others – such as his theory of Ideas – that he sees as his own task to extend and improve).[50] But it is equally clear that these elements do not exhaust Deleuze's thought (there is too much empiricism and affectivity there as well), and so to inflate them into the totality of his work (or even its essence) is to create a monster no less monstrous than the ones Deleuze fathered through Leibniz, Nietzsche, or Bergson (to name but three of his amours).[51]

The significant fact is Badiou's rejection of Virtualism *per se* as quasi-spiritualist rather than truly naturalist, it is a 'wild empiricism disguised as science'. Deleuze was right to think in terms of multiplicities, Badiou admits, but he wasn't successful in his pursuit of this endeavour. He missed the correct starting point for thinking the multiple because his work on mathematics contained a poorly thought-out polemic against sets that quantified them too much, erroneously reducing them to number (whereas number actually reduces to sets). The 'vitalist notion of the open is ultimately only thinkable as virtuality . . . [while] the set-theoretical or ontological open is entirely contained in the actuality of its own determination'. For Deleuze, actual multiplicities are always *only* 'purely formal modalities', whereas this formality is precisely their power for Badiou: multiplicity must be homogeneous and empty to be the basis for universalist politics. If multiplicity is heterogeneous, it leads to hierarchy and dualism (the duality of the actual and the virtual for one).[52] In the words of two of Badiou's commentators, Ray Brassier and Alberto Toscano, immanence must be 'handed over to the actual'.[53]

The politics of the virtual that we discussed in Chapter 1 re-emerges now in connection with the fact that Badiou and Deleuze are both thinkers of immanence. For Badiou, the univocity of the virtual provides Deleuze's political ontology with a shaky foundation. And we would have to agree. As we saw in Chapter 1, being ontological, Deleuze's duality of the actual and the virtual does sunder univocal being into real and less real, more or less becoming (and so returning), more or less creativity, and so on. Hence, there is an element of equivocity rather than pure univocity (being is said in different senses and not in a single and same sense). Deleuze says that monism = pluralism, and that the only (necessary) enemy is dualism.[54] This is his 'magic formula', but, we must ask, isn't Deleuze a monist in ontology *in order to be* a pluralist in politics? Different things *nonetheless* express being in the same way. But how is the 'equal' or 'same' established, if not empirically (whether it be through radical or mundane experience)? Is it on account of our God-given souls, our species-being, our conventional human rights, our genome, or now, in another magical vein, our virtual underpinning? But, on the other hand, if we do embrace the equivocity of the actual and the virtual, we are able to establish a politics (because, God knows, we don't want being to be said in the same way of National Socialists, who don't become, create, practice the third synthesis of counter-actualisation, and so forth).

Significantly, the equivocity and duality that creates this moral hierarchy is reflexive: what exists less (has less or even no being) is what doesn't become, what is essentially re-active, what suppresses (others') active becoming.[55] To be is not simply to become, but to meta-become, because not to be is not to *allow others* their becoming (in reactive judgement). It is the transgression of the formula that we are all (virtually) equal and should be left alone in our sovereign individuality, becoming on our own 'line-of-flight'. The link between reflexivity and value is evident in this part of Deleuze. Even the very idea that 'dualism is the enemy' is paradoxical – setting up an instance of the very duality it renounces. But it can be resolved by invoking a theory of types because it is reflexive, instancing itself amongst the things to which it refers. What it implies is that there are types of dualism, a good and a bad type. The bad type is of all the traditional dualisms of mind/body, man/woman, human/animal, and so on. The good type is of the virtual (monism) and the actual (wherein all the bad dualisms reside). The reason why the dualism of virtual and actual is the sole good one is because 'politics precedes being' according to Deleuze: his ontology is overtly politicised, as we learnt earlier.[56] Deleuze announces this relation between politics and being in the context of equating pragmatics with schizoanalysis in *A Thousand Plateaus*, but this is not an equation, it is a priority – politics *precedes* being.

According to one Deleuze scholar, Claire Colebrook, equivocity leads to relativism, a position that is incompatible with Deleuzian univocity. Likewise, François Zourabichvili describes Deleuze's work as a non-relativist perspectivism.[57] It is obvious that Deleuzians want to be pluralist but don't want to be relativist: their pluralism should fall short of accommodating, as a paradigm case, a fascistic way of living. Now Badiou's Actualism goes in the opposite direction to Deleuze, *but for a similar political purpose*. Instead of setting up a (Virtualist) ontology of the One (univocity) to underpin a politics of the Many (equality), we *begin* with plurality in ontology: 'plurality is the ground of being in general'.[58] We don't need a virtual to guarantee our *becomings*, and likewise we don't need univocal being as a guarantor either, be it of our happiness or our rights (through a virtual sovereign or general will – a virtual-Hobbes, or a virtual-Rousseau). We axiomatise the multiple: there is no-One that may be said in a single and same sense. There are only the multiples, each of them the same *qua* multiple, with no individuating quality other than their sheer quantity or cardinality.

The limits of a politics stemming from an Actualism of mathematical hue remain to be investigated, especially for those traces of the virtual latent within it. Such traces will be especially evident in Badiou's use of abstraction, human intelligence, and even the infinite itself (irrespective of it supposedly being an actual infinite). But before we can examine that, we must look at the evidence put forward by Badiou for what is his specific contribution to philosophy, namely, his theory of the Event, Truth and Subjectivity. These ideas are all interlinked, but resting behind them is the most important (mathematical) axiom in all of Badiou's work, that of the void-set. Even more than the virtual, it is the void that fundamentally separates Badiou from Deleuze.

NULL *AND* VOID?

In his outline of the history of post-war French philosophy, Badiou positions his own thought on one side of a fundamental division: a line is drawn between philosophers of the formal concept – Althusser, Lacan and (amongst others) himself, and philosophers of the interior life – Sartre, Foucault and Deleuze.[59] Curiously, this both follows and doesn't follow a similar line drawn by Michel Foucault himself in his own mapping of the field: on the side of knowledge, rationality and the concept, he placed Cavaillès, Bachelard and Canguilhem; on the side of experience, meaning and the subject, he put Bergson, Sartre and Merleau-Ponty.[60] What is curious about this is that Foucault places himself in the *conceptualist* lineage of Cavaillès, whereas Badiou places him with the vitalists. It seems that Foucault's concepts are not formal enough for Badiou. This is a noteworthy difference when it comes to the origin of abstraction, a discussion we must leave for later. Vincent Descombes, however, has written a history of recent French philosophy that begins with a possibly more productive distinction that sees *nothingness* as the centre of the French schism. Following Hegel (or rather, Kojève's Hegel), we have those philosophers who give nothingness an ontological bearing: Sartre and Lacan in particular. Lack is fundamental to desire. Philosophers who equate nothingness with a psychological act of negation, by contrast, are represented by Bergson and Deleuze. For them, desire is first and inherently productive: desire only gives rise to (the illusion of) lack derivatively.[61] Nothingness is not ontological. We have had to invent zero, the void, or nothingness from a desire. Desire creates, it is productive, even going so far as to producing its own sense of lack: man is in love with his own desires.

Where does Badiou stand in all of this? Certainly, proclamations such as 'within its [truth's] heart, there is a lack, a hole', give the impression that Badiou comes closest to some kind of Hegelian stance – nothingness is fundamental. Yet, the term Badiou uses for negativity is 'void' and, in his later work especially, he is always careful to distinguish the void from nothingness.[62] The void is always particular, it is not a universal null or *nihilo*: it is the negation-of-a-situation, a localised voiding of a situation made possible on account of the void immanent to every situation. We must never forget where Badiou's pluralism stems from: there is *no-One*, no thing that anything has in common save its membership of a plurality. The other way of saying this is that the only thing that multiple things have in common is their plurality and *nothing* else. Their plurality is built on a void – their not-being-one is their (relation to) nothingness. Consequently, where the void is on the side of the (ontologised) subject for Lacan and Sartre, it is on the side of being for Badiou – indeed, it is the birthplace and destiny of any event: the being of the event is a void. As such, the event is quite 'evanescent', a chance moment whose inevitable disappearance is only tempered by the 'linguistic trace' left of it in its name.[63]

Another way of looking at this is that there is a nothing in every situation – what must go uncounted – namely both the *operation* of the counting and the situation's ground in an inconsistent multiple: both are necessary to but unpresentable in the situation – they are its void. The void supports Badiou's subtractive ontology because it is the void that is subtracted from the situation and is precisely what the situation is not – its negative identity (though not by mere opposition). The void indicates 'the failure of the one'. It is neither the *ex nihilo* nor the *Ab-grund*: as Oliver Feltham and Justin Clemens affirm, it 'is simply what is not there, but what is necessary for anything to be there'.[64] In terms of set theory, there is only one null set, a multiple of the void, that is the ground for every situation. So far, so ontological. But note the term 'operation' above and in the following quotation:

> Nevertheless, its count-for-one being an operation indicates that the one is a result. Insofar as it is a result, by necessity 'something' of the multiple does not absolutely coincide with the result. ... the law in which it is deployed is discernable as operation. And although there is never anything other – in a situation – *than* the result, (everything, in the situation, is counted), what thereby results marks out, before the operation, a must-be-counted. It is the latter which causes the structured presentation to waver towards the phantom of inconsistency.[65]

The void is operational, a *voiding*, an extraction or subtraction, a process. But it is not the gift of the subject, of *poursoi*, nor the derivative of desire: it is rather this voiding that allows for the possibility of a subject at all (more of this later). The void supports the event and so the subject. The void is what shatters, explodes and exceeds any situation, and so it is not (what is a situation). It is 'omnipresent', an errance in every presentation, both inside and out: the void is a sub-set of every set, while also being reiterated as its own sub-set. And yet there is no set to which the void alone belongs and that might present it. As Badiou puts it: 'It would already be inexact to speak of this nothing as a point because it is neither local nor global, but scattered everywhere, nowhere and everywhere, it is such that no encounter would authorize it to be held presentable.'[66] These theses all stem from the 'axiom of the void-set' that asserts that every non-empty set is constructed from a set that contains no elements, the unique empty set. In other words, Badiou is a meontologist: everything is made out of nothing.

One more point before we finish with Deleuze and Badiou. In Badiou's eyes at least, the void, far from reducing difference to one hypostatic pole of a dualist ontology, actually supports multiplicity. We always have a beginning, or a halting point, with a multiple of nothing. It is the ontological atom. For if the 'first' presented multiplicity was not a multiple of nothing – if it was a multiple of something – then that something would be a One. But the One is not. Hence, there is only one void (this 'unicity' of the void can thus be compared to Deleuze's univocity of being): '*it is because the one is not that the void is unique*'. Additionally, the void must have a proper name, for if its name were a type, it would place the void under a category that would subsume it and so re-establish the One: 'the name of the void is a pure *proper name*, which indicates itself, which does not bestow any index of difference within what it refers to, and which auto-declares itself in the form of the multiple, despite there being *nothing* which is numbered by it.'[67] The void is self-referential. Yet it is also ubiquitous – everything refers back and forward to it.

So can we then say that the void is the point of genuine difference between Badiou and Deleuze, or is it just another incarnation of the virtual and so what actually binds them together – the void being to Badiou what the virtual is to Deleuze? Undoubtedly, the void is described as an 'almost-being', and, despite its operational, processual nature as *voiding*, it does play a role of containing and limiting process similar to the way the virtual *can* act in Deleuze (as we argued) as an eternal support for change. Let me explain a little further this connection between the void and the virtual. When writing about the 'axiom of union', Badiou asks if it is possible to count the decomposition of multiples into sub-multiples so that every multiple would be a multiple of multiples *ad infinitum*? The answer to this conjecture is no: there must be a halting point, every presentation must be sutured to 'some fixed point, to some atom of being that can no longer be decomposed'. The void is that atom. But here is where we can venture a criticism. Isn't the notion of a 'multiple *of* the void' already a hypostasising of the void in terms of this use of the preposition 'of'? It is arguable that by claiming that presentation *per se* is his theme, Badiou simply sidesteps a substance metaphysics (of the One) at the expense of introducing an exotic *nihil* of sorts. Henry, by contrast, avoids the 'of' by saying that presentation is self-presentation (it is 'of' itself), though as we saw, this needed further specificity in its internal structure if it were not to be reduced to the mere tautology of A = A. All the same, in rejecting indefinite composition and instead invoking the void to halt any downward spiral, it seems that Badiou has been unfaithful to his own pluralism, that 'every multiple is a multiple of multiples'.[68] For isn't the void, after all, simply an inverted One?

We have seen how a logical regress does not necessitate *aporia* when it is a natural *progress*, an indefinite growth. Badiou's natural atomic order could consequently be deemed a construct, a projection from an immanent perspective (a virtualisation creating a void). The axiom of the void-set, as a virtualisation, can be understood thus as relative and not absolute. *The axiom is itself contextualised as immanent to the system.* Yes, this creates a paradox (it is both within the system *and* outside it – what it is *and* what it is about), but the system (such as Badiou's philosophy), as we will see, can be viewed as a set of meta-theoretical mutations driven by paradox. The system is inconsistent just when it is consistent.

Another example of this was in Henry's conclusion that the only way to understand *aporia* is through affect, which is also both what it is and *about* what it is: Life is equally ground and element due to its 'phenomenological duplicity' – the affection that also affects itself. More broadly still, in fact, consciousness as such is often marked by a self-referential structure that allows it the paradoxical status of being part and whole, as when, for example, we refer to our future and in so doing immediately enact a self-fulfilling prophecy or self-negating prophecy. Or in Deleuze's concept of the double-life of sense that, as part and whole, leads to the proliferation of the paradoxical name.[69] The paradoxes of self-reference, in other words, play themselves out in numerous domains. The anti-phenomenological stance of *Being and Event*, however, will only allow Badiou to understand inconsistency through sets alone. Other implementations would have to be derivative. When we come to Laruelle in the next chapter, on the other hand, we will see why *aporia* can be thought through affect, sense and sets together, such that none has any pre-eminence. All that counts is the philosophical regress itself.

INFINITISM *IN EXTREMIS*

'It constitutes a rupture to say that situations are infinite and that human life is infinite and that we are infinite. It is a new axiom and we have to explore its consequences.'[70] More than any other philosopher of the post-war era, Badiou champions the infinite against the philosophies of finitude, historicism and death, as well as the limits of reason.[71] Deleuze too gives a home to the infinite, but in a naturalised fashion that Badiou judges to be insufficient. Only through mathematics is the purity of the infinite fully supported. As Hallward tells us, with the work of Georg Cantor (1845–1918) and his notion of transfinite or 'suprafinite' sets, we get for the first time a concept of an actual or *completed* infinite that is more than merely potential, but is still of human measure. Previously, only something unnatural – God or some form of disguised divinity – was allowed actual or self-embracing infinity: with Cantor's set theory, we have the actual infinite in our grasp.[72] *Being and Event* is clear on this: monotheistic infinitism was an illusion because it was actually beholden to a Greek *finitism* (Aristotle's especially), in that its concept of the in-finite was still dependent on our human (epistemic) finitude. The infinite God of Christianity, is, *qua* being, essentially finite. On the contrary, the 'effective infinity of being' only comes to light with post-Galilean mathematics. To this day, admittedly, the infinity of multiplicities is not fully understood by mathematics, but nonetheless mathematics is the sole preserve of being *qua* being (even with its paradoxes).[73]

Badiou breaks down what we need, to think this ontology of infinity, into four elements: to commence at all, we need a point of being (a starting point); secondly, we need a procedure or rule to pass from one presented term to the next; thirdly, we need the report of the invariance of the next term to be traversed; fourth and finally, we need a 'second point' to act as the 'cause of the failure of the procedure of exhaustion', that is, a cause to ensure passage, a 'rule of passage'.

This second point will always be something 'presented "elsewhere"' – as 'Other'. Interestingly, this is the only alterity allowed into Badiou's thought: 'Infinity is the Other on the basis of which there is ... a rule according to which the others are the same.' The Other is what enables us to say that there are 'still more' others of the same type, 'over there' while we are still counting 'here'. It is the infinity of a here and a there, a double. The Other is also what allows others to be accorded to the same, to be the 'still-more' enabling us to traverse the here to the over there. 'The Other', basically, is Badiou's equivalent of synthetic perception. It allows repetition, but it is also an 'existential seal' that forbids the derivation of the infinite from the finite. It is what overarches any others and allows them be made-same, for if there were just others and no Other, then their infinitude could be deduced from the finitude of the here and already (by negation). But the Other is not related like that to the here, and in fact, neither are the others: the Other makes them all relate to the same, it *makes* them repeat. The question might arise, of course, as to whether the Other is itself just the infinite in new guise, and so a deferral of any explanation of the infinite. Yet this charge is beside the point, for Badiou admits that the 'infinity of being is necessarily an ontological decision, which is to say an axiom'. Any (non-axiomatic) rule generating it would always be relatable to others and so to the same (by negation). Infinity cannot (yet) be defined, but it can be decided, which is something different.[74]

Indeed, whereas any mechanism of natural finitude is empirically observable, mathematical infinity is not, so it must be embraced through a decision. In subtractive ontologies like Badiou's (as opposed to generative ones like Hegel's), there is always 'some exteriority, some extrinsicness' to them, and hence infinity must be a *decision* of ontology. Significantly for us, Deleuze's would be another, Virtualist and generative infinite like Hegel's, based on 'pure presence, interior virtuality, the subjective'. But this is an inadequate conception of the infinite for Badiou because the 'same of the quantitative One also proliferates inside itself'. Generative ontologies confuse a *qualitative* science of finite quantity (with which Badiou has no quarrel, he says) with the idea of the *infinite*, which is pure quantity, something altogether different. In fact, the quality of quantity is a 'hallucination' of infinity in Badiou's view. Only the second place of Other deserves the name of infinity.[75]

When we come to examine the *Logiques des mondes* in Chapter 5, we will see that Badiou tempers his views of phenomenology, quality and even the virtual: these are no longer hallucinations, though they are still not properly real either – they merely 'exist' rather than have being. For now, however, we will commence an investigation into whether, on the one hand, Badiou has been truly able to think infinity on the basis of pure quantity (and its paradoxes) without also secreting a qualitative element into the infinite and its avatar in the event, and, on the other hand, whether Badiou's notion of 'the Other' – the guarantor of passage to completed infinity in his Cantorian approach – is not itself also paradoxical. Isn't the Other prone to a further, third place rule of procedure in order to guarantee its process (and so on, *ad infinitum*)? There are shades here of Plato's Third Man argument, of course, and not so surprisingly. But the regress of The Other, concurrent with the problem of passage or procedure, need not have to be sidestepped by axiomatic decision when such a regress and apparent *aporia* can actually be a non-decisionistic basis for the infinite – one within a natural, indefinite and *incomplete* progress.

EVENTS AND PROCESSES

The philosophy of the event (or events), can be as abstract as anything in philosophy. Its many facets and perspectives have origins in Anglo-American philosophy of mind (Donald Davidson in particular), in the process philosophy of Bergson and Whitehead, and in the ontologies of Deleuze and Heidegger. It asks questions such as whether beyond (or beneath) the beings that make up events (people that do things, objects which cause other objects to do things, and so on) there is the independent reality of the events themselves. It also asks whether these events are objective or subjective, mental or non-mental. Are they individuated by their causes, their effects, or their spatio-temporal location? Are they empirical or non-empirical, actual or virtual? Central to the theory of the event is the question of whether events are subjective impressions or objective realities. This is often the first kind of question asked about events. For example, what is the reality of a process like 'raining' beyond the drops of water falling? At another level, we might ask what is real about the event of my turning forty years of age, or the fall of the Berlin Wall; that is, what is real about both personal and historical events beyond our own *subjective* impression of their significance? After all, it is not just that the unification of Germany might be described as an act of liberation by some or an act of capitalist imperialism by others: in terms of its historical importance, it may well prove significant mostly as the transformation of a large amount of post-industrial real estate, given the alternative view that it is global warming that will prove to be the death of us all rather than the advance of capitalism or the fall of communism. Events seem so subjective, and yet they are also based in reality.

According to Oliver Feltham, Badiou's enduring problem across all of his work is 'thinking the relation between change and being'. For Badiou, as we saw, the difference between the natural and the historical amounts to the problem of the emergence of the new. Such novelty needs a number of conditions. Change arises from an anomalous position within any situation, what is called an 'evental-site'. Evental sites are always local, *in situ*, at 'site-points'.[76] The existence of an evental-site does not guarantee a change in the situation, however: it merely outlines the event to come. Hence, the need for a twofold supplement to bring about lasting change: an *actual* event, which is 'completely unpredictable', and 'someone [who] must recognise and name that event as an event'.[77] Subject and event are tied together in the decision of the former to name the latter. The subject is not connected to the event as the one that pre-exists it, but as the one that comes into existence with that nomination (as well as a continuing fidelity to that nomination, as we will see).

However, we are getting ahead of ourselves again. We have examined how mathematics deals with being: the event, by contrast, is what concerns trans-being, the new, what ruptures a situation. The event belongs to the situation but also supplements it by transforming it. It is both *in* it and *of* it — and this duplicity *is* its power of transformation, given that it is the paradox of quantity that leads to disruption and change. The event, then, does have *some* relation to mathematics, for it concerns sets that are, paradoxically, elements of themselves. At this level at least, Badiou is close to Deleuze: the event is about change.[78] But it is an odd temporality. An event is what will *come to be*. An event is a be-coming. The only temporality, therefore, is future anterior — purely formal and non-durational. An event is 'decoupled' from temporality.[79] The idea should be familiar from our analysis of Deleuze's *Aion*: if the event *did* have its own temporality then it would need another series of meta-events or *Ur*-events to periodise its progress, and so on to infinity. And this is the kind of regress that Badiou cannot accept (at least in *Being and Event*). So the truth (of and in an event) for Badiou is neither temporal nor atemporal but, he claims, the 'interruption' of 'a time ... of the situation'. Unlike Deleuze, however, Badiou says that he cannot 'think that the new is a fold of the past. ... This is why I conceptualize absolute beginnings (which require a theory of the void) ...'[80] Here we see signs of ambivalence in Badiou, on the one side echoing Deleuze's fundamentally timeless theory of the *Aionic* event, on the other, rejecting the basis for that timelessness in the virtual (the fold of the past).

Another apparently strange facet of this theory is that Badiou doesn't properly (non-circularly) account for eventuation – how and why events occur. But he not only admits this omission, he makes a virtue out of it. This emerges from the fact that the event maintains an odd relation to mathematics, despite being a trans-being. An event pertains to a set that belongs to itself – an excess-of-one or 'ultra-one'. It is *ultra* because the same thing is counted *twice*: 'once as a presented multiple, and once as a multiple presented in its own presentation'.[81] Or, in other words, the 'State' of a situation is quantitatively larger than the situation itself. And here we return to set theory and inconsistent multiplicities. An inconsistent multiplicity's *actual* status is 'undecidable' – it is a limit of thought, like the Lacanian Real – and ontology cannot describe it in virtue of the fact that it only uses the language and names of consistency. An event is being as it is not, and ontology can say nothing about it other than this.[82]

Remember that there were two relations in set theory – 'belonging', where a multiple is counted as an element in the presentation of another multiple; and 'inclusion', where a multiple is a sub-multiple of another multiple. In the first, elements of what belong are counted as one by the multiple they belong to; in the second, every element of the first is only presented by the second. The important point is as follows: multiplicities which do not belong to themselves are called 'ordinary' by Badiou, while ones that do, are called 'evental'. They are evental because they are abnormal, unnatural, paradoxical, or excessive: 'inclusion is in irremediable excess of belonging'. They present both their entire site *and* themselves.

For instance, when two lovers utter the phrase 'I will always love you', a naming-event takes place of their eternal love that is both a part, the actual utterance, and the whole, that theirs *is* an eternal love (the truth of which *will* only ever be known to a third-party in retrospect after both lovers are dead). Or when a militant declares something 'in the name of the revolution', a part – the utterance – is also the whole – the revolution. At the time of the utterance, the militant's declaration is purely speculative from the point of view of the State – the revolution *may* occur – but from the perspective of the militant, the revolution is actual. Yet the revolution's eventual reality (should it be deemed that there had been a revolution by the [new] State or some third-party) would have been impossible without the ('speculative') faith of the militant that it was actual already at the moment of the declaration. It is this paradoxical self-belonging that generates excess and rupture.

One of the axioms of set theory, the Axiom of Foundation, says that every multiple is founded by one of its elements with which it has nothing in common: for instance, a cat is founded by its cells, but it is not a cat-cell. The implication is that no multiple can be an element of itself. But an event is composed not only of the elements of a site, but also by itself. Hence, it 'departs from the laws of being' (it is trans-being). The event is a one-multiple made up of all the multiples belonging to the site and itself; but of course, as we know already, 'it is unthinkable that a set belong to itself'.[83] As Badiou puts it:

> I will term *evental site* an entirely abnormal multiple; that is, a multiple such that none of its elements are presented in the situation. The site, itself, is presented, but 'beneath' it nothing from which it is composed is presented. . . . I will also say of such a multiple that it is *on the edge of the void* or *foundational* . . .[84]

The evental site is 'on the edge of the void' because, just beneath the site, the multiple, there is *nothing* – no terms that can be counted-as-one.[85] Hence, evental sites block the infinite regression of multiples (because they rest on the void). Each multiple has its own beneath, immanent to it, such that 'belonging cannot infinitely regress'. There is a halting point or original finitude. Where Badiou places the image of the void, Henry placed the affect. Both act to create a point against which the new can rebound (Badiou even calls it an 'ontological anchor').[86] In their purity, however, both are virtuals.

To conclude this part of the exposition, there are two things that we should note: The first is that the event is born out of the paradoxes of quantity. Indeed, we *need* paradox and can only get one from an indiscernible within the situation.[87]

> It is clear that absoluteness does not suit pure quantity (except if it is finite), nor does it suit the state. There is something evasive, or relative, in what is intuitively held, however, to be the most objective of givens: the quantity of the multiple. This provides a stark contrast with the absolute solidity of the ordinals, the rigidity of the ontological schema of natural multiples. Nature, even infinite, is absolute: infinite quantity is relative.[88]

What is clear is that paradoxes are productive. As we have seen, Badiou keeps coming across circularities in the progress of his investigation and dissolves them by stratification, ordered around a base level emanating from the void. In fact, Cantor's major innovation, according to Badiou, was the notion of different *types of* infinity – 'the infinite proliferation of *different* infinite quantities'.[89] Paradoxes lead to proliferation and circularity is resolved by typing. To quote Badiou one more time:

Within the framework of ontology, however, the circularity can be undone, and deployed as a hierarchy or stratification. This, moreover, is one of the most profound characteristics of this region of thought; it always stratifies successive constructions starting from the point of the void.[90]

But we must again ask: isn't the void posited in order to avoid the possibility of (indefinitely growing) tiers of presentation, all of them becoming real, as opposed to a Manichaeism of pure, real and potentially revolutionary 'presentation', versus impure, unreal and tyrannical (stately) 'representation'? Within a complete prolif-eration of tiers *every moment* would be an event in the making – pure process – and not just heroic ones like the French or Cultural Revolutions.

Second point: despite the quality of quantity being a 'hallucination' for Badiou, the fact that events emerge from the paradox of quantity speaks for a type of asubjective quality as real. In this light, the following quotation from Badiou is telling:

> The halting point for this dissemination [of facts about an event like the French Revolution] is *the mode in which the Revolution is a central term of the Revolution itself*: that is, the manner in which the conscience of the times – and the retro-active intervention of our own – filters the entire site through the one of its evental qualification.[91]

'Evental qualification', 'mode', 'manner'. We have seen this language before in Henry. Indeed, Badiou's event, being so political in inspiration, is oddly molar in its trans-being, for it is at this political level that it is rendered in set theory (adequately or not), without reducing it to economics, biology, or some other relatively molecular stratum.[92] Nature, meaning non-human nature, has no events. By being molar, I mean that Badiou's use of renowned historical moments to depict events (the French Revolution, the Chinese Cultural Revolution, the invention of set theory) is indicative of a peculiar kind of anthropocentrism. We will soon look at his elitism of the event and especially his qualification of it as inherently political qua 'emancipatory': but the events named in this qualification are socio-historical and heroic, and therewith, entirely molar.[93]

Badiou's is a politicised ontology as much as a political ontology. What is vital for him is that events are always for the good (whether it is achieved or not), they concern emancipation and, as such, equality. Hence, there is an element of self-fulfilling, Whiggish historicism in his classification of events. I don't mean this in the sense of *a* regime proclaiming that its present age is an absolute good, and so whatever brought it about is for the best as well (the pure Whig view). Rather, it is Whiggish in as much as it is retrospective from a frame of reference (ours) that makes *us* think that we are 'modern', that we have changed, and so that at least one 'event' must have taken place, *as Badiou defines it*. For, *ex hypothesi*, to believe that there has been *any* history at all (that is, any events for Badiou) is to believe that equality *has been* at some time in the making. But why should we think that an event, as Badiou defines it, and so any history, has ever happened? When has the 'universal' ever been truly emancipated (even if only programmatically)? Making events rare makes them elite but also partisan in their nomination. Badiou would not dispute this – the subject is always inside the event. But Badiou's general *theory* of the event is outside any one event, yet he has so designed the theory that a whole set of changes (those relating to natural processes) *can never* be plausibly nominated by any subject. Was the founding of the first national animal protection society in the world, the Royal Society for the Prevention of Cruelty to Animals, for example, an event? It concerns emancipation too, and at a level of universality broader than that found in any anthropocentric endeavour. Yet because Badiou restricts events to the human realm, any concerning nature (or a concern for nature) will be entirely bogus. The answer to *why* the creation of the RSPCA cannot be an event for Badiou will expose another Virtualism in his thought after the void – that of the intellect, of 'infinite thought', which remains the exclusive *supernatural* power of human beings, something we possess, he says, only '*by grace*'.[94]

THE CHOICE OF A SUBJECT

The history of twentieth-century philosophy – in hermeneutics, analytic thought and post-structuralism – amounts to a litany of attacks on truth, in Badiou's view. In their different ways, all three say that 'we are at the end of metaphysics' and that meaning must take over from truth: philosophy becomes a meditation on language, be it through Greek etymology, science, or disseminating signs (Badiou is clearly thinking of Heidegger and Derrida for two of his targets). But, in essence, they are not so different, for all three concern flux: for them there is only 'the general circulation of knowledge, information, merchandise, money and images'.[95] For Badiou, though, the irony is that there must be a point of immobility for a philosophy of change to begin – a 'point of interruption' amongst these flows if we are even to try to think the *possibility of* the new. This is no easy challenge, as Badiou realises. Against a nominalism of the new (based on language), one cannot simply invoke an easy transcendentalism as the answer. The outside, the objective, cannot *pre-exist*, for otherwise we end in a circularity as old as Locke's theory of abstraction (that Berkeley so quickly pointed out as question begging). It is all too easy to become trapped in the impasse between an empirical object formed by abstraction and a pre-existing abstract idea.

It was while Badiou was thinking of the problem of the continuum, of the multiple and the set of its parts, however, that he says he was led to a new solution to this dilemma: the multiple is not formal but 'a real, whose internal gap, and impasse, were deployed by the theory'. The circularity, paradox and stalemate between old and new, between pre-existence and construction, is itself the solution.[96] Immanence. This is Badiou's notion of the *generic*: there are names that we impose in infinite fidelity to the event that creates a truth.[97] It is the imposition that is real and is founded on an 'evental site'.

Going against the idea of a 'pure empiricity of what happens' (Badiou probably has Deleuze in mind here), *Being and Event* opts for this conceptual construction of the event because 'it can only be *thought* by anticipating its abstract form, and it can only be *revealed* in the retroaction of an interventional practice which is itself entirely thought through'. Thinking and revealing are intrinsic to the constitution of the event (out of an evental site); in fact, the axiomatic nature of set theory crystallises this ontological necessity and makes a virtue of it. The subject *must* intervene within the indiscernible and decide for the undecidable – the subject *must* choose for the event, that an event *will have happened* (in set theory, this is termed the 'axiom of choice').[98] As Hallward puts it, 'being and thought are actively indistinguishable'.

> Badiou himself associates this axiom [the axiom of choice] with the possibility of a purely generic or 'anarchic representation', a 'principle of infinite liberty'. It provides him with the precise concept of the *being* (as opposed to the act) of subjective intervention.[99]

In Badiou's eyes, this reverses the problematic of subjectivity: it is no longer the question of how an ineluctable subject is made to tally with being (how does the Cartesian subject interact with a world), nor how being generates subjectivity (how can brute matter have a 'to be like'), but how subject and object, subject and event, come into being *together* as precisely what ruptures being through a process of naming.[100] It is the performance that is real: naming forces the indiscernible to add itself to the situation in a performative, immanent action (presentational, not representational).[101]

Hence, the two other fundamental theses of *Being and Event*, following the outline in Badiou's introduction: that 'a subject is nothing other than an active fidelity to the event of truth', and that 'a truth does not retain anything expressible from that situation'.[102] Where Deleuze gave *experience* the transcendent function of constituting the subject, for Badiou, truth and subject come together so that neither reigns over the other as objectivism or subjectivism would respectively entail.[103] There is an identity of being and thinking, but only via events and the decisions immanent to them – they are co-engendered through one process. *Qua* a non-processual state, the subject is indeed transcended by truth – 'every truth is transcendent to the subject' – but *qua* process, it is through subjectivisation that a truth is possible.[104]

As Hallward further explains, far from seeking to limit the radicality of choice, Badiou invokes it in order to situate the irreducible decision that distinguishes the fundamental orientations of ontology such as subjectivism and objectivism. Rather than seek to evade the implications of decision – arbitrariness, circularity, contingency and so forth – he embraces them as the unique vantage point from which it is possible to explore the exceptional *being* of a truth.[105] However, the process of decisions and namings brings forth another circularity with respect to the being of the subject. Jean-François Lyotard was amongst the first to alight on this problem: to say that the subject is created in the naming of an event is to embark on a hopelessly circular explanation, as naming is already a form of subjectivisation. In other words, naming, choosing, or commitment cannot create a subject if these acts already assume a subject. Acknowledging the criticism, Badiou's later work claims that 'the infinite capacity of subjects can be maintained in an immanent fashion, because the notion of a consequence will be constantly bound to the subject him- or herself'. *Consequences* are the active decisions and procedures that embed the subject in being, and create an event out of being.[106] The key neutral term is the *process* of choosing, which has different sides, not all of them individuated or voluntaristic, and which interact dialectically with a world that fleshes out the consequences of commitment in bodily forms that then feed back into the process.[107] In this new regime, one cannot isolate a clear relation of antecedent and consequent between the subjective and the evental that would then make any circularity evident.

TRUTHS, SUBJECTS, FORCINGS

Badiou's return to the subject may be on new ontological grounds (certainly not 'self-identical substance'), but it is still a return, and one that does not diffuse the subject by *immersion* in a differential or libidinal ontology, but generates it from a *tension* within ontology. At times, this sounds Sartrean – the subject as a hole in being. But, against the idea of a given self, it is also very Kierkegaardian – we *become* subjects. Hence, just as Badiou's events are heroic (and so rare), so also his notion of subjectivity is elitist (subjecthood too is rare), sporadic (infrequent), and haphazard (it relies on chance encounters). The subject effects an 'intervention', the first moment of a fundamental change that Badiou calls 'fidelity' or a 'generic truth procedure'. It is neither a result nor an origin, but 'the *local* status of a procedure'.[108] A generic truth procedure is an investigation or set of enquiries into the consequences of an event by the militant faithful, the object being to transform the situation 'in line with' how the event belongs to it.[109] Walking this line faithfully, though, is a complicated process with it being unclear when the subject or the event has priority.

Ultimately, Badiou's is a radicalised conservativism as regards the decentred subject. Yes, the subject is derivative, but it is not a victim of any transcendental process (Language, *différance*, Power); it is immanently co-authored with the truth that it makes and conserves (of itself and the world). The subject is now a '*fragment* of the process of truth'; a post-Cartesian *and* post-Lacanian thesis that distances the subject from any substance, but without either reducing or eliminating it. A Post-Continental subject. To learn more of this relation between fragment and process, however, we must accentuate the 'object-side' of the event, to wit, Badiou's theory of truth. As we have seen, any truth itself is undecidable: truth begins as an axiom in that *we* must decide, groundlessly, to affirm that an event has taken place. Given that 'a truth arises in a novelty ... a truth begins by surging forth', it is this surging forth that 'provides the basis for the undecidable'. Hence, we have what is further described as a 'desubstantialization of the Truth, which is also the auto-liberation of its act'. All of these aspects of truth can be summed up in the following motto: 'Truth proceeds'. Here again is the central idea for Badiou: truths and subjects *come together* – the truth of a multiple is produced *immanently* to this multiple, with our intervention. That is why there is no need for a dogmatism of *static* correspondence to re-assert the claims of truth. The process of truth doesn't lead to relativism, but a new kind of absolutism of immanence: truth instantiates a being or situation to-come. As Henry might say: many affects establish the becoming of affect at another level, auto-affection, the feeling of Life feeling itself; so also for Badiou in his argument contra relativism (or what he calls 'sophism'): many truths does not equal no truth at all but the process of truth, the procedure of truth, 'local truths', the 'becoming of truths'.[110]

For Badiou, then, truth is its own standard (it 'is the proof of itself'), for as new, the true simply cannot *correspond* to anything (to any *previously* existing standard), but 'depends on its own production'.[111] When a truth is 'forced' to become *knowledge* it *will* correspond to something, as a standard or referent is created out of it. But the truly new just is what is too quick (no matter how slow) to fall into a subject-sign and object-referent split that may or may not correspond to each other. A forced statement concerns knowledge – what is actually known – but not truth, which concerns a break with what is known. The new-truth comes before subject and object in 'a single process'.[112] As such, genuine change is unrepresentable, for it is what happens just once and so is not repeatable – it never stands *still* long enough to allow a split-relation of standing *for* (of sign to referent, of subject to object) to emerge. Novelty is non-relational, immanent to itself alone.

Naturally, we might wonder whether the immanence of truth renders both itself and falsity redundant, for we know from Nietzsche that when the true world becomes a fable, so too does the apparent one. Perhaps this explains why Badiou is sometimes equivocal in his use of the term 'truth', using it as a non-correspondent novelty immanent to itself in his own theory, but then also as a support for judging other philosophies (or sophistries) as *doxa*, as mis-representations or non-corres-pondences.[113] Once again, the absence of an error theory is felt. In fact, however, this *inconsistency* of Badiou is inevitable given his metatheoretical task, and we will see that it may well be the sign of his own philosophy's novelty and truth, given that inconsistency or paradox is the mark of an event. But we must leave this thought for later.[114]

There are analogues for Badiou's position on the be-coming of truth. Obviously, its distance from knowledge makes truth non-epistemic, but whereas in Heidegger this distance is measured by an ontologised truth, truth as *alētheia*, for Badiou it is beyond both ontology and epistemology, as event. Badiou's is an adventist or futurist theory of truth, and the event is subjective in a special way, for it does not concern (objective) being but that which is not being. Kierkegaard is therefore closer to Badiou when he wrote (citing Lessing), 'if God held all truth enclosed in his right hand, and in his left hand the one and only ever-striving drive for truth, even with the corollary of erring for ever and ever, and if he were to say to me: Choose! – I would humbly fall down to him at his left hand and say: Father, give!

Pure truth is indeed only for you alone.'[115] Truth is a striving, a becoming, and a fidelity. But Badiou's theory is neither passionate nor predicated on a (seemingly implausible) psychology so much as a non-psychological decision for the future.[116] Where Kierkegaard (like Henry) places the *passivity* of passion first (which for Henry is a *higher type of* activity), Badiou puts the *activity* of choice to commit to an event.

Because their verification is always in the future, truths are infinite procedures, and (like subjects), are also rare. So if there is a truth, then it must be an *infinite* part of the situation, that is, 'its procedure contains an infinity of enquiries', as '*a truth groups together all the terms of the situation which are positively connected to*' *the event.*'[117] But there is also an added element, that of self-belonging: a generic procedure is consequently an excrescence – it is included in but does not belong to the situation, it is solely represented not presented therein. This is, at base, Badiou's mathematised variant of Marxist class-consciousness (we might call it 'set-consciousness', except that Badiou wants to naturalise consciousness through mathematics); for it is self-belonging that sets alight the possibility for revolution, for change. 'No revolution without class self-consciousness' becomes 'no event without set self-membership'.

Two final points concerning truth and forcing. Firstly, Badiou uses *forcing* as the ontological model for the faithful's investigations of an event's consequences. Indeed, in his later work, 'forcing into existence' takes over from naming altogether. It is the process by which the situation is made to 'recognise' the transformation it is undergoing, such that it is no longer indiscernible but actually verifiable.[118] Forcing is also another term for this process beyond subject and object. Indeed, it is interesting to contrast Henry's subjective use of force (as *idée force*) and Deleuze's quasi-objective use of force (as Nietzschean dynamism, as the force of sensation), with Badiou's use of the process of forc-*ing* through a mathematical model that is both intellectual in form, and ontological in content (mathematical form *is* reality). Secondly, a problem that we have touched on before. Badiou writes: 'if a truth is something new, what is the essential philo-sophical problem concerning truth? It is the problem of its appearance and its "becoming".'[119] But isn't it highly arguable that if the 'new' is a becoming first and foremost and a being only secondarily, then the possibility of any categorisation for it has been usurped? Certainly, Badiou's naming of truth as 'new' means that it *doesn't* correspond to anything (any extant situation), which is what he would want anyway. Moreover, Badiou's new absolute of truth is always to-come, and thus we might say that it is virtual. Yet, in actual fact he opposes *this* to the actual interpretations (*doxa*) of the sophists. How is this sustainable? It neglects the possibility of another, new, type of (meta-) absolute, that is, an absolute always renewed, *doxa* replacing *doxa* in a *movement* of becoming that is absolute. The becoming is not simply of subjective attitudes or affects, but also the 'objective' *multiplicity* of *doxa* adopted. Para-dox is resolved as multiple meta-*doxa*. More of this thought later when we look at the democratic theoretics of François Laruelle in opposition to Badiou's elitism.

TWO KINDS OF FRENCH PHILOSOPHY

Without a doubt, Badiou lies at the pinnacle of one kind of French thought – the mathematical Cartesianism of *res extensa* re-conceived through set theory.[120] Michel Henry, by contrast, lies at the pinnacle of the other, internalist Descartes – of the *res cogitans* (though one must read the *cogito* as a *felt* certainty rather than a represented one). In this respect, then, Badiou and Henry represent the two most extreme extrapolations of the Cartesian project in no less radical a fashion than their extensions of the Deleuzian one, pushing its tendencies to their farthest limit. This is all the more ironic given Deleuze's own attitude to Descartes. Like Foucault, he wants to overcome the legacy left to French thought by Descartes: the dualisms of mind and body, civilization and insanity, human and animal, representation and world, are all to be abandoned as enemies of immanence. Nonetheless, several philosophers have defended Descartes, sometimes as a radical (Derrida contra Foucault), sometimes as a traditionalist (Badiou).[121] Henry straddles both positions by taking an orthodox element of Descartes – interiority – and radicalising it as an all-pervading passion: *'the essence of subjectivity is affectivity'*.[122]

As mentioned earlier, Badiou's own reading of the history of French philosophy is similar to Foucault's, placing himself in a line of thought emphasising the concept over life. The very last meditation in *Being and Event* (the thirty-seventh), is entitled 'Descartes/Lacan', encapsulating the French lineage Badiou wants to continue. For Henry, however, Badiou is more Greek than French, for the Greek tradition ignores life and prefers to define 'man through thought'. But we must always remember that there is a 'pathos of thought' for Henry, of the 'obviousness' and the 'self-evident' that explains the Greek captivation with vision and *theōria*. Quoting Husserl approvingly, Henry takes the phenomenological view that 'the consciousness which judges a mathematical "state of things" is an impression.'[123] Abstract knowledge has *'the particular pathos of its own certitude'* that stems from rest, that is, from *stasis* (which is ironic given Badiou's processual tendencies). Henry continues as follows:

> If, in a general way, in the history of philosophical thought, triangles play a role which is obviously out of proportion to the interest which we accord them in our concrete life, it is because the species of necessity which their properties imposes upon us signifies . . . a type of rest, an *assurance*, a sort of ecstasy within the assurance which Descartes sought so much.[124]

In the mathematical immanentism of Badiou, there is only the matheme: feeling or 'assurance' is the furthest thing we can have from ontology, from the real – there is no possible equivalent in a patheme. Henry, on the contrary, takes mathematics as but a *view* taken on affectivity, an illusory outside, a virtual image of affect. Both see the *cogito* as an exception to (a certain image of) the world, through concept and affect respectively.[125] Yet both Badiou and Henry are philosophers of the actual and of immanence. Moreover, the two not only mirror but also merge into each other on account of a monistic reductionism – 'everything is *x*' – which leaves no room for alterity, even if only the *illusion* of its other, 'non-*x*' (the affect that must falsely *appear* as non-affect for Henry, that is, the World as virtual image). For Badiou, as we will see, that other is what must falsely *appear* to condition mathematical being and its events – that is, affect.

The lesson to be taken from this could be as follows: philosophies of pure immanence, that leave nothing outside of themselves, by the same token find it difficult to explain their other as anything but error, illusion, or misrepresentation. But what's more, they cannot even explain *the emergence of* this meagre outside of error, illusion, or misrepresentation, this virtual outside. One might invoke a difference between being and its merest *mode* in order to explain such errors – but this would be another virtualisation in the guise of modularity (where 'mode' simply becomes a body-double for the virtual). What we will eventually argue is that both poles or limits of philosophy – in this case pure felt-quality (Henry) and pure thought-quantity (Badiou) – are haunted by their meta-other, that which makes their own thought both possible and impossible.

Let me explain further. While articulating the meaning of 'situation' (or presented multiplicity), Badiou describes the work of Jon Barwise and John Perry as a 'positivist version of my enterprise'.[126] He quotes their definition of 'situation' as follows: 'we mean a part of reality which can be understood as a whole, which interacts with other things'. Now according to Barwise and Perry themselves, awareness of the situations in which statements are 'embedded' and of the different uses to which they are put, some value-free, some value-laden, demotes the ascendancy of truth-values in the philosophy of language. Differences between utterances that were originally thought reducible can be reinstated by paying proper attention to these situations:

> In many contexts embedded statements seem to contribute something more specific than their truth-values to the embedding statement. Frege's choice of the truth-value as that which belongs to the statement in virtue of the references of its parts precluded taking this appearance at face value. His approach was to look to another aspect of meaning for the specificity provided by the embedded statement.[127]

The other aspect Frege found, of course, was sense: our personal take-up of a Third Realm objectivity. If statements can be in touch with physical reality, they will be so in view of this communication with the Third Realm rather than any intrinsic feature of their own. Resisting this move, Barwise and Perry attempt instead to take subjective appearances at 'face value' and in accordance with the attitude of our 'common-sense world'. They call this strategy (after Donald Davidson) 'semantic innocence.' This innocence is a 'pre-Fregean' stance rediscovering the 'old idea' that statements stand for 'situations, complexes of objects and properties in the world'.[128] The meaning of 'unicorn', for example, becomes the property *unicorn* that exists in the real world independently of whether or not it is exhibited by any real objects. 'Situation' here is used ultimately to save a singular reality.

But an attempted return to semantic innocence is not without its obstacles. One problem in particular lies in wait for any theory trying to delimit the notion of context.[129] Context is not a separate variable upon which, for instance, the meaning 'within' the context is dependent or independent according to one's theoretical stance: the meaning is a part of the context. Meaning does not reside *in* the situation, it emerges *as* the situation. For Henry, for example, no representation will ever be particular enough to depict it effectively, and a perfect singularity will embroil the entire universe. The most universal is literally the most singular as well – the outside is the inside.[130] What entails this expansive enfolding, and what keeps on being left out otherwise, is the *affect* of the singular rather than its concept (as in Hegel's 'concrete universal'). It is the quality, the 'what it is like', that demands ever more analysis: and the more you go into its detail, the more you go out into its context. But no context short of the universe is ever specific enough. The outside really is integrated into the lamina of the inside.

Badiou would place things exactly the other way around. The mathematical presentation of situation *is* particular enough, and indeed embroils all of being (which ultimately means the void) by its subtraction of any specific properties. Hence, we can remove the rest of the context, its qualities, from our considerations.[131] The singular being is its multiplicity and nothing else, but this singularity is tied to every other multiple: the inside (singular quality) is really outside (subtracted universality). Badiou's and Henry's philosophies are 'literally' inversions of each other (the meaning of this 'literal' will be unpacked later), Henry standing to Badiou much as the latter relates himself to Hegel and his 'interiorization of Totality into every movement of thought' such that the two are 'radically opposed'.[132]

But perhaps this polarity is based on axioms, for Badiou's subtractive ontology rests on an implicit axiom of abstraction wholly opposed by Henry throughout his work: in other words, the one's subtraction is the other's impoverishment.[133] Subtractive ontology says that a being is not accessible to experience because being rests on a void rather than the fullness of sensation or affectivity. Presence is (a)voided, and this allows us to schematise the structure of any possible situation. Set theory is a subtractive ontology in not speaking of any being's qualities or identity; to get back to reality means to strip off rather than to dress up. But this is the contentious point: even if one accepts the axiom of abstraction, one must still ask whether abstraction does actually leave perception behind. Milič Čapek, for instance, reminds us that the increasingly imageless nature of modern mathematics does not preclude the existence of '*far more subtle and more elusive elements* [of spatiality] *even in the most abstract mathematical and logical thought*'. The mathematical intuitionist L.E.J. Brouwer similarly believed that the principle of the excluded middle arises in part out of 'an extensive group of *simple every day phenomena*'. In a similar vein, one might ask to what degree the logical continuity of a mathematical series is totally free from our understanding of a spatial continuum. Peter

Hallward, on the other hand, while pointing to Berkeley's critique of infinitesimals as 'ghosts of departed quantities', nonetheless follows the abstractionist line, taking discoveries such as the non-Euclidean geometries to indicate the transcendence of mathematics over perception.[134] But though such mathematics may 'passeth all understanding', it is debatable whether this is only an issue for a normative use of *human* cognition. Both Spinoza and Berkeley argued for types of mind that would have the power to conceive *and* perceive objects beyond our understanding; while some intuitionists, like Bergson, see a natural geometry arising from perception in its *pre-human* form.

Crucially, though, Badiou claims that this is *not* an axiomatic issue, for it is not just a question of different starting points: the empiricist approach (broadly speaking) is simply *wrong*. Intuitionism, for instance, is just plain mistaken for

> trying to apply back into ontology criteria of connection which *come from elsewhere*, and especially from a doctrine of mentally effective operations. In particular, intuitionism is a prisoner of the empiricist and illusory represen-tation of mathematical *objects*. ... All the 'objects' of mathematical thought – structures, relations, functions etc. – are nothing in the last instance but species of the multiple.[135]

Yet, if his theory of truth is immanent in principle, how can Badiou claim a *non-correspondence* between intuitionist thought and mathematical objects, even at a meta-level (for truth is not confined just to object-languages)? Again, how can he found a theory of error when any axiomatic approach can only claim more or less *productivity* for a chosen set of axioms? Is there something more that he hasn't explicitly stated, some other overarching value?

We'll return to the issue of a transcendental vector in Badiou's thought when we look again at his politicisation of ontology, but, for now, the central question for Badiou and his disciples is as follows: what is it that makes the abstract abstract? Where, when and by what is the abstract abstracted? Where is its *own* event? Badiou would answer that the abstract is wholly non-subjective, real, and *non-evental* because it is the mathematical condition for any event. To provide the event of abstraction would be to provide the event of the condition of the event, and so enter a regress. To this response, Henry would reply that such a non-evental condition is impossible. The abstract is itself a type of seeing and a type of affect, a viewing-event: it is formed through at least one particular quality that cannot be neglected – the invisible, hypersubjective affect. Indeed, in true phenomenological spirit, a mathematical set would be a psychological residue, a ghost. A patheme must lie behind the matheme. For Henry, set theory would be the ultimate virtual-isation and contradiction – an objective phenomenology. It is with this connection between the event and affective perception that we will conclude this chapter, not to indulge Henry's views, but because truth emerges with a subject's *fidelity* to the Badiouian event. What is the nature of this fidelity? It is modelled on mathematical deduction alone, we are told, yet it is a strange word to choose for something that is supposedly not *at all* affective in form. Badiou does, of course, talk of the 'affects of truth' (happiness in love, joy in science, enthusiasm in politics, pleasure in art) when 'a truth seizes me', and there is an almost religious sense in his depiction of the passive seizure by the event.[136] But all the same, fidelity itself cannot be religious or pathetic in nature. The question remains open, then, on whether the affect of truth restores a common ground between Badiou and Henry, and if so, whether it also has a connection with Deleuze.

REAL EVENTS

For Badiou, truth appears via a subject's fidelity to what it creates out of a non-subjective, real evental site – some unpredictable change within a situation that, with further investigation, may eventually come to be an event.[137] Badiou's evental fidelity can thus be contrasted nicely with Quine's ontological commitment: where the one is a relation to 'what there is', the other is a relation to what *will have* been. Fidelity thus embodies Shaw's famous line, 'Some look at things that are, and ask why. I dream of things that never were and ask why not'. But the faithful are not dreaming – they believe that what they want is actually happening: their subjectivity only appears as *merely* subjective from the perspective of the non-faithful.

Throughout Badiou's exposition of an event, its conditions and its effects, there is an ongoing mix of subjective and objective predicates. For instance, the event is characterised by the dice-throw (a very Deleuzian approach too), in order to capture its 'purely hazardous' form as well as its fixity as a multiple (there are only so many sides of each die). As such, chance is conjoined with necessity. It is the objective chanciness of the event that calls for the 'activism of intervention' – the intervention that recognises and decides on the very basis of this undecidability. But there is a paradox of action here. The paradox is that the decision to think of a site as having an undecidable element actually cancels out that property, and annuls itself in a 'disappearing gesture' by being subsumed within the structure of the situation.[138] Immanence again. The '*x*' which 'indexes' the event also belongs to 'X', which names the site, even though it is what ruptures it, even though the 'name of the event must emerge from the void'. The name is an 'indistinguishable' *of* the site, but also something 'projected' by the intervention.[139]

All Badiou's manoeuvrings here are to keep everything immanent all of the time, subjective and objective intertwined. The intervention too, for instance, is also undecidable, being only recognised in the situation through its consequences (rather than a transcendent variable). What counts are the consequences of an event and so the 'organized control of time' that Badiou eventually calls fidelity. Fidelity is the name for that set of procedures which discern the multiples within a situation created by an evental multiple. And though the term fidelity does indeed refer to the 'amorous relationship', Badiou argues that the amorous relationship itself ultimately refers 'to the dialectic of being and event'. Mathemes over pathemes.[140] Likewise, while referring to a 'phenomenology of the procedure of fidelity', Badiou claims that terms like conviction or enthusiasm or conversion are too concrete at this level of abstraction. Rather, the sole two minimal values are 'connection and non-connection'. So now, we can discern what is really at play here. Indeed, in his later work, Badiou retreats from the tendency to think that the event is affirmed solely by our decision; rather, 'the event has consequences, objective consequences and logical consequences'.[141] But while the event may have once had what appears to be a more subjective element of intervention, it was always asubjective in essence, for the subject comes alongside the event, in fidelity to it. The event transforms the logic of a situation objectively, and so it is to this transformation that the subject is faithful, even as it is its own fidelity to it that partly gives the event the power that it has to transform. This is the zigzag co-engendering of the two.

We can make two related points about this attempted alloy of object and subject within the event, one concerning the process of events and the other our fidelity to them. The first observation is with regard to the position Badiou takes over the *individuation* of an event. Badiou's is a heroic theory of the event: only the best in science, art, love and politics will do.[142] But what if every moment to some degree – that is, to some frame of reference – is an event? From this position, being must supervene on process, and indeed many would see this as a necessity in any rigorous theory of the event, for otherwise events will only ever be forms of being, re-structurings of the present, and so on. In Whitehead's words, 'wherever and whenever something is going on, there is an event'.[143] Compared to this, Badiou's events seem all too *objectively* obvious (political revolutions in particular, but also heroic *scientific* revolutions, especially those in mathematics, are all too often the favoured examples). By contrast, a process philosopher like Whitehead or Bergson proliferates change: at every moment, there is creation to be seen (whether we can see it or not).[144] Bergson's theory of 'Fabulation', for example, empha- sises the construction of significant events out of more basic processes from an inhuman though nonetheless subjective stance.[145] But these values of 'significant' and 'basic' are avowedly partial. Fabulation is an 'as if' composition, and Bergson acknowledges that it is when a process first strikes our affects that we are then able to declare an event. Unlike the composed event, however, processes really are everywhere. Deleuze, as we saw, is closer to Badiou in thinking that events are not constructions; but unlike Badiou, Deleuze allows events to multiply endlessly in truly Bergsonian fashion.

Whether Badiou actually needs a stronger process view like this to ground his own valorisation of radical novelty will be discussed in a moment, but before that, we come to our second, related point. Fidelity is the subject's relation to the event. But if the event is not punctal but stretched out over a series of enquiries as Badiou contends, isn't there then an *event* of fidelity too, such that it cannot be objectively determined (through 'connection and non-connection', objective consequences, and so on) without *petitio principii*. Tellingly, a similar question can be raised with respect to Donald Davidson and his related theory of events.[146] In his attempt to found a mind–body identity theory, Davidson aims to show that *all* mental events are really physical events. Yet he himself asserts that events are mental *or* physical only when *described* as such. When an event is described as mental, it is given an intentional or quasi-intentional character which enters it into a holistic structure incapable of being divided according to the atomistic nature of the physical.[147] But the same event can also be put under a non-intentional description involving deterministic laws of cause and effect. Neither of these two descriptions can be reduced to the other, yet they are descriptions of the same event. Hence, we have Davidson's characteristic 'anomalous monism': a monism which cannot be stated in any law-like way. But the mystery at the heart of this theory (that connects Davidson to Badiou's theory of the event) is how and why Davidson should believe that this same event that can be put under various descriptions, intentional and non-intentional, *is* the one and same event. How can Davidson go beyond description (to a *real* mind–body identity) *when it has yet to be confirmed that description is not an event too?* At its heart, the issue is whether it is possible to transcend descriptions to arrive at an objective determination of an event, if only in principle.

For example, I place my lips on the cheek of another person; I kiss a friend in a public garden; I greet a friend; I betray a friend; I cause a friend to be arrested; I start a world-religion; I become synonymous with treachery. Of these various descriptions of the one apparently singular event, all are brought to bear on the momentary act retrospectively. The moment can only be taken for a key event in the development of a world-religion, for instance, from the *retrospective* perspective of those of us who have seen Christianity rise to that status. But the other descriptions are not therefore rejected because of an asserted identity between the moment and one privileged description (a monism); nor is there a dualism of the moment (now termed the 'event') and *mere* descriptions: there are only the descriptions *that are the events*. If there are seven equally possible descriptions then seven different events have taken place. That's a big 'if', of course, but any description that might decide which one (if just one there be) of the seven is true and which are not, would have to prove its own transcendence over the others as a master-discourse.

And how would it do this? In this second case, there would not be one event, a monism, but many events, namely the various descriptions. Such events are always retrospectively generated from a particular frame of reference. In other words, the event is something subjectively constructed and yet also real. Any attempt to individuate events objectively through, say, their putative causes and effects, will have no guarantee that it is not using the wrong kind of language, one that illegitimately discriminates against the event being possibly intentional. Trying to quantify over their causal relations will invoke a partisan non-intentional description. And simply assuming that 'sentences about [the] identities' of events are not themselves events, uttered from a particular situation, will always risk circularity as to the nature of an event. In fact, Davidson may well have tripped over the most notable thing about descriptions, the one that Henry advocated: the essence of phenomenology as a form of passive descriptivism, of letting be, shows description to be both passive ('merely' descriptive) *and* active (revisionary) at once, for passivity is the highest form of activity. The description of an event is another event, or rather, it is a part of the event it describes, it fabulates it.[148]

Of course, this is partly Badiou's view too: the subject's co-engendering comes with its intervention upon an evental site. But, all the same, the evental site is real and fidelity is distinct from it. So the response to Davidson is salient for Badiou as well, the point being that fidelity is not ancillary or 'supplementary' to the evental site but constitutive of it, a part of it: at the very least, it is an event – or set of events – all its own.[149] Fidelity, like description, is both subjective *and* evental. And the event of fidelity is affective as much as it is mathematical *even in Badiou* (as much as he would wish it were *only* the latter), as I'll now try to show.[150]

THE AFFECT OF THE EVENT: VIRTUAL THOUGHTS

'Let us say that not everything that changes is an event, and that surprise, speed, and disorder can be mere simulacra of the event, and not its promise of truth.' Given this selectivity, what then is the real, non-subjective mark of the event for Badiou? Or to put the question in answerable form, why are events rare? The answer rests on the multiple, on the abstract, and on the universal. An event concerns *all*, so that a political event, for instance, concerns the *liberation* of all: 'Every historical event is communist, inasmuch as "communist" designates the trans-temporal subjectivity of emancipation.' The generic, as Badiou says, is '*egalitarian*'.[151] Let us examine this politics more closely as an example of the limits of marking the event through universality. If the event is egalitarian, only a *wholly inclusive* event (infinite openness, without object) would be an event of the highest order. It would be one that liberates all. But all what? Does this include animals, the last zone of our expanding ethical regard according to Peter Singer? Equality is the central term for an event (in ideal form), but equality between who? Those who have interests (Peter Singer), or those who can respond (Emmanuel Levinas), or just those who were not counted before? In other words, how is equality fleshed out – in welfare, in rights, or just in counting?

Clearly, it must be counting that counts in Badiou's mathematicism, for his events are ones that admit into representation what was previously discounted.[152] But then who or even what counts? If the event that brings forth the uncounted is *haphazard and unpredictable*, couldn't the state-advocacy of vegetarianism, anti-vivisectionism and/or animal rights be events precisely because they are *not* on any current political agenda in any state? This would tally with Jacques Rancière's notion of genuine political transformation, wherein to include a previously ostracised group requires a transformation of the rules of political inclusion, given that the group was so radically excluded before. And Badiou admits that he is in great accord with Rancière.[153] In *Saint Paul*, Badiou's idea of the multiple 'as in excess of itself' *vis-à-vis* any represented whole or state, would approximate this notion: the part cannot be assigned to any whole without also reconfiguring it. The criticism we would still have of Badiou is that, not surprisingly, he has failed to think through just how radically the whole might be reconfigured once the universal has been adopted, for doesn't the enfranchisement of animals, like that of children, the insane, or criminals (out-laws), instance one of these rare reconfigurations, one of these genuine political events?[154]

But now the problems are only beginning. The political impetus of truly *universal* liberation is problematic in the extreme when it comes to counting both the cancer cell and the cancer cell's host, as John Llewelyn has shown so well (though we only have to think of the incompatible claims of the *foetus* and its mother to reach the same conclusion).[155] Its rigorous implementation leads to a paradox of thought and an impasse of action. The pure equality of the multitude, like pure quantity, brings with it its own dilemmas: an immobility in ethics and politics akin to Zeno's paradoxes of motion. The paradox of charity, for example, is twofold – not just that if I give to the poor, I become one of the poor, but also that if I help my friend's enemy, I also attack my friend.[156] Put more formally, if the answer to the question of *extent* with regards to politics ('who belongs to the *polis*?') is *subtractive* – the *polis* is simply made up of whatever can *belong* at all (the *polis* is a set) – then the multitude covered is infinite. The city includes all, internally (cancer cells) and externally (the enemies of the city).[157] This leads to stasis as regards principled action (what Badiou calls 'thought-practice'), the impotence of an infinite task. How can the thought that founds the event be 'for all', if *all* should genuinely mean everything?[158] No events at all, *or*, events everywhere. As Slavoj Žižek puts it, 'the limitation of Badiou is nowhere more perceptible than in his positive political program, which can be summed up as unconditional fidelity to the "axiom of equality"'.[159]

Of course, there is no set of all things for Badiou – the One is not – and so the universal is a political impetus rather than an actuality. But Badiou wants to shut down the political process of the event at a seemingly arbitrary stage, human emancipation, even though his notion of the universal is *unqualified* precisely because its impetus is mathematically grounded: it is infinite. For Badiou, false events (simulacra) do not lead to changes in the situation and new forms of counting. True events (a tautological phrase for him) do. But does Badiou ever count sheep? The rise of National Socialism in Germany is paradigmatic of a false event for Badiou because it didn't count all, indeed, it explicitly *discounted* some who had previously been counted (the Jewish community). But didn't the Nazis inaugurate an historical event by being the first state to ban vivisection? Let's pursue this extreme thought, if only to show up an important weakness in Badiou. As a political phenomenon, Nazism was about one level of inequality (of Aryan and non-Aryan); and yet it *restricted* vivisection in the name of a greater continuity and universality – that we are all animals (though some are more noble than others, irrespective of their species-membership).[160] Yes, of course, they treated (some) people 'like animals', but they also initiated the state into treating (some) animals 'like people' (minimally by simply not using them for vivisection).[161] Equality, or at least less inequality on a certain level.

The point I'm making is that the *application* of eventhood accords with Badiou's own political *eros* and/or assumed definitions (as one would expect from an axiomiatic thinking), but in such a way that contradicts his own characterisation of an event. I might just as well have pointed to the founding of the RSPCA in 1824 by Richard Martin, or the publication of Singer's *Animal Liberation* in 1975 as other events of similar import. Yet even in the *Logiques des mondes*, Badiou rejects as the 'contemporary *doxa*' the 'humanist protection of all animals'. Over the rights of Life, Badiou prefers the 'rights of infinite thought'.[162] It is ironic, then, that Badiou's nomination of the French Revolution as a true event goes even further than he thinks, for during its very inauguration a number of Revolutionaries liberated some of the animals from the royal menagerie, 'in the name of their revolution'. Badiou, presumably, would have left them in their cages.

There is, of course, a built-in circularity explicitly *posited* by Badiou's theory of the event – events are made by our intervention to declare an event as having occurred – but there should be no circularity in this theory of circularity. Yes, we decide groundlessly to affirm *that* an event has taken place, but *what* an event is, is not groundless, for Badiou gives it a clear characterisation in terms of universality. Yet the *way* Badiou implements his theory, is, I believe, (necessarily) selective, there always being an element of *eros*, of affect, in the constitution of any *polis* – not just his – because the recognition of an event needs affectivity. As Henry put it, we can suffer with all that which suffers because there is a 'pathos-with' that is the 'largest form of any conceivable community'.[163] Badiou's theory, however, claims to be non-subjective or Real:[164] a 'genuine event' is based upon the void, he says, and the void 'neither excludes nor constrains *anyone*. It is the absolute neutrality of being', such that fidelity to an event is 'universally addressed'.[165] So in this respect – its attempt to found a theory of non-subjective eventhood through transformations that act for the universal – Badiou does contradict himself by privileging the human, by speaking of 'any*one*' as if this didn't exclude that which we name 'any*thing*'.

So why does Badiou resist such an 'absorption of humanity into animality' as the *Logiques des mondes* condemns?[166] His reply would be that animals are not political and so cannot concern events: 'politics, ultimately, is the existence of the people'. 'We' and 'all' still excludes some: 'total emancipation' is not for all. And in a crucial *property*, humans are not animals.[167] The universal quantifier, this one time, is qualified and filled in, the principle for this exceptional exclusion being *thought*.[168] Politics is about nothing other than itself, a 'collectivisable thought', and, as we all know, pigs don't think. But this crypto-humanism rests uneasily with Badiou's anti-humanist tendencies. In fact, in the absence of God, it is arguable that Badiou deifies human thought as an ideal: 'Noumenal Humanity'. What makes us human, for Badiou, is our 'capacity' (another virtual) for thought and 'thought is nothing other than that by which a truth seizes and traverses the human animal'. Humanity is what provides the support and locale for truth procedures. This is not a conservative rationalism on Badiou's part, for just what counts as thought is mobile or 'aleatory' in his work: but whatever thought is or becomes, it does so only for humans, who alone are the bearers of thought and constant re-inventors of reason.[169] Badiou's speciesism allows him to politicise his ontology of the pure multiple for a very specific set, given that his *polis* is built exclusively around a human *eros*.[170] Indeed, there is an economy of thought to Badiou's ontology that is very reminiscent of Heidegger's. Despite eschewing any confusion between being as such and the particular being of human existence, Heidegger's *Being and Time* still opts to approach the question of being through human *Dasein* as the most appropriate method because only humans ask the question of the meaning of being (though we saw Henry earlier criticise this move as logocentric).[171] Likewise, Badiou justifies his anthropocentric ontology because only humans can count (in every sense of the term). Despite subtracting the concept of the subject from any empirical or historical humanism, that is, one based on identitarian thinking through biology, gender, ethnicity, or religion, Badiou continues to valorise the human subject. Mathematical thinking is the one property allowed to adjudicate membership (exclusion and inclusion) because it is the basis of set theory – the theory of what it is to be a member *per se*. Hence, Badiou is able to have his anti-humanist cake and eat it anthropocentrically.[172]

But to say that only those who think are included is begging the question – who thinks? Don't animals think? Are the findings of modern evolutionary epistemology, ethology and neuropsychology on primate intelligence wholly pointless because great apes don't do degrees in mathematics at the Sorbonne?[173] But neither did I. And neither, I suspect, could I. *That is why there is no pretence of mathematics in this presentation of Badiou's thought.* I am actually not a mathematician. I can do some maths, as can a chimpanzee. I may be able to register for a degree in mathematics (unlike a chimpanzee, of course), but this is a technical difference: in order to define humans as an inclusive group, Badiou has had to ignore our individual differences, our individual empirical and *actual* differences, in order to establish a *virtual* ideal. He has also had to ignore our continuities with non-human animals, as well as our entire material embodiment. So far, so Platonist: Badiou is obviously proud of not being a philosopher of the animal like Deleuze. And though he may protest at being called a 'pre-Darwinian', in his theory of truth at least, he leaves the human in splendid isolation from the evolution of all other animals.[174]

Were Badiou to retort that the continuities established by evolutionary episte-mology, ethology and neuropsychology are all the findings of pseudoscience, it would seem that the philosopher is *judging* science and refusing to let its findings, its truths, challenge philosophy's thoughts. To admit only the science that leaves one's philosophy intact is tantamount to admitting no science at all. Badiou is clearly political in his use of science, which brings me back to my point about mathematical training. The sad fact is that, even in the ideal situation, I suspect that I could never graduate with a degree in mathematics and could certainly never be as good a mathematician as, say, Henri Poincaré, *no matter how hard I tried*. This is because of empirical differences. Mathematical creativity, novelty, or even 'genius' cannot be determined simply through the definition or axiom of all humanity, 'generic humanity', as mathematically gifted.[175] Mathematical power comes in degrees (no less than the mastery of German or Ancient Greek). The *Meno*'s slaveboy and I can both do some maths, but there will be differences between us (his is a younger brain) and Poincaré, as there is between us and the chimpanzee. Differences of degree.

The point being made here is agnostic as to whether mathematics is subjectively constructed or transcendentally empowered – the *source* of the differences is immaterial: all that counts is that there are *always actual* differences, be they of active creation or passive reception.[176] To shut out all non-humans as bare life and include all humans, despite a shifting empirical ability, is, *following Badiou's own thought*, to re-qualify the multiple in an illegitimate manner. Defining humanity by its purported ability to think mathematically (to the very *same* degree) is to virtualise an actuality and homogenise a heterogeneity. The generic is the generic, no more and no less: to qualify it as generic humanity is surely to appropriate it in a Sartrean and Cartesian dualism that expels too much being. Indeed, it is here in this philosophical apartheid that the seemingly absent *philosophical* subject effectively resides in Badiou's thought, albeit surreptitiously. Though he seeks '*subjective forms that can be neither individual nor communitarian*', at crucial moments Badiou individualises his theory in the direction of an unnecessarily anthropocentric dogmatism that also covers over a highly dubious induction, to wit, that animals don't think.[177] Being equals counting (ontology equals mathematics), and so animals (and everything non-human) are discounted because they supposedly can't count.

What we have analysed here concerning political events could just as well be performed on Badiou's characterisation of artistic, scientific, or amorous events. The general criticism is that, contra Badiou's elitism of the event (in every sense), change is everywhere, but change is discerned by some *as events* because of their *interests* or what Badiou himself calls a 'mode of discernment'.[178] In the specific case of politics, it is our affective, embodied, worldly situatedness that facilitates a feasible (that is, a difficult but not impossible) charity of mind: we delimit our 'others' (and their claim on us) by sheer situatedness – we can see, feel and think *only so far, and not to infinity*. The claim of quantity, the universal, is only perceived (as a quality) within a frame, even if, perhaps, a growing one: there is no view from nowhere, no God, not even by proxy of (Platonist) mathematics.[179] But now we are veering too far back to the position of Henry (though in a secularised version of his emotivism); and we already saw in the previous chapter that equivalent criticisms can be mounted against Henry's own excessive valorisation of pure affect and the claim of quality, of the self.

WHENCE COMES THE NEW?

If mathematics is to be a thought at all, according to Badiou, then it must be through an impersonal, asubjective thought. But what will Badiou's bridging mechanism be between this asubjective and the subjective; how do we think infinite mathematical thoughts with our finite psychological and biological brains? As Frege might have asked, how do we subjectively think such objective (or non-subjective) thoughts? It cannot be by *deduction*, for that is already a party to the dispute (being mathematical) and so is as inadequate for the role of neutral mediator as Descartes' pineal gland. Badiou's later work in the *Logiques des mondes* does broach the issue of phenomenology, of how things appear (in every sense of this 'how'), but it does so at the expense of the ideal purity of being. Bodies, spaces and living organisms have an impure and dirty 'existence', as do the sciences that study them (when compared to the mathematical study of being). So now, we have a duality of being and existence. And, moreover, Badiou's human ideal remains virtual, not actual. Is evolutionary biology thus to be denied in favour of the human ideal, this paragon of animals?

In truth, the virtuality of noumenal humanity is just one more virtual to be added to the others in Badiou's philosophy – of thought, of being and the void, and of the event – though in fact they are all simply the different faces of the one Virtualism, of psychology (thought), of life (humanity), of time (the event), and of the world (being and void). All of them fulfil crucial roles of inclusion and exclusion both at the margins and at the centre of his system. In *Being and Event*, Badiou's Actualism, immanence and deductive rigour come at the cost of huge delimitations and omissions. Badiou's definition of ontology is the thought 'of what is sayable as be-ing'. This reflects the traditional Parmenidean equation of thought and being: Badiou believes that what is conceivable is what exists. But this assumes so much on the issue of what is sayable *vis-à-vis* what is possible, conceivable and imaginable, or even whether any of these are tenable distinctions, and are not wholly interconnected in actuality.[180] Pure thought and pure being, both of them immaculate conceptions, may well have messier origins.

In sum, Badiou has a paradox of quantity as the generative force that creates novelty (events), but we've seen that what counts as an event is arbitrary (Badiou glosses the event as equality, yet this is highly problematical). *All* that can be said of the event is that it occurs, that there is something new, but its external details, outside of the frame of reference of the one who names it, are arbitrary. Yet does this make the event wholly subjective? Are events constructed relative to our interests? The answer is only a qualified yes in both cases, because the subjective and these interests are not only intellectual, voluntary or human: they are also embodied, involuntary and inhuman (though without being essentialist either – bodies are unpredictable processes too). There are subjectivities that are 'outside' relative to our own subjective 'inside'; there are diagonals that run across the theoretical lines of immanence and transcendence, and subject and object. Interests are everywhere *yet* selective. Indeed, novelty is what is experienced *as* new, it is what stands out to someone *against* the familiar, what *transcends* the familiar.

This is what Jean-François Lyotard meant in his critique of Badiou when he said that 'one must have particular affection for the void' (or the evental site at the edge of the void), one must be 'affected' by it.[181] Of course, Badiou admits that the event is always *in* a situation, but he adds that the event's relation to its situation is *wholly* unconditioned.[182] Absolute novelty. We have ourselves stated exactly this point earlier when amending Deleuze's appropriation of Bergson: novelty needs no constitution in the virtual-past (even by a relation of 'different/ciation'). The new emerges from itself, *de novo*. But whereas novelty is auto-conditioning, this doesn't mean that it is a pure *punctum*, an island unconnected to any other ground. It is not a present *state*, but a *continuity* of change. Its connection *precisely is* the contrast it makes, given that the contrast can only be to a point of view or frame of reference: novelty is perspectival and affective. There is a continuity of hetero-geneity. Absolute or pure novelty makes no sense, for it has nothing with which to contrast or stand out as new. Novelty needs some form of generality or continuity to be novel (or be fabulated as an event). And it is affectivity, or shock, that also provides that back-ground – the frame of reference that sees something *as* old and *as* new, as present and as past ('my past') – that virtualises other processes into immobile states in the very same procedure that allows other processes to stand out as novelties. All of this is done by affectivity. The affect is not *of* the novelty, it *is* the novelty (otherwise, affectivity would become one more virtual ground again). This is the affective mirror Henry (and to a degree Lyotard) hold up to Badiou's theory of change.

A final defence of absolute, non-affective novelty could be mounted through Badiou's use of chance in his theory of the event, which is predicated on *pure* randomness. He thinks of the cast of dice as emblematic of the event 'because this gesture symbolizes the event in general; that is, that which is purely hazardous, and which cannot be inferred from the situation ...'. As pure randomness, hazard, or chance, the event is this 'supplementation of being'. But *pure* chance too is itself a fabulation, a construction.[183] Words like 'chance', 'luck' and 'accident' are names that already indicate an anthropomorphisation of events reflecting our interests ('lucky for me that the bullet went over my head') and allowing us a possible magical influence on the future ('I better keep my head down from now on'). Improbability is subjective (as Bernoulli – who knew more about gambling than most – Bergson and Sartre showed in their different ways) and so cannot be the source of the subject.

In this sense, change is everywhere (as the philosophers of difference would claim), but events (lucky or unlucky) are not (as Badiou would claim). However, a number of arguments can be mobilised to explain the rarity of the event in terms of affective perspective, as we have seen with both Henry and Lyotard. The decision that an event has taken place, if decision it be, need not be non-psycho-logical through and through: there is a place for bodily recognition.[184] This renders the status of the event as new, the *event-qua-event*, bear also on its own qualitative difference, its *qualia*. Quality, not e-quality. The fundamental issue is that Badiou still thinks of the event too much in terms of being, even if by negation, that is, as 'what-is-not-being'; hence, novelty is based on the void and, despite his protests to the contrary, comes perilously close to being formed *ex nihilo*.[185] In other words, Badiou doesn't think of the event *per se*, event-as-event, as intrinsic novelty, coming positively *de novo*, out of itself, autocatalytic, unfounded (in substance *or* in thought), that is, as new. Badiou thinks of the being *of* the event rather than the event of being.[186] But the event, *qua* new, cannot be explained through anything other than itself. Novelty is irreducible to what is the same, be it matter, structure, or principle.

In other words, Badiou makes the choice for being before becoming, as a Platonist must. But doing so makes his explanation of change truly untenable because it is explained through an outside (being). Yet his stated view *is* that the new 'can only be thought as process'.[187] What we have argued instead is not that the new is inexplicable in principle, but simply that it is only ever explicable immanently (*de novo*), through itself and its interior properties, properties that can be described in different ways, but whose basic structure – the structure of novelty – remains the same. The new reduces, relates, or refers only to itself – it is auto-affective *or* self-belonging. Indeed, it is not 'self-belonging', an oddity of set theory, that generates novelty, but novelty that *is* (in one description) self-belonging *or* (in another) auto-affection.[188] And this duality is an inclusive, not exclusive, disjunction. It is perhaps a little incongruous that Henry and Badiou have revealed this common structure of novelty precisely in virtue of their wholly opposed philosophies. According to François Laruelle, however, that incongruity is totally unwarranted: if we look hard enough at any philosophy, we will see the same structures mounted and remounted, time and again, be it on the subject of novelty or anything else. It should consequently be no surprise that, no matter the topic, philosophers always say the same thing.

CHAPTER 4

From Philosophy to Non-Philosophy: François Laruelle

> It is a question of knowing if immanence will be the Real itself as being only (to) itself; or if it remains finally the property of a plane, of a universal, etc., and even of an Ego.[1]

ON FIRST PHILOSOPHIES: MATHEME OR PATHEME?

Time after time, we have witnessed an especially peculiar parallel between Badiou and Henry. To think, according to Badiou, means to 'break with sensible immediacy'. The name of 'stellar matheme' has been applied to his work in as much as it refers to Mallarmé's symbol of the star as constituting 'a reserve of eternity' beyond any empirical limits. Badiou's definition of evil, in fact, is where 'something that was invisible must now become visible'.[2] Something is forced into the light, either by naming or being made existent. But this is also Henry's definition of the barbaric virtual – a forcing into visibility. Henry and Badiou are both philosophers of the unseen. The making visible to all, the forcing out of invisible and immanent being into a transcendent world of specular control; this is what is essentially barbarous for Henry and evil for Badiou. But what it is that is forcibly revealed is different for each of these two philosophers: the evental site within a set for Badiou, the affective state for Henry. Where Henry derives fundamental layers of hidden self-affection, Badiou derives fundamental layers in hidden sets of sets. Both believe that there are layers or levels to actuality, and though their composition is quite different – pathetic and mathematical respectively – they still have the same invisible structure of *reflexivity* (the feeling of feeling, the set of sets).

To crystallise the difference between Badiou and Henry we might even paraphrase Kant and say that affectivity without mathematics is blind, and mathematics without affectivity is empty. But Henry welcomes blindness and Badiou resolutely grounds his ontology on the empty set, that is, on the void.[3] From the point of view we articulated in the previous two chapters, though, both forms of the actual – patheme and matheme – are needed as ideal poles between which a movement is installed. Each pole has what the other needs, the view that affectivity takes of itself (in Henry) and the affect that makes any view possible (Badiou's abstract views of mathematics and the event). Where Badiou's mathematical

Actualism falls over especially is in its need for affect (to register an event). And where Henry's affective Actualism falls over is in a need for objective views. These two stark and reductive philosophies seem to be caught in a prison of their own making that fails to provide an explanation both as to how their other might exist (even as an illusion), and also thereby of their consistency. Each reduces the actuality of the other's position to the virtual in order to banish it. Only together, however, in the lines of metaphilosophical movement that bring us from the one to the other (through implication, omission and *reductio*) do we adequately picture a reality that is beyond pure immanence (of any one type) or pure transcendence. All-or-nothing philosophies ('everything is *x*, nothing is *y*') are inexpressible, or rather, once they are expressed, they auto-ramify into *x* and *y*. One becomes two, *monism dualises*.

Let me explain further. Henry has shown us how *qualia* can be felt and yet not be anthropocentrically subjective – they are of a world (the cosmos as auto-affection). Henry's problem was the paradox of quality: why is there any specificity at all, whence comes the world's structure, details, quantities? Is the predictive success of applied mathematics simply a product of chance? And why must there be just *one* God (mono-theism), why is there not a number of lives 'higher' than ours? Henry rejects ontological monism (Heidegger) for losing the specificity of affect, but what of his own lack of detail? What of his own affective monism? Alternatively, Badiou claims that the 'One is not' – there is no God. Monism is false (if only by being able to state it, it sets up its counter as an illusory-being, but still a being). But then Badiou installs the infinite and void as purities in place of the One. Yet a true theory of the multiple, or true pluralism, must think of *its* novelty, *its* differences directly *through themselves* rather than through being (or ontology) at all (even a being masquerading as multiple). Both the One and its mirror-reflection, the void, are the virtual images between which real, actual becoming becomes.

In a thoroughgoing Actualism, the multiple, as becoming, as indefinite growth rather than infinite and eternal concept, needs nothing else but itself for its ground. There is no need for either an ontology of being or a meontology of nothingness. It is a reflexivity: it relates to the 'more' of itself, to its own growth, its own novelty. This is not to reject the One *simpliciter* in favour of the many, because the plural here is not quantitative, but reflexive – it is always an ongoing meta-pluralism: that which generates 'the one' and 'the many' in a dualising process of differentiation and integration across types that are logical, psychological and cosmological. Henry reduced this reflexivity to quality (auto-affection); Badiou reduced it to quantity (set theory): both miss the issue of structure/detail (quantity) and novelty/event (quality) their theories respectively needed in order to sustain themselves. Their two theories outline a duality that only works by integrating them together as metaphilosophical processes: they sustain themselves only as movements out of each other, movements that are quantitatively and qualitatively reflexive at the same time. I will venture later that the metaphilosophical discourse that can best embody this threefold demand (for reflexion, quantity and quality), one that is formal *and* concrete, mathematical *and* affective, is the philosophical diagram. But this is all a little premature.

In his attempt to sequester novelty to quantity alone by infinitising it (albeit to an untenable political end – the liberation of *all*), Badiou neglected the need for quality (the excessive quantity exceeds *a point of view or frame of reference*), no less than Henry neglected the need for quantity (a world) in his valorisation of quality as affectivity alone. But Badiou might protest that the infinities discovered by mathematics are excessive enough to count as truly novel – there is no need for change to be felt in order to be radical. We are seemingly faced, then, by a simple choice: novelty as quantity or novelty as quality. Perhaps all we have here is one dogmatism pitting itself against another. Naturally, Badiou would want to rephrase the discussion in terms of axiomatics rather than dogmatism, that is, he would say that he adopts the axiomatic approach at the outset because there is *no way* of deciding the matters at hand other than by an original decision (that will only establish its efficacy subsequently).[4] Why might this be so? Because there is no way to choose between Badiou and Henry, between the *matheme* and the *patheme*, given their all-encompassing and hence self-fulfilling ontologies: everything that is, is set theory, or everything that is, is auto-affection. What is often said of Berkeley's similarly all-embracing philosophy, that it is as impossible to believe as it is to refute, seems no less true of these positions. Of course, everything could be mathematical at base, if one understands a thing *as such* as what can be quantified. Or obviously everything could be affective, given that it is absolutely certain that everything feels a certain way to the subject first and foremost. When Byron writes, 'To me, high mountains are a feeling', even to try to argue the contrary would be churlish – there is strictly nothing one can say against this idea. All the other reductionist philosophies, both naturalist and anti-naturalist, be they based on physics, biology, cognition, culture, language, thought, or spirit, could be strung between these two deltas of pure quantity and pure quality, but none would match their single-mindedness. But perhaps they are impossible to believe *because* they are irrefutable on their own terms, their purity and perfection allowing for no further movement into or out of them. With that unalloyed purity comes a certain sterility, as Bergson once wrote:

> To place will everywhere is the same as leaving it nowhere ... It makes little difference to me if one says 'everything is mechanism' or 'everything is will': in either case everything is identical. In both cases, 'mechanism' and 'will' become synonyms of each other. Therein lies the initial vice of philosophical systems. They think they are telling us something about the absolute by giving it a name ... But the more you increase the extension of the term, the more you diminish comprehension of it. If you include matter within its extension, you empty its comprehension of the positive characteristics by which spontaneity stands out against mechanism and liberty against necessity. When finally the word arrives at the point where it designates everything that exists, it means no more than existence. What advantage is there then in saying that the world is will, instead of simply saying that it is?[5]

But Bergson's refutation here is a metaphilosophical one (it concerns systems *per se*). It is only metaphilosophically that we can escape the logic of such totalising philosophies and so put them back in motion. What some call 'Popperian falsifiability' is not epistemic alone, but also marks the movement of thought opposed to its hypostasis.

With regard to Badiou and Henry, then, it must be an axiomatic stance that infinities of quantity can generate novelty, no less than the idea that only qualitative difference will suffice must remain an unproven assertion. For if they were falsifiable, what empirical difference (of degree or of kind) *could distinguish and arbitrate between them?* That is to say, how can we differentiate qualitative difference from quantitative difference? It is impossible to say what *type* of difference, of degree or of kind, differentiates the set of all differences in kind from the set of all differences of degree. To attempt an answer is to cite a difference that must fall into one of the two sets rather than a third that separates them. Hence, one must state by fiat that either quality or quantity alone is fundamental – a reductive strategy despite all appearances to the contrary. Admittedly, in *Bergsonism* Deleuze proposed the virtual as precisely the place where all the types of difference, of degree and of kind, coexist 'in a single Time, which is nature itself'.[6] That this solution is less than adequate becomes clearer when, in *Difference and Repetition* and other texts, this virtual coexistence is adumbrated as a 'transcendental Difference' or as 'degrees of difference itself and not differences of degree'.[7] Radical though the solution is, one cannot help noticing that part of the *explanandum*, 'degree', reappears in the *explanans* (unless, that is, one is positing the virtual as a regress of actualities, which Deleuze is not).

Of course, Badiou decides to give the name of 'indiscernibility' to such a 'difference without a concept', and this may well tackle the point a little better. But axioms (decisions) have to pay their way in explanatory power (be it deductive or hermeneutical), not pave a circular path.[8] The axiomatic method is supposed to avoid covert circularity in favour of being open and productive. But how is production quantified, or rather, how is the unproductive quantified without invoking a new level of circularity? If the quality of quantity is a 'hallucination', to use Badiou's term, then so is the quantity of quality, if by hallucination we mean the psychological affects of quantity. Either this, or Badiou must give us a non-psychological theory of hallucination, that is, he must explain the possibility of both his philosophy and others' sophistry. Why is his thought true and others' false? As mentioned earlier, philosophies of *pure* immanence, leaving nothing outside of themselves, cannot explain their other as anything but illusion, or even the emergence of this illusion. But then they cannot explain their own possibility or emergence either. They must be axiomatic. However, they are incomplete in as much as they are axiomatic, indeed, the axioms are their assertoric point of emergence. Badiou calls this a decision. Henry calls this incarnation. Neither can immanently judge the other as sophistry or barbarism, for there is no *deciding* between them. And there is no *affection* between them either. And this 'between them' is neither decision nor affect. The purpose of this chapter, in effect, will be to elucidate the meaning of this 'between'.

Ultimately, then, Badiou (no less than Henry) needs to provide us with an account of the event of his own thought, and the non-event of all other competing philosophies. This he fails to do.[9] The philosophy that can depict quality and quantity equally, on the other hand, has the greater explanatory scope, and Badiou himself sets scope or 'maximal extension' as his criterion for theoretical preference.[10] This is what we will be examining in what promotes itself as the most powerful and rigorous thought of immanence imaginable, that of François Laruelle's non-philosophy. Philosophy can be about both quantitative and quali-tative difference together, not because one of the two is really *reducible* to the other (this is exactly the move being resisted), but because the two are held in a 'unified theory', a 'democratic' exchange. Because quantitative and qualitative difference are irreducible, the vocation of theory (non-philosophy) remains separate from but nonetheless engaged with both *matheme* and *patheme*, once they have been divested of their pretence of absolute authority over reality.

TOWARDS A NEW METAPHILOSOPHY

Before embarking on this non-philosophy, however, we must supplement our investigation of Badiou with a metaphilosophical examination of an Ayerean problem (of another kind). A.J. Ayer used his 'principle of verifiability' in *Language, Truth and Logic* to establish an anti-philosophy that is in some ways not so different from Badiou's position.[11] Admittedly, Badiou is neither an anti-philosopher nor a scientific positivist, but by leaving ontology to mathematics he demotes *prima philosophia* in a fashion similar to the line taken by empiricists from Hume to Ayer. Like Badiou, Ayer rejects the idea that the function of philosophy is to propose a complete picture of reality based on first principles. Reality is best left to science. But this leaves Ayer with a problem that is essentially that of his own philosophy. Given that in his view meaning is either synthetic or analytic, made up of either verifiable empirical statements or mathematical tautologies, then his own philo-sophical statements on these fields, being neither empirical nor mathematical, are meaningless. In other words, his representation of the situation is either meaningless or a new, third type of meaningfulness created by exceeding itself in self-belonging (by referring to itself). A meta-meaning.

In turn, Badiou's dilemma is that his discourse concerns being and truth. Given that it is not mathematics but philosophy he writes, then, *ex hypothesi*, it is not ontological; but given that it is not any one of the four conditions of philosophy either, then it is also not true. Of course, Badiou describes his own work as a 'meta-ontology'. But does this mean that it is a new, different type of existence, or that it is simply a piece of knowledge, and so not true and new? Presumably, Badiou believes there is something new and true in what he writes, but then it must indeed be, as a discourse, instantiating a new type of existence. It is its own event (referring to itself), only one that doesn't rupture or negate being, but simply *qualifies* it into different kinds by representing it. This is a conclusion his mathematicism could not tolerate, for it would contravene the unicity of being (the void is unique) and the homogeneity of nature (history alone is eventful), by setting up a kind of existence that is *both being and event, presentation and represen- tation*. A being which is a process. Morever, it would be a kind of being generated by philosophy and so not wholly captured by set theory. None of this would be acceptable. But for now, let us explore its possibility further.

The issue is whether philosophy generates truth, and so whether it has its own kind of subjectivity. Badiou says that it doesn't, because this would allow philosophy the power of auto-positioning itself above all other enquiries. This sovereignty would be totally unwarranted (there is no intuition, perception, or deduction which could support it), and so it is better to begin with the axiom that philosophy is conditioned by an outside, in particular the axiom that the One is not, that there is no 'all' or whole on which philosophy could pitch its absolute perspective.[12] In these generic terms, Badiou is seemingly more open to the possibility of his *kind of* philosophy than to the possibility of his own specific implementation of it. And quite rightly. For the feasibility of Badiou's philosophy as meta-ontology relies on an overarching truth: that of a meta-meta-ontology of this *kind of* philosophy being possible. But Badiou's philosophy incorporates this overarching truth too (being 'meta-'), and so is both element and set, that is, it is a set of which it is itself a member (auto-reference/auto-affection again). In other words, meta-ontology exceeds ontology as an event – the 'meta-' is the excess. In Badiou's own terms, it is a decision marking the event of the axiomatisation of set theory, and so it is new. Prior to the decision, its status is undecidable; but, and this is also vital, if Badiou's theory concerns the Whole of philosophy, then no philo- sophical decision could render it consistent because there is no 'Truth of Truth', that is, there can be no truth to the Whole when the Whole does not exist.

So is Badiou's philosophy new? Going by Badiou's own stipulations, the response must be negative, for compossibilising (the function of philosophy) is not an event. But then, given that his philosophy is conditioned like every other, while at the same time presumably new (unlike every other), we have something both arbitrarily novel (an event) and conditioned. But how? Monique David-Menard calls this duplicity a 'savagery', by which she understands that the junction of Badiou's discourse to the matheme 'is neither thematized nor transcendentally regulated; and that it is this excess of the practice of thought over the rules that it defines that gives it its philosophical scope'.[13] But here, *in this description*, it seems that the creation of Badiou's philosophy is actual and immanent to itself, *but only if also transcendentally true*: for otherwise, *how* did David-Menard assert this of Badiou's philosophy? Is hers a spontaneous creation? How is it consistent or corre- lated *as a truth* with Badiou's philosophy?

We are going around in circles here created by the paradox of Badiou's own philosophical authorship, its own self-reference: it refers to all philosophy in such a manner that either its status as philosophy is in peril or its truth is. If it is true (about its conditioning), it is untrue (for what is conditioned cannot be true). *Or* Badiou's philosophical self-reference creates a new kind of truth, philosophy, and being at one and the same time. To put the matter anew: If 'philosophy is no longer sovereign' for Badiou, what is its new role?[14] It cannot judge or predict fidelities in the four fields that condition it, but it can attempt to construct a 'space of compossibility' for all of them in its contemporary era. Yet if poems, say, are no more fundamental than mathemes, then what is Badiou's philosophical language of compossiblity composed of – what is its vocabulary? Perhaps it is of a new kind. Indeed, we saw that a new language is precisely what an immanent theory of truth needs to replace any traditional theory of error, where error is understood as misrepresentation. Truth as presentation (not representation), as emergence, as novelty, and as performed or instantiated (in the discourse of mathematics or *pathos*, but also, I've claimed, in Badiou's meta-ontology and Henry's philosophy of affectivity), must look to other normative criteria. Norms rest on normality, and normality doesn't lie well with novelty. But perhaps there is a beginning for such criteria to be found in Badiou himself.

There must be a 'point' for philosophy to begin, Badiou says, a point of interruption amongst the flows of meaning.[15] Again, he could be trying to think the *possibility of* the new here (and thereby undoing it, as we have argued), but he may also be thinking of the possibility of (his own) philosophy. His thinkable, pure inconsistency, now renamed truth, is a retort to the flux of post-modern *skepsis* (of unthinkable flows). Like Descartes, Badiou turns the doubt against the doubters as a new instrument of truth: the truth that emerges in fidelity to an event is an irruption of *inconsistency* within consistency. The vice becomes a virtue. If ontology can think its own refutation through set theory, then so too can metaontology (genuine philosophy in its unique capacity to *think* truth).[16] Now recall that philosophy is conditioned by an 'outside'.[17] Significantly, Badiou's philosophy of philosophy is also outside philosophy *per se* and so must belong to one of these outer fields. If it does, though, it is not the metaphilosophy it hoped it was because either all philosophy is Badiouian (there never was a genuine philosophy beforehand), or his philosophy both is and is not philosophy – paradox. But this conundrum could actually mark the truth of (Badiou's) metaphilosophy. By his own lights, non-contradiction cannot be proven from within a systematic thought – so his own philosophy, whilst it remains immanent itself, must acknowledge its paradoxical powers.[18] Let's look at these powers closely. For Badiou,

> The specific role of philosophy is to propose a unified conceptual space in which naming *takes place* of events that serve as the point of departure for truth procedures. Philosophy seeks to gather together all the *additional-names*. It deals within thought with the compossible nature of the procedures that condition it. It does not establish any truth but it sets a locus of truths. It configurates the generic procedures, through a welcoming, a sheltering, built up with reference to their disparate simultaneity.[19]

Philosophical operators are not 'summations, totalizations' but subtractions. They concern the 'conjunction' of truths or (after Heidegger) their 'compounding'. Philosophy constructs a category of 'Truth' (without itself creating truth) by seizing and being seized by the truths of its conditions: it creates 'a space of thoughts' or makes truth 'manifest'. But as compossibility entails that only what can co-exist exists, such that contradictory beings cannot exist, what is to be made of actual contradictory beings such as the waves and particles of quantum mechanics, say, or contradictory claims, such as for the political equality of the cancer cell and its host (or the *foetus* and its mother)? Doesn't compossibility flout the idea of novelty, that is, new forms of co-existence? Moreover, given that philosophy cannot create truths and only names events, how can it fathom *novel* compossibilities? Badiouian philosophy appears to exist only in a space of pre-existing rules as to the nature of compossibility, for instance, the law of non-contradiction. But events may involve situations that breach such laws (as wave/particle complementarity does): if we can compossibilise them, it will only be because we are forced to think in new ways, with new *images* of compossibility.[20] Hence, thought must be eventful too in order to compossibilise truths previously deemed incompatible: it must be meta-eventful (*vis-à-vis* these 'lower order' events), which is only to say that it is an event of another kind.[21]

And what would these new images be? More specifically, what is this 'space' of co-existence? 'Conceptual space', 'points of departure' (or 'immobility'), the generic procedure as a 'diagonal of the situation', the 'locus of truths', 'a space of thoughts', and 'torsions': such spatial metaphors are doing a great deal of work here for Badiou, the most obvious being the notion that the void might have an 'edge'.[22] He also talks of philosophical 'pincers' that seize the truths of its conditions under the sign of Truth. And, of course, a subject is formulated as 'a point of truth' – the 'local existence of the process that unfolds generic multiplicities'. Philosophy is the 'place' where the truths of, say, love and art are 'crossed'. Finally, when again writing of compossibility, Badiou talks of that most Lacanian of spatial images, knots:[23]

> It is necessary to elaborate a general theory of the connections of knots between different procedures but the difficult point is to have criteria for such an evaluation: however, it is possible once you have categories for the different steps of the procedures. I am working on this point.[24]

In this and the next chapter we will examine two attempts to resolve the matter of compossibility (the being of philosophy) through immanence: one will be the 'non-philosophy' of our fourth and final philosopher of immanence, Laruelle – 'the most important unknown philosopher working in Europe today'.[25] The other comes by way of a mutation of Laruelle, conjoined with Badiou's latest thinking on spatiality and the appearance of being. The conditions that make philosophy possible are themselves made possible *together* through a spatial relation rather than a conceptual one.

In works subsequent to Badiou's *Being and Event* such as *Conditions*, *Metapolitics*, and *Handbook of Inaesthetics*, there is a much more detailed elucidation of the non-philosophical materials feeding into philosophy: love, literature, politics, mathematics, in various guises and personas (Rimbaud, Beckett, Mallarmé, Mao, Plato, Hegel, Lacan), are all examined with a view to exposing their own specific truth procedures, their subtractive methodologies or styles. The neologisms of 'metapolitics', or 'inaesthetics' indicate the new relationship between philosophy and its non-philosophical conditions, one of submission to their truths, to their modes of thinking. But it is still their numericity that counts throughout (the Two of Love reaching to infinity beyond One, Beckett's Two 'in excess of solipsism' tying all of his work together, the three infinities of politics moving towards One, and so on). This is the case even while Badiou avoids offering an explicit synthesis of the different numerical procedures once and for all.[26] This evasion is all to the good in that it indicates the transitional character of any one philosophical compossibilising, such that setting down the metatheory of all such compossibilising would be obtuse in the extreme.

But there is still the implicit reduction to the *mathemic form* in virtue of this constant motif of numericity coming to the surface. So why shouldn't this not be regarded as another *suture*? To this 'obvious objection', Badiou has replied that his use of mathematics is a 'protocol of distinction' and not a *suture*, and that 'the mathematical thread' is not in everything he writes.[27] But the impression is that the philosopher doth protest too much. Alternatively, what would a space of compossibility look like were it not *sutured*, tied, or knotted to any one condition: in other words, what would philosophy *look like* if spatial terms like *suture*, knots, and so on, were not always words at all? Philosophy would then be a space of moving, provisional synthesis that must unknot, or *de-suture* itself from any one non-philosophy in the most perspicuous manner possible lest it fall back into reductive ties.

With the idea of non-philosophy in our minds, we have already entered into the domain of Laruelle, for his approach purports to maintain a completely immanent position by abstaining from philosophy as such while simultaneously taking it as its own raw material. Philosophy conditions non-philosophy, but, as we will see, not in anything other than an occasional way. Non-philosophy rejects both *matheme* and *patheme* as irrevocable because they both follow the transcendental outline of all philosophy. Transcendence is the very form of philosophy.

Badiou, on the contrary, maintains that there is no need to side-step philosophy *tout court* in order to avoid transcendence, for ontology can think its own refutation – that the indiscernible is – and so can immanently condition philosophy with new ideas without negating it. But this still rests on his decisionism – wagering on the unpredictable. One last way of looking at decisionism is captured in Jakob Fries' famous 'Trilemma' of epistemic foundations: in its organisation of the question of foundations, it states that a philosophical position (a statement) is justified either by another statement, which itself will need another statement to justify it in turn (and so on *ad infinitum*, equal to a proliferation of names), or by dogmatic assertion (axiomatic decision), or by a percept (or some psychological state).[28] Regression, Dogmatism, or Psychologism. We have to choose. Deleuze, Badiou, or Henry. But is the choice itself between a percept and a decision really a choice, or is it actually a percept? We can see the proliferation of the dyad of *matheme* and *patheme* begin again in new guise. In fact, the dyad's movement is never-ending, it simply renames itself whenever it seems on the brink of dissolution. In Chapter 1 we portrayed Deleuze's thought as this endless process of renaming, as a circulation of names.[29] Both his novel word-mergers and their swift replacement were themselves a process that made Deleuze's philosophical practice an instance of the natural processes he describes. An alternative to these circulating names, however, is to depict the proliferation in a way that eludes the terms of the dilemma, making the regress real rather than aporetic, or rather, the *aporia* is positively realised in a medium other than conceptual philosophy. Laruelle attempts this materialisation of dyadic regress with his non-philosophy.

For Laruelle, the establishment of a radically immanent philosophy, one which escapes transcendence, cannot be achieved in and through traditional philosophy at all: it can only be instituted through a 'non-philosophical' thought whose subject-matter is the history of philosophy itself. This non-philosophy will thus appear similar to philosophy, but only because its raw material is traditional philosophy in all of its inevitable intermixtures with, and consequent corrupting transcendentalisation of, the 'Real' or 'One'. Echoing the ideas of Derrida, Laruelle claims that transcendence is the fundamental shape of all philosophy. But Laruelle's escape is not into the formalities of writing – philosophy as literature – nor a restituted (negative) theology. Non-philosophy is not just a theory but a practice. It re-writes or re-describes particular philosophies, but in a non-transcendental form – non-aesthetics, non-Spinozism, non-Deleuzianism, and so on. It takes philosophical concepts and subtracts any transcendence from them in order to see them, not as representations, but as parts of the Real or as *alongside* the Real. This practice is called 'cloning', 'determination-in-the-last-instance', or 'force (of) thought'. In this respect, Laruelle's non-philosophical discourse would be a *movement* between any polarised philosophies, given the subtraction of the representation of the Real from their positions.

We will describe how non-philosophy operates later as each of its ideas is unpacked. Through the course of this, however, we will also see that Laruelle retains philosophy as a static, regulative ideal rather than as an immanent process, that is, as virtual rather than actual. His own philosophy is open to the same critique placed at the door of traditional philosophy (despite the prefix of 'non-'). However, such a 'retortion' – the implication of non-philosophy within its own critique of philosophy – will not be offered as a means to surpass Laruelle in one more gesture of prescriptive superiority, but rather to render his ideas more productive through a new kind of description that maps his thought back onto philosophy.

WHAT DOES NON-PHILOSOPHY DO?

In his course at the Collège de France for 1958–1959 entitled 'Our State of Non-Philosophy', Merleau-Ponty addressed the crisis in which philosophy had seemingly found itself (once again). In reality, he argued, it was only a temporary phase, and genuine philosophy will be 'reborn' as it re-engages with its non-philosophical resources in literature, painting, music and psychoanalysis.[30] Laruelle, by contrast, takes the view that any liberation of philosophy from torpidity will entail something much more radical than the renewal of its conditions: it requires the overhaul of *thought* itself. It is not less theoretical consistency or rigour that is required but more rigour, more consistency. This is what his non-philosophy pursues as the condition of philosophy. How can we produce new thoughts and new texts given the exhaustion of the orthodox form of thinking at the end of twentieth-century Continental philosophy? But the 'non-' in non-philosophy is not, as we will see, either the *Destruktion*, deconstruction, withdrawal from, or end of philosophy. It implies the generalisation, universalisation and most consistent implementation of theory; one that rethinks the history of philosophy in a radically new style. His is a 'post-deconstructive' or 'non-Heideggerian deconstruction' searching for the means, tool, or *organon* by which we might renew theory without contenting ourselves simply with deconstructing philosophy.[31]

In this respect, Laruelle stands with Badiou in that both authors pose the same problem: which direction must we take after the 'death' or 'end' of philosophy? That the one will look to Real Identity and the other to Ontological Multiplicity for the means of answering this question should not tempt us to think that they are easily opposed, for each radicalises what he means by Identity (the One or Real) and Multiplicity by giving them an internal structure – the 'One-in-One' for Laruelle and the 'multiples of multiples' for Badiou. Indeed, what Laruelle wants is nothing less than a '*mathesis transcendentalis*', a kind of mathematicism for all knowledge. In this, Laruelle shows the lineage he shares with Badiou – that of a post-Lacanian thinking that connects the Real with science and mathematics. Of course, Badiou's philosophy says that the One-is-*not*, and Laruelle's *non*-philosophy is (of) the One. The One is not just a number for Laruelle, however. Thinking the One is thinking the radicality of Identity, the sovereignty and unconditionality of the Real, its autonomy from *all* philosophy. No, the main dissimilarity between these two philosophers is more fundamental than number because, for Laruelle, Badiou remains a philosopher. As such, his most radical innovation – the equation of mathematics with ontology – misses the chance of being a true non-philosophy for the simple reason that it retains just enough philosophical dominion to rupture this audacious equation. The sign of this dominion comes in Badiou's definition of philosophy itself as meta-ontology.[32] In other words, meta-ontology (Badiou's philosophy) continues to condition its world (in this case, the world of mathematics as ontology).

We saw for ourselves that this equation led Badiou into interminable circles and it is with this symptom in mind that Laruelle brands him a typical philosopher. His missed opportunity is due to a lack of rigour in thinking about the meaning of immanence and what the transcendence of immanence entails. For Laruelle, philosophy is simply a superior form of common sense, so a true heterodoxy to get philosophy moving again will require an even greater shift in philosophical territory. Badiou does indeed initiate this process by replacing aesthetics with inaesthetics, political philosophy with metapolitics, and ontology with meta-ontology. For Laruelle, these could well have been essays in non-aesthetics, non-politics and non-ontology.[33] But Badiou is not radical enough. If Badiou had pursued the consistency of his thought to the end (to rid philosophy of all right to truth), he would have replaced philosophy with non-philosophy, for he still conditions his scientific, political, artistic and amorous truth conditions *in the name of philosophy* – he still prescribes transcendentally (that, say, neurology is not a genuine science) rather than describing them immanently. When Laruelle writes of his own *mathesis transcendentalis*, the transcendental never means the conditions of possibility, it means the immanent 'force (of) thought'.[34] Non-philosophy makes no truth claim at all. It is instead a thought *alongside* the Real, not *about* the Real. And it is this abstention from reference, this epistemic passivity alongside the Real, that makes it the most rigorous thought conceivable.

To pursue this project of renewal, for Laruelle, means moving away from both Greek thinking about being and Jewish thinking about alterity, going beyond both Being and Difference – two last co-ordinates of Continental philosophy. The Greeks fixed philosophical practice in a way that has remained to this day 'curtailed, repetitive, and superbly sterile'. And we still live in the era of the 'Greco-unitary' closure and enclosure of thought. If thought is to move forward out of this circle, it must move away from the '*Gréco-philosophique*'. Not that there have been no attempts at all to make this break in the past. According to Laruelle, non-philosophy has a heritage going back through Feuerbach, Hegel and Fichte to Kant. For them, nonetheless, it designated 'a pre-speculative state, of the absence of philosophy', a 'momentary ignorance', destined to be surpassed by philosophy itself. Here non-philosophy means a 'sur-philosophical state'. Each philosophy thus defines a margin of non-philosophy that it tolerates, circumscribes, or reappropriates. Deleuze's 'plane of immanence' belongs to this tradition of non-philosophy, as the outside that makes the inside possible. But such differentialism is still too embroiled in the philosophical form, in the form of a representational decision, which we will see Laruelle describe as the hallmark of transcendence. The philosophies of difference, of deconstruction and of the multiple have only inverted rather than transformed the philosophical cause. Neither Derrida (nor Heidegger) nor Deleuze have escaped this (en)closure of philosophy; in fact, the philosophies of difference have given philosophy new life, they have perpetuated it rather than transformed it. So when Deleuze considers the two rival formulas, 'only that which resembles differs' and 'only differences resemble each other', as the choice between privileging identity or difference, we are never given a non-question-begging reason why the latter should be embraced. It is a pure decision.[35] Likewise, Badiou's philosophy of the event still 'posits the event as a real in itself but in reality it is the effect of a philosophical decision, inscribed within the order of possibilities proffered by philosophy ...'.[36]

What makes Laruelle's non-philosophy the favoured form of the practice over its historical forebears is that philosophy here becomes the material of non-philosophy rather than its object, an 'occasional cause' (more on this later) rather than its core. Non-philosophy no longer comes either before or after philosophy, is neither a celebration of its death nor its historical re-affirmation: it is no longer a 'simple rebellion from the margins'. Non-philosophy, rather, is an *experience*: 'an experience of the Real that escapes auto-position, that is not a circle of the Real and of thought ... a Real that is *immanent (to) itself rather than to a form of thought*, to a "logic".'[37]

As regards our theme of immanence, non-philosophy is presented as an immanent thought precisely *because* it does not try to think of the Real but only alongside or 'according to' it. Theirs is a relation of non-relation, a meta-relation, what is called a 'unilateral duality'. Like Henry, there is no intentionality; like Deleuze, there is no structure Other. Yet Laruelle is not disavowing all thought for immanence (as it is arguable that Henry does), but using immanence to think philosophy. He has nothing to say *about* radical immanence in itself, but only something about philosophy in the light of there being a limit to it, namely not being the Real.[38] Non-philosophy cannot be representational, therefore, because that would once again virtualise or mix the Real with what is unreal. For immanence to be radical, it must not be *mixed* with any kind of transcendence, any reflection, representation, or any decision as to the nature of the non-philosophical. There is no '*mixte*' (to use Laruelle's vocabulary). The Real can neither be known nor even thought, but can only be 'described in its axioms'. In fact, even 'immanence' cannot be a *name* for the Real – it can only be described. The Real is not even the condition of possibility for non-philosophy, for, as Laruelle admits, this would be a Kantian formulation. The Real is, however, its *presupposed*, and 'unlike a condition or presupposition, which disappears into the conditioned, the presupposed has an autonomy that is irreducible to the conditioned'.[39]

Non-philosophy, then, has a complex aetiology: it uses philosophy as material, but, unlike philosophy, it acknowledges the unthinkability (of) the Real; because it re-writes philosophy, its final product can appear to be simply *more* philosophy. But it is a crypto-philosophy that is written under a different sign because philosophy's representation of the Real has been phenomenologically reduced. Transcendence has been bracketed and so Laruelle's non-philosophy only *appears* similar to philosophy. It is, in a very technical sense, a pseudo-philosophy.

THOUGHT-WORLDS

In an attempt to go beyond any quasi-dialectical play that would render one philosophy of immanence (Henry's for example) a transcendental hinter-world relative to another (Badiou's), Laruelle steps in to claim that *all* philosophical systems are infected with transcendence. For Laruelle, there is an 'idealism at the heart itself of thought' such that every decisional, representational thought colours its world with its own chosen ideas – be it the plane of immanence, the event, or auto-affection. What philosophy calls 'reality' is first and foremost a *concept of* the world: 'through this concept, philosophy projects *a reality in itself, which is to say, one that has been constructed in the realm of operational transcendence ...* '. Every philosophy

137

is a mixture of reality with a pre-decided interpretative schema, be it substance and accident, subject and object, phenomenon and noumenon, difference and repetition, and so on. Philosophy becomes (despite every cosmology, such as Deleuze's) a negation of the Real (world) since it is an affirmation of an infinite '*arrière-monde*', namely, philosophy itself regarded as the 'thought-world'. Hence, Laruelle can make the rather startling declaration: 'I postulate that philosophy is the form of the World'.[40]

His position as regards the truth of these 'thought-worlds' is agnostic: we cannot know the Real, and any philosophy that does claim to know it is virtualising the Real through its own conceptual schemas. Non-philosophy, by contrast, works by positing the equivalence (as regards the Real) of all philosophical positions. The autonomy of the Real leaves all philosophies relative. So there can be no hierarchy between a 'fundamental thinking', say, and 'regional ontologies' (biology, physics, and so forth). Non-philosophy demands the identity of the philosophical–fundamental and the regional, be it art, science, ethics, or technology. But it demands this only 'in-the-last-instance': it is not interested in their *immediate* confusion or the collapsing of one into the other in conformity with any of the laws of their *philosophical* association or mixture. Rather, it postulates their 'identification-in-the-last-instance', a kind of *hypothetical* identity of philosophy and world. This is the practice Laruelle calls 'cloning'.[41]

Let me explain further. As a consequence of seeing each and every philosophy fabricate a thought-world out of itself, the totality of all philosophies, *as a totality*, is affirmed. All theory is equivalent *when regarded as* (in the last instance) raw material for non-philosophy. This is why it is emphatically not a 'philosophy of the no', according to Laruelle: the 'non-' in non-philosophy should be taken in terms similar to the meaning of the 'non-' in 'non-Euclidean', being part of a 'mutation' that locates philosophy as one instance in a larger set of theoretical forms. The philosophical decision is not deconstructed, disseminated, or dispersed, but integrated within a wider paradigm. Non-philosophy is a '*generalisation*' of philosophies that may even allow us, according to Laruelle, to find peace amongst them.[42] For this reason, non-philosophy can be looked upon as the fullest possible implementation of Badiou's subtractive ontology, in that it applies to *all* philosophy in a true catholicism:

> Non-philosophy is not an intensified reduplication of philosophy, a meta-philosophy, but rather its 'simplification'. It does not represent a change in scale with respect to philosophy, as though the latter was maintained for smaller elements. It is the 'same' structure but in a more concentrated, more focused form.[43]

This last point is crucial: non-philosophy is not a meta-language, it is not a metaphilosophy. In fact, every philosophy always already plays a metaphilosophical role for itself – it is nothing special. More significantly, where metaphilosophy is hierarchical, non-philosophy instead offers a '*unified theory of science and philosophy*' without hierarchy, without pre-conditions.[44]

But non-philosophy is also a *gnosis of itself* – a kind of Gnosticism, 'first science', or a 'science of science'. All the same, it emphatically does not regard itself as a foundation of science: rather, it is a knowing (science) that is auto-foundational.[45] That is why Laruelle's thought purports to have the status of a *discovery*, that of the Real, rather than being one more philosophical decision, one more representation. Non-philosophy's discovery of the Real is the opening in thought that will allow new ideas to develop. But this is no naïve exit or way out (*sortie, Ausgang*) from philosophy, a going outside in order to join with the Real in an experience of oceanic thinking. The notion of an exit, or even a twisting free, is already too reflective, too philosophical in Laruelle's view. Non-philosophy is not an *Ausgang* qua decision and reflection: it is a given. A non-reflective *sortie* is the real aim of non-philosophy. There is no (simple) exit.[46]

THE PRINCIPLE OF SUFFICIENT PHILOSOPHY

Philosophy originates with one fundamental principle: that everything is philosophisable. This is philosophy's narcissism, its philocentrism. Laruelle calls this the 'Principle of Sufficient Philosophy'. Parmenides is rightfully the (covert) patron saint of all philosophy in seeing a perfect adequation between being and thought (that we saw Badiou, for one, endorse). Taking exception to this, Laruelle playfully asserts that 'not everything is philosophisable, such is the good news I bring'. Philosophy must have a *limit*, namely whatever is non-philosophy, which must itself exist at least in principle (or as a last resort), on pain of otherwise assuming that philosophy is indeed the measure of everything. In place of this principle of self-sufficiency or auto-positionality, non-philosophy sees no justification for philosophy's supposed ability to apply itself to everything – the philosophy of art, the philosophy of science, and so on – in a manner that allows it a fundamental status in the discourse of those subjects. It has limits: its autonomy is relative (to the Real) and not absolute (to itself). For Laruelle, the conditions of possibility of experience and the object of experience are the same. As a consequence, there is no first philosophy. Non-philosophy accordingly installs an equality between the 'fundamental' and the 'regional' – though without losing their heterogeneity – in a drastically anti-hierarchical approach.[47] What Foucault found for the human sciences – that their theoretical failures are only ever taken as a spur for more theory rather than less – is also true for theory (philosophy) *per se*: but given this irrepressibility, the limits (failures) of philosophy must not become the rationale for even more philosophy, they must instead be *used*. This is what non-philosophy endeavours to do.

Of course, the first response to this attack on philosophy will be that of *tu quoque* – that Laruelle's is a very typical philosophical point in as much as it argues for consistency and rigour and against circularity and presupposition (wherein the empirical and the transcendental are illegitmately established and then mixed together). And yet the retort of hypocrisy is itself a key thesis of non-philosophy: if Laruelle's depiction of the principle of sufficient philosophy is correct, then philosophy *must* counter-attack with this form of riposte: its 'resistance' is necessary and the very proof of philosophy's narcissism, the way it sees itself mirrored in everything it looks at (even the rejection of itself), conducting its 'own interminable self-interpretation'. The idea that non-philosophy is not *more* philosophy is simply impossible for philosophy to understand. Hence, Ray Brassier will write that resistance to non-philosophy is 'wholly and legitimately necessary', and that it is 'precisely what non-philosophy requires in order to operate'.[48]

THE SYNTAX OF DECISION: MIXTES, DYADS, OR AMPHIBOLIES

Let's turn to specifics by looking at two ways of interpreting Laruelle. One way of reading the non-philosopher's claims about philosophy is as a version of the Duhem–Quine thesis – not in terms of the underdetermination of theory by putatively neutral 'evidence', but rather as regards the nature of *any* evidence as such (the 'thought-world') being wholly definable by philosophy. Theory is saved by a world that theory has already cast in its (reverse) image. This is how Laruelle puts it when he says, for example, that each philosophy will define objectivity, communication, and so on, in a way to save the theory and render it coherent.[49] Hence, *any* philosophy is unfalsifiable because it is circular. So what we discovered about Henry and Badiou – that their thought is so fascinating and yet so sterile, so irrefutable and thus so unbelievable – is applicable to all philosophy if one looks hard enough. The scholarly champions of Derrida, Heidegger, or Deleuze can interminably analyse their masters' texts such that, under interrogation, terms discover nuances nobody else (outside) could have guessed ('ah! you see, by 'event', 'writing', or 'science' *he* means . . .'), so building up ever-growing chains of deferred explanation (or 'unscientific postscripts'). But this is not a cynical point concerning the self-defence mechanisms of academic industry; it is simply an illustration of the interchangeability of philosophical language.

Here's a second way of seeing non-philosophy. As we discussed in our chapter on Henry, in the post-Freudian world-view, we commonly say to the neurotic that his or her symptom is not about *x* (the manifest content), but about *y* (the latent content). When I meet someone who is fearful of flutes, I'm more likely to judge him or her to be a phobic rather than re-examine my ideas about flutes. Henry *generalises* this to say that the affect, the fear, is not about anything worldly at all, but only about itself. Now philosophy, in a like manner, *judges* common sense, saying to it, as to a neurotic, that its thought is not about *x* but really about *y*. The 'hermeneutics of suspicion' is not a modern invention – it is central to philosophy's disassociation from *doxa*. But Laruelle, like Henry (to whom he comes closest amongst our philosophers of immanence), aims for a radically unworldly thought.[50] In pursuit of this, he implements a further generalisation of Henry by treating philosophy like a phobia, saying that all philosophical thought is really about itself, it is auto-sufficient. Its so-called world – *x* – is actually a mirror of itself. A *mixte*.

On the one side of the *mixte* we always find a 'common world'. The *mixte* is hierarchical: the common world (of *doxa* or even '*Ur-doxa*') is surpassed by the philosophy when renouncing it, even as it is actually its own mirror, its own specular alter ego and bogeyman. On the other side is the essential, philosophical reality (be it deemed metaphysical or not). Plato's dyad of the sensible/intelligible for instance, or Deleuze's of the actual/virtual would be typical of this manoeuvre. Sometimes things will be left in some kind of inarticulate monism – a philosophy of immanence that cannot explain its Other. That it has an Other may even be denied in an eliminative ontology. Sometimes, though, the philosophy might try to 'articulate' its two worlds with some bridging mechanism, the 'common' one that is its own projection (for instance, the 'derivative' nature of the matheme or patheme) and the 'essential' one (the 'fundamental' domain of the patheme or matheme).[51] Deleuze's bridging mechanism is actualisation or different/ciation, which is given a certain amount of ontological integrity within the Deleuzian system. Henry's and Badiou's bridge is a making 'visible' that is given the more lowly status of hallucination or illusion (the conditions of which are inexplicable *sensu stricto*). But whether it be a two-world or one-world ontology, there is always a prescription that is illegitimate because it is built into the presuppositions of the theory rather than being founded on the Real. Laruelle simply exposes these by judging the judgements: he eradicates all judgement or prescription. There is no one Genuine Philosophy, there are only philosophies, plural, with no one having privileged status over the other, none that are merely empirical while others are *a priori*.

Such *mixtes*, dyads, or amphibolies function throughout philosophy. They are not restricted to 'concepts of reflection', however, as is the case with the Kantian notion of amphiboly whereby the origins of 'inner' and 'outer', say, are judged through a confused amalgamation of sensibility and pure understanding. An amphiboly or *mixte* is a function of any philosophical *reflection* as such. In this sense, all philosophy is anthropomorphic, mixing the human with, as Erik del Bufalo puts it, 'something other, with the Other-than-Real'.[52] Anne-Françoise Schmid puts it even more succinctly while also linking the *mixte* to Laruelle's egalitarian epistemology:

> All discourse is a combination. The only thing that can be opposed to a combination is another combination. A scientific concept can be deconstructed only by opposing another combination of science and philosophy to it. Non-epistemology generalizes this state of affairs, but only by first being a practice that ensures the identity of combinations.[53]

Philosophical dualities can play games of mutual supplementation of their terms, move in circles *ad nauseam*, invert their duality, overturn their duality, and so on, but they always perpetuate the duality nonetheless. Philosophy never goes beyond a widened *cogito*: any putative immanence it might have is limited to a self-reflection or self-affection. To think 'of' the Real is to miss it for the representation itself. Deconstruction tried to break the mirror of representation by substituting the Other for Being. But still the dyadic relation – and the decision – is there. A genuine transformation of thought, by contrast, will not consist in playing new games with representation, but rather in determining representation through, as Laruelle himself puts it, 'a radically un-representable agency or instance – more precisely, through a without-representation that allows itself to be thought by means of representations which have been reduced to the status of philosophically inert material'.[54]

In effect, all philosophy is tautological (and not just Henry's). Circularity is ubiquitous and every philosophical decision has the form of a transcendental deduction, be it overt or covert. Hence again, the parallel with Foucault, his empirico-transcendental doublet being just one form of *mixte*, however.[55] Hence also, Ray Brassier again, this time highlighting what I imagine many readers of philosophy have always suspected: 'philosophy manages to interpret everything while explaining nothing, because the structure of the *explanans*, decision, is already presupposed in the *explanandum*.'[56]

There is a structural homology, then, between philosophical systems, namely their form as '*mixte*'. This *mixte* is an 'in-between', an '*entre-deux*' or dyad that attempts to undo (in a dualism) or conceal (in a monism) the necessary weakness that is endemic to philosophy, namely, that of mixing the Real with its own transcendent structures (the decision to be a philosophy of *x*, *y*, or *z*). The *mixte* is the eternal between, between the conditioned and the condition, between the given and the *a priori*: it is what both binds and distinguishes the two. In other words, the *mixte* is both a dyad and its (attempted) undoing, with the result that philosophy becomes self-fulfilling prophecy – it is circular – setting up the very (straw man) duality (whether or not it is avowed) it magically has the power to overcome. Philosophy always reproduces its own structure reiteratively: that is, a philosophy of *x*, *y*, or *z* is a *mixte* of what it deems real – *x*, *y*, or *z* – and itself (deemed pure philosophy). But the *x*, *y*, or *z* is always the 'philosophy-of-*x*-*y*-or-*z*', it is never the Real. Its syntax betrays it as regressive, internally begging the question in virtue of its very form. Every philosophy contains, somewhere, in some guise, a *petitio principii*. In other words, philosophy is always representation. The essence of reflection is specularity such that philosophy is even responsible for the 'specularisation' of the real. Non-philosophy, on the other hand, 'de-specularises' philosophy, turning it from a view of things to a thing itself, as we'll explain soon.[57]

EXEMPLARY EXAMPLES OF PHILOSOPHY

Which dyad philosophy constructs is always a *decision*. Laruelle's basic question is as follows: what is philosophy? This is not asking for the nature of just logocentric or differentialist philosophies, nor philosophy as fundamental thinking, or the creation of concepts, or wonder: it is simply asking, what is philosophy *qua* philosophy across every actuality? And the answer is: the decision as occasioned by the Real. The decision is the 'invariant or principle and formalised structure of philosophy'. It is what 'homogenises, idealises, quantifies, or qualifies the Real and forecloses it'. Let's turn to some examples to see how this works. Laruelle knows full well that Henry is his closest philosophical antecedent who has taken immanence to the extreme, and done so at the expense of representation too. And yet he remains a philosopher (like Badiou) with a philosopher's weaknesses, according to Laruelle. No less than his forebear Descartes, Henry works *between* psychology and metaphysics in as much as auto-affection is a 'philosophical semi-mechanism' that Laruelle also describes as the 'ultimate amphiboly'. Yes, it is an improvement over Descartes in ridding itself of an explicitly representational structure, but Henry still makes auto-affection *follow thought* – it still serves philosophy.[58] He remains a cogitative philosopher. In defence of Henry, one could ask whether Laruelle has taken account of his clear depiction of the *cogito* as affective, vitalised, and much more than just reflective (which for Henry is a derivative illusion). But this is not the point. Henry retains *a depiction*. He may renounce representation, but as Laruelle says ominously, 'one does not destroy the reality of philosophical *mixtes* by dissociating one of its sides from the other'. Simply by writing in the syntax of philosophy, 'Henry posits in a quasi-transcendent fashion the unekstatic immanence he objectifies.'[59] It's the positing, the thetic or depictive nature of philosophy, with its attendant decisions, that is at fault.

Laruelle reserves even harsher words for Deleuzian immanence. Peter Hallward puts it bluntly: Deleuze's is a two-term philosophy; Laruelle's is a virulently one-term non-philosophy. Not surprisingly, therefore, the stage is set for a complete mismatch. Deleuze's concept of the virtual and the actual is *the* example of a decisional thought with its own *mixte* – different/ciation, which (dis)joins the virtual and actual. When ontology becomes an ontological plane of immanence, there is, in the words of one Laruelle commentator, an 'osmosis' of thought and the Real. So Deleuze remains Greek.[60] In fact, there is an ongoing history to Laruelle's critique of Deleuze. As early as his 1971 work, *Phénomène et différence*, Laruelle accused him (particularly in *Difference and Repetition*) of falling into an abstraction equal to the Platonism he hoped to reverse.[61] But it is in his 'Réponse à Deleuze' following the publication of *What is Philosophy?* that he is most vociferous, reducing Deleuze's thought to the adage '*philosophia sive natura*'. To Laruelle's obvious annoyance, the plane of immanence, the event and so on, still tend to 'Platonise in an unbridled manner'.[62] The plane itself is, syntactically and reflectively, what qualifies pure immanence such that it becomes 'the property of a plane, of a universal, etc. and even of an Ego'. Deleuze's continual invention of anti-dualistic terms – '*entre-deux*', '*entre-temps*', '*entre-multiple*', '*devenir éternel*' – will not conceal the arbitrary decision to denounce transcendence as theological. They are themselves *mélanges* of the transcendental and the empirical:

> Concepts of fusion, penetration, indiscernibility, of consistency, that doubt-lessly oppose transcending existence only by globally interiorising the whole or the essence of transcendence to immanence, by a new type of *relever*, non-dialectical or non-Hegelian.[63]

The plane of immanence, in its very syntax of being 'to' something (even 'to itself'), gives it away as an 'axis of transcendence'. Of course, there is no standard, metaphysical 'hinter-world' in rhizomatics, but there is a 'pure form of the hinter-world in the plane of immanence ...'. Deleuze fools himself into thinking that empiricism goes beyond transcendence when in fact it is simply another form of it, perhaps the most dangerous form because of its self-misunderstanding. 'Experience', writes Laruelle, 'is the suicide of philosophy itself'.

Clearly, then, Laruelle is anti-Virtualist. As del Bufalo describes it, 'the World is the actual of philosophy, philosophy is the virtual of the World'. Both actual and virtual (world and thought) need and mirror each other. Laruelle's meta-level Actualism, then, accounts for how every philosophy tries to mix its representational decisions with the Real, to virtualise the actuality of the Real by refracting it through its own representational schema and so produce a virtual image of the Real (which is actually of itself). But Laruelle's is not a two-world view, or so del Bufalo claims: his Real is not an 'arrière-monde' despite taking the 'cracked form of the *virtuality* of decisions and of philosophical *actuality*'.[64] We ourselves will be more sceptical, however: the very fact that the Real needs, as raw material, the virtual/actual form of philosophy is a sign of retortion in Laruelle's thought. But even more pressing for now is an examination of his use of the Real, and in particular his idea of it as an *experience* (that which was, in Deleuzianism, supposedly the death of thought).

PASSION ACCORDING TO THE REAL: GNOSIS AND VISION

In *Le Siècle*, Badiou makes a rare reference to Laruelle, counting his critique of decisionism in favour of vision, and of being in favour of the Real, as part of the century's 'passion for the real'.[65] Doubtless, Laruelle would take exception to this characterisation of his work, for it is the mark of *philosophy* that it desires the Real: non-philosophy has no desire or passion *for* the Real, it simply thinks according to the Real. We will examine this syntactical difference here.

In an extremely significant dialogue between Derrida and Laruelle, Derrida finally asked him, in some frustration, from where he got his idea of non-philosophy if not from philosophy itself. Laruelle responded in the following, remarkable manner:

> *I get it from the thing itself.* This is as rigorous an answer as I am able to give. Because the criterion for my discourse was a rigorously immanent or transcendental criterion, there is no other answer I can give.[66]

One must admire Laruelle's audacious consistency: of course this is the only answer he can give without becoming philosophical again, that is, without showing some sufficient reason, for that would reduce immanence, in this case, to a logic. Laruelle takes non-philosophy as absolutely self-sufficient, his starting point in the Real, and as such it is a thought without any conditions at all. Naturally, the *philosophical* reply will be, how does he know this? How does he know that non-philosophy is 'alongside the Real'? And his answer will be, *because it is*. He starts, as he puts it, 'directly from the One, which is to say from the most radical experience there is. You have to start from the real, otherwise you'll never get to it.' One might describe this as an ultra-Humean stance: because any explanation only ever defers our ignorance, why not avoid what must always and ultimately be an arbitrary decision as to which *particular place* to begin with, by hypothesising a beginning with the Real itself and seeing what happens. What would thought look like if it was a thing itself and not a picture, name, simulacrum, affect, call, destining, appearance, and so on, *of* the thing.[67]

Indeed, it is because philosophy seeks and desires the Real that it never gets it. It is not possible to think the Real philosophically as a *problem* — that is too active, too interventional; rather, one commences non-philosophically, unproblematically, passively. It makes no non-philosophical sense to ask what the Real or the One is. Oddly enough, then, Deleuze takes on immanence 'too quickly' by deeming it a philosophical *object* — it must firstly be 'given and secured' by taking it as a non-philosophical Real.[68] One must be passive before the Real, letting it be, thinking alongside it, not prescribing or judging it. Through pure description (another ultra-Humean stance), one actually partakes in the Real. By taking the route of radical passivity, albeit of another kind from that of Henry, non-philosophy begins with the Real and progresses *to* philosophy, rather than the other (problematic) way around — going *from* philosophy (or the transcendental) to the Real.

This unproblematic starting point (in every sense of the term) is called the 'vision-in-One', which is described as 'the being-given which is without-givenness'— a givenness *without* a 'background' of givenness (in case any theological interpretation is suspected).[69] It is a heretical, Gnostic knowledge, a science in the pure sense, an experience of the Real.[70] And though one might regard this Real as an abstraction, we cannot accuse Laruelle of not accounting for this abstraction (as we charged Badiou), for he openly nominates it as one of his axioms: 'I lay claim to the abstract — the Real or One — rather than to abstraction. The One is an abstract-without-an-operation-of-abstraction.'[71] Where Badiou still lacks a philosophical (meta-ontological) subject and the operations of that subject, Laruelle does not, even if it is at the expense of a most hyperbolic axiom, that of simply *being* (according to the) Real. And, as we saw earlier, we are not allowed to say that this starting point was *decided* by Laruelle either. Rather, it was 'discovered' — that is why it is immune from the 'philosophical circularity' that marks the philosophical decision.[72]

So this is the vision-in-One. But why is the experience of the Real an experience of One, of Identity, why is it a vision-in-*One*? Because of immanence. The One is highly *non-relational*: even refusing the world (as illusion in Henry) or refusing phenomenology (as hallucination in Badiou) is a kind of relation (and one we've sought with difficulty to explain in their philosophies). The One is indifferent to all. It is not immanent *to* anything, but immanent *in* itself. Hence, the experience or vision-in-One cannot be intentional or representational in any way. Nor is it a perception (if we understand perception as representation).[73] As a non-relation, then, vision finally bypasses the problems connected with error-theory that we encountered in the thoughts of each of the other philosophers of immanence we've studied.

CLONING PHILOSOPHY

That non-philosophy is not related to the Real and yet accords with it, can best be understood when one remembers that non-philosophy is a practice first and foremost: 'non-philosophy is "performative"', Laruelle is careful to repeat, 'and exhausts itself as an immanent practice rather than as a programme'. It is a new practice of philosophy rather than a new, reforming theory of it; or better again, it is a new *usage* of philosophy. Hence, it is better to ask what non-philosophy does, rather than what it is. Its being is its actuality, that is, its performativity.[74] The method this practice follows has various names, 'Cloning', 'Unilateral Duality', and 'Dualysis' being the terms most often used. As explained earlier, it has roots in phenomenology, the purpose of the process being to find the

> true minimal phenomenological essence or *identity of the double*, its identity without synthesis or its *being-in-One-in-the-last-instance*. It is the *real* critique of specularity and of philosophical speculation.[75]

But remember that this is a performative essence that passively, that is non-decisionistically, allows the Real to act on thought. Through giving up the desire for the Real, the Real acts on philosophy, though in a special form of causation, as we'll see.

Non-philosophy must use philosophical language as its material – its 'symbolic support' as Hughes Choplin puts it – but it 'de-*mixtes*' it, transforming its syntax into what we might call a new 'uni-tax'. By cloning philosophical statements shorn of their transcendental ambition, 'a work of transformation' occurs. It is admitted that cloning will seem mysterious to philosophy, but it allows us to 'explain' representation in an arguably less mysterious fashion than that of the philosophical Decision. The first thing to do is de-*mixte* the philosophical dyad. This is performed by breaking it apart by isolating the virtual term (the decision philosophy made at the outset). Then, at a meta-level, the isolated term is identified *as the Real*, an 'as if' identification that *performs* rather than represents the Real. In other words, philosophy's transcendental desire is replaced with a Real identification, only one that is hypothetical, so to speak.[76] In cloning, non-philosophy experiments with philosophy: it tests the hypothesis, 'what follows from thinking of a philosophy *as belonging to* the Real rather than as about the Real' through varying the significance of its terms from representing reality to being (according to) the Real. Wherever there was a *circular* synthesis in the original philosophy, this Real identification installs a relation of 'determination-in-the-last-instance', a kind of occasional cause of philosophy by the Real.[77]

Thinking of this in terms of a 'unilateral duality' brings out more of the egalitarian nature of the operation. If philosophy is usually vertical, with some bilateral plane of inequality/normativity (for instance, of the virtual and the actual), then a unilateral duality places the philosophical dyad on a *horizontal* plane of equivalence – equivalence relative to the Real. A unilateral duality is a non-relational 'relation' between the Real and philosophy. This sounds paradoxical, of course: if one asks the question, 'what is the relation between relation and non-relation?', one might at first simply refuse to answer (no less than we seemed to be at an impasse when we asked 'what is the difference between differences in degree and differences in kind?'). Or one could venture the following response: 'it is a unilateral duality', by which Laruelle appears to mean another order of relation. This special relation renders philosophy level (*lateral*) with all other thought – save non-philosophy itself of course. It also uni-versalises (unilateralises) thought relative (or according) to the Real.[78] And finally, this non-relation *just is* non-philosophy, it is what it does.

To reiterate: non-philosophy works by taking a philosophical dyad as its material, not by thematising it (for this would only be a meta-duality or representational duality, another piece of philosophical bilaterality), but by *visioning* the philosophy *as* real just when it gives up its mantle as sole truth (the representation of the Real). It is notable that the more thoroughgoing pluralism of Laruelle is founded on a spatial signification (*laterality*), while that of Deleuze, which is still home to a distinction between common *doxa* (or *Ur-doxa*) and true philosophy, is founded on language and the voice (*univocity*). In our concluding chapter, we will consider further whether there is indeed something inherently less normative in spatial inscriptions – *figures* of speech – than there is in verbally informed writing.

This determination-in-the-last-instance or 'as if' causality must not be thought of as a mysterious causality from an 'ulterior' world, some 'world-behind-the-scenes'.[79] It is not *causa sui*, but determined 'before all determination'. It is the causality specific to non-philosophy in general; an immanent, occasional causality. Being wholly uni-directional, from the Real to the thought-world, it is 'rigorously irreversible' (and not just empirically so, but conceptually too). And being a kind of occasional cause means that determination-in-the-last-instance is a causality of the moment (in-the-last-*instance*). This singularity of the 'last-instance' indicates that the Real is the unique real cause (as the void is for Badiou) and is 'occasional' because it is tied 'to the moment where it manifests itself'. But this moment, though singular, is not in the present. The temporality of the occasion is futural and explains why this determination is hypothetical, following the deductions of a 'what if' thinking ('what if thought was a thing').[80] The event of thought is the advent of thought, its manifestation-in-the-last-instance, the force (of) thought.[81]

FROM DESCRIPTIVE PHENOMENOLOGY TO THE DEMOCRACY OF THOUGHT

The practice of non-philosophy, as Laruelle's *Philosophie et non-philosophie* phrases it, 'is only the unlimited redescription ... of the vision-in-One itself' – its redescriptions are its performance. Erik del Bufalo goes so far as to assert that 'philosophy is the world *phenomeno-logically* given to non-philosophy'.[82] And indeed, Laruelle's liking for presuppositionless rigour, the apodeicity of vision, his use of free variation (experimentation), his search for invariant essences (*mixtes*), and his bracketing of transcendence in favour of description, appear all very phenomenological. And yet he claims that 'non-philosophy' is 'at its starting point, a "transcendental science" in a sense which is no longer Husserlian or philosophical, but rather that of an identity-in-the-last-instance of science and philosophy'.[83] Laruelle's rigorous science is 'non-Husserlian' in the same manner in which non-philosophy is a 'non-': the Husserlian project is 'integrated' and so transformed within a broader, unified theory.[84]

By comparison with this egalitarian descriptivism, philosophy is 'intrinsically anti-democratic' and judgemental. It begins by putting itself on the same level as the 'common world', but this is done only so as to 'raise itself above it ... turning itself into an exception'. This exception is ascribed 'to its own thought'. Philosophy always has an 'over-ethic', manifesting a pretension to domination, legislation, foundation and critique. In our own studies of Deleuze, Henry and Badiou, we have seen something of this duplicity in the warring tendencies between descriptivism and prescriptivism. As we saw with Deleuze and Badiou especially, ontology is always politicised. By contrast, non-philosophy denies nothing and affirms everything as every-thing: it seeks a 'democracy between philosophies, and between philosophy and the sciences, arts, ethics, etc ...'. Laruelle says that he wants to avoid all synthesis, all authority of philosophy over science; indeed, the alternative, 'philosophy or science', is for him a 'false choice'. Against synthesis, non-philosophy pursues a *unified* rather than *unitary* theory of science and philosophy. A unified theory will entail that philosophy is uprooted from its foundational status, it is regionalised or localised (laterally) alongside science in a more encompassing perspective. Unification commends universality and laterality; unity concerns transcendence and hierarchy.[85]

Here is an analogy: many of the established psychotherapies seem to work equally well: behaviourist, Freudian, Jungian and cognitivist practices all have levels of success sufficient to make them believe they are helping their patients.[86] Yet the respective metapsychologies of these therapies imply that *only one should work* – their own. Their claims to truth are mutually exclusive. Freudians, for instance, will say that if cognitivism *seems* to work, that is because Freudian structures like transference operate latently within the cognitive encounter, so-called, between patient and therapist. But the Freudian methodology of transference is not just about any kind of relationship, and clearly, the relationship within a cognitivist analysand/analyst pairing is not run according to Freudian lines. *And yet they still do both work.* It seems that there is something effective about the therapeutic relation as such, but if we try to define it exhaustively in any specific relational terms, as Freudians or cognitivists, say, we are only left with question-begging arguments, that is, virtualisations or mixtures of the relation with our own metapsychologies. There is only the occasional cause of the Real – that is the 'relation' that can be no particular relation. Now in Laruelle we have a theory of why all philosophies work (in the sense of 'operate') to the same degree: there is a pure equality between the founding choices.

Laruelle's project can best be summed up as a thought-experiment in the fullest meaning of this phrase – the experience of thought and the thought (of) experience – the experiment being concerned with what philosophy would become were it not representational *at all*, but rather the thing itself. By this I don't mean to take philosophy as an aspect of Mind that is the Real (even if its most 'complete' aspect), for that would be just one more idealism, one more philosophical positing. Rather, the question is: what would we find if *all* philosophies, *in their plurality*, were real (and so *not* in accordance with their mutual exclusivity, their exclusive claims on truth and reality)? In this sense, Laruelle provides us with an application of Badiou's subtractivism to philosophy *per se*, that is, in place of being as such equalling sheer quantity or set-membership (Badiou), what philosophy is as such becomes sheer decisionism, that is, the pure attempt to *evaluate* the Real. This collective form or structure is both that which all philosophies have in common and that which makes them real. There is consequently no fallacy in going from fact to value because values (transcendental evaluations) are types of facts once they've been reduced *en masse to all there is* (the totality of philosophies each trying to establish its 'truth' as the one that *ought* to be true). As the most rigorous thought of immanence possible, non-philosophy allows every philosophy its truth and reality, not in the name of an epistemological relativism (more Continental philosophy), but through a hypothetical Real-ism (a kind of Post-Continental naturalism).

TOWARDS A NEW PHILOSOPHICAL INCOMPREHENSION: CIRCULAR RIGOUR

Both Badiou and Deleuze are renowned for disliking dialogue as a model of philosophical procedure: theirs is the aristocratic style of *disputatio*.[87] But only to a degree. Neither have stepped beyond all discursive norms to the point where philosophical comprehension itself was an issue. Yet Laruelle's heresy is such that he voluntarily gives up the idea of philosophical engagement *tout court* in favour of elaborating his ideas on a '*unilateral front*'. No philosophical arguments are given, allegedly. They have had to be supplemented here using philosophical parallels (with Foucault, Henry and Badiou), analogies (with psychotherapy), and resemblances (with the Duhem–Quine thesis or Humean naturalism), that I'm sure many non-philosophers will find inadequate because they *are* typically philosophical stratagems. And such supplementation is necessary, given Derrida's complaint to Laruelle (to take only one example) that non-philosophy is like a 'kind of violent shuffling of the cards in a game whose rules are known to you alone'. And, indeed, we have already seen how Laruelle insists that cloning will (or must) seem mysterious to philosophy, or how philosophy will consider non-philosophy naïve, even to the point of irritation. It is claimed that all of this is necessary:

non-philosophy is utterly 'unintelligible' to philosophy, though this unintelligibility 'implies a very profound communication, but only on the side of non-philosophy'. That 'non-philosophy is constitutively unintelligible to philosophers' is something that constitutes non-philosophy as much as it does philosophy.[88]

There is a certain pride to be found, it appears, over the incommunicability of non-philosophy to those who have not yet made the 'unilateral leap'. But its starting point is not the leap of faith (although the problem of communicating non-philosophy might warrant comparison to that of Kierkegaardian subjectivity), nor, obviously, a decision. It is a vision. To the philosopher, this vision can seem at best to be only a glimpse, a *soupçon* of comprehension. There is always the suspicion of having missed the point, given the non-philosophers' insistence on philosophical incomprehension.[89] From the philosophical point of view, however, the 'vision-in-One', taken literally, points to a rehabilitated optics being the only means adequate to understand Laruelle's non-philosophy. Or rather, its philosophical understanding will not be a representation or optics of reflection at all, but a mutation, a *dioptrics* of *refraction*. It will be at best a vision of the vision-in-One, a glimpse or glimmer of understanding trying not to resist or re-assimilate, to reflect or retort.

It will be with an attempt to enhance this glimpse or glimmer that this chapter will draw towards a conclusion. In fact, if philosophical understanding *per se* could be said always to begin with just a glimmer, then Laruelle's thought may not be so wholly outside of and transcendent to philosophy after all. In as much as I have expounded Laruelle philosophically, it is obviously a moot point whether I have understood him at all (no less than it is debatable whether my non-mathematical exposition of Badiou understood a word of his thought, or only the words of his thought). Naturally, I think that I have grasped something of Laruelle's ideas, which, at a minimum, must not be impossible *de facto* given that the subtitle to one of Laruelle's own key-texts, *En Tant Qu'Un*, is '*La non-philosophie éxpliquée au philosophes*'. Explanation may be possible after all. But how? I believe that the answer lies with those terms prevalent in non-philosophy that are *not* given a non-philosophical treatment (for instance, circularity, rigour and consistency), concepts that are critical to any exposition of Laruelle (as well as any philosophy in fact). On these terms, then, I will try to build an understanding of this flimsy understanding.

What philosophers do see first when reading non-philosophical writing is the laboured use of prepositions, hyphenations and parentheses ('in-the-last-instance', 'force (of) thought', and so on). These are not there simply to compose legitimate compounds and decompose illegitimate ones, but also to defamiliarise the noun they qualify with their twisting, contorted attempts to re-describe philosophy. But, of course, this is the crucial issue of trying to replace syntax with unitax, both literally, as in Deleuze's 'immanence *to* itself' or 'the plane *of* immanence', or figuratively in the dyadic structure of every philosophical decision. The very fact that immanence was 'to' anything at all (even itself) is to have missed the radicality of immanence, says Laruelle, which must only be parenthetically 'to', that is, '(to)'. It would be even better if it was 'in' itself, as in 'in-the-last-instance'. 'In' is better that 'to' in non-philosophical writing. The trouble with philosophy, even its deconstruction, therefore, *seems to be* (philosophical) *language itself*. Syntax. Language is inherently con-fusing, equivocal rather than genuinely univocal. After all, an amphiboly is originally an ambiguity founded on grammatical word-play: 'if you think Derrida is confusing you should read Laruelle'. Deconstruction, to stay with this example, by only inverting philosophy, was said to retain its primacy. It worked on the relation of hierarchy within philosophy and not on the terms of its dyads – a highly contentious accusation, of course, but one Laruelle seems assured of.[90] That assurance, I suspect, comes from deconstruction still using a recognisably philosophical grammar. In his ambition to leave this grammar behind, Laruelle *brackets* the prepositions of philosophical syntax in both a phenomenological and literal action, that is, in a writerly act – a kind of retention and removal, a crossing out.

Consequently, the issue is not just to do with a particular syntax but with linguistic grammar and philosophical writing *per se*. It is this that needs to be transformed. But the question is, *how much?* The title of one of his early edited works, *Le Déclin de l'écriture*, may come close to the crux of the problem. We intend to show that there are resources in Laruellean thought to take this decline further and transform writing *at a wholly graphical level*. The constant references to non-Euclidean geometry when explaining non-philosophy, as well as the plane language of laterality, being 'alongside' the Real, and so on, may be more literal, that is, spatial, than first understood. Non-philosophy is not '*hors-langage*', but it is '*sans-langage*' – a '*sans-signifiant*' set of signs.[91]

Here is what we are going to venture. Laruelle seems at once to be a critic of philosophy (under its traditional mark of transcendence) and an anti-philosopher, while also instantiating an immanent thought 'alongside' reality. He yokes together apparently irreconcilable positions located on either side of the critical turn Continental philosophy has been taking over the last two decades: Derrida and Deleuze, deconstruction and immanence. With careful interpretation, however, his category of 'non-philosophy' can be retrieved for a (non-transcendental) *graphical metaphilosophy*. In pursuing this line, Laruelle's rigid demarcation of philosophy from non-philosophy must itself be reduced, bracketed, or put in motion. This is not because transcendence is inescapable philosophically or *non-philosophically* (an ultra-Derridean position), but because the transcendence of transcendence (immanence) occurs as *movement*. Of course, Laruelle would most likely reject this move: all philosophy for him is already metaphilosophical, and that is precisely why it is inadequate (and *not* non-philosophy). He would point out that Kurt Gödel had long ago exposed the limits of logicism and thereby showed that metaphilosophy is impossible (whereas non-philosophy escapes Gödel's critique because it is not foundational). As Lacan had also already said, 'there's no such thing as a metalan-guage'.[92] But the *graphical* metaphilosophy that we will propose is not logicist or foundational at all, it does not concern reflection – it does not have a two-tier structure of object-language and meta-language with the latter reflecting statically on the former. There is an alternative approach where non-philosophy would be understood as metaphilosophy in the etymological sense, that is, as what designates the continual transformation of philosophy, the perpetual self-overcoming of *philosophia*. And it does this through movement.

Thinking *alongside* the Real and *in* immanence could consequently be a *naturalised* metaphilosophy that is naturalistic because it instantiates an immanent, spatial flux, and metaphilosophical because it moves in and out of transcendent, or *static*, philosophy. Laruelle's impression that metaphilosophy is simply more philosophy ignores its potentially creative, transitory and provisional nature *qua movement*. In its movement, there is still an inside and an outside to philosophy such that a reflection on philosophy (metaphilosophy) can be non-philosophical, if only momentarily. But while the inside–outside dichotomy is a real boundary, it is also dynamic, multilayered, and porous, so that what may begin on the outside may eventually be incorporated under philosophy's skin. That is how such a metaphilosophy can accommodate the impossible purities of Henry's and Badiou's *patheme* and *matheme*. For these ideals are also describable as attractors within a phase-space of philosophical thought, with a sketchable, diagrammatic, movement existing between them. It is this kind of non-philosophy – a rejection of first philosophy – that we have been practising all along *vis-à-vis* the Virtualisms of Deleuze, Henry and Badiou. The concern with reflexivity (Henry's auto-affectivity and Badiou's self-belonging sets), and circularity (Badiou's criteria for an event), with monism and dualism in Deleuze (the dyads of molar and molecular, difference and repetition) and Badiou (being and event), with sufficient reason (Deleuze's ground for process), with the spatiality of compossibility (Badiou), with philosophical descriptivism (Deleuze and Henry), and finally with the autonomy and irreducible actuality of novelty throughout (a variant of the non-relational Real) – these are all themes that could have been culled from non-philosophical texts. But they are also mutations, as we will discover.

Going back to the analogy with psychotherapy, Laruelle actually imitates the Freudian move to explain all other theories in his own terms. By this I mean that he tries to totalise the equality between philosophies by describing their modes of operation and conditions of possibility entirely through non-philosophical terms such as the Real, '*mixte*', decision, and so on. There is a virtual in Laruelle too – that of the *essence* of philosophy itself as inherently and statically dyadic, specular and decisionistic. In Badiou's terms, it is both an element and the set (or theory) of its own procedural logic. Philosophy is the actual term of the *mixte* that non-philosophy is both a part of (as the virtual term) and determined to overcome. By contrast with the virtualisation of philosophy by Laruelle, I would say that any attempt to describe how or why all philosophies are equal is itself another momentarily transcendental move that must eventually be internalised as more philosophy. To think in metaphilosophical terms means that we do not so much oppose philosophy, *à la* Laruelle, as keep it moving beyond any perfectionist account that might claim the mantle of first philosophy. And this is true of what I have just said myself. Such a recursive claim as this ('this is true of what I have just said myself'), being both element and set, must border on paradox too. But as Quine said, paradox does not have to lead to the end of thinking; it can also be the source of its renovation.[93] My wager is that renewal is possible by materially rethinking the paradox of circularity, of recursion and self-reference, in general.

Naturally, this depiction of non-philosophy as itself dyadic can be read non-philosophically as 'retortion', the same *tu quoquo* counter-move typical of philosophical resistance.[94] But this is not an attempt to reduce non-philosophy to philosophy by showing that it begs the question, that it is circular, and so on. It is rather to show that, *because it too is circular*, it can be depicted as a kind of metaphilosophy, that is, a graphical or diagrammatic metaphilosophy. Throughout his middle to late work, Laruelle defines non-philosophy by its rigour, that is, its non-circularity.[95] This is its virtue. But his own earlier work on Félix Ravaisson – another of the French 'spiritualists' haunting Post-Continental philosophy – saw something more powerful and even rigorous in circular thought. Here, on the topic of Ravaisson, is where we will draw this chapter to a close.

THE FLEXUOUS LINE

Many believe that non-philosophy is unthinkable *per se*. Laruelle says it is unthinkable philosophically. Why can philosophers only glimpse (in moments) Laruelle's thought? Why does it seem to border on nonsense almost instantly, that is, not through the paradoxical implications of its argument, in the manner of Derridian aporetics, but through what seems like impenetrable and mutating jargon *ab initio*? It is arguable that what greater consistency it supposedly attains comes at the price of understanding. But non-philosophy is not perfectly consistent (it is prone to the retort of being dyadic too) and it is not wholly incomprehensible either (we can glimpse its point). What is this glimpse, this vision? Perhaps non-philosophy is indeed unthinkable, as a *thought* of thought, but does work as a *vision* of thought. The vision is a *diagram*. The mutations of philosophical writing must be seen as sketches. The idea is that non-philosophy strives to reform syntax to such a degree that it verges on the pictographic. Following on from Laruelle's work on Ravaisson, we can see the 'non-' of non-philosophy as substitution, as displacement, as movement, as the first swerve away from ordinary thought and transcendental philosophy. *Through drawing*. Deleuze's 'image of thought' must be taken literally as *image*. An image of thought that is seen firstly as a *thought* of thought does indeed lead to mere logical regress (which, in its own terms of sufficient reason, is a failing). But an image of thought that is seen as an image first, stays in immanence by *sketching its own movement of regress*. The regress is viewed 'in-one' and so remains non-transcendental – it is materialised, naturalised.

These ideas are to be found in Laruelle's first work, *Phénomène et différence: Éssai sur l'ontologie de Ravaisson*. Here we find his major treatment of Ravaisson's theory of the 'serpentine' or 'flexuous' line, taken from two articles he wrote on art and drawing in 1882. The basic idea is that drawing is a kind of metaphysics no less than orthodox philosophy, it is a figured metaphysics (to use Bergson's famous description of Ravaissonian thought). And conversely, metaphysics is a written drawing. The serpentine or animal line 'operates a passage' from the conceptual to the real affirmation of the identity of being and movement.[96] And here we are brought back to the crucial title of Laruelle's study. The flexuous line *is* difference. If it embodies a (philosophical) concept, it is because it is a concept. More than that, for Laruelle, *as drawn* the line is superior to orthodox philosophy because it is not a 'construction of a concept of difference'. The line is not forged from '*mixtes*'. There is a primacy of the line over the concept because it is a source 'anterior' to the 'scission of concept and of experience'. Flexion over re-flection. Or rather, reflection need no longer be cast off as specular, but now, along with metaphilosophy, integrated into a broader, spatial, paradigm. It is not going too far, then, to say that the line is the naturalised, metaphilosophical analogue to Laruelle's later non-philosophy.[97] In other words, if metaphilosophy is material, then it is *not* specular reflection and *is* identifiable with non-philosophy. The new rigour would be in the consistency of the viewed drawing, its 'force (of) perspicuity', rather than in any logical clarity, any deduction from a decision.

It is notable that there have been other writers interested in Ravaisson's line, but Laruelle is determined to resist what he feels are their misinterpretations. In particular, he opposes what he takes to be Bergson's Virtualist reading of the line. The flexuous line is not an invisible crypto-conceptual source, as Bergson seems to think (according to Laruelle).[98] It is neither 'thought concentrated in a virtual moment, nor thought as transcendental'. The line is actual, 'always already deployed and deploying itself in the space where it is engendered'. The visible and being are adequate to each other immediately.[99]

But what is of equal importance to the nature of the flexuous line as actual is its shape as a 'mode of circularity': its shape affirms both difference as well as the unity that expresses itself in difference. The synthesis of the two is made in a 'modality of circularity – not a circularity, still and homogeneous to itself, but circularity "in movement"'. The moving form of the circle is simultaneously graphical, metaphysical and logical. The core problem for Ravaisson's philosophy was (following Aristotle) the 'circularity' of nature and soul being both 'principle' and 'end'. In attempting to solve the problem, however, Laruelle stipulates that we cannot simply 'break the circle' in absolute opposition to a logical *aporia* – there is no simple exit. The solution comes non-conceptually through the serpentine line that is a synthesis of circular movement and the straight line, of 'finality' and of 'diffusion', of being and difference: 'it is movement . . . that reduces antinomies'. In this 'aesthetic of torsion' or 'torsion of grace', we can step aside from logical regressive movement to find a material progressive movement.[100]

Complex as it is, then, serpentine circularity cannot be reduced to simple (Euclidean) geometry, which comprises ready-made positions. In its 'self-decentring', it 'creates difference': 'the serpentine line *shows* that difference is not mediated by alterity, but differentiates itself immediately and manifests itself immediately ...'. And this line comes directly from a vision, a 'view', a showing, that must be understood in Ravaisson's terms as expression rather than phenomenologically. It is not yet the vision-in-One; nonetheless, the viewed-line is already a move towards a more graphical and less linguocentric approach to philosophical expression. Finally, the circulating, flexuous line is part of Ravaisson's 'preontological' understanding of being, which Laruelle asserts is the only one possible for philosophy. Philosophical method will always make a 'circle with its object', for philosophy cannot 'develop, define or describe this precomprehension of Being'. We cannot get rid of this circle and must return to it always – a far cry from the anti-circularism of later non-philosophy. Laruelle is careful to specify that this is not the hermeneutical circle, however: it is the movement of all thought and not just interpretative thought, a serpentine circularity whose non-Euclidean curves bypass what linear thought cannot encompass.[101]

It is odd that the flexuous line could lie so close to what would become the core themes of Laruelle's later thought – pre- or non-ontology, materiality, unified theory (before science and philosophy), actuality, difference and identity, the impasse of the concept, and (of course) circularity. And yet its graphical resources were displaced in favour of Laruelle's later, rather more orthodox rewriting of philosophical language (at some cost to comprehension). Published in 1971, perhaps *Phénomène et différence*'s vision of positive circularity came too close to Heideggerian hermeneutics and the circular being of *Dasein* – something of an orthodoxy at the time. But this would only be to take the serpentine line as a thought concept. As an image of thought, it comes near to Deleuze's zigzag of thought and Bergson's zigzagging of philosophical doctrine.[102] Yet in Laruelle's later work on Deleuze, the diagram was actually disparaged as that which 'organises the philosophical decision'.

Nonetheless, we believe that there is reason for hope. According to Laruelle and his most sympathetic commentators, non-philosophy is not a discipline with pre-established models – it operates without paradigms. It may even find within itself 'aspects or moments' that might develop into 'independent disciplines'.[103] As one of these new disciplines, a mutation or refraction of Laruelle, a graphical non-philosophy or diagrammatic metaphilosophy will be sketched in the concluding chapter. There are no drawings in Laruelle's book on Ravaisson, but we will supplement this lack with some of our own in order to gain a glimpse of what we are proposing – not an image (of) thought, but an image-thought. And we need not depend on parentheses, prepositions, or hyphens – some things have to be drawn to be understood. Indeed, Lacan himself, who originally said that there can be no 'metalanguage' on account of the fact that we would still need a language to transmit it, nonetheless *creates* another type of language to do just that: a metalanguage can still be 'put in shape' (*mise en forme*) using topology and, therewith, 'is capable of being integrally transmitted'.[104] In looking at such diagrams – topological as well as non-topological – we ourselves will also be able to tackle the problems left in our previous chapter to Laruelle's fellow post-Lacanian, Badiou, especially as regards the nature of philosophical truth and the spatial appearance of compossibility. For what are Lacan's knots if not serpentine lines, the same lines that Badiou, in works both previous and subsequent to *Being and Event*, uses to illustrate the interweaving regimes of truth?[105] It is hugely significant that even greater emphasis is put on the diagram in the sequel to *Being and Event*, the equally monumental *Logiques des mondes*.

CHAPTER 5

Thinking in Diagrams

When everything appears similar,
nothing really is (Alain Badiou).[1]

THE JOURNEY OF THE DRAWING

Let me commence with the following notice: there is no Truth in diagrams, nothing sacred in geometry. Laruelle's use of the flexuous line is not an intimation of the divine (as it was for Ravaisson); its immanence, its materiality, keeps it at some distance from the infinite lines, pure circles and perfect triangles of Nicholas of Cusa, for example (his own possible pantheism notwithstanding). Such infinities, purities and perfections smack of the virtual, the transcendental, 'the vision of God'. The Ravaissonian line is actual in its drawing, finite, or perhaps indefinite, metaphysical without being immaterial: it is the real in view. Nor is the diagram a way out of philosophy (*sortie*, *Ausgang*), for there is no easy escape through art, no with-drawal. But it is the *out-line* of philosophy, what picks philosophy out from the non-philosophical background while also tying its figure to its background conditions. As we would render it, the philosophical diagram is the pre-philosophical, meta-philosophical and ante-philosophical all in one – the moment between being exclusively outside or inside philosophy – not the subject leaving philosophy but unforeseeable subject-matters becoming philosophical. And it works as a drawing, a process, a procedure, a temporary moment in between; not the shape of a thing but the outline of a process (of thinking). Hence, dia-grammes should be always seen as moving forms, whether or not they are static. These are the ideas that we will examine in this chapter.

There is no Truth in diagrams, but there may be the diagram of a truth in some. In the introduction to this book, we considered the consummate Continental thought of Jacques Derrida on the experience of the *aporia*, the experience of impossibility and the impossibility of experience that his later work on hospitality, forgiveness and mourning explored. Though we should not conflate the different phases of his work too neatly, we shouldn't disassociate them entirely either, for in the early undecidable non-concepts or quasi-concepts of *différance*, trace, or *pharmakon* there is, prefigured, the experience of *aporia*.[2] Derrida is a self-confessed literalist – he 're-literalises' language, words becoming things again by exposing their metaphorical roots in spatiality, *'espacement'*, graphemes. Hence, if the 'sign is that ill-named thing', then it must be crossed out: the 'sign ~~is~~ that ill-named ~~thing~~'. However, this crossing out, according to Derrida's own *Of Grammatology*, is invisible because the 'graphic image is not seen'; the trace, the original difference between the appearing and the appearance, is virtual.[3] Derrida virtualises the trace. But what is *différance*, what is a non-concept, if not an actual and visible *picture*, a non-philosophical 'outline' (in the French a 'contour' or *'tracé'*)?

Of course, when Heidegger crossed out being, marking the *aporia* of his own late-ontology, he only localised what Derrida does for every concept. ~~Being~~ is a visible graphic, a drawing that *takes* one mark *before* another (*con-cipere* – the root of 'concept'), condensing them into a figure-ground image that leaves the background visible. Echoing this gesture, we can also over-layer the phases of Laruelle's thought, early and late: the Ravaissonian line and his own non-philosophy, translating the latter into the graphic ~~philosophy~~, the 'non-' being a productive substitution rather than an erasure, a ✕ in front of 'philosophy', blocking it out and yet also letting it be seen, used and mentioned at the same time. Crossing out makes the indiscernible partially discernible, indefinite; the marks of both the cross and its background are each only partly occluded, so we are never completely blind and the background is never fully erased. Derrida, naturally, would never define these terms, 'blindness' or 'erasure', as absolutes either, yet *their* initial lexical definition is absolute in its finitude (if their dictionary entry was not *literally* finite there would be only one *actual* entry in the dictionary and this one dictionary [for there could only be one] would be infinitely long).[4]

Doubtless, *we* can lexically qualify such terms (through word association, polysemy and etymology – the whole disseminating play of language), but by then they are no longer the terms we *began* with ('ah! but you see, by 'blindness' he means …').[5] If this is the case, then Derrida could just as well have begun by lexically qualifying 'vision' or 'One'; indeed Laruelle does just this using hyphens (the vision-in-One). And yet Derrida didn't choose these words. He *decided* to start with words of lack, difference and absence, all the privatives of 'de-', 'in-', and 'un-', and so, as Laruelle would add, perpetuated the game of philosophical dyads.[6] Where you begin always determines where you end when the game is circular. And you must begin *somewhere*. To both endorse and revise Badiou: every flow needs a *provisional* point of immobility, an 'as if' *starting* point whose hypothetical status is irreducible. The start may or may not be a decision, but it is a start. Even for process thought, there are a plurality of flows, not just one flow, not just one continuum (just as there are many actual entries in the dictionary and many actual dictionaries, despite the virtual chain of endless signification connecting them – 'see also …', 'see also …', 'see also …').

But perhaps *ostensively*, as shown, words can be tempered and given degrees of meaning no longer based on the bi-valent logic of either/or, presence or absence. It is not that ostension is natural or True, bringing us into a pure presence. But it does work analogically in degrees and so can be neither just true nor just false, but always in between. Of course, it can never be completely *clear* whether it is a rabbit, say, that is being pointed out, or a temporal phase of a rabbit, or a rabbit-part. As Quine well explained, even as regards perception, our ontological commitments load the dice and make communication mis-fire. But not in the same way as with the symbol. In the realm of analogical appearances, the act of pointing, like the act of drawing, is a physical connection with a world that cannot miss its target completely; indeed, its possibility of error by degree (and the possibility of there being quantitative difference at all in fact), rests on *already* being part of that world (just to look at my act of pointing *as an act of pointing* is to enter my world to some degree). The ostensive, the 'stretching out', is a showing with the hand that is also a drawing-in. In *The Logic of Sensation* it is what Deleuze names the 'haptic'. It is a part-icipation rather than a representation, a material belonging and becoming of one part in another rather than by one specular whole of another. Analogy is less prone to the errors of representation because it embodies its 'object' rather than depicts it. In the *Logiques des mondes,* Badiou calls this the 'differential degrees of appearance', as we will see. And this is what Merleau-Ponty explained as 'perceptual faith', which was never a clear definition of representation, but an ambiguous, indefinite relation of subject–world intertwining. The diagram is that kind of intertwining.

Derridian erasure or crossing out also has another power: it can visually decide the undecidable. Let me explain. What is the concept of a non-concept or quasi-concept? It cannot be in terms of another concept *simpliciter*, for such an explanation would be circular. But the elucidation could involve a diagram, namely one depicting the circle of the concept of a non-concept. The paradox of *aporia* cannot be removed (*aporia* – 'difficulty of passing', from *aporos,* 'impassable'), but it can be mobilised if one materialises the circles it creates. One explains by showing, one decides the undecidable by experiencing, because experience is, in the words of Bergson, 'a realised contradiction'.[7] The *aporias* of thought, its impossibilities, are realised in a vertiginous picture.

Certainly, Derrida knows about pictures, about their inclusions and exclusions, the traces and traits of representing the Truth in art. These too need to be deconstructed: the permeable borders of the picture, the osmotic edges of the frame, the *parergon*, the *passe-partout*, the circle (and the 'circle of circles').[8] The frame is what is supposed to keep the inside in and the outside out. The outline is what *creates* a provisional outside – a transcendence – and an inside – immanence. But the frame and the outline bleed. Immanence is never perfect, the transcendent leaks in. All the same, it is always only a relative transcendent that impinges, *one* outside relative to *this* inside, never The Outside. Throughout this study, I have continually used the term 'frame of reference' interchangeably with 'point of view' or 'perspective' when elucidating Deleuze, Badiou and Henry. This was not merely to avoid naïve subjectivism (in favour of situated being), but also to indicate the transcendence of transcendence: if 'reference' specifies representation and transcendence, then the frame is what relativises it to a situation, to a point (of view). In a frame of reference, 'Reference' is enframed in a *locus* and transcendence is naturalised in a *Gestell* (framework), which puts a different spin on Heidegger's name for scientific naturalism. But as a diagram, the deconstruction can also be experienced in a view, a 'glimpse' or '*clin d'oeil*' (to use Derrida's reworking of Heidegger's *Augenblick*), that is, not as a representation, but a presentation, a movement that perpetually crosses itself out in a dissolve – a realised, moving contradiction.[9]

Before proceeding any further, the reader may well be wondering why we are having this engagement with Derrida, the pre-eminent figure of Continental philosophy, at the conclusion of a Post-Continental survey. Why this play with language, especially the constant and irritating punning, when I should be drawing to an end (finally, no pun intended)? The first reason is in order to resist any easy, sub-Derridean deconstruction of (diagrammatic) showing into just being a type of saying.[10] That there may only be degrees of difference between lexical and ostensive definition does not license the reduction of the one to the other. The sheer excess of quantity can lead to a qualitative difference (that Badiou would call an event). And while every degree of difference is a degree *of some kind* of thing, it is not of the same thing. That they are of *one* kind of thing means that a multitude is being 'counted as one', *as if* it were one, from some frame of reference. The reduction, the deconstruction, is perspectival.

The second reason is because of metaphysics. Continental philosophy is not negated by what follows it, but simply crossed out, and as such, remains visible beneath. None of our philosophers of immanence, we have argued, have eliminated the virtual, the transcendental from their thought. Taken together, in this survey, this over-view, we can see that they have relativised immanence and transcendence to an interplay between different frames of reference, biological, affective, mathematical and epistemological. Beyond the myriad differences in approach, what is left in common is *this* interplay, both within each of their works and between each of their works. It is this interplay that we intend to depict through their use of diagrams – another thing all four philosophers have in common – and our own diagrammatic interventions. Those amongst our quartet who do welcome the name 'metaphysics' for their work, nonetheless always keep it at a distance from transcendental being, which in the second half of the twentieth century means keeping a distance from Heidegger or his French avatar, Derrida.

If Heidegger was Continental in his proximity to transcendence, to ontology, then it was lexically so, for we know that he battled with language no less than Deleuze, constantly reinventing synonyms for being, even going so far as crossing it out. Of course, Heidegger also tried to suture philosophy to the poem, and perhaps this was his own dead-end given the subsequent and inevitable rendering of his thoughts into prose in what is called 'Heideggerian philosophy'. But nonetheless, it is the mark of Post-Continental philosophy to think in terms of tendency, in vectors and directions, rather than in absolutes (it is analogical rather than digital). Heidegger points to what comes after him. And even more so Derrida, with his discovery of the grammatology that was so graphically realised in later works like *Glas*. The two 'exemplary' Continental philosophies cancelled themselves out, not just in the *cul-de-sac* of aporetic thinking, but also, at least nascently, in their forms of expression, the graphical mark of crossing out. And such crossing out or erasure is part of the meaning of the diagram – a movement that constantly redraws itself.[11] Auto-transcendence leads to immanence.

If Laruelle is right in saying that written (and comprehensible) philosophy will always fall into transcendent thinking, then Post-Continental philosophy, as a rigorous and productive philosophy of immanence, must invent a new form of expression if it is to be understood. That is, it must concern itself with new media of meaning. Derrida's grammatology points to just this possibility. We cannot transcend transcendence with words, but we might be able to do so with new images, at least for now or for as long as they remain *new* images (words were once graphemes too). There is no *arguing* with Heidegger or Derrida – language (transcendence), even their own *anti-logos logos*, will always win. Even the statement above, 'it is the mark of Post-Continental philosophy to think in terms of tendency ... rather than absolutes' is highly deconstructible ('is this mark absolute or not?') and leads to more circles. So enough of this logic, it is time to begin again with an emphasis on another form of experience than that of words. Our diagrams will replace conventional words and concepts with lines, arrows, shapes and spatial arrangements, not as a 'pure' language of form – what transcendental phenomenology desperately needed to render self-presence possible in the face of differential language – but as the depiction of the very regress that plays itself out in the paradox of presence, a depiction that both repeats the dilemma and moves it forward: when materialised, regress is a kind of progress.

OF DIAGRAMMATOLOGY

In Alexandre Kojève's celebrated lectures on Hegel, the ones that helped to prepare for the French reception of German phenomenology, the lectures for the academic year 1938–1939 contain something special. Noting Plato's remark in *Parmenides* that if 'Being is the One, a man could not *speak* of it', Kojève goes on to adumbrate Hegel's concept of time with eighteen figures that position the Hegelian system within the history of philosophy. Relativism, Mysticism, Platonism, Aristotle, Kant, Spinoza and Hegel are all depicted in a rogues' gallery of lines, angles, arcs, circles and the famous 'circles of circles'. No possibility is left unschematised, the shift from Plato/Theology to Spinoza/Acosmism, for instance, being the detachment of a small circle from intersecting the circumference of a larger circle. Two pages of graphs cover the history of philosophy from Plato to Hegel (see Figure 4).[12]

The relationship between text and image, word and graph, has been a recurrent theme in the recent study of cultural representation from Nelson Goodman and Ernst Gombrich to Roland Barthes and W.J.T Mitchell (who coined the phrase 'diagrammatology').[13] Even the best and most zealous of those who employ graphical images, however – Randall Dipert (whose 'world as graph' thesis is as all-encompassing as Badiou's view of set theory), Gilles Châtelet (who has probably done more than any other figure to theorise the philosophical use of the diagram), or C.S. Peirce (whose use of existential graphs borders on the metaphysical) – all

161

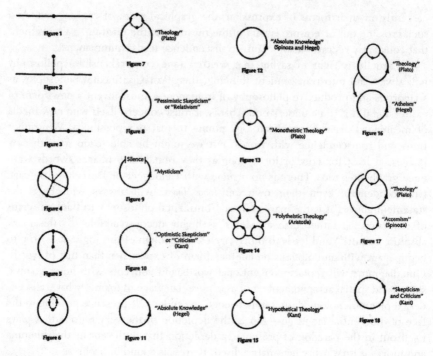

Figure 4

caution us in their use.[14] The ideological effects of image-rhetoric were clearest of all to Barthes. Yet the temptation remains amongst Phenomenologists and Deleuzians alike to employ visual metaphors or 'allegories' liberally. We talk of the 'arrow' of intentionality if we're Husserlian, the 'turn' (*Kehre*) in Heidegger's work, 'chiasmic' reversibility in Merleau-Ponty, or the 'cone' of the World if we follow Deleuze. And such images are never mere ornament – they are often frames around which whole arguments are set. Michèlle Le Doeuff, in particular, has done important work charting the influence of imagery (of islands and maps, windows and doors, statues, clocks, horses and forests) in guiding the history of philosophical argument.[15] But not only are philosophers so seduced. Work on 'envisioning information' has taken huge advances in recent years and across a range of disciplines.[16] Diagrams have long been useful in teaching and learning logic (Euler and Venn diagrams), computing, economics, architecture, physics and learning itself ('mind-maps'), of course, but now their foundation to all under-standing has been highlighted through research in cognitive science and visual studies. Diagrams are 'problem solvers' because they 'automatically support a large number of perceptual inferences, which are extremely easy for humans'.[17] The use of diagrams in the philosophy of science has also been gathering interest, especially in the work of Bruno Latour and Gilles Châtelet.[18]

The diagram may be just one aspect of the general 'scopic regime of modernity', but it is one that is increasingly evident within both discourse and theories of discourse. Certainly, the everyday practice of philosophy often involves drawing simple diagrams, using a pen and paper to sketch the relationship between ideas, objects, or philosophers that would otherwise be too difficult to realise 'in the head'. Diagrams are indeed part of the 'external mind', sometimes even to the extent of railroading our thoughts. Circles with arrows do seem to capture continuous cycles, while concentric circles direct the eye from a marginal to a core idea; tree diagrams are good at indicating hierarchies, while sectioned triangles are better at depicting foundations, and so on.[19] No doubt, some of this works through cultural convention, but not entirely – nature is not wholly reducible to culture. Nonetheless, we will not speculate here as to how diagrams may work in psychophysical terms, be it through intuitions, mental imagery, or bodily schemas.[20] What is notable is that they *do* do conceptual work.

Consequently, whether their use is positive or pernicious, we can still ask if graphic images simply help us to understand (or be seduced), or if they stand in a more literal relationship with the concepts to which they are bound, as ends rather than just as means. And why not as ends? To Richard Feynman, for example, the diagrams he employed to teach physics *actually showed* what happens in the quantum-mechanical world. For him, there was a physical being to the diagram. And for some philosophers this may be true in the metaphysical sense as well. In what follows, we will look at the philosophical 'dark side' of Badiou, Henry and Deleuze, that is, we will re-examine their thought with regard to what they showed as much as what they said. Whilst each of these philosophers of immanence regards what the others are saying as still transcendental, some common ground does appear between them in the guise of the philosophical diagram, something that each of them uses to show what he means by immanence. For some, the diagram will indeed have metaphysical bearing, though again, this is not our interest (diagrams do not have a Truth). *My* question is only metaphilosophical: how do the diagrams of immanence express their philosophy, and how do they relate to each other?

THE LOGICS OF WORLDS

Badiou is one of the most graphical of contemporary philosophers. His language is already replete with spatial metaphors, as we mentioned at the start of Chapter 4, though they remain for him metaphors for the most part. He even crosses words out when analysing one of his favourite subtractive artists, Mallarmé, in *Conditions*.[21] But he also supplements these proto-drawings with numerous figures. In the essay 'What is Love?' (also in *Conditions*), Badiou offers two diagrammatisations of the 'humanity function' (H) according to which 'Woman' and 'Man' knot together the four types of subject: artistic, political, scientific and amorous (see Figure 5).

H according to Woman

H according to Man

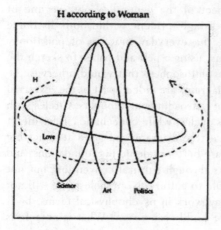
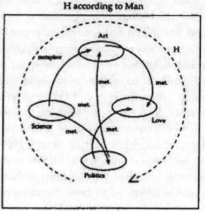

Figure 5

Similar Lacanian knots, of the genuine Borromean variety, also appear in his *Théorie du sujet*, written a decade earlier (see Figure 6).[22]

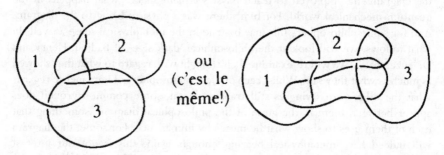

Figure 6

Lacan himself, of course, infamously brought the use of the diagram to its pedagogical and therapeutic limit, his final seminars being practised in silence while he drew intricate knots on the blackboard for his audience. Unilateral surfaces like Klein bottles and Möbius strips had always interested him for their paradoxical form, but from 1972 onwards, the renowned 'rings of string' had largely usurped the place of language in his model of the mind.[23] And this mathematicism has clearly influenced Badiou's trajectory – there is no doubting his desire to pursue Lacan's goal of 'mathematical formalization'.[24] The diagram can easily be seen as a subtractive art in this light, for what is it to map, sketch, or outline a thought if not to eliminate its qualitative content in favour of its co-ordinate form? But Badiou did not follow Lacan's topological matheme, favouring rather the numerical over the 'geometrical' (broadly speaking) and the set-theoretical even more over the numerical.[25] Being as being is expressed most purely through sets alone, anything else is appearance.

Yet, in Badiou's latest thinking, in the *Logiques des mondes*, he has supplemented his set-theoretical ontological base with a theory concerning how that base is linked to our phenomenal worlds. Appearances have returned. In doing this, however, he has remained faithful to his belief in the power of mathematics, only now through the field of 'category theory'. Category theory provides him with a mediating logic (for situations, worlds, or appearances) that is born out of modern algebraic geometry. It is composed of 'objects' and 'arrows' or 'morphisms'. The morphisms connect the objects and together they form geometric relationships depicted by lines and arrows.[26] See Figure 7 for a graph made up of three such objects and morphisms.

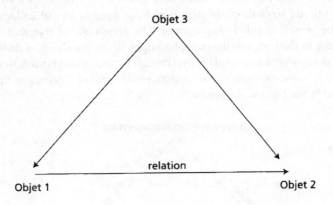

Figure 7

Significantly, Badiou's categories are *descriptive* rather than axiomatic (as set theory was), that is, they are not based on a decision or ontological commitment to found the world in such and such a way, but on a description of the world, what Badiou also calls a sort of 'geometry of truth'. As such, he has at last embraced a 'minimal phenomenology of appearance, an abstract phenomenology of locali-zation'. Moreover, in this light, Badiou sees no difference between a transcendental logic and formal logic: 'every logic, he says, is a logic of appearance'. Badiou wants to fuse together what Kant held apart: the phenomenon is the noumenon. I quote again from a preparatory study for the *Logiques des mondes*: 'Formal logic is a diagrammatic approach to transcendental logic: a particular section of transcen-dental logic.'[27]

The *Logiques des mondes* adds more to Badiou's thought than the addition of a phenomenology, however (already no small thing). It also supplements a number of the theses from *Being and Event*, there being a new complexity to the situation (it is now more than just 'multiple' in a non-relational sense but also composed of a network of relations as they appear in the situation), the subject (who now is not conceived solely through a single, decisionistic fidelity to the event, but through different spatio-temporal relations with it, there being three figures of the subject now: faithful, reactive and obscure),[28] and truth (which, like the event, now concerns the transformation of the logic of a situation rather than its being, which remains the same). All in all, myriad worlds of points, organs, bodies and relations appear alongside pure being to create a beautiful mess.

The nuances this sequel brings to *Being and Event* will not be our worry here – they are at once too numerous and too subtle to digest in any quick time. Moreover, they would deflect our attention needlessly, given that the essentials of *Being and Event* remain intact (immanence equals mathematics equals ontology, the event stands over lesser kinds of change).[29] Our primary concern with Badiou, however – the metaphilosophical issue of Truth and the role of his philosophy in elaborating a theory of Truth – does have a new light brought to it by Badiou's shifting attitude towards phenomenology from being a virtual hallucination to now being a well-founded phenomenon. The philosophy of that shift is argued for directly in the text, but the metaphilosophy of the possibility of Badiou's own thought is explicated more indirectly, through his use of diagrams.[30] Reproduced as Figure 8 is one example of the diagrammatic logic of a particular incident as portrayed in the *Logiques des mondes*.[31]

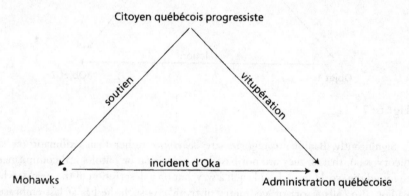

Figure 8

What is interesting is that Badiou believes that in his latest work he is proceeding from being (ontology) to appearance (phenomenology) by going from set theory to category theory, that is, by going from sets to diagrams (like Figure 8). From the perspective of a phenomenologist like Henry, of course, he is simply moving from one more abstract spatialisation of reality to another less abstract one, that is, to one that is still and always a phenomenal experience, albeit with slightly more affective, useful, perceptual concreteness. They are simply two different frames of reference. Hence, despite appearances, we should not get carried away: these diagrams are far from being a common meeting ground as far as Henry (or Badiou) would be concerned. For a start, category theory may *look* like a phenomenological topology, but it is not. It is not about *spatial* relations but relations understood in the most abstract form possible, the universal components of any group of structures, physical or mental, concrete or abstract, natural or cultural, real or fictional. It is a phenomenology without either intentionality or subjectivity, an asubjective phenomenology, or non-phenomenal appearing that is not *for* a subject, but appearing as localisation itself. Pure localisation or pure 'Being-there'.[32] For Henry, this non-phenomenal appearing would be a contradiction in terms.

From his own, mathematical perspective, on the other hand, Badiou has entered into a debate concerning foundations, for it is possible to think of category theory as *the* fundamental mathematical discipline, given its ability to represent or package not just political or artistic situations, say, but *any* world, including that of any other branch of mathematics (algebra, topology, group theory, and so on), in terms of categories (with objects and morphisms differing depending on which branch it is describing). A category can exist with such a rich logical structure that it can even envelope set theory! These are called '*topoi*' in the literature. More worryingly still for Badiou, category theory has links to intuitionist and, more generally, constructionist approaches to mathematics that, were its primacy to be established, would run wholly counter to Badiou's Platonist preferences. The *Logiques des mondes* has a twofold purpose in this arena, therefore, both to establish a relationship between Badiou's ontology of being as being and the appearance of being (the existence of worlds), as well as to decide upon the rival status of the mathematical expression of appearance, category theory, *vis-à-vis* Badiou's own meta-ontological fidelity to set theory as the foundation of all mathematics. As he puts it elsewhere, the question is to decide between Plato or Aristotle. Badiou's decision is clear: he remains an ontologist and not a phenomenologist. Category theory has its place (literally) for the 'working mathematician', but it is not at the centre. It allows us to understand the logic of appearances as a theory of relation as relation, but not their being as being. Set theory remains central, and what Badiou really proposes in the sequel is 'an "ontologization" of the phenomenological'. As Peter Hallward puts it, only set theory can *decide* what is real.[33]

From the metaphilosophical point of view, finally, things are different again. It is not the conjecture that, because category theory *does* look like topology, Badiou might now be returning to the Lacanian *matheme* and giving shape to a possible metalanguage of being that is not set-theoretical. This would still be far too phenomenological and, as such, already biased towards the appearances of category theory and not its possible mathematical basis (to say that a category is identical to its diagrammatic appearance is already to decide against any non-diagrammatic basis for it, be it in set theory or anywhere else). Rather, my interest is strictly metaphilosophical, that is, neither exclusively in the being of category theory (Badiou's frame of reference) nor exclusively in its graphical appearance, but rather in its usage in both domains – the specific *philosophical* use of the diagram that is *both* material *and* conceptual, *both* immanent appearance (or inscription) *and* symbol referring beyond itself (putatively to sets, in Badiou's case).

One other, but significant philosophical outcome of the *Logiques des mondes* is a new place for the analogical world. Alongside the bivalency of being and void, digital ones and zeros, there are the subtle shades of *existence* and *inexistence*, the appearances of worlds. Things can be more or less alike, they can have *degrees of identity* stretched between a minimum and a maximum (but never a zero or one). This is how the world appears, how we have a consistent or coherent world, and so how the One, despite really being multiple, appears *as* One. In elaborating this coherence of worlds, then, has Badiou embraced a two-world ontology – being *and* being-there? Certainly, the category-theoretical paradigm is about construction over decision, about the primacy of the virtual over the actual, of intension over extension. The Deleuzian virtual (as a kind of superior phenomenology) is placed at least alongside the actual (preferably without being subordinated to it), yet ontology remains 'indifferent' to the 'localisation' of multiples. Badiou's commentators seem at odds as to whether this amounts to the theoretical bridge we needed to allow communication between the 'actual and the virtual' (to keep to Deleuze's language). On the one hand, Toscano and Brassier argue that 'Being appears precisely because there is no whole.' On the other, Hallward stipulates that '*how* something appears is not deducible from its ontological profile'.[34] In one view, being necessitates a being-there, in the other, being-there is wholly contingent. These positions can be reconciled (*that* something appears is because there is no whole), yet phenomenology is supposedly about the *how*, about the appearance. As Henry noted regarding Heidegger: the ontological is indifferent as regards the different phenomena's modes of appearing because the generality of ontology (being *as such*) cannot create specificity. So, in as much as set theory subtends our phenomenal worlds for Badiou, but does so without the means for generating the specificity of worlds (their transformation is a pure contingency), the category theorist with a foundationalist streak will naturally reply to Badiou as follows: why must we keep being at all? As Berkeley said in his critique of Lockean substance, we must look elsewhere to account for any specific world-order if that order's particularity cannot be explained by substance.[35]

But let us not re-run that dialectic, the dyad of virtual or actual, nor, aside from Deleuzian immanence, that of Henry or Badiou. Either regime can be in the ascendant depending on how one loads the dice. What is interesting is that, in his theory of appearances, Badiou accommodates 'differential degrees of appearance' that are at the same time linked to the fact that 'there are many transcendentals'.[36] The transcendental is for him a matter of degrees. This is not such a controversial point though. What is most notable is that the multiplicity and relativity of transcendence and, as a corollary, of immanence as well, *is* captured by the graphs Badiou uses in the *Logiques des mondes* and elsewhere. These diagrams depict existence in varying shades, with degrees of difference rather than binaries of black or white: they depict them through embodiment, for they are not *metaphorically* shaded, merged and folded onto each other, *they are* shaded, merged and folded onto each other. The diagrams *are* appearances with 'differential degrees' (colour, texture, shape).

For instance, in *Conditions*, Badiou presents a diagram of truth, the 'gamma diagram' that supposedly 'represents the trajectory of truth, regardless of type' (see Figure 9).[37] This diagram, if it really did account for every truth-trajectory, could well be taken for the answer we were seeking at the start of the last chapter – the spatial compossibility of all four of Badiou's truth procedures being actually depicted in a graph (ironically one that mimics the shape of its name – a letter in the Greek alphabet, Gamma γ). And it seems that this is indeed Badiou's purpose for it: 'my diagram is philosophical', he says, 'in that it renders the four types of truth compossible through a formal concept of Truth'. Compossibility *is* spatial. But given its totalising nature (it is One diagram), how can it possibly accommodate (depict) the *degrees* of difference between the different truth procedures in a single, static image? From the one extreme of the four regimes having a truth procedure specific to themselves (how art makes new art, politics makes revolution, science discovers laws, and lovers make love is entirely heterogeneous and incommensurable), yet somehow seized together within the 'pincers' of philosophy (but without that metaphor ever being cashed out in anything other than merely programmatic form), we now have the opposite extreme of every specific, local truth being pinched to nothing, reduced to one image. And this one image, that of gamma γ, does also look like a set of pincers (Figure 10)![38]

Alternatively, hasn't the diversity and equivalence of these truths, their multiplicity and coherence, always been captured most adequately by the diagrams Badiou has produced of them throughout his writings, diagrams that finally

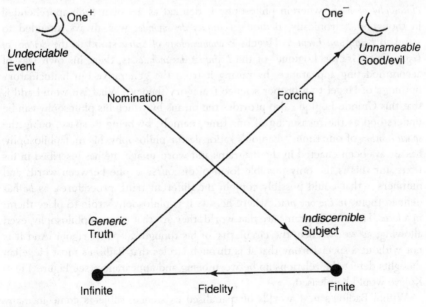

Figure 9

Figure 10

approach the metaphysics they need only in the *Logiques des mondes*? Not the mark of the void, or the infinite, or gamma, but the indefinite marks strewn throughout his works; these are the actual components of a feasible language of immanence for Badiou's philosophy.

Apart from his spatial metaphors, the other way in which Badiou describes the role of philosophy is as the temporal summation of the truths of one period, the 'measuring [of] our time'.[39] This alludes, certainly, to Hegel's preface to *The Philosophy of Right* wherein philosophy is defined as 'its own time apprehended in thoughts'.[40] Ironically, Badiou's *Logiques des mondes* was always intended to stand to *Being and Event* as Hegel's *Phenomenology of Spirit* stood to the *Science of Logic*. This 'Grande Logique' of the *Logiques des mondes* is, then, his own way of accommodating appearance, by raising it from the generative but hallucinatory ontology of Hegel to a proper science (category theory). What we would add is that this Grande Logique also provides the means by which his philosophy can be understood as the measuring of our time, namely, by being in space, being the *spatialisation* of our time.[41] Badiou's rationale for philosophy, his metaphilosophy, has always been enacted in the diagrams and word-images he has inscribed in his texts, for this is the only possible form of discourse – one between words and numbers – that could possibly conjoin the different truth procedures, as *he* has defined them, *in the one place* where he says it is philosophy's role to place them: in a *locus*. His own diagrams are that world, they are that (meta-) philosophy, even allowing, as we will see, the circularity of his thought a spatial rigour. And it is not without a special irony that it is through circles that Badiou's most Hegelian thoughts depict the relationship between being and appearance (see Figure 11).[42] Kojève would be pleased.

Within Badiou's new worlds of spatialised existence, subjects come in many forms: faithful, reactive and obscure. But if philosophy is itself the most compre-

Being and Appearance

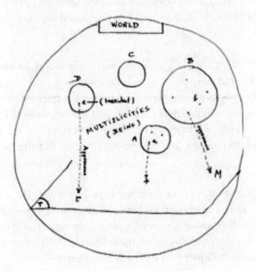

Figure 11

hensive spatialisation, then the philosophical subject might also come in different *types* which may form spatial relationships amongst one another. Badiou's own thought would create a visual world for other philosophers to relate to – reactively, faithfully or obscurely. Lyotard cuts one such figure over the matter of incompossibility in his own work and his later reaction to Badiou's *Being and Event*. In his 1971 *Discours, Figure*, Lyotard cites the Freudian picture of the unconscious as ignorant of contradiction; because it *doesn't* allow negation, it *does* allow the 'incompossible'.[43] Opposites unite in an analogical universe. Of course, Lyotard in this text is arguing against, amongst other things, the linguistic approach in Lacanian psychoanalysis (it still being a year before Lacan's discovery of topology). He wants to deconstruct the difference between discourse and figure, to show how figural and sensual experience can form a discourse all its own. Only through discourse are the compossible and incompossible dichotomised. Within the figural, however, they are mutable categories; what was incompossible can become compossible, in the 'same motley world', as Deleuze would say.[44] And it is worth recalling that it was Lyotard who later criticised Badiou's *Being and Event* for ignoring the pathetic and sensual basis to registering an event: that the new, the impossible or incompossible, is what we are 'affected' by when it is figured as compossible, as possible. It is the sensuous figure that can render the heterogeneous in one place, that can give us a vision-in-One. Hence, it can be seen that Lyotard's *figural* is a reaction against Badiou's non-figurative *matheme*, but in a way that we could ourselves diagrammatise in terms of Badiou's later work (though we won't sketch this interplay here just yet).

The faithful subject could also be sketched. In an article on Badiou, the significance of which the *Logiques des mondes* itself acknowledges, Justin Clemens argues for a 'topology of Truth' in Badiou, but it is one based on the *letter* rather than the diagram:

> This literality of mathematics should be understood as the production of material marks that have nothing whatsoever to do with ordinary language: mathematical symbols are not signifiers, they are letters. Mathematics and logic are formal languages in which there is no latitude whatsoever for hermeneutics. Numbers — which are marked by arbitrary letters — are not linguistic. A mathematical letter marks, not any positive entity, but the lack of objects and objectivity.[45]

The letters of mathematics enact their negative reference (the void). But also, in his philosophical nexus of the procedures of all four truth conditions, Badiou's philosophical act is the construction of a place, 'the place of Truth' that operates through letters, through the ability to trans-literate.[46] Clemens takes this notion of the letter from the following in Badiou's *Inaesthetics*:

> This would then be my definition of an egalitarian freedom within thought: A thought is free once it is transliterated by the small letters of the matheme, by the mysterious letters of the poem, by the way in which politics takes things literally, and, finally, by the love letter.[47]

From which Clemens concludes:

> The letter is not an *epistemological* category for Badiou: it is *simultaneously* an integral moment in a truth process, marking its inaugural act of decision or intervention, *and* the matter of the knowledge of being. The disposition of letters involves a supernumerary *act* that at once founds the work of truth *and* the extension of being beyond its previous limits. Truth *and* being, name *and* number, quality *and* quantity: this is the irreducible double destiny of the letter in Badiou. Being *and* the knowledge of being, truth *and* Truth, all meet in the materiality of letters.[48]

After this faithful crystallisation of Badiou's philosophical act of transliteration, Clemens admits that Badiou himself can have no definition of what a letter is, in anything other than a 'metaphorical fashion'. And we can see why Badiou can never *say* what a letter is as such. On the one hand, he constantly privileges mathematical transliteration such that the modes of transformation in the other three procedures all seem to be transferred (*metapherein*) from mathematics metaphorically, and, on the other hand, it is obvious that a *literal* definition of the letter would only be a circular definition. However, there is a depiction of the letter, an indefinite appearance rather than definite definition, available to Badiou on the basis of his new work: this would be predicated on letters, plural (not just one letter singular, even gamma γ) understood grammatologically from the outset, that is, as diagrammatic. The diagram is exactly the letter that shows itself in a multitude of spaces through Badiou's various philosophical drawings. And it is the spatiality of the letter that we can use, not only to tie together the four corners of his own thought, but also to link his theory of immanence to that of his most estranged others. In other words, we can relate Henry and Deleuze to the diagrammatic space of Badiou's thought through their own diagrammatic thought. It is notable that both Lyotard and Clemens, whether reactive or faithful, use only words when writing about the figural and the literal (letter) in Badiou. By contrast, Deleuze and Henry form both a clearer and a more ambiguous *spatial* relationship with him.

BADIOU'S META-OTHERS: HENRY AND DELEUZE

We saw already from Henry's work on Kandinsky that, despite his differences with Badiou, he does not reject abstraction all out. Rather, he affectivises it. In *Voir l'invisible*, the force that we experience as pathos '*is also the force that produces the line ...*'. Kandinsky's abstraction, his graphs, are not abstracted *away* from life, *they are a mode of life*: it is 'the pathos of force that produces this graphism, which is its interior sonority. This is supported on itself, on the pathetic diversity of life and its indefinite modalisations – *on the abstract content of art ...*'. At once painterly and geometric, Henry sees diagrams display the facets of auto-affection immanently through their abstract form. A painting like *Black and Violet* or *Yellow, Red and Blue*, as Henry regards it, simply *is* a fragment of immanent life, not a representation of it.

The form of a Kandinsky 'possesses its own proper interior, it is a spiritual being ... a triangle is a being'. Similar vitality is attributed to each of the components of the graph: the point (it has an interior sonority and pathetic concentration), the line (possessing movement and tension), and the plane/plan (its unity is dynamic, interior and pathetic, it breathes, it is sonorous). And, to be sure, the colours too are vitalised in the diagram. Obviously, the synaesthesia that informed both Wassily Kandinsky's art and writings may be at work here (Henry remarks on how 'the unity of the colour yellow and the figure of a triangle is precisely a unique reality, one and the same affect in us, a single emotion'). Or, it could be that Henry is transforming this so-called psychological condition into a metaphysics: the sonority of the plane is at once the point, horizontal line, vertical, circle, yellow, and blue. Despite their 'objective difference', they are actually the same subjectively.[49] Pluralism = Monism.

Clearly, the painterly qualities of *Black and Violet* make of it a different kind of diagram from that of a category relating three objects with three morphisms. The latter effaces its own materiality – texture of lines, colours, shades, scales – as best it can in favour of the mathematical meaning inscribed by the diagram (especially the more complicated ones that involve algebra as well). But this is to think too readily of the category as a symbol and not a letter, making of its actuality something pointing away, a reference to a virtual. Indeed, this can be done to the actuality of a painting no less than to a mathematical 'symbol'. Deleuze, for instance, also writes of Kandinsky in *The Logic of Sensation* but mostly to disparage what he regards as the actuality of his work.[50] It is precisely what Deleuze reads as the virtual being of Francis Bacon's art that explains his preference for it over Kandinsky. This is because, in fact, Deleuze tends to think of the diagram itself as virtual or as a virtual process – only *potentially* concrete or actual.

Stepping back from the artwork a moment, this Virtualism first re-emerges from Deleuze's general theory of the diagram, the scope of which is both metaphilosophical and metaphysical. We can look to both *The Logic of Sensation* and *A Thousand Plateaus* for this rendering. For him, a diagrammatic depiction of a theory is one that modulates a theory, that is to say, it abstracts a theory. A philosophy has its own 'abstract machine' or 'diagrammatic machine' that dynamically outlines the functions or processes, the relations or differences, within and between theories. The famous abstract machines of *A Thousand Plateaus* are also diagrams, that is, 'the aspect or moment at which nothing but functions and matters remain. A diagram has neither substance nor form, neither content nor expression.' The diagram is a purity, and as pure, it must be virtual. The diagram is what 'retains the most deterritorialized content and the most deterritorialized expression, in order to conjugate them'. Diagramming raises a trait to its highest power, it 'carries it off'. But if we ignore this Virtualism and look at the diagrams Deleuze uses throughout his works in their own actuality on the page, it is striking that they are neither wholly iconic nor symbolic. They neither fully resemble nor represent anything, but rather, in their in-between depiction, instantiate that which they supposedly look like or symbolise. The examples from *A Thousand Plateaus* on the topic of facialisation are fascinating to look at and think with in this regard (see Figure 12).[51]

In *The Fold* as well, Deleuze provides diagrams, hand-drawn in the original French text, that are further examples of this in-between state, being neither icons nor symbols of Baroque architecture (see Figure 13).[52] They simply are little pieces of the Baroque that also tell us something about the Baroque, about what the Baroque *does*. But, despite this clear role of instantiation in his usage of the diagram, the diagrams are still not theorised as actual in Deleuze. As he writes in *The Logic of Sensation*, diagrams are at best proto-actual, a 'germ of order or rhythm', and that which 'begins the act of painting'. The diagram 'is a possibility of fact – it is not the fact itself'. It is what modulates or subtracts from the virtual.[53]

Indeed, Deleuze's diagrammatology might even remind one of some aspects of Badiou's diagrams if one reads them in terms of their self-proclaimed Virtualism (that is, as *mere* appearance). Yet, Deleuze contends that diagrams are *concrete* conditions of the actual, whilst still not themselves being actual. It is again in Deleuze's work on Bacon that this comes out, if a little obscurely. His approach is

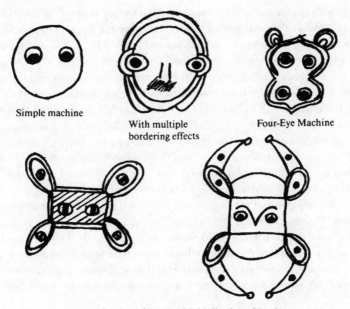

Simple machine

With multiple
bordering effects

Four-Eye Machine

Proliferation of Eyes by Multiplication of Border

Figure 12

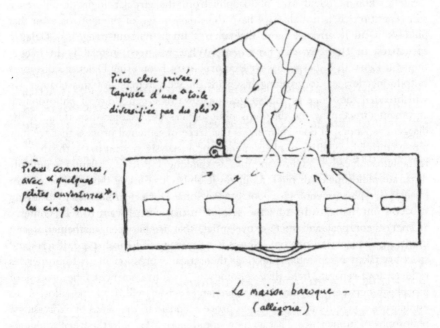

Pièce close privée,
Tapissée d'une "toile
diversifiée par des plis"

Pièces communes,
avec "quelques
petites ouvertures":
les cinq sens

- La maison baroque -
(allégorie)

Figure 13

taken up with prolonged reflections on rhythm theory in art – the coexistence of all movements on a canvas. Subtending the concrete machines of each canvas is the abstract machine, a diagram of spots, lines and zones. The language of the diagram is analogical, working productively through modulation. The diagram is again irreducible to either symbol or icon. And it is not a code: Bacon's geometry 'attests to a high *spirituality*, since what leads it to seek the elementary forces beyond the organic is a spiritual will'. These forces are haptic rather than optical, tactile rather than visual. Such diagrams can actually fill the whole canvas as a set of suggestive traits, a graph of potentials. The diagram is not just an outline, but involves the fullness of colour – as sensation – too. Following Cézanne, Bacon pursues an analogical use of geometry, but analogy here is not understood as resemblance so much as modulation, subtraction. The Diagram subtracts.[54]

Given the filling out of the diagram and what we might describe as its painterly Actualism, Deleuze pushes a little against his own Virtualist theory. And with his own diagrams, especially the hand-drawn ones that mark themselves wholly as diagrammatic *processes* of drawing, Deleuze provides a figural and actual geometry that (on the page) is between abstraction and resemblance, between symbol and icon, between mathematics and art, and, we would say, between Badiou and Henry.

Proper abstraction for Deleuze, then, is singular and real, a non-organic life and a type of line passing between things: a zigzag, a transversal. Is this transversal not also close to the serpentine line that, at once actual and metaphysical, Laruelle thought could save philosophy from the circular logic of difference and repetition? It is not that we have the *wrong* image of thought, or even that philosophy might advance more through a 'thought without image', as Deleuze speculated in *Difference and Repetition*.[55] What we need instead is an image-thought. Kenneth Knoespel has written productively on using Deleuze's diagrams as 'piloting devices' for reading his work: in what remains of this chapter we will broaden the scope of this suggestion towards a genealogy of philosophical argument directed by the diagrams philosophers use. Rather than think of the diagram as Knoespel does, namely as the 'trace of a mental process that we may pursue through cognitive or phenomenological analysis', I want to see the diagram metaphilosophically and immanently, as thinking for itself, relating seemingly disparate philosophies through its intrinsic ability to outline thought.[56] I am not trying to re-phenomenologise geometry in some Husserlian manner by bringing it back from mathematics to some original experience; I want to see geometry as meta-theoretical and meta-experiential, that is, between mathematics and intuition, concept and percept. Nor is it a topology of logical space, if *topos* and space are taken as separable from their theoretical expression and with properties reduced to a separate field (like topology or cognitive science). The process of morphism between diagrams across time and register will, we hope, allow us to establish an image-thought that might prove adequate to the needs of expressing a philosophy of immanence. That is, they would neither fall into the usual problems of representation, nor reduce the diagram to some transcendent Outside. This would not be a Badiouian morphism of appearance but a meta-morphism between different theories of appearance.

METAPHILOSOPHICAL DIAGRAMMATOLOGY

This book has tried to establish Badiou, at least in *Being and Event*, as the thinker of the pure outside and Henry as the thinker of the pure inside: in terms of their purity, their puritanism even, they merge into each other. As an alternative to this dualism, I am trying to establish metaphilosophy as a *diagrammatic* movement of thought from inside to outside, and back again. In spatialising thought, this is clearly a subtractive, privative process. It ignores content but only because content, when it tries to represent immanence, falls into dyadic thinking (as Laruelle has shown). Needless to say, then, the diagram is not some Absolute Truth: spatialisation is unReal in terms of content and only Real in terms of form. All the same, the dia-gram, the moving form, is a between-form, and embodies real and actual connections. Like Kandinsky's abstract points, lines and planes, the diagram is a living, philosophical abstraction, but one that remains *actual so long as its outlines keep moving*. This insistence on movement is there because metaphilosophy (like meta-ontology) is itself a paradoxical self-belonging (it refers to itself all the time as a truth-bearer and truth-maker in one). Hence, it stands only for the moment, and not for the eternal (as with Laruelle's essentialism). The moment I say *this* is a metaphilosophy, or even show it, it shifts again. Ostension creates its own outside in the act of pointing out. Form becomes content when its movement is arrested to stand for something beyond, a virtual. Hence, the diagram will have to alter perpetually. And while it does, at least for a moment, the diagram's actual movement eludes the trap of virtualisation, of standing for Truth as and when the letter becomes the symbol. Eventually, we will illustrate the way in which a diagrammatic metaphilosophy might progress, using a thinking that is both formal *and* also aware of its affective and perceptual origins (as spatialised thought), to see the relationship between Virtualist and Actualist philosophies, and finally to outline the pure Actualisms of Henry (pure Affect) and Badiou (pure Idea) as virtual poles between which a metaphilosophical movement, itself actual, can run.

There are various sub-routines to this method, that, though seemingly different, still deserve to be called diagrammatic. Focusing on the abstract, subtractive vocabulary that a philosopher utilises is one important dimension: the pared-down rhetoric he or she employs could, with some work, be schematised into geometric forms (no less than Badiou renders it as numerical forms).[57] Or there is the very spatial origin of many word-meanings, by which one could create pictures of a thought using the Derridean method of re-literalising (metaphorical) words into their spatial roots (whether or not that basis is itself rooted in the movements of our body). The same can be done at one further remove from the individual words and their etymology, by looking at the diagrammatic structures of writing: the narratives of beginning, middle and end (not necessarily in that order), the

177

openings and closings, departures and returns, the complications and reversals of the (philosophical) plot – all of these could be graphed (as Sterne's Tristram Shandy does in one beautiful moment of compression).

There is also a kind of intentional diagrammatic writing, a preparing of the way for the diagram by invoking all of the routines just sketched and then accentuating them, either by inflation or deflation, so that they become self-conscious (or at least secretly so). Derrida's *Glas* or some works of the 'Oulipo' group (*Ouvroir de Litterature Potentielle*), would be different examples of this. Founded by Raymond Queneau in 1960, Oulipo embrace abstract restrictions in their writing in order to energise it, constrained literature being the mother of invention (the most celebrated example is George Perec's lipogrammatic novel *La Disparition*, written without the letter *e* appearing in it at all, and translated into English with equal ingenuity as *A Void*).[58] I wrote an introduction to Bergson in 2000, *Bergson and Philosophy*, the (unannounced) constraint of which was having to follow the diagram of a diploid. I say it 'had to' follow this diagram, but only because I realised two years earlier that, given the inconsistency of Bergson's texts, this shape best accounts for the evolution of his thought across forty years, his own spatial metaphors and diagrams, and the movement of the key ideas in his philosophy.[59] It was an account that materialised that inconsistency and rendered it intelligible to the eye. I have reproduced it here (Figure 14) to save the reader from reading the verbal rendition.

There are two problems with the diploid that are instructive. Firstly, the interpretation of the diagram is still dependent on the text that accompanies it (such textual neighbours were also seen above in the diagrams of Badiou and Deleuze

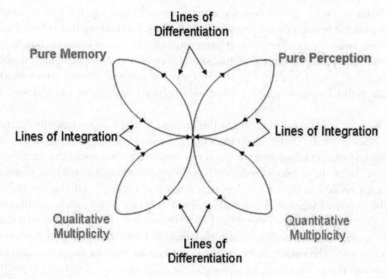

Figure 14

in Figure 8 and 13). A purist might think that this text invites the viewer to think that the diagram needs to be interpreted, to be decoded, and as such, is actually a symbol to be read and not a diagram to be seen, at least as we have described it. The discursive paradigm would thereby re-assimilate the diagram. However, it is precisely to avoid this that the diagram should be dynamic. In theory, any textual accompaniment could be rendered as *another* diagram or some kind of mutation of the original diagram. For instance, in the diploid graph, each leaf is a vortex (and so should be moving) that is reiterated on various orders from the psychological (Bergson's *Time and Free Will* and *Matter and Memory*) to the cosmological (*Creative Evolution*) and even the metaphilosophical (*The Creative Mind*). One way (but not the only way) that this might be shown without being said, is by literally reiterating the diagram (Figure 15). Animation software might also be introduced to allow the complex morphing of shape into other forms (sometimes with more dimensions), each 'child-form' taking on a relationship with its 'parent' that would stand for a sophisticated conceptual development. This would obviate the need to front-load the diagrams with textual keys. Some of this work in 'philosophical animation' is already being done (Figure 16).[60]

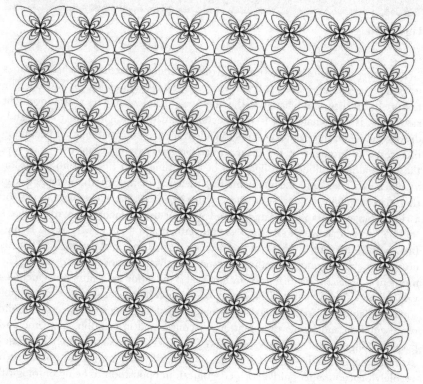

Figure 15

Figure 16

Enriching the life of the diagram to avoid its reduction to the text that enframes it, is not just about movement, however – it is also about *what* is moved. The texture of the diagram, what gives the lines weight and what gives their movement *momentum*, is also vital. That is why certain animations might have to be hand-drawn, taking on the painterly traits of Deleuzian diagrams without yet becoming pictures. The moment of the diagram can be heavy or light; to assume always the pure, almost unbearable lightness of an outline with (ideally) no extension would be to take only the mathematical meaning of a diagram. Retaining also the relative weight, colour, scale and texture of a *particular* movement allows for a richer range of graphic meanings (and without using algebra, as with Badiou's '*topoi*').[61] Not that we should *dissociate* movement and form either: as Pia Ednie-Brown says, 'texture is a kind of consistency or pattern of variations'.[62] There is no movement 'in general' in the diagram, but always a movement of sorts. The moment is a *moment-um* that only grammar and reflection split into 'movement + vehicle' or 'velocity + mass'. We must keep in mind the status of the metaphilosophical diagram as an indefinite set of materialised 'betweens': between symbolic representation and iconic presentation, discourse and inscription, matheme and patheme, digital and analogue, geometry and art, internal representation and external picture, audience and artwork. Finally, the diagram should not be seen as solely procedural, cognitive, or pedagogical, in opposition to being ontological (or at least ontical, a being rather than Being). The diagram is both de-scriptive and re-vision-ary – both script and vision, symbol and icon, in-one. We will especially address this double facet of the diagram as active intervention and passive depiction, given that it has also been a recurrent theme for a number of the figures in this study.

THE OBJECT O: A NEW FRAMEWORK FOR THE DREAM OF EXPERIENCE

The last feature of diagrammatology is genealogical, or what Gilles Châtelet and Kenneth Knoespel refer to as an 'archaeology' of diagrams.[63] This is not about diagrammatising thought, but looking at extant diagrams for their philosophical bearing. Here we look at them partly in relation to the philosophers whose thought they are linked to, but partly also as works with independent lives and visual lineages all their own. This kind of diagrammatology follows the lead of Aby Warburg's anarchistic 'iconology' or 'montage-collision'. As a method of decontextualisation, it marginalises historical provenance and cultural context in favour of sheer appearance, uncovering kinships between images based on their elements, their relative motions, and their juxtapositions in an almost cinematic manner.[64] Likewise, we can create interesting links between the diagrams of, for instance, Bergson, Deleuze, Lacan, Badiou and Merleau-Ponty, mostly on the basis of their shapes, in this case, that of cones and diploids. This will be a rhizomatic rather than arboreal genealogy (or rather, it will unearth the rhizome in every family tree).

Recall the conical diagrams used in Chapter 1 to distinguish Deleuze's Virtualist reading of Bergson from the Actualist one. The second, Actualist diagram doubled the layout to create two cones facing each other (see Figure 17). Be they one-dimensional lines, two-dimensional planes, or three-dimensional cones, the figure of two triangles meeting (or intersecting) at their apex is one of the most prevalent in theory (as we saw Henry note earlier: triangles play a strangely disproportionate role in philosophy). In both science and art, in the light cones of relativity theory, the triangles formed by Greimas' semiotic square (not unrelated to Badiou's gamma diagram), and the gyres of Blake and Yeats, perhaps only the circle and spiral is used more widely. After *Bergsonism*, Deleuze himself re-uses the single cone or pyramid image in the *Anti-Oedipus* (depicting the three bodies of earth, despot and capital) and *The Fold* (understanding the Baroque world as cone).[65] But the *double*-cone has resonances in philosophy beyond Deleuze. In fact, the cones take a mad itinerary from Lacan through Merleau-Ponty and then back to Bergson that is instructive for Deleuze's canonical reading of the virtual.

Visually, there is a clear if arbitrary similarity between the double cone and Lacan's famous cones or 'triangular systems' sketched in *The Four Fundamental Concepts of Psychoanalysis* (Figure 18, p.183). Of course, what is symbolised in Lacan's illustration is somewhat different at face value, namely, the geometric field that locates the subject of representation on the one side, and the same field that turns 'me' into a picture on the other. The fact that the two triangles must

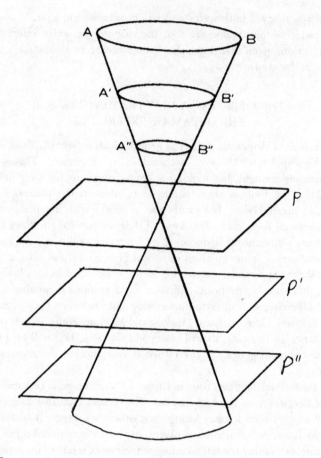

Figure 17

be superimposed in the 'scopic register', shows for Lacan the truth that the 'gaze is outside', that I am a picture. No doubt (if we wanted to), we could generate a theoretical overlapping between Lacan's picture theory and Bergson's theory of the image, arguing from more or less scanty analogies. But even more interesting for now are Lacan's other references when he discusses these triangular systems. For, lecturing in 1964, he had recently discovered Merleau-Ponty's *The Visible and the Invisible*, and peppers his talk continually with references to intertwinings, interlacings and, of course, Chiasms.[66] Which brings me to the next part of the genealogy. Figure 19 (p. 184) reproduces Merleau-Ponty's chiasm in the flesh. The intertwinings and reversibility characteristic of the chiasm are clearly visible if we follow its outline, of course. But, if we also take in the planes that lie within those lines (swapping figure and ground), we equally see two cones meeting at their apexes. So, building on an analogy between diagrams and using our liter-

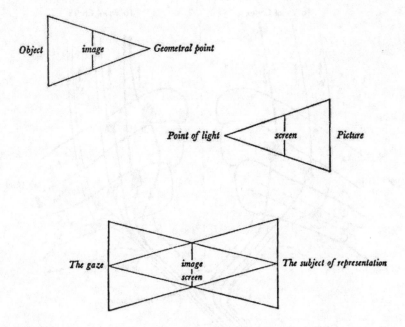

Figure 18

alist imagination, can we find a new meeting-point between the double-conical understanding of the virtual–actual and Merleau-Ponty's theory of the flesh in *The Visible and the Invisible*? Certainly no such legitimation can be found in the text, for Merleau-Ponty does not refer at all in *The Visible and the Invisible* to the conical diagrams in *Matter and Memory*. However, in the chapter on 'Interrogation and Intuition', he alludes to another Bergsonian diagram in *Matter and Memory* that favours the Actualist reading of Bergson even more. Here Merleau-Ponty writes of the dream 'of finding again the natural world or time through coincidence, of being identical to the *O-point* which we see yonder, or to the pure memory which from the depths of ourselves governs our acts of recall ...'.[67] This Bergsonian dream is supposedly only a dream because, like the dream of Levinasian 'pure experience' that Derrida banished (while also tracing it back to Bergson), language forces such empiricism to awaken from the chimera of coincidence with the world.[68]

Few today would argue that Bergsonism was ever a philosophy of *pure* experience and coincidence,[69] but of greater interest here is the provenance of this 'O-point' to which Merleau-Ponty refers. It stems from the second chapter of *Matter and Memory* when Bergson gives a different but not unrelated diagrammatisation of our temporal experience from that of the cones in his third chapter (see Figure 20, p.185). Significantly, too, this diagram depicts the *lines* (rather than planes) of influence or force between self and world in a manner which is both an interlacing or chiasm (a graphic refutation of Merleau-Ponty's portrait

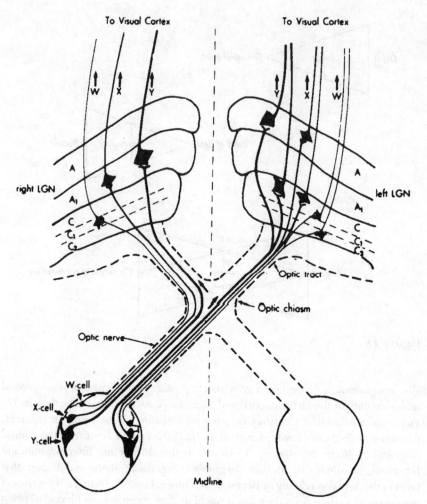

Figure 19

of Bergson), and a haploid (half-diploid). The geometrical double-cone morphs into the biological haploid. Figure 20 represents the dialectical tension between the object of our recognition and the memories which facilitate our recognition of this object. It is a recognition enabled by an attention that involves *our entire past* (hence Merleau-Ponty's reference to 'pure memory'). Bergson describes it as a 'kind of *circuit*', in which '... the external object yields to us deeper and deeper parts of itself ...'.[70] '*L'objet O*' (as Bergson calls it) is not an object at all, but the *disturbance* within an object; *A* is our nearest sensation of it; *B, C, D*, etc., are our ever-widening and more meaningful spans of attention that embrace the disturbance with larger and larger portions of our past. Complementary to these

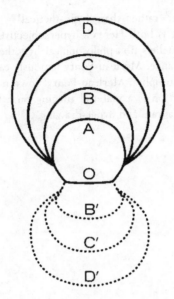

Figure 20

spans, B', C', and D' symbolise the 'deeper strata of reality' on the side of the object (its 'deeper parts'), as Bergson puts it. This diagram testifies, therefore, to a clear Actualism in Bergson, even in his most Virtualist text *Matter and Memory*: the greater depth of the object, its revealed virtuality (so-called), *belongs to the actual disturbance in the object, to the actual itself* (it originates 'from the object'). Indeed, if one were to superimpose Bergson's first diagram (Figure 19) upon the diagram of the double-cones (Figure 17), 'the object O', would be placed at the apex, the pure present on the plane *P*. Then, taking the widest diploid formed by DD' or one of the more restricted ones formed by the smaller circuits CC', BB', or even the object O itself, one would have a representation of *multiple* presents ranging from the broader expanses to an *ideally* pure and immediate form. *In other words, the object O — qua present — can exist on any of these circuits, at various depths or levels.*[71] The *O-point* or *object O* would now even more clearly represent, not a static object, but a relation, a mediation, a disturbance or novelty: it is not a place but a moment, an anoriginal, anomalous present, the paradoxical present (paradoxical because these actual disturbances *multiply* the present by typing it circuitously, in circles, and so discharge any need for a virtual behind the present).[72] The *object O* is what Badiou calls an event, but it is not a thing, a void, or a zero (Bergson is against all negativity); it is one moment in a positive, indefinite regress of processes.[73]

And, in the end, what is so wrong with regress anyway? In pluralism, immanence materialises the regress as types.[74] The *object O* is an 'as if' perspectival frame: the hypothetical point of immobility that is neither presence nor void, but the reality of regressive frames, the reality of a lucid dream within a dream. Perhaps it should be called 'hyper-thetical' rather than 'hypo-thetical' – *more* theoretical rather than under-theorised. It is both Henry's hypersubjective (where *'feeling as'* is a hyperknowing) *and* Laruelle's non-philosophical hypothesis of the Real's determination-in-the-last-instance. Merleau-Ponty famously called it 'hyper-reflexion' – the basis of his 'a-philosophy', Merleau-Ponty's own non-philosophy.[75] For us, that reflection on reflection is a material turning on a turning: the non-philosophical as serpentine diagram and hyper-drawing.

CONCLUSION

The Shape of Thoughts to Come

THE DELEUZE PARADOX

'Thinking by analogy' can often lead us into errancy when it relies entirely on word-associations. We can easily be led off on a tangent no matter how sophisticated our theory of what it means to be 'alike'. But *seeing* analogies can be temporarily *less* corrigible (we are in the realm of degrees here, not right or wrong). Badiou goes too far when he says that 'when everything appears similar, nothing really is' (but as a recent phenomenologist only on sufferance, he would say that). For Deleuze, however, almost the opposite is the case: when nothing appears similar, everything really is (pluralism = monism). Between his works *Difference and Repetition* and *Francis Bacon*, Deleuze sharply altered his views about analogy. Between his most Platonist, Virtualist text and his most graphical one, analogy is rehabilitated. It is no longer rejected for working in the economy of the same or representation, but accepted as productive, modular, embodied and sensual.[1] As we discussed at the start of Chapter 5, seeing and touching by analogy (ostension, drawing) is *less* prone to the errors of representation than thinking by analogy, for it embodies its 'object' in a physical continuity rather than depicting it 'outside'.

Admittedly, both Deleuze and Badiou have always had issues with language. Deleuze can at times be hyper-linguistic in practice, with a glossomaniacal invention of words across his texts. At other times he seems in denial of the power of language in theory, seeking a non-linguistic semiotics of direct sensation. Badiou is more consistent in having always underscored the textual letter with the mathematical inscription. Where Deleuze's non-linguistic signs are prone to being reduced to language (on the basis that if you can say it in a philosophy text, then it is sayable *per se*), set-theoretical inscriptions seem impervious to reduction, and that is why Badiou believes that they are *the* language of immanence – there is no 'outside' beyond them. Or at least there wasn't any outside until the rise of category theory, which suggests, for some, another kind of analogical inscription. But it was this realm of the diagrammatic that facilitated a better account of the function of philosophy for Badiou, quite literally as the space of compossibility. And with the *Logiques des mondes*, he even accords some reality (or 'existence') to analogy, to appearances and differences of degree.

In one way of seeing things, 'Deleuze' is the anomalous, anoriginal point of 'origin' for Henry and Badiou – he is their *Object O*. As a Virtualist of the One, of the Idea and the mathematical, he leads to Badiou (and his own selective reading of Deleuze). At the same time, as an Actualist of the many, of the affect and the empirical, he leads to Henry. But we have seen how Badiou needs Henry and Henry needs Badiou in as much as their errancy from Deleuze pushes his thought towards untenable extremes. We need the *two* Deleuzes together. What I have described as the tensions in Deleuze's thought – the constant renaming in the face of dualities continually re-appearing – may well be the paradoxical nexus of his creativity. The tension is a creative tension: the paradox is 'Deleuze' as such, who is *both one* (Deleuze) *and many* (Henry and Badiou). And this paradox is 'resolved' by, or rather *creates*, different types of 'Deleuze' whose names are 'Henry' and 'Badiou' (themselves the names of philosophies that have their own impurities, despite all efforts to the contrary). Of course, paradox is central to Deleuze's thought. In *The Logic of Sense*, the productivity of paradox is affirmed, not by dissolving it through synthesis or explanation, but by means of creativity. New things are created through paradox, and one can say the same about philosophies in a metaphilosophical understanding, namely that the paradox of Deleuze creates and affirms Badiou and Henry.[2] Their lines of flight emerge out of Deleuze, head towards pure quality and pure quantity as two attractors in the phase-space of thought, only to miss their impossible destinations and fall back into Deleuze again (with the acceptance of abstraction in Henry and phenomenology in Badiou).

This movement from the One (Deleuze) to the Many (the double-life of the Deleuzes) and back again is not a qualitative movement alone – this would reduce it to Henry's hypersubjective affect or pure quality with no purchase on others; nor is it solely a quantitative one – Badiou's pure quantity of the multiple that, in any case, generates quality as a result (whether Badiou acknowledges this aspect of the event or not). The movement to Deleuzian plurality is meta-plural: it is a pluralism of *types of* plurality, quantitative and qualitative (an 'of' that is also generative of the terms it is about). It is reflexive in regard to quantity and quality, in regard to sameness and otherness, in regard to outside and inside, and in regard to concept and feeling. And this reflexivity, this turning, is neither purely (psycho-)logical nor geometrical, but both – a *moving* diagram, seen and felt simultaneously. The re-flexuous line, the Deleuzian fold, *vinculum*, or *lekton*.

This line, finally, can be given a shape: that of a Bergsonian haploid (see Figure 21) – the alternative to Agamben's spider diagram that I promised at the start, with Deleuze replacing Heidegger at the centre and the direct lines of influence becoming circuits of reciprocal determination. These circuits embody the circular logics that make Henry and Badiou circulate around both each other and a centre, 'Deleuze', that, far from being virtual and One, is replicated in their works as many and actual. Badiou and Henry *come out* of Deleuze and *push* him to extreme limits, though subsequently they are brought back together again, back into Deleuze. The regress, the circles in their thought, is not an obstacle to rigour but the means of seeing what is happening in their work. The circles also duplicate Badiou's pincers of philosophy: only they are open pincers that cannot seize anything without also changing, widening and perhaps even breaking their clasp.

Certainly, Figure 21 is a spatialisation and so a simplification; as such, it neglects the impurities of Henry and Badiou. For this reason, where we see names written on the diagram, we would prefer to have other diagrams, or the mutation of this diagram, morphing into other circles, angles, lines and other, unpredictable forms (on Badiou's side, for instance, the relations with Lyotard and Clemens might transform the haploid into a diploid).[3] A simplification is a kind of subtraction or condensation, not to an essence, but to a glimmer of understanding. But a simplification is not a falsification. Bergson himself, for instance, famously scorned the image of a time-line as a spatialisation of duration, yet he felt its threat precisely because lived-time *can* approach the state of a homogeneous line: we *can* tend to live unilinear psychic-lives. This is the rationale behind *Time and Free Will* – that a description of life could become a revision of life because descriptions are immanent to what they describe. The increasingly explicit and graphic quality of our lives indicates a real line of development in our being, one where spatiality is not just revealed in the spatial metaphors lying at the origin of language and spreading throughout it, but also in the nature of our spatialised, homogenised existence. Outside of philosophy, the power of the diagram is not always benign. In Milan Kundera's *The Unbearable Lightness of Being*, the character of Tomas bemoans our existential fate as beings without any full view of our own being. For us mortals, caught within the flow of life, we can only glimpse the barest 'outline' of being. But it is an outline with no interior: 'the sketch that is our life is a sketch for nothing, an outline with no picture'. Yet there is no need for despair. The lack of a picture, the lack of being in other words, need not licence a meontology, a sketch 'of nothing'. We can also embrace the lines of flow in their own processual lightness and actuality.[4]

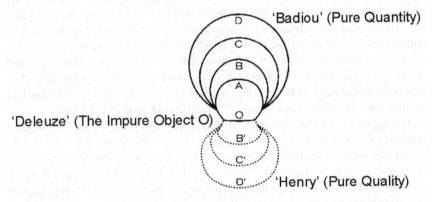

'Badiou' (Pure Quantity)

'Deleuze' (The Impure Object O)

'Henry' (Pure Quality)

Figure 21

THINKING OUTSIDE-IN

I've said that the diagram can be read as a subtractive reading of theory (in Badiou's sense). Reducing quality (though never eliminating it), the diagrammatic ensures that no particular theory is privileged and so every particular theory is affirmed equally, universally. The diagram can be as egalitarian and democratic as Badiou and Laruelle respectively see mathematics and non-philosophy. But we must consequently ask the opposed question: isn't diagrammatology ontologically reductive? Doesn't it boil everything down to 'the same'? After all, we never hesitated in pointing out when others were being reductive – Henry's philosophy embodied everything as affect and the objective is only a false aspect of life feeling itself; Badiou said that only quantitative multiplicity combines all into all, *qua* their being. These are indeed both totalising and reductive philosophies. But doesn't the diagram that connects their philosophies together not itself reduce the extreme singularity of their thought to a common essence? Is it not another totality? These philosophies *say* their point so differently, so how can *we say* that they are the same.

The answer is that we don't say anything like this. In fact, we don't *say* anything at all. All we do is *show* that the one thing these mutually exclusive philosophies do have in common is *our* ability to *see* a 'likeness' when we cannot think or say it. What they have in common is what *allows them* to be spatialised to another frame of reference. A diagram does not say that Henry = Badiou. Henry is Henry. And Badiou is Badiou. But Henry and Badiou can be transformed into each other, for the very transform-ing is its own actuality too, not *related* to the theories in their singularity but acting on them, *seeing* them in a certain way. Diagrammatology only shows that there is a *parallel* between them, in the literal sense of the term. It is just that a pure, totalising thought like Henry's or Badiou's, because it is so pure and simple, makes the process of rendition appear rather straightforward (rather than reductive) where other, more hybrid philosophies would require more intermediary translation and so much more complex diagrams (that would consequently seem less reductive). Diagrammatology is always optical, always perspectival. There never is a *real* emergent so much as a new uptake (or frame of reference) of the relationship between *relata* (that then relates them differently). Deleuze called this the 'system of reference' – how the same elements are taken up *as* nomadic, polyvocal and rhizomatic, or *as* sedentary, biunivocal and arborescent. There is never a real synthesis or emergence on the same level, but always the maintained dichotomy that is taken up (virtualised) at another level, at another scale. The diagram is not reductive of others but productive of itself.

The figure or outline, we must remember, is always to a specific frame of reference *which is itself an outline or frame*. Hence, the figure does not wholly cut its ties with the background and so reintroduce transcendence (because it is supposedly free to represent that background); it is figured to a figure (frame). And this circularity (of being a figure to a figure) is itself enframed by the diagram as it continually changes shape. The diagram is not the universal 'underneath' – a new hinter-world – but one shifting point of view (for each philosophical moment there are different frames, different diagrams, perhaps ones that are no longer diagrams at all). Still and all, when words do have little in common, there is a way in which the most general, least partial account of philosophies comes through their implicit or explicit diagrams.

Indeed, the diagram may be the ultimate form of descriptivism. Diagrams don't judge – they intervene, they depict, making a picture and then breaking it through the movement of redrawing. And yet they force their account on us, being descriptive and revisionary simultaneously through their sheer perspicuity; as Henry writes of the line: 'it is this joy, it is the feeling that life has of itself that justifies the line, its choice, its particular trace ...'.[5] But revision is not judgement. The diagram *shows and thinks* the between rather than constantly re-naming it as Deleuze and Derrida do. The problem with names (rhizome, virtual, *différance*, trace) is simply that making any one term stand for the between will invariably polarise the dispute; terms are terminals and so partisan to one end. Alternatively, if hyphenated or conflated terms are used ('desiring-machine', 'movement-image'), then the monism is established in a movement, a hyphen between meanings (rather than through one new name). But the hyphen is already a diagram. It is the diagram as an extended and contorted hyphen that keeps meaning in motion best because it is just abstract enough to allay contamination, but just concrete enough to carry meaning (though these levels of 'just enough' are not fixed, they too are enframed). Deleuzian word-combinations, by contrast, inevitably fall apart into their contradictory aggregates because, with habit, the mind hypostasises the movement between them as a new noun and, as such, a substance allied to one side or the other. This is the dilemma of the dyad. Diagrams can be substantialised too, of course, but so long as they move between icon and symbol in their form and movement, scale and texture, they can be a genuine '*entre-deux*'. A fluid representation, 'almost matter ... and almost mind', as Bergson himself once defined the philosophical image.[6]

As such, the diagram, like change, is a realised contradiction. In one respect, Parmenides was right: change *is* contradiction. Likewise, for Kant, time *is* antinomical. The inversion of Kant or Parmenides simply reverses the formulation to say that inconsistency is the mark of the Real. That is why Badiou remains a Parmenidean thinker and must see the event as inconsistency in person. But the dilemma of change mostly concerns reflective, discursive thought. Against the Real, the Virtual, or Being, as the intelligible source of contradiction, there is the actuality of change itself without need of sufficient reason (even in the form of contradictories). Diagrammatology is perhaps the only consistent mode of expression possible for an immanent thought of process because it depicts change *together* in the diagram. This is not to say that it captures process exhaustively, but that its lines and turns *are* the extremes of concrete-movement-affect (Henry) and abstract-stasis-thought (Badiou) in one moving *mise en scene* (what Lacan called a *mise en forme*). Any more iconic (thickness of line, accuracy, and granularity of detail) and the abstract is lost; any more symbolic, and the concrete is lost. But the forces acting upon us not to symbolise the diagram come from its movement even more than its iconicity. An icon is always interpretable. Without movement, the diagram would be too easily made to stand *for* something when it stands *still*. The diagram is always between the digital and analogical, conventional and natural, symbolic and iconic, as the two-in-one, because the lines ('standing for . . .') keep shifting.

The paradox of representing immanence was that of being both prescriptive and descriptive, that is, pertaining to both representation (truth as correspondence) and being (truth as novelty, process, event, or affect). Dualism and monism. This emerged in different ways in our studies of Deleuze, Henry and Badiou. Only Laruelle avoided the circle, but at perhaps too high a cost in his later work. The paradox of self-belonging is also one of being and representing (being *about* oneself). But self-belonging comes in different types – in Henry as Life and life (auto-affection), in Badiou as set and sub-set (self-membership). It is neither quality nor quantity alone, but the dynamic between the two. The diagram, as an unconventional form of representation, is a dynamic monism or dualysation – dualism and monism in movement, that is both itself and movement beyond itself in a graphical self-belonging. It perpetually perishes as it indefinitely re-draws inside and outside, immanence and transcendence.

The interminable lists of 'in betweens' that we have continually attributed to the diagram, vertiginous and nauseous, can be cast aside once we stop conventional writing and start unconventional drawing. *Do* something new, *do* something renewable. I'm willing to bet that, at *this* point in time, the best philosophical way to prove the possibility and reality of movement is not to walk away, as Bergson recommended to Zeno, but to take the line for a walk, as Paul Klee said. This optimism is not misplaced. There is no need to withdraw from philosophy altogether by letting action 'break the circle' of Parmenidean and sufficient reason, when we can enact a new kind of philosophy through drawing new kinds of circle.[7] It is through such action that we may begin to meet the challenge that immanence and process spell for thought and so forestall the drift to anti-philosophy, 'sophistry', or the 'end of philosophy'.

There may be other kinds of action, of course, other ways in which inside and outside, container and contained, are shown to have 'no precise limit', as Deleuze once wrote. The diagram is not to be fetishised as the poem or the Venn diagram has been in the past. The nature of the subject-matter that comes in to renew philosophical expression may be diagrammatic now, but it will take on totally alternative forms using different, renewable media in due course. Are we asking for a wordless philosophy, then? Not at all. There can be no *a priori* outline of the philosophical future given that the *a priori* itself has been re-integrated into experience in a special refraction or 'turning of experience' back on itself.[8] But what those experiences are is unforeseeable because experience is always multifold. This, in broad outline, is the implication of a Post-Continental understanding of philosophy: thoughts which are under conditions that are not of their own making, thoughts that are a shock to the System, thoughts that are democratised, and thoughts that are affects. Philosophy is not a sovereign state of mind, but part of a process immanent to experiences of many kinds.

When philosophers are 'generous' enough to say of literature, painting, film, architecture, science, or the Internet, that they too think, what is mostly meant is that they are capable of illustrating philosophical concepts. It is the conceptual artist's or the scientist's kinship to something called 'philosophy' that elevates his or her subject-matter to the conceptual level. What we are saying – and what a Post-Continental thought indicates – is that philosophy must take up the challenge of renewal and acknowledge the possibility that art, technology and even matter itself, at the level of its own subject-matter, in its own actuality, might be capable of forcing new philosophical thoughts onto us. With that, however, there might also come a transformation of what we mean by philosophy and even thought itself. The non-philosophical condition of thought, so-called, is not a discrete state or privileged domain, but a contingent and indefinite process. It is the process whereby *any* subject-matter can facilitate philosophical reflection, be it through folding back on itself, belonging to itself, or affecting itself. The medium or language of the process keeps changing; only the flexuous shape of the process remains constant. If we have discovered anything, it is that transcendence, that which is the outside both literally and figuratively, is multiple and relative, and comes in types that depend on one's frame of immanence. And that frame, the place where one takes a stand, is never permanent.

Notes

INTRODUCTION

1 As just a sample of this literature, see Tranoy 1964; Grene 1976; Margolis 1985; Owens 1993; Biletzki 2001; and the articles by Rosen, D'Agostini, Philipse, Ophir, Matar, and Picardi, edited by Biletzki in the *International Journal of Philosophical Studies*, Vol. 9, no. 3 (2001).

2 Papineau 1993, p.1. However, the line continues saliently 'but the aspirants to the term nevertheless disagree widely on substantial questions of philosophical doctrine'.

3 See Mulligan 1993.

4 See Mullarkey 2004.

5 Badiou 2000, p.99.

6 The philosophical school of French 'spiritualist' thought denotes something quite different from the Anglophone sense of the term, meaning an anti-reductive view of the mind rather than anything to do with spirits surviving post-mortem of the body.

7 See Alliez 1995.

8 Prusak 2000, p.108; Rockmore 1995, p.2.

9 Heidegger 1993, pp.433–435. I say 'most' because Henry, as a phenomenologist, remains guarded towards science even as he rejects Heidegger's ontology in favour of embodied thought.

10 Heidegger 1993, p.434.

11 See Lawlor 1999.

12 See Barbaras 1998.

13 Merleau-Ponty 1964, p.16. See also Merleau-Ponty 1996. This is also the reason why Jean-Luc Nancy's philosophy of immanence is not treated here: given his residual Heideggerianism, Nancy's project doesn't explore the tensions that arise from attempting to redefine transcendence *completely* in terms of immanent thought, which is the theme we have taken upon ourselves.

14 Derrida 1978, p.79.

15 For Laruelle this is more problematic: certainly, he wants to renew thought more than philosophy as it is currently practised, but this new thinking will then be as much *for* philosophy as it is for any other kind of thinking. Moreover, Laruelle never leaves philosophy for literature in this project: the call is for a heightened level of abstraction, for hyper-philosophy rather than the poetic or messianic Word.

16 See Wood 1989, p.312 on the generative role of *différance* only making sense within 'the language of transcendental causation'.

17 Badiou 1999, p.31.

18 Deleuze 1992, p.180; Deleuze and Guattari 1994, p.48. See also Kerslake 2002 and de Beistegui 2005.

19 Deleuze too projects a transcendence onto others, phenomenology in particular, only he retains the name of transcendence for this.

20 Derrida 1993a, p.13.

21 Agamben 1999, p.239.

22 This particular bet is not at all faithful to Badiou's conception of an event, which for him can never apply to philosophy itself but only to the conditions of philosophy. The problems this restricted view of the event brings to Badiou's thought will be tackled in Chapter 3.

23 The reference to 'moment' reflects the idea that twentieth-century Continental philosophy can be understood in terms of crucial moments, 1900 being the first. See Worms 2004.

24 These consequences are also being investigated in various different traditions, as can be seen in the increasing trend of practitioners in Nietzschean, Hegelian and Phenomenological circles towards a critical, non-reductive naturalism, be it in the French-speaking world by the likes of Renaud Barbaras and Natalie Depraz, or beyond by Keith Ansell Pearson, Babette Babich, John Protevi, Brian Massumi, Manuel DeLanda and David Morris. For just a sample of this work, see Babich 1995; Barbaras 1998; Ansell Pearson 1999; Depraz and Zahavi 1998; Hass and Olkowski 2000; Morris 2004; Protevi 2001; Petitot 1999; Massumi 2002; DeLanda 2002.

CHAPTER 1: DELEUZE AND THE TRAVAILS OF VIRTUAL IMMANENCE

1 *Anti-Oedipe et Mille Plateaus*: Cours Vincennes: Dualism, Monism and Multiplicities – 26/03/1973.

2 May 2004, p.67.

3 Deleuze and Guattari 1994, p.47; see also Deleuze 1990, p.308.

4 Deleuze writes of his mentor, Jean Wahl, that he wrote on 'the possibilities within empiricism for expressing its poetic, free and wild nature' (Deleuze 1994, p.311). The very same can be said of Deleuze.

5 See Deleuze 1994, pp.164, 140ff. Each faculty is borne from a peculiar violence, 'involuntary adventures', and only operates fully in that mode (Deleuze 1994, pp.143, 145). Thinking is not the natural, well-intentioned exercise of a faculty: it depends on forces to take hold of it; it is the *n*th power of thought (Deleuze 1983, p.108; see also Deleuze 1988a, p.117). A shock: 'thought is primarily trespass and violence. ... Something in the world forces us to think. This something is an object not of recognition but of a fundamental *encounter*' (Deleuze 1994, p.139).

6 Deleuze 1991b, p.87.

7 Baugh 1993, p.22 and see Deleuze 1991b, pp.103, 66, 109, 119. In his *French Hegel*, Bruce Baugh claims that the phrase 'transcendental empiricism' first appeared in

Wahl's work. But the idea of a superior empiricism goes even further back than Wahl, to Bergson, Marcel, James and, of course, Schelling.

8 Deleuze and Guattari 1987, p.146.

9 Badiou 1994, p.63.

10 Deleuze and Guattari 1994, p.40.

11 Deleuze 1990, p.91.

12 Deleuze 1973, p.91. See Deleuze and Guattari 1987, pp.75–110 and Massumi 1992, p.177. The *locus classicus* for Deleuze's rejection of objectivism (along with subjectivism) is found in *Proust and Signs*, Chapter 3, by recourse to 'essences' which 'transcend the states of subjectivity no less than the properties of the object' (p.36). Realised through involuntary memory, the Proustian essence is both real and ideal though without being either present or abstract: it is virtual (p.60). But whether the virtual is an adequate response to objectivism remains to be seen.

13 See Deleuze 1990, p.142.

14 See Deleuze and Parnet 1987, p.115. Abstract machines, or diagrams, are 'the aspect or moment at which nothing but functions and matters remain. A diagram has neither substance nor form, neither content nor expression' (Deleuze and Guattari 1987, p.141). It is not necessarily abstract in the Platonic sense of a 'transcendent, universal, eternal' idea, for it only operates within concrete assemblages, and describes their becomings, re/over/de/codings, or re/de/territorializations. But there can be a transcendent model, the idea of the Machine (Deleuze and Guattari 1987, pp.510, 512).

15 Deleuze and Guattari 1987, p.330.

16 Braidotti 1993, p.44.

17 Deleuze 1993a, p.6; Deleuze and Guattari 1987, pp.406–407; Deleuze 1990, p.22; Deleuze 1988b, p.127; Deleuze 1994, pp.183, 190. Though Deleuze makes extensive use of Bergson's images from *Matter and Memory* in his *Cinema* books, Bergson himself eventually thought that his choice of the term 'image' was a poor one.

18 Deleuze and Guattari 1984, p.2.

19 Deleuze and Guattari 1984, pp.1, 181, 288; Deleuze and Guattari 1987, p.141. An abstract machine has actually two levels of functions. An example of one such abstract machine comes from Deleuze's treatment of Foucault's work, which we may describe as the 'discipline and punish' machine. At the level of its content, there is the function of the panoptic prison where one is seen without being seen, and which works over the matter of a human multiplicity (the prisoners). At the level where this content is expressed, we have again a function, 'penal law', whose own matter is 'delinquency'. The discipline and punish machine can best be understood, then, as a giant process capturing numerous other machinic beings, living and non-living, in its net of functions (Deleuze 1988a, p.47).

20 Deleuze and Parnet 1987, p.104; Deleuze and Guattari 1986, pp.29, 39, 40, 45, 57, 82; Deleuze and Guattari 1984, p.109. Of course, this is tempered, as it nearly always is by Deleuze and Guattari, with the cautionary distinction between these machines and the merely technical machines which are only components of larger machinic assemblages; see Deleuze and Guattari 1986, p.57.

21 Eventually in *Capitalism and Schizophrenia*, the notion of 'desiring-machine' was replaced by the terminology of 'assemblages' because 'no assemblage can be characterized by one flux exclusively' (Deleuze and Parnet 1987, p.101). The move from *Anti-Oedipus* to *A Thousand Plateaus* is simultaneously more physicalist and less psychosociological: ethology replaces ethnology (Deleuze and Guattari 1987, p.328); schizophrenia expresses nomadology only at the level of *pathos* and not universally (Deleuze and Guattari 1987, p.506); and 'lines of flight' and rhizomatics take over from schizophrenia. The translator of *Negotiations* points out that 'desiring' was abandoned from *Anti-Oedipus* to *A Thousand Plateaus* due to its 'residual subjectivism' (Deleuze 1995, p.184).

22 Deleuze 1995, p.143; see Deleuze 1992, p.12, and Deleuze and Parnet 1987, pp.5, 15; Deleuze 1997, p.4. For a thorough analysis of the short essay by Deleuze, 'Immanence. A Life ...', that links together immanence, life and emanation, see Agamben 1999.

23 Deleuze and Guattari 1984, pp.44, 285–286.

24 Badiou counts ten such pairs; see Badiou 2000, pp.28–29.

25 Deleuze 1991b, p.91.

26 Deleuze and Guattari 1987, p.49; Deleuze 1990, pp.87, 103.

27 Deleuze and Guattari 1987, p.217. This problem echoes a classic one in Spinoza-interpretation: the Spinozist Attribute is defined as 'that which the intellect perceives of substance as constituting its essence'; hence, some think that attributes are not real but subjective for Spinoza. Yet Spinoza adds that 'it is in the nature of reason to perceive things truly, to wit, as they are in themselves' (*Ethics*, 2.44, Spinoza 1992, pp.31, 92); so now what is perceived rationally is objective. The analogue for Deleuzian molarity/molecularity will emerge later.

28 See Deleuze and Guattari 1984, pp.70, 280, 342. Not that all reductionism is a demotion solely in scale – economic reductionism, Platonist reductionism and structuralist reductionism would be obvious counter-examples; but in Deleuze's case, his materialist language and sporadic anti-molar analyses do invite micro-reductionism.

29 See Deleuze and Guattari 1984, pp.42–43; Deleuze and Guattari 1987, p.33; Deleuze 1988a, p.84. Massumi 1992, p.64 writes as follows: 'Stability is always actually metastability, a controlled state of volatility. No body can really *be* molar. Bodies are *made* molar, with varying degrees of success.' But Deleuze and Guattari (1984, p.340) continue: 'At times we contrasted the molar and the molecular as the paranoiac, signifying, and structured lines of integration, and the schizophrenic, machinic, and dispersed lines of escape; or again as the staking out of perverse reterritorializations, and as the movement of the schizophrenic deterritorializations. At other times, on the contrary, we contrasted them as two major types of equally social investments: the one sedentary and biunivocalizing, and of a reactionary or fascist tendency; the other nomadic and polyvocal, and of a revolutionary tendency. ... And why are there two types of social investment ...? The answer is that everywhere there exist the molecular *and* the molar.'

30 Bogue 1989, pp.104–105.

31 Deleuze and Guattari 1987, p.54. Compare this tempered view of deterritoriali-

sation in *A Thousand Plateaus* with the last passage from *Anti-Oedipus* (p.382): 'We'll never go too far with the deterritorialization ... this process that is always and already complete as it proceeds, and as long as it proceeds.'

32 Deleuze 1986, pp.92, 80; see also p.84.

33 Deleuze and Guattari 1987, p.275.

34 Irigaray 1985, p.141.

35 Grosz 1994, p.189. Deleuze's attraction to writers like D.H. Lawrence and Henry Miller cannot have helped their cause with feminism, nor for that matter the reading of anorexia as a positive act of becoming a body without organs (see Deleuze and Parnet 1987, pp.43, 90, 110).

36 Deleuze and Guattari 1987, pp.275–276.

37 See Buchanan and Colebrook 2000. See also Colebrook 2004.

38 Deleuze and Guattari 1987, p.276; Deleuze and Guattari 1994, p.20; see Deleuze 1995, p.149.

39 Deleuze and Guattari 1994, pp.209–210.

40 Deleuze 1993a, pp.112, 8.

41 See Deleuze 1993a, p.115.

42 This is why François Wahl is right to contrast Deleuze with Badiou by nominating the former as descriptive and the latter as foundational in their styles: see Wahl 1992, p.10.

43 Massumi 1992, p.106; Deleuze and Guattari 1987, p.335. Indeed, a molar form can be generated by two types of molecular force that themselves have properties normally associated with the molar: covalent, arborescent, mechanical, linear, localizable relations ... or indirect, noncovalent, machinic and nonmechanical, superlinear, nonlocalizable bonds' (Deleuze and Guattari 1987, p.335).

44 Deleuze and Guattari 1987, p.33.

45 Deleuze and Guattari 1987, pp.36, 502.

46 Deleuze 1994, p.183.

47 Žižek 2003, p.3.

48 See de Beistegui 2004, p.16, who views Deleuze's project, like Heidegger's, as an attempt to renew 'ontology at the end of metaphysics'. Though this is not a 'fundamental' ontology (p.22) – it leaves room for empiricism and science. See also Leclercq 2003, p.188 on the Deleuzian project of creating 'transcendental being'.

49 de Beistigui 2004, p.21.

50 Deleuze 1994, p.36.

51 Massumi 2002, p.38, argues against seeing transcendence and immanence spatially, and that, through the 'productive paradox' that puts them together (as either 'an infinite interiority or a parallelism of mutual exteriorities'), one must think beyond the contradiction.

52 Henry 1973, p.42.

53 Williams 2005, p.78; see also May 2004, p.72.

54 See Ansell Pearson 2002; DeLanda 2002; and Massumi 2002.

55 Though 'the virtual' appears in a number of recent Anglophone dictionaries on Deleuze, it is noteworthy that it has no entry in either *Le Vocabulaire de Bergson* (Worms 2000) or *Le Vocabulaire de Gilles Deleuze* (Sasso and Villani 2003).

56 Deleuze 1994, p.208; Deleuze 2002, p.148.

57 See Ansell Pearson 2002, pp.171ff.

58 Ansell Pearson 1999, pp.37, 38.

59 Williams 2003, pp.11, 7, 13. It should be stated that Williams is here writing directly of Deleuze's handling of the actual and the virtual, rather than of his appropriation of the terms from Bergson. As excellent a reading of Deleuze as his work is, Williams' interpretation still illustrates the one-sided value given to the virtual, despite its more even-handed provenance in Bergson's work.

60 See Ansell Pearson 1999, p.87.

61 Massumi 2002, p.15 talks of pastness as the 'condition of emergence for determinate memory' but also as the condition of the present (with which it is contemporaneous) and contemporary with a 'futurity' that allows us to understand tendency as futureness.

62 See Parr 2005, p.297. This is the definition of the virtual most prevalent in Deleuze's cinema books, especially *Cinema 2: The Time-Image* (Deleuze 1989) – there are others. The past is certainly how Badiou reads Deleuze's virtual: see Badiou 2006, p.404.

63 As Sartre previously said of Bergson's virtual, if it already has perfect existence, why does it need to actualise itself? See Sartre 1962, pp.46ff.

64 Deleuze 1994, p.79.

65 See my *Bergson and Philosophy* (Mullarkey 2000), Chapters 2 and 8 for more on this.

66 See Smith 1994, pp. 180–194, who argues that this regress can be infinite and benign.

67 As Jean-Louis Vieillard-Baron notes, 'il use fréquemment d'images empruntées à la geometrie, comme la rotation ou la projection, ou à l'optique comme la réflexion et la réfraction; et, on ne comprend rien à sa pensée si l'on prend ces images en un sens vague et banal' (Vieillard-Baron 1993, p.23).

68 Gunter 2007.

69 See Deleuze 1998b, p.72.

70 See in Deleuze and Parnet 2002, p.148.

71 See Bergson 1946, pp.130–158. When writing for or against the power of the past one must be aware that most Virtualists use the Bergsonian term 'the past in general', which has important distinguishing features. For this notion, see Bergson 1975, pp.134–185.

72 Ansell Pearson (1999, pp.70–71) takes the Virtualist line against Bachelard to show how a continuity with the past does not undo novelty.

73 See Bergson 1911, p.30; see also 'pure heterogeneity' at Bergson 1910, p.104; '*moving continuity*' at Bergson 1988, p.260.

74 Lawlor 2004, p.27. Lawlor reads the 'past in general' in the light of the phenomenological notion of an immemorial past or a past that was never present. It is again Deleuze who points towards this reading: Deleuze 1994, p.83: 'all the levels and degrees coexist and present themselves for our choice on the basis of a past which was never present'. For my treatment of it as still belonging to a false reading of Bergson see Mullarkey 2005. It must be remembered that, for Lawlor, Bergson prefigures Heidegger in his critique of the present (see Lawlor 2002b, p.28); this reading moves too far into the retrospective light of Heideggerian phenomenology.

75 In *Bergsonism* (Deleuze 1991a, pp.110–111), actualisation is a 'genuine creation' because it involves the creation of 'divergent lines' with 'dissimilar means' – and the directions of these lines are not ready-made, but created '"along with" the act running through them'. But if they are *so unrelated*, how exactly are they related?

76 Massumi 2002, p.200.

77 See Whitehead 1978, pp.22–23. That Whitehead's own Actualism (of actual occasions in perpetual becoming) is supported by eternal objects rather than the positive regress of other types of change (wherein logic and world unite by materialising the regress), shows how even a process thinker as rigorous as Whitehead tempers his views in order to save a certain kind of logic.

78 In fact, in the second chapter of *Matter and Memory* Bergson gives just such a doubled depiction in a quite different diagrammatisation of our temporal experience. We will examine this further in Chapter 5.

79 Deleuze 1973, p.17; Deleuze 1994, p.276, see also p. 284.

80 Guattari 1984, p.128.

81 Deleuze 1995, p.141.

82 Deleuze 1988b, p.63.

83 Deleuze 1990, pp.1, 5. See also p.75: 'The paradoxes of sense are essentially that of the *subdivision ad infinitum* (always past-future and never present), and that of *nomadic distribution* (distributing in an open space instead of distributing in a closed space)'.

84 Deleuze 1990, p.63. In *Cinema 2* (Deleuze 1989, p.81) what allows us to see this eternally split time directly is called the 'crystal-image' (Guattari's idea), but also a 'ritornello' or 'refrain' (p.92 – see also Deleuze and Guattari 1987, p.348).

85 Deleuze 1983, p.108; Deleuze and Guattari 1987, p.313; Deleuze and Guattari 1994, p.90; Deleuze and Guattari 1987, p.153. See also Deleuze and Guattari 1987, pp.503, 512.

86 Badiou 2000, p.33. Laruelle's critique of Deleuze, as we will see in Chapter 4, rests entirely on its dyadic structure.

87 Laruelle 1995b, p.56.

88 Evidence of indefinites ('dynamic definitions' in Bergson 1911, pp.89, 90, 111–112) are throughout Bergson. Reality, says Bergson, is neither finite nor infinite but 'indefinite'. See Bergson 1946, p.211; Bergson 1977, p.296. The 'Indefinite' occurs sixty-three times in *Creative Evolution* alone and forty-nine times in *The Creative Mind*.

89 Deleuze's use of the indefinite tends to remain too close to its linguistic origins, using the indefinite article, as in '*a* life', to make a point against subjectivity and even to link it to the event as an infinitive: see Deleuze 1997, p.5. For two other rather ill-matched treatments of the indefinite in Deleuze, see Deleuze 1993a, p.43 where it is taken logically, and Deleuze and Parnet 2002, p.148, where it is taken cosmologically.

90 Dummett 1977, p.32.

91 Deleuze 1994, p.67; Deleuze 1993a pp.42–43. See also Deleuze 1994, p.91 on layers or orders of time, or series upon series, defined by the task of remembering what a lower order forgets.

92 As Massumi points out, Prigogine and Stengers too would allow the virtual 'its own contractions'; hence, there is no unified field; whereas Deleuze sees it as 'neutral, sterile, impassive, eternal', and posits a matter-energy monism; see Massumi 1992, p.169.

93 Deleuze 1990, pp.28, 29, 36.

94 Deleuze 1990, p.40.

95 This proliferation or regress should be endless. There are thresholds, but none is higher or lower: 'Each individual is also himself composed of individuals of a lower order and enters into the composition of individuals of a higher order', see Deleuze and Guattari 1986, p.41. Yet Deleuze can also talk of 'simple animals' with only three affects (the tick): see Deleuze 1988b, pp.59, 60.

96 Ansell Pearson 2001, p.234.

97 See Deleuze 1989, p.172.

98 Deleuze 1998a, pp.134, 135.

99 Divorcing emergence – in Deleuze's languages, 'actualisation', 'expression', different/ciation, 'unfolding' – from emanation is as vital as is divorcing the virtual from the possible: emanation still has a 'minimal transcendence' to it that a rigorous theory of immanence cannot tolerate. It still concerns a relationship of *likeness*: see Deleuze 1992, p.180. Whether the other relations still avoid an ontological reduction is an open matter, however.

100 See Deleuze and Guattari 1984, pp.26–27; Deleuze 1986, p.56.

101 This phrase is an allusion to Laruelle. See Laruelle 1999b, p.141.

102 See Nietzsche 1974, no. 276; *Philosophical Investigations*, §124. See also 'We must do away with all *explanation*, and description alone must take its place' (§109), or 'Philosophy just states things and does neither explain them nor deduce anything from them. – Since everything lies open to view, there is nothing to explain' (§126), and so on; see Wittgenstein 1967, pp.49, 47, 50.

103 To show, for instance, that all films are about the body with illustrations taken from the work of David Cronenberg verges on question begging. To illustrate the argument with films by Woody Allen would be more impressive. See Shaviro 1993.

104 Deleuze and Guattari 1987, p.95.

105 Deleuze 1983, p.61.

106 Deleuze 1983, pp.123, 124.

107 But this is the Deleuze of his Hume days, before he rediscovered Substance through Spinoza. The Humean idea that relations are external is precisely the opposite of Spinozist 'capacity': the latter is only epistemically sceptical about power ('you don't *know* until you try') where Hume is more ontologically sure: 'power', 'force', etc. are meaningless terms.

108 Badiou (1998, p.68) turns around the Nietzsche quote – 'become that which you are' to 'you are only that which you become' – thus inverting the Deleuzian formula as well.

109 Descombes 1980, p.180.

110 Deleuze 1992, pp.258, 225, 102. Before consigning Deleuze's reading of Spinoza to the same problematic as that of his reading of Nietzsche (making power or force a

rightful potential), it ought to be noted that Deleuze describes *potentia* as completely 'act, active, actual' (ibid., 97): but he then immediately depicts action itself as a 'capacity for being affected … constantly and necessarily filled by affections that realize it': hence, 'potentia' has simply been replaced by the equally offending 'capacity'. These problems might be resolved at least for Spinoza by realizing that his notion of substance does not stand alone separate from its modes, in that the expressed and expression are one and the same. Thus, the action and what is activated are not distinct. Still, there does remain some sort of difference between the two and a further difference between the expressed (or what is activated) and substance itself. Substance (singular) with its modes simply reiterates (or foreshadows) the problems of the virtual and the actual too well.

111 May 1994, pp. 38, 49.

112 May 1991, pp. 24–35: pp. 24, 28. See also Zourabichvili 1998, pp. 335–357.

113 Badiou 2000, p. 97.

114 Deleuze 1990, p. 149; Deleuze and Guattari 1987, p. 203. See John Protevi's *Political Physics* (2001). Protevi uses the Deleuzian concepts of stratification and networking to naturalise political ideas such as servitude and freedom.

115 Massumi 2002, pp. 11, 1. Compare the identical statements in the opening of Bergson's *Matter and Memory*. Almost automatically, however, Bergson is invoked as the philosopher of the virtual: Massumi 2002, p. 31.

116 Massumi 2002, pp. 3, 5 (second emphasis mine). He defines emotion (p. 28) as 'a subjective content, the sociolinguistic fixing of an experience which is from that point onward defined as personal. Emotion is qualified intensity, the conventional, consensual point of insertion of intensity into semantically and semiotically formed progressions …'. Other purities loom large too: 'pure relationality of process'; the virtual 'whose reality is that of potential, pure relationality' (p. 58). Also the 'space of sheer transformation', 'relationality in itself, freed from its terms' (p. 51).

117 Massumi 2002, pp. 7, 9. He calls the issue of potential the problem of 'the void' (for his 'next project', p. 21).

118 Massumi 2002, p. 33.

119 Massumi 2002, pp. 57, 58, 62. And at this point, we must ask how this thought could ever be called Bergsonian. Manuel DeLanda also faces the same dilemma of the empirical and the superempirical, describing Deleuzian difference as a Kantian noumenon that is nonetheless *not* beyond 'human knowledge', that is, a completely unKantian use of the term. See DeLanda 1999, p. 31. He is following Deleuze (Deleuze 1994, p. 222), who states that difference is not given but is that by which 'diversity' is given.

120 Massumi 2002, p. 217.

121 Massumi 2002, p. 215.

122 Massumi 2002, p. 216.

123 Deleuze 1990, p. 261; Deleuze 1994, p. 222.

124 Bergson 1988, p. 206. It is reflection that clarifies resemblance into the general idea as memory narrows it into the perception of the individual. This clarification, this narrowing, is formed through refraction, in this case the dissociation of a hybrid mix (or earlier refraction) of difference and repetition into two respective purities, that

is, of pure difference and pure repetition. The primal perception underlying this, in contrast, is a 'discernment of the useful' without need of abstraction. The similarity with which we begin this work of discernment is not the same as the similarity the mind arrives at when it consciously generalises (pp. 208–209). The first is a similarity 'felt and lived', which seizes us through our bodily interests (p. 208). It is a bodily recognition. The second is a thought-concept that is as interested in the similarity it sees as it is in the difference that this implies.

125   That is why Deleuze is wrong to look to the past or memory as the basis for a 'new monism' in Bergson (Deleuze 1991a, p. 74) – it stems from affect and movement (as Massumi reflects) and the new monism, in any case, is a meta-monism or dynamic monism that generates plurality.

126   Massumi 2002, p. 220.

127   Bergson 1988, pp. 206, 207: 'Hydrochloric acid always acts in the same way upon carbonate of lime whether in the form of marble or of chalk yet we do not say that the acid perceives in the various species the characteristic features of the genus.' Perhaps Massumi *would* say that the two sense each other.

128   There are other ways of reading Deleuze's internal tension: James Williams reads these tendencies as follows: 'He can be interpreted – either sympathetically or not – as depending on a strong materialism that brings him close to positions in contemporary science, thereby devaluing his work on Ideas in *Difference and Repetition*. Or he can be interpreted as over-emphasising a new Ideal and virtual field at the expense of the actual, thereby leading to accusations of an anti-Platonism that merely replicates its biggest fault, instead of inverting or correcting it' (Williams 2005, pp. 78–79).

129   Badiou's theory of the event, where novelty does *appear* in a situation, is wholly accounted for by his mathematical ontology, that is, the event's possibility is ontological, whereas its appearance in a world is only phenomenological. For Deleuze, the actualisation process is centrally ontological – the virtual is its actualisation. The paradox of this asserted identity is also the Deleuzian dilemma.

130   Deleuze and Guattari 1987, p. 34.

131   It is the frame of reference that sees and defines the 'indefinite' (smooth–striated, time–movement, rhizome–tree) as either one or the other, smooth or striated, time- or movement-image, and so on, in a perception always 'finer' than one's own, a perception that Deleuze believes is even capable of perceiving the so-called imperceptible (see Deleuze and Guattari 1987, p. 287).

132   See Deleuze 1989, p. 280.

133   Deleuze 1993b. See also Alliez 2005, p. 106.

CHAPTER 2: HENRY AND THE AFFECTS OF ACTUAL IMMANENCE

1   Henry 1988, p. 91.

2   See Deleuze 1993a, pp. 41–43.

3   While Deleuze allows that Leibniz's Principle of Sufficient Reason entails that everything has a concept, he adds that 'the concept is not a simple logical being, but a metaphysical being' (Deleuze 1993a, p. 42).

4 See Derrida 2005.

5 Henry 1990, pp.44, 45.

6 Admittedly, in various guises, as Heidegger's being is also an event and Merleau-Ponty's Flesh is also a style of behaviour.

7 The paradox generated in the use here of the term 'appear' with regard to phenomena will be an issue that will return.

8 Henry 1973, p.324; Henry 2003a, p.159; Henry 2003b, p.104.

9 Henry 1973, pp.453, 478; Henry 1993, p.7.

10 See Deleuze and Guattari 1987, p.506.

11 Susan Emanuel, the translator of *I am the Truth*, tells us (p.ix) that Henry uses *pathos* and *pathétique* according to Greek etymology, that is, as 'anything that befalls one' or 'what one has suffered, one's experience', or 'any passive state or condition'. See too Henry 2000, p.237: 'Suffering and joy are the fruits of life'. There is an 'ineffable happiness of the ordeal and of living'.

12 Henry 1990, pp.171, 172; Henry 1973, pp.70–71, 84.

13 Henry 1990, pp.11, 54. Henry's own early thesis, *Le Bonheur de Spinoza*, already sketches the important influence Spinoza will have on his thought.

14 Henry 1973, pp.230, 231; Henry 1990, p.26. Henry, as a good empiricist, then, defines the horizon as a privation of the actual.

15 Henry 1973, pp.191–193, 364ff, 668.

16 Henry 1990, p.80; Henry 1973, pp.486–487. See also p.485: 'every tonality … is … an understanding tonality'; 'affectivity does not consist of an ensemble of modifications or subjective qualities of themselves opaque, irrational, inexpressible … consequentially deprived of "sense" …'; 'because in itself affectivity is understanding …'.

17 Henry 1975, p.186; Henry 1988, pp.102, 120–121. See also Henry 1990, p.177: The 'mystery' of life is that the living is 'coextensive' with the Whole of life in it, that all in it is its own life. The living is not self-founding – it has a 'Fond' which is life, but this Fond is not different from it.

18 Henry 1993, p.62.

19 Henry 1993, p.63. 'Actuality' is the translator's rendering of '*effectivité*' in the French (linked to *affectivité*) which we regard as wholly appropriate.

20 Henry 1993, p.321. See also Henry 1973, pp.471–472: 'the "already" of the Being-given of feeling does not concern the past of feeling or anything which presents itself as already there to the power which discovers it. It concerns this power itself, its Being here and now given to itself … that feeling be always already given to itself …'.

21 Henry 1975, p.119; Henry 1990, p.38: indeed 'the condition of experience is no more than a "source" posited by reflective thought' that Henry also calls 'virtual'.

22 Henry 1973, p.64. Given that genesis is arguably the basic problem of phenomenology (see Lawlor 2002b, pp.11–23) this neglect makes Henry's heresy even clearer.

23 Henry 1973, pp.288, 296; Henry 1993, p.294.

24 Henry 1993, pp.20, 21, 29. Henry quotes Descartes saying (in *The Passions of the Soul*) that 'all our perceptions … are indeed passions'.

25 Henry 1973, p.727, Henry 2000, p.227.

26 Janicaud 2000, p.31.

27 Henry 2003a, p.50.

28 Henry 2003a, p.247; Henry 1990, p.176. Also Henry 1990, p.9: it is reflexive life (what refers [se refere] to nothing but itself) which makes any intersubjectivity possible – and this appears less paradoxical when one understands that it is in the experience of a radically immanent subjectivity that life comes [parvient] to itself. *Ego and alter ego have a common birth and can only communicate on account of both being alive.*

29 On Henry and Bergson, see Yamagata 1999. On Henry and Levinas, see Forthomme 1986; and Guillmard 1999.

30 Henry 1990, pp.25–26, 107. The prevalent use of reflexive verbs by Henry is not just a peculiarity of his mother tongue but highly motivated in philosophical terms: see Henry 2003b, p.109n1.

31 See Deleuze 1986, p.56 and Deleuze 1990, pp.307–310.

32 Henry 1973, p.265.

33 Henry 1990, pp.5, 6; Henry 2003b, p.100; Henry 1973, p.233.

34 See Badiou 2005d, pp.153–154 on Hegel and Henry on manifestation. This is one of the few places where Badiou mentions Henry by name.

35 Henry cites *Being and Time* section 7 approvingly: there is a relation between the object and the method of phenomenology. But Heidegger gets this immanence wrong, making it an identity when in fact it is a self-relation, or non-logical reflexivity. See Henry 1990, pp.112, 117.

36 Henry 1990, pp.128, 129.

37 See Hallward 2003b, pp.22–23; Henry 1973, p.45.

38 Henry 1990, pp.58, 27–28. For a critical analysis of Henry on Husserl, see Kelly 2004 and Choplin 1997, pp.33–49.

39 Henry 1990, p.16. Henry prefers to think of such sensibles (or 'primary contents' in the language of Husserl's *Logical Investigations*) as '*impressional*', as '*affective et volitive*', where 'pulsions' play a large role. In lived affects, their 'radical immanence' is their impressional quality as such, excluding all transcendence from itself. See Henry 1990, p.20. For Derrida's similar use of the '*anarchy* of the noema' against Husserl, see Derrida 1978, p.163.

40 Henry 1973, p.464: 'this is why the proposition such as "I feel in me a great love" or "a profound boredom" is equivocation at its highest degree. For there is not, there never is, as far as love or boredom is concerned, something like the power of feeling different from them which would be "commissioned" to receive them, namely, to feel them as an opposed or foreign content. *Rather, it is love or boredom, it is the feeling itself which receives itself and experiences itself in such a way that this capacity for receiving itself, for experiencing itself, of being affected by self, constitutes what is affective in it, this is what makes it a feeling.*' The Deleuzian idea of an 'intensive magnitude' could not be further from Henry's understanding of affect: yet their theories of affect do overlap in many other ways (in being non-representational, for instance).

41 See Tillette 1980, pp.633–651.

42 Henry 1973, p.473.

43 Henry 1990, pp.64, 67, 98, 100; Henry 2000, p.84. However, Janicaud argues that Husserl too, in texts like the *Crisis*, moves phenomenology away from the essentialism where Henry wants to pigeonhole it. Whether either Henry or Derrida are fair to Husserl's notion of the present is a moot point, but we won't enter that debate here. For instance, as Prusak writes: 'whereas Derrida reads Husserl as a prisoner of the metaphysics of presence … Marion reads Husserl as showing the way out of the metaphysics of presence and thus beyond deconstruction' (Prusak 2000, p.9). For close readings of Husserl and Derrida on auto-affection, see Lawlor 2002b and Tereda 2001.

44 See Derrida 1973 and Derrida 1978, pp.154–168, for the classic expositions of his critique of Husserl.

45 Henry 1990, p.8; Henry 2000, p.230; Henry 1973, pp.187–190.

46 For instance: Henry 1990, p.30: 'The more the analysis regresses towards archaic forms of constitution, the more this material element calls out to it and constrains it.'

47 Henry 2003a, pp.56, 62. For more on Henry's notion of movement, see Yamagata 2000. For a critique, see Bernet 1999, p.341n10.

48 Henry 2003b, pp.101, 102, 103; Henry 1973, p.35; Henry 1990, pp.117, 118. Janicaud argues that Henry is unjust to Heidegger: reducing his ek-static to the worldly or visible, even as Heidegger himself questions 'bringing to sight' in certain texts like the Zähringen seminars (though in fact Henry cites these too). See Janicaud 2000, p.83. See also McNeill 1999.

49 Henry 2003a, p.55.

50 On this relation, see Zahavi 1999, p.227; see also Radcliffe 2002 comparing Nagel to Husserl.

51 Henry 1990, p.164.

52 Henry 1990, pp.7, 127. Henry cites Didier Franck approvingly on Heidegger's inability to account for his ontological categories, and Henry says that the life he regionalises is *biological* life.

53 Hence also, a critique of Henry from the position of any anti-privacy argument becomes problematic. For Wittgenstein, most famously, the depth grammar of a 'pin in box' is not same as a 'pain in knee': it's behavioural. Hence, *Philosophical Investigations*, §303, famously asks after the sense of saying that I *know* I am in pain (Wittgenstein 1967, p.102). But Henry never says we can *conceptualise* interior 'states', for that notion of knowing that comes *after* affect already introduces the gap between self and affect that begs the question and makes the anti-privacy argument possible. On this front, Wittgenstein's anti-privacy argument is linked to Hume's argument against the intrinsic connection between cause and effect because both desiccate the processes they are trying to explain (away) into states. Hume makes cause discrete from effect and so cannot find a way to reconnect them. Likewise, Wittgenstein can't see how a memory of an internal language rule could be retained or remembered. Both analyse mind into parts and find trouble in trying to recombine them.

54 Merleau-Ponty 1962, pp.xvi, 327, 426, 430; Merleau-Ponty 1963, p.169.

55 Henry 1973, pp.376, 377, 394, 260n.

56 Henry 2003b, p.108. For a defence of Merleau-Ponty against Henry's reading, see Barbaras 1998, pp.137–155.

57 See Zaner 1971, pp.204–206.

58 Henry 1973, p.326.

59 There is an 'original body' presupposed by this constituted body, an original body that always assumes the ultimate donation – one with this sensibility of 'I can'. It is this body which enables my experience of the world, and of others, not a body for *my* sensibility but my sensibility itself: see Henry 1990, p.149.

60 Henry 2003b, p.105; Henry 1975, p.142 ('thought is affective'); Henry 1990, p.170; Henry 1975, pp.73, 82, 83.

61 The unity of the body is not a transcendent unity, but the unity of the power which moves the different parts of organic space (Henry 1975, p.124). Henry cites (p.182n) a commentator who notes a 'transcendent empiricism' in Maine de Biran, but Henry rejects this: Maine de Biran's is an 'internal transcendental experience', neither empirical nor transcendent.

62 See Žižek 2002, p.263n10.

63 See Lawlor 2002a pp.62, 63; Barbaras 1998, pp.15ff.

64 Henry 1973, p.506.

65 Janicaud 2000, p.73. See also Valdinoci 2001, p.224n on tautology in Henry.

66 Henry 1993, p.26. Henry 1990, pp.58–59: we are no longer talking about 'the laws of the world and of thought, but the laws of Life'. See also Henry 1973, p.252: '*The structure of reason is the structure of phenomenality. Because it is the structure of phenomenality, the structure of reason is a phenomenological structure.*'

67 Henry 1973, pp.666–667.

68 Henry 1973, p.492.

69 Henry 1973, pp.559 (my italics), 618.

70 In Damasio's case, it would most likely be his use of neurological correlates to locate conscious affect in a 'core' that Henry would object to first (in a long list of objections).

71 Henry 2003b, p.106: 'If our various tonalities find their ultimate possibility in the essence of life, it follows in the first instance that they can never be explained solely from the worldly events that we interpret as their "motives" or "causes".' An event can cause suffering only in a being capable of suffering.

72 Henry 1990, pp.111, 173.

73 Henry 1993, p.297.

74 Henry 1973, p.547.

75 *Tractatus Logico-Philosophicus*, 6.43 (Wittgenstein 1961, p.72).

76 Badiou's theory of the subject is also one of 'uptake', which is another name for the process by which fidelity constitutes a subject: see Badiou 2005a, p.406: 'It is abusive to say that the truth is a subjective production. A subject is much rather *taken up* in fidelity to the event, and *suspended* from truth, from which it is forever separated by chance.'

77 Wittgenstein 1994, p.137.

78 See Henry 1988, p.219.

79 Hence, the similarities between Henry's *Essence of Manifestation* and Bergson's most Actualist text, *Time and Free Will*, which connects process directly to the flow of consciousness (as does *The Essence of Manifestation,* Henry 1973, pp.364ff). See also the similarities between the latter's critique of psychophysics and the following in Henry 1973: pp.464, 498–99.

80 Henry 1990, pp.12, 123. For two views that say that Henry can only but fail to think his own philosophy, see Kelly 2004, and Depraz, Varela, and Vermesch 2003, p.70.

81 Henry 1973, pp.158, 152, 160, 10.

82 According to Prusak (Prusak 2000, p.5).

83 Henry 1993, p.10.

84 Henry 1973, p.42.

85 Henry 1973, pp.42, 43, 291.

86 *Ethics*, 3.6 (Spinoza 1992, p.108). When writing about error, Henry refers to adequacy a number of times at Henry 1973, pp.567, 568.

87 Henry 1973, p.576. The circularity of this explanation will be addressed soon.

88 See Critchley 1992.

89 Henry 1990, p.131: 'All Speech is the speech/word [*parole*] of life.' 'Parole de la vie' is the pathetic auto-revelation of the absolute subjectivity which is the Saying [*dire*]. Language is the language of real life. It is in this sense firstly that the logos can be true and that, in a certain manner, *it always is true*. The word is not in Greek (in the sense of a 'view'), but the arrival of the world itself as such.

90 Henry 1973, pp.299, 544.

91 Henry 1973, pp.661, 684.

92 Henry 2000, pp.218, 219.

93 And so the explanation of error as 'badly understood feelings' need not be circular if we understand 'badly understood' here to mean an inadequate level of pathos-thought.

94 Henry 1993, p.xiv.

95 See Henry 1987. 'Virtual reality' in particular (in contrast to Virtualism as such) is just the latest phase of this making-visible (though perhaps the most sophisticated yet, in as much as it pretends to depict the virtual as reality and not representation).

96 Henry 2003b, p.103; Henry 1988, pp.33, 32, 236, 219. Also p.29: the pure abstraction of Mondrian and Malevitch makes the object disappear altogether, and yet, coming from geometry, it too still belongs to the world. Following a kind of 'transcendental' light (p.30).

97 Henry 1988, p.37.

98 Henry 1983, pp.306, 116, 240, 244, 212, 193. And these different kinds of work 'find their *actuality*, precisely, in the irreducible, unrepresentable, and indefinable subjectivity of the absolute monad': (p.194).

99 Henry 1983, p.13: 'the concepts upon which the analysis in *Capital* is based are exclusively philosophical concepts, and in a radical sense as *ontological concepts*.'

100 As he doesn't tackle the issue directly, it would be interesting to know Henry's attitude to the theory of *immaterial* labour that places art and research, for example,

at the intersection between economic production and consumption: see Lazzarato 1996.

101 Henry 1983, pp.297, 298, 300.

102 Deleuze and Guattari 1987, p.40.

103 See Lambert 2005; see also Sellars 1999.

104 Bergson 1977, p.208.

105 See Valdinoci 2001, p.244. For Henry's important references to Fichte, see Henry 1973, pp.66, 79, 303, 409.

106 Henry 2003b, p.107.

107 Henry 1973, pp.268, 269.

108 This divinity seems to fall into the world from the virtual; incarnation understood as condescension, a product rather than a process. For Henry's complex notion of incarnation and its relation to his Spinozism, see Longneaux 2004, Chapter 4.

109 Henry 1990, pp.8, 176.

110 Whitehead 1978, p.80. For supermole, Whitehead would say 'subject-superject'.

111 Henry 1973, p.621.

112 Henry 1973 p.502: See also pp.498–499: 'Certainly feeling cannot be reduced to sensation nor enclosed in it: Sensation passes and feeling endures, sensation is simple and superficial whereas feeling is complex and always has a certain depth. But sensation, even though it is called simple, furtive, etc., the isolated sensation is but an abstraction which is never realized even in the abstract conditions of the laboratory.'

113 Henry 2003b, p.103; Henry 1973, p.519.

114 Massumi 2002, pp.13, 14.

115 Massumi 2002, p.1.

116 In *The Essence of Manifestation*, Henry distances himself from the idea of levels of affectivity, as found in the work of Max Scheler, for instance (Henry 1973, p.674n), but this has more to do with a hierarchisation of more or less authentic/fundamental levels of affect – anathema to Henry – rather than a rejection of the very notion of internal structure.

117 As regards the return of affect, even in post-structuralism, see Terada 2001: as she writes (p.3): '[Poststructuralism] has reason to stress emotive experience, for far from controverting the "death of the subject", emotion entails this death'.

CHAPTER 3: ALAIN BADIOU: THE UNIVERSAL QUANTIFIER

1 Badiou 2005a, p.423.

2 Badiou 2005a, p.123. Nature is understood in these ontologies, not as objectivity nor even the given, but as the gift, the mysterious gesture of opening, and this is Badiou's primary complaint against them.

3 Feltham 2005, p.xxiv: 'set theory ontology may be said to be an ontology of immanence, retaining being *within* its inscriptions'.

4 Brassier and Toscano 2004, p.21, describe his work as an 'anti-naturalist materialism'.

5   Badiou 2005a, p.124; Badiou 2004a, p.64. This is the crucial difference between Number and numbers, the true ontological difference.

6   Hallward 2003b, p.19.

7   Badiou 2003a, p.165. The essence of science, for Badiou, is the matheme. This identification will come to haunt Badiou's attempts to secure his philosophy from itself being reduced to its scientific condition.

8   Badiou 2005a, p.28.

9   Badiou 2003a, pp.14, 19; Badiou 2005a, p.9, 10.

10 The mathematisation of the real is not a quantification, statistical averaging, numerisation (in the normal sense), says Hallward (Hallward 2003a, p.78): true, but it is a homogenisation – a making same – and quantification does not lead to (the paradoxes of) *pure* quantity. Badiou 1999, p.105: in Badiou's system, pure quantity is termed the 'power' of a set.

11 Wahl 1992, p.30.

12 Brassier and Toscano 2004, pp.6, 15. They refer to this outside as indicative of Badiou's materialist stance (p.6). See also Feltham 2005, p.xxvii.

13 See Hallward 2003a, pp.181–182.

14 Badiou 2005a, p.xi.

15 Badiou 2003a, p.50; Balibar 2004, p.30; Badiou 2005a, p.250. See Feltham and Clemens 2003, p.10: it is irrelevant if what is presented is physical or mental, possible, actual or virtual, a thing or a predicate. For Badiou, there is no unity, no 'unified totality' (no intension), just multiples of multiples.

16 Badiou 2005a, p.8.

17 Feltham 2005, p.xxiv. It is said that the rise of category theory over set theory as the foundation of mathematics may render *Being and Event* redundant – see Meillassoux 2002; and Brassier and Toscano 2004, p.4, on Badiou's principle of continual amendments, though always within 'basic axiomatic coordinates'. We will look at this issue of foundations in Chapter 5.

18 Badiou 2004a, pp.3, 4; Badiou 2003a, p.21: The translation of set theoretical terms into philosophy – situation, presentation – is *meta-ontological* rather than ontological proper.

19 Badiou 2005a, pp.xiv, 8, 18.

20 See Badiou 2005d, pp.153–154.

21 Badiou 2004a, p.xv; see Badiou 1999, p.62; Feltham 2005, pp.xviii, xix; Wahl 1992, p.31; Brassier and Toscano 2004, p.8.

22 See Badiou 'The Scene of Two', p.2, on Badiou's play with 'I love you' reducing to 'I matheme you' in the French thus: '*Je t'aime*' / '*Je te mathème*'. Love is here described as subtractive, the lowest common denominator between a two as 'Two', not an emergent or transcendent third element fusing one and one into two. It is immanent, actual, and a non-relation ('non-rapport'). It is symbolised thus: $(u \leq M$ and $u \leq W) \rightarrow [(t \leq u) \rightarrow t = 0$, where M and W are the generic positions of 'man' and 'woman']. See also Badiou 'What is Love?', pp.39ff, where love as a process and not a sum product (of $1 + 1$) is articulated.

23 Henry 1975, p.142. See also Badiou 'What is Love?', p.40: 'no theme requires more pure logic than love'.

24 Badiou 2003a, p.93. The term 'matheme' comes from Lacanian terminology (see translator's note at Badiou 1999, p.156), and in Greek *mathema* means 'learning'.

25 Feltham 2005, p.xvii. See also p.xxiii: 'in Badiou's reading the extension of the set theoretical universe is strictly equivalent to the actual writing of each of its formulas: it does not preexist set theory itself'.

26 Badiou castigates Heidegger's linguistic exoticism at Badiou 2003a, p.48.

27 Badiou 2005a, p.34: 'the inconsistent multiple is actually unthinkable as such'; 'inconsistency' simply states that, because all thought presumes a situation that can have a consistent identity, then an event, being what ruptures a situation with inconsistency, is unrepresentable, at least for normal thought.

28 Badiou 2003a, p.184. See also p.185: 'There is no intrinsic relation between science and philosophy. Philosophy is not an interpretation of science. Philosophy is the method for organizing the discussion between science and science, science on the side of specific production and a science as a part of the thinking of being *qua* being.' However, in the following chapter we will discuss the nature of philosophy and its conditions in terms of compossibility, which will be more a spatial relation than a discursive one.

29 I will, however, provide some exposition of his mathematical ideas where necessary, but mostly in the endnotes.

30 Badiou accuses readers who proclaim any such mathematical reticence of disguised 'laziness' (Badiou 2004a, p.18), missing the point that being able to follow (with help) a mathematical proof is not the same as understanding its global significance, which needs an altogether higher level of expertise. Being able to follow an elegy by Rilke (Badiou's own comparison) is not easy either, of course, for its minimal comprehension appeals to a knowledge of German. However, the only other requirement to understand it is, *prima facie*, automatically universal, namely, being human. In other words, its significance is (at least putatively) a form of given global knowledge rather than an acquired one (even Meno's slave-boy had to be taught what he already 'knew').

31 'Let none enter here who is not a geometer' was the inscription over the entrance to the Academy. Badiou is fond of quoting Plato's interdiction (see Badiou 2004a, pp.14, 168, Badiou 1999, p.34).

32 Quentin Meillassoux asserts that Badiou's meta-ontology 'is another name for "philosophy"', but we will see that this cannot be assumed given Badiou's own idea of what philosophy is. See Meillassoux 2002, p.44n.

33 See Sherry 1988. See also Brassier and Toscano 2004, p.20, on the 'intensification and purification of thought' that *may* be consequential upon following Badiou's axioms. The issue will be whether the characterisation of this intensification and purification is not already coloured by these axioms. I suspect that they are.

34 Badiou 2005a, pp.xii–xiii; Badiou 2003a, pp.11, 12. Brassier and Toscano 2004, p.9, discount the possibility of any kind of ontological difference in Badiou, but this is surely over-stating the case given his new category in *Logiques des mondes* of existence alongside that of being.

35 Badiou 2005a, p.23.

36 The *Logiques des mondes* revises Badiou's position on appearance, but only by making a new distinction between being and existence, the latter alone concerning appearance directly.

37 Badiou 2005a, p.27.

38 Badiou 2005a, p.27.

39 'The multiple from which ontology makes up its situation is composed solely of multiplicities. There is no one. In other words, every multiple is a multiple of multiples' (Badiou 2005a, p.29). See also Badiou 2005a, pp.95–99, and p.44: there is no distinction even between elements and sets, 'all is multiple, everything is a set'.

40 Badiou 2005a, p.29; Badiou 2003a, p.15; see also Badiou 2005a, pp.41–2; p.44: 'What is counted as *one* is not the concept of the multiple; there is no inscribable thought of what a *one*-multiple is. The one is assigned to the sign $\in$ alone'.

41 Badiou 2005a, p.38. As Hallward writes: 'The extensional or "combinatorial" conception of set proceeds instead from the bottom up; such a set is simply a result, the result of collecting together a certain bundle of elements [ignoring all properties]. In contemporary set theory (and in Badiou's ontology), the extensional approach prevails, largely because Russell's famous paradox concerning sets belonging to themselves demonstrated the vulnerability of any set theory which tries to *define* the notion of set' (Hallward 2003a, p.333). The effect of paradoxes (like Russell's) was the need to abandon all hope of 'explicitly defining the notion of set. Neither intuition nor language are capable of supporting the pure multiple'. Instead, an axiom system is used.

42 Badiou 2005a, pp.44, 66.

43 If Badiou's Platonism is at the limit of naturalism, Descartes' purely geometrical *res extensa* was already heading in that direction – algebra: 'What Descartes did was to begin to eliminate the intuitive aspect of geometry, in favour of a purely numerical description of forms and curves, that is, a description that allows us to reduce the expression of a form to the calculus of its coordinates' (Hallward 2003a, p.325). In short, Cartesian geometry numerises space, the infinitesimal calculus numerises movement; and (for Badiou) set theory numerises being (while being much more than just arithmetic). But the counter-possibility of a constructivist, intuitionist theory of number remains, as we will see.

44 Badiou 2000, p.46.

45 Cited in Hallward 2003a, pp.298–299.

46 Badiou 1998, p.23; Badiou 'The Scene of Two'; Badiou 1999, p.108; Badiou 2000, p.53. See also Badiou 2004a, p.56, 'The idea that actuality is the effective form of being, and that possibility or potentiality are fictions, is a profoundly Platonic motif'.

47 See Hallward 2000, p.28. Against this form of Actualism, Henry would say that understanding does not exclude the possibility of an affective form of non-symbolic knowing. Moreover, to say that everything is actual to every intellectual point of view, which is Badiou's position, need not equate with saying that everything is actual to *some* intellectual point of view (through virtualisation).

48 Badiou 'What is Love?', p.41. Or p.51 where the noumenal 'possibility' of the human is the translator's rendering of '*virtualité*'.

49 Badiou 1994, p.55.

50 This reading has not altered during the time since Badiou published *Deleuze: The Clamor of Being* in 1997: the *Logiques des mondes* still talks of the 'eternal truth of the One' in Deleuze, of 'the One as ontological condition', or difference as only a 'variation on a theme' for him, and so on: see Badiou 2006, pp.404, 407, 406.

51 One primary objection is that Badiou thinks of Deleuzian actuality, ontical beings, as 'simulacra of Being' (e.g., Badiou 2000, p.26), that is, as representational, and so in a relationship of inequality with being (equivocal), rather than as productive and genuinely univocal. See Toscano 2000, pp.232–233. For a thorough appraisal of Badiou's relationship to Deleuze (albeit from the Deleuzian side), see Smith 2004, and for a more bi-partisan approach, see Tarby 2005, Chapter Four.

52 Badiou 2004a, pp.16, 67, 70, 72, 79, 99.

53 Brassier and Toscano 2004, p.15. They add, like Deleuze, that there can be no 'immanence *to*'. Badiou refers to the 'scission of immanence' that separates his own philosophy from the Deleuzian one (Badiou 2004b, p.235). Such a scission is not between their types of immanence, vitalist and mathematicist, but between a unitarist immanence for Deleuze (of the univocal) and a dualist one for Badiou (being and event). And yet it is Deleuze's monism that relies on the virtual *and* the actual.

54 Deleuze and Guattari 1987, p.20. Of course, this being *equals* difference for Deleuze, such that the 'sameness' *is* of one transcendental Difference. He envelopes all the different types of difference into one transcendental type. We will return to the subject of this 'transcendental Difference' (Deleuze 1994, p.86) in Chapter 4, for it is highly problematic.

55 See Deleuze 1995, pp.172–173; Deleuze 1983, pp.111–145.

56 Deleuze and Guattari 1987, p.209.

57 Colebrook 2004, p.294: 'Univocity or one being enables real difference, for difference is no longer differentiation *of* some being that is other than the differentiated'; Zourabichvili 1994.

58 Badiou 2005c, p.21. He goes on to add that 'there is no simple plurality, there is plurality of pluralities ...' but this is not any 'plurality of opinions' (p.24) – it is sheer multiplicity of being.

59 Badiou 2005e. See also Badiou 2006, p.16/Badiou 2005g, p.24, and Badiou 2000, p.98.

60 Foucault 1994, p.430.

61 See Descombes 1980.

62 Badiou 1999, p.126; Badiou 2003a, p.176: 'In *Théorie du sujet* I thought that negativity was creative in itself and I don't think that now. I think that creativity is a sort of affirmation and not a sort of negation.' That said, with the *Logiques des mondes* we see the negative dimension to novelty return to Badiou's thought – for something to appear, something else must disappear. As such, this text pushes Badiou further away from Deleuze on the subject of negativity (despite coming closer in many other areas).

63 Badiou 2003a, pp.86–87; Badiou 'Being by Numbers'.

64 Badiou 2005a, p.56; Feltham and Clemens 2003, p.16.

65 Badiou 2005a, p.53.

66 Badiou 2005a, pp.55, 86, 87, 88.

67 Badiou 2005a, pp.57–58, 69, 59.

68 Badiou 2005a, pp.77, 63, 29.

69 Henry 1988, pp.120–121. See also Henry 1990, p.177. See Deleuze 1990, p.77.

70 Badiou 2003a, p.182–183.

71 See Badiou 2004a, pp.26, 27.

72 See Hallward 2003a, pp.328ff.

73 Badiou 2005a, pp.142, 143, 145.

74 Badiou 2005a, p.148; see Badiou 2005a, pp.151–160 and pp.142–149 respectively, for the four elements of an ontology of infinity and Badiou's theory of the Other.

75 Badiou 2005a, pp.163, 168, 169, 164, 170.

76 Feltham 2005, p.xix. Badiou 2005a, p.176: 'Every radical transformational action originates *in a point*, which, inside a situation, is an evental site.'

77 Badiou 2003a, p.27.

78 See Massumi 2002, p.215, on the Deleuzian event as novelty: '... an event has transpired. Something new has arrived in the world ... a new singularity has irrupted. ... "More" has come. A new life: more to reality.' The event is excess to context (pp.216, 223).

79 Badiou 2005a, p.179 'The site is only ever a *condition of being* for the event.' But we know a site is a site only ever retrospectively (because there *was* an event). See Toscano 2000, p.223, and Lecercle 1999. p.8: the event has no duration – it has a retrograde temporality of 'after-the-event'.

80 Badiou 2000, pp.64, 91. See also Badiou 1994, p.56, Badiou's argument for the rarity of the event: Deleuze's proliferation of the event only renders it void, empty of any singular meaning: the event is simply 'whatever happens'.

81 Badiou 2005a, pp.189, 182. Badiou 2003a, p.32: an event is an unfounded multiplicity – it transgresses the 'axiom of foundation', because it is its own element 'it belongs to itself' – hence it is called 'ultra-One.'

82 Badiou 2003a, p.13. Dimitry Mirimanoff (1861–1945) called such sets that belonged to themselves 'extraordinary'. So 'an event is ontologically formalized by an extraordinary set'. The question now becomes, how can a *set* be new? And the answer is: via a generic or indiscernible set, that is, one without any possible discernible property. One can define a concept of a generic subset within a situation (amorous, artistic, political, scientific), but one cannot not know if it ever exists in that situation because it is an 'excrescent multiple' that is presented (rather than represented) at the level of the situation. A generic subset is only present through inclusion and cannot be known via any properties. When a set is modelled, its sub-sets and elements are fleshed out by giving values to the variables. If you add its generic set to this model, it is supplemented. Badiou 2003a, pp.29, 30.

83 Badiou 2005a, pp.81, 82, 84–85; Badiou 2004a, p.100; Badiou 2005a, p.134.

84 Badiou 2005a, p.175.

85 In music, for example, 'at the heart of the baroque style at its virtuoso saturation lay the absence [*vide*] ... of a genuine conception of musical architecture. The Haydn-event occurs as a kind of musical "naming" of this absence [*vide*]' (Badiou 2001, p.68).

86 Badiou, 1990, p.91.

87 Badiou 2005a, p.375.

88 Badiou 2005a, p.362.

89 Badiou 2005a, pp.379–382, 273.

90 Badiou 2005a, p.376.

91 Badiou 2005a, p.180.

92 It would be reductive or not depending on whether one's view is that explanation must always be a *simpler* discourse and so a dumbing down. By contrast, the Deleuzian event is molecular in being *and* rendering (sometimes, though, with tensions, as we saw for instance with 'atoms of womanhood').

93 Badiou 2001, p.113.

94 Badiou 2001, p.133.

95 Badiou 2003a, p.49.

96 Badiou 2005a, p.5.

97 Badiou 1999, pp.80–81.

98 Badiou 2005a, p.178. Also Badiou 2005a, p.407: a subject is 'that which decides an undecidable from the standpoint of an indiscernible. Or, that which forces a veracity, according to the suspense of a truth.' Or, p.417: 'support of a faithful forcing, it articulates the indiscernible with the decision of an undecidable'.

99 Hallward 2003a, pp.337, 339. See Badiou 2004a, p.54: Mathematics envelopes a 'coordinated movement of thought, co-extensive with being'.

100 Badiou calls this a type of 'ontological argument' (pp.372ff) where it is the name that creates the thing. So it is no longer the question of how pure mathematics, say, is possible that is then answered via the Kantian Transcendental Subject. The question is turned around: 'pure mathematics being the science of being, how is a subject possible?' (Badiou 2005a, pp.5–6).

101 See Badiou 2005a, p.379.

102 Badiou 2005a, p.xiii

103 Badiou 2005a, pp.xii–xiii; 406. Here is Deleuze: 'Experience, then, being immanent to itself and not to an individualized subject, *is thereby transcendent*. One does not ask how the subject gains its experience but how experience gives us a subject' (Deleuze 1991b, p.87).

104 Badiou 2005a, pp.397, 392. Because the subject is local, truth is equally indiscernible for him or her, because truth is global.

105 See Hallward 2003a, p.348.

106 See Lyotard 1989, pp.238, 240; Badiou 2003d, p.132. Also Badiou 2003a, p.173: 'I don't attribute the decision to the name of the event, but to the event directly and, finally, to the logical consequences of the event. ... So I am not decisionistic at all ... now.'

107 See Badiou 2006, Book VII, pp.471ff, on the topic, 'What is a Body?' See also Bruno Bosteels 2004, on the rise and fall and rise again of the dialectic across Badiou's works.

108 Badiou 2005a, p.392: 'The subject is *rare*, in that the generic procedure is a diagonal of the situation.' The subject – in its operation (p.395) – is qualified as artistic, amorous, etc., or mixed. Subjectivity can also be collective, of course, as in politics.

109 Badiou 2003a, p.28. The indiscernible and the generic are related, but the former is negative and connotes what is subtracted from knowledge, while the latter is the positive, 'what does not allow itself to be discerned' – 'what makes a hole in knowledge' (Badiou 2005a, p.327).

110 Badiou 2005a, p.15; Badiou 2003a, p.62; Badiou 2004a, p.112; Badiou 2003a, p.168; Hallward 2004, p.9; Badiou 1999, pp.106, 133, 128. But Badiou admits that philosophy does need its other, its sophist outside, to maintain its dialectic – it cannot proclaim sophism annihilated. The sophist reminds us that the category of 'Truth is void', and in Badiou 1999, pp.135ff, Badiou provides an almost frenzied (dialectical) account of how Truth must now be deployed against its sophistic other.

111 Badiou 2001, p.117; Badiou 2003a, p.173. Badiou says that he has the same conception of truth as Spinoza in his later work

112 Badiou 2004a, p.128, 53. One can force a new situation to exist – a 'generic extension' – containing the whole of the old situation and to which the generic procedure *belongs* (is presented and represented), Badiou 2005a, p.342. See also Lecercle 1999, p.8: truth is to knowledge what the event is to the situation, the former is in the latter (it has a site there) but exceeds or supplements it.

113 Brassier and Toscano 2004, p.18: Badiou clearly abandons the critical method of supplying an 'account of the generation of *doxa* or the sources of representation'.

114 Obviously, we will have to set aside Badiou's *stated* objective of dissociating philosophy from truth in pursuing this thought.

115 Kierkegaard 1992, p.106.

116 I say an implausible psychology, for how can one truly strive for what one believes *at all levels* cannot, and should not, be found? How can one believe in the existence of the impossible (an event)? Badiou often cites the end of Beckett's *Unnameable* in answer: 'You must go on, I can't go on, I will go on': see Badiou 2004a, p.133.

117 Badiou 2004a, p.114; Badiou 2005a, pp.333, 335, 340.

118 Badiou 2003a, p.31; Badiou 2003d, p.131: disaster [evil] is no longer forcing a name onto the unnamable, but making something pass from inexistence to existence. Badiou 2004a, p.115: forcing 'represents the infinitely generic character of truth in the future perfect'. See also Hallward 2003a, pp.135–139.

119 Badiou 2003a, p.61.

120 Badiou remarks on matter, extension, as 'on the border of the mathematical', at Badiou 2001, p.130.

121 Badiou rejects Deleuze's reading of Cartesian clarity as merely 'brilliance, that is as transient *intensity*' (at Badiou 2000, p.35), though Deleuze used it in order to disparage Descartes. See also Badiou 2006, p.12 / Badiou 2005g, p.22 on Descartes' funda-mental dualism as one of things and truths (a very familiar sounding formulation).

122 Henry 1973, p.475.

123 Henry 2003b, p.105.

124 Henry 1975, p.143. The irony is now for Henry given his subsequent passionate reading of Kandinsky's triangles.

125 See Badiou 2006, p.14 / Badiou 2005g, p.23.

126 Badiou 2005a, p.484n.

127 Barwise and Perry 1990, p.403. See also, for a more general overview, Barwise and Perry 1983.

128 Barwise and Perry 1990, pp.392–393.

129 Work by Gregory Bateson, Terry Winograd, and most famously Derrida, warns us of the danger of contextual representation. See Bateson 1972, p.338; Winograd and Flores 1986, p.43n7; Derrida 1982.

130 See Badiou 2004a, pp.144–145.

131 The ethical ramifications of ignoring situation qua environment will be shown later: Badiou has never had time for environmental politics (e.g. Badiou 2001, pp.106, 115), and this is not unconnected to his subtractive, decontextualising political ontology.

132 Badiou 2004a, p.221. But Hegel and Badiou are only opposed in their positioning of the subject with regards to thought (whether it is interior and antecedent or exterior and subsequent), not the value of thought *per se*, which makes Henry (and his primacy of affect) the more complete alter-ego to Badiou. Indeed, the *Logiques des mondes* is Badiou's most Hegelian text.

133 Badiou 2003d, p.124: 'Abstraction is the foundation of all thought'.

134 Badiou 2003a, p.23; Čapek 1971, p.182; Brouwer 1975, p.492; Hallward 2003a, p.326.

135 Badiou 2005a, p.249.

136 Badiou 2001, p.53.

137 Badiou 2005a, p.230: An event contravenes the axiom of extensionality – what it picks out has no contours or edge – it represents nothing and is unconstructable. Disorder. And yet it creates '*the very height of order*' for all other sets. The axiom of choice is needed to establish that every multiplicity allows itself to be well-ordered. In Sartrean terms: by his choices, man brings order and value to an inherently meaningless universe. Because Badiou, like so many Parmenideans, give us no other choice than between being or nothingness (given their onto-logical precedence over becoming), the truth emerges with a subject's fidelity to the product of an evental site, namely out of a void. (At least until the *Logiques des mondes*, whereafter degrees of existence are admitted as well).

138 Badiou 2005a, pp.193, 197–198, 202. Also Badiou 2005a, p.203: 'The act of nomination of the event is what constitutes it, not as real ... but as susceptible to a decision concerning its belonging to the situation. The essence of the intervention consists ... in naming this "there is" and in unfolding the consequences of this nomination in the space of the situation to which the site belongs'.

139 Badiou 2005a, pp.204–205.

140 Badiou 2005a, pp.207, 211, 232. In mathematics itself, the 'operators' of fidelity are (amongst others) deduction, reasoning by hypothesis, and reasoning by the absurd (Badiou 2005a, pp.240, 245ff).

141 Badiou 2005a, p.330; Badiou 2003a, p.172.

142 Hallward 2000, p.29, cites Critchley approvingly on Badiou's heroicism. Badiou also individuates the event through heroes (in his heroicism of the event), though it must be added that the names of heroes such as Cantor or Schoenberg stand as much for an individual as they do for a set of inquiries around the name of an individual.

143 Whitehead 1920, p.78.

144 Bergson 1946, pp.91ff.

145 His is a non-anthropological approach that is still, oddly enough, psychological while also being objective (or, if you prefer, beyond the objective and subjective). Contra Badiou, we are each of us already Subjects, to some more or less profound degree. See Bergson 1977, Chapter Three, and Mullarkey 2007. This theory of events being created out of traumatic encounters with processes of disaster bears comparison to Žižek's Lacanian theory of the event as something forged from an encounter with the 'undead/monstrous Thing' which he contrasts explicitly with Badiou's conception: see Žižek 2000, pp.162–163, as well as Žižek 2001, p.65, on creating meaning out of catastrophe. See also Žižek 2003, p.107: 'the materialist solution is that the Event is *nothing but* its own inscription into the order of Being' – this is Žižek's Actualist theory, albeit one couched in the Lacanian framework of 'real-imaginary-symbolic'.

146 Though some would beg to differ about this relation: see Norman Madarasz' Introduction to *Manifesto for Philosophy* (Madarasz 1999, p.4).

147 See Davidson 1980, pp.215, 221.

148 Davidson 1980, pp.163–180: pp.178–179, 163. So, following one of Davidson's own examples, if I flip a switch, and in doing that, also turn on a light, illuminate a room, and inadvertently alert a prowler in my house, it is not that there has been one event of which four descriptions could have been given (Davidson's view), but rather that there have been four events, namely the various descriptions which must be performed at different times. Description can no longer be seen as an innocent and purely speculative action. See Davidson 1980, pp.3–19.

149 Badiou does consider that fidelity might be conceived as a second event (Badiou 2005a, p.239), but leaves the matter open so as to take up the dualism of event and fidelity as his main theme. See also on this possibility taken more seriously, Düttmann 2004, p.203.

150 In fact, Badiou does at times allow that there is an element of mannerism in his theory of the event too, again resting on the function of fidelity: the 'operator of faithful connection designates *another mode of discernment*'. A mode of discernment, and not just *what* is discerned ('connection and non-connection', objective consequences . . .). See Badiou 2005a, pp.329, 180 (on 'mode' and 'manner').

151 Badiou 2003a, p.129; Badiou 2005a, pp.210, 409. Though Badiou will also say that 'equality is subjective' (for instance, Badiou 2005c, p.98) by this he means that it is not objectifiable, it is not realised in any 'empirical world' (p.99): it is subjective in the Platonic sense, ideal, yet real; an asubjective subjectivity, or a 'disinterested subjectivity' (p.100).

152 There is also the matter of *how* one is counted, of course (how does the boss count the workers' time, for example – see Badiou 2001, pp.101–102), but in a minimal matter, if '*every-one counts as one*', the most important manner of counting is surely just to be held as 'one' *qua* what might ever be counted at all, irrespective of specifics, that is, not to be absented from the count – to count 'for something, or for nothing' (p.103). But having interests (something, Badiou admits, humans share with other animals – Badiou 2005c, p.97) is not important: what must be important is what is

unique to the human: thinking, understood as that through which 'the human animal is seized and traversed by the trajectory of truth' (p.98).

153 See Badiou 2005c, p.116.

154 Badiou 2003c, p.78. He makes a similar point in Badiou 2001, p.109.

155 See Llewelyn 1991, p.263.

156 See Badiou 'The Scene of Two', pp.3–4 on the dilemmas surrounding the Christian maxim of loving another as oneself being born from the misconception that self and other are original rather than derived from a primordial two-ness. See also Badiou 2003c, pp.89–90, on the 'false love' that puts the other over the self.

157 Žižek posits universality not as a universal 'encompassing' but as 'a line that cuts universally' and so what legitimates certain discriminations (Žižek 2004). And, of course, one can define the universal in ways that will lead to limited groupings, as when preference utilitarianism defines the scope of ethics in terms of those who can have preferences or interests.

158 See Badiou 2003c, pp.2, 91, 96–97.

159 Žižek 2003, p.104. Daniel Bensaïd calls this his 'pure maxim of equality' (Bensaïd 2004, p.102).

160 Badiou 2001, pp.72, 74. Also p.65: 'The Nazi category of "Jew" served to name the German interior, the space of a being-together.'

161 Of course, vivisection continued to be practised in Nazi Germany, but we're in the realm of events-to-be here, and inaugural changes that might inspire a certain fidelity, not to National Socialism clearly, but to an aspect it might share with other movements and events. After all, they famously introduced the *autobahn*, but that has never stopped non-Nazis using the motorway.

162 Badiou 2006, pp.10, 15/Badiou 2005g, pp.20, 23.

163 Henry 1990, p.179.

164 See Badiou 1991: 'l'événement est en position de réel … Le procès de vérité est matériel … '. This materiality testifies to the material Real working in Badiou.

165 Badiou 2001, p.73. My italics.

166 This is a phrase he uses in *Logiques des mondes* to characterise what amounts to the crypto-fascism of democracy: Badiou 2006, p.10/Badiou 2005g, p.21.

167 Badiou 2005a, p.348; 'One Divides into Two', p.5; see 'Does Man Exist?', in Badiou 2001, p.11: man has an animal 'substructure, he is mortal and predatory, but this is not his distinguishing feature'. To simply be taken as one of the living, is to be '*held in contempt*'.

168 In his book on Saint Paul as the founder of universalism, Badiou points to the 'entirely human connection' between the 'general idea of a rupture' (the event) and a 'thought-practice' (Badiou 2003c, p.2): the universal here is anthropocentric, the sets it subtracts a subject from are all human — Greek and Jew, male and female, the slave and the free man (p.9). Though Greek and Jew, for instance, are not supposed to be 'objective human sets' (p.40) understood in terms of *nations* (they are actually 'regimes of discourse' (p.41), nonetheless, *as forms of discourse*, they remain human. See also Badiou 2001, p.16: 'Man is to be identified by his affirmative thought …'.

169 Badiou 'One Divides into Two', p.6; Badiou 'What is Love?', p.41; Badiou 2003a, p.71. On Badiou's 'aleatory rationalism', see Brassier and Toscano 2004, pp.13–14.

170 No less than dull and rather average Europeans were nonetheless regarded as superior to the 'the rest of the world' in virtue of their ideal rather than real status for centuries (Paul Valéry, quoted in Derrida 1992, pp. 64, 112–113).

171 Heidegger dismisses the circularity of his position rather too quickly as merely a 'formal objection' with little purchase on a concrete investigation such as his: Heidegger 1996, p.6.

172 Moreover, while Heidegger's strategy is methodologically motivated – of whom better to ask the question than the one interested in answering it? – Badiou's discounting of those who cannot count is not so simple because it implicitly derives a value (the non-ethical status of animals) from a purported fact (the non-mathematical abilities of animals).

173 See Dehaene 1997. Of course, there are differences: even the famous case of Sheba, which resolutely shows that a chimpanzee can manipulate *abstract* number – it is not a case of conditioning – is still behind the mathematical abilities of a human child. But it is not an *absolute* difference: mathematics is not unique to the human, and humans do not all have the same *actual* mathematical prowess. Indeed, 'even' rats can represent number 'as an abstract parameter that is not tied to a specific sensory modality, be it auditory or visual' (p.24). Deleuze would be proud.

174 See Badiou 2001, pp.131–133.

175 Badiou 2005a, p.353: 'Rousseau's genius was to have abstractly circumscribed the nature of politics as generic procedure.' Badiou also refers to Leibniz's genius, but, crucially, refers neither to his own genius (that is, how his philosophy is possible), nor how genius operates within generic humanity.

176 Badiou asserts that mathematics itself thinks, and does so outside of the knower/known dyad (Badiou 2004a, pp.50, 53). This is similar to the Heideggerian claim that Language speaks us rather than vice versa, but whereas Heidegger invited an ontological elitism amongst human languages (German 'speaks being'; all the others merely 'speak of being'), Badiou ignores the actual differences amongst mathematician-humans as well as the mathematical abilities of non-humans.

177 Badiou 2006, p.17/Badiou 2005g, p.24. On the question of the absence of any philosophical subject in Badiou's thought – be it Badiou or other philosophers – see Brassier and Toscano 2004, p.19. At issue is really whether philosophy generates truth, and so its own kind of subjectivity. Badiou says it doesn't.

178 Badiou 2005a, p.329.

179 See also Žižek 2000, pp.163–164 on the necessary connection between registering the event and trauma and finitude (though he puts more of an emphasis on mortality than on affect, despite the event being 'a traumatic intrusion', that is, what is registered by a being *capable of affect*, and not simply a finite, mortal being). Yet it is via Lacan that Badiou sees 'the real' as the impossible (element) of a situation – 'present but unrepresentable' (Hallward 2003a, p.14). The event is a traumatic encounter. But Badiou's subject is pure consciousness (decision, action, fidelity), not a traumatised unconscious. It is more Sartrean than Lacanian in this respect.

180 See Tye 1986.

181 Lyotard 1989, pp.230, 240. Badiou rejects this, seeing Lyotard falsely 'patheticising'

his concepts in his requirement of a 'first affect' (Lyotard 1989, pp.268, 269). But where Lyotard thinks of the affective in terms of self and 'Other' (p.238), Henry's more challenging position is of a hypersubjective affect – one that would thereby elude Badiou's refutation. See Critchley 2005 for further analysis of pathos in Badiou.

182 Brassier and Toscano 2004, p.22n1: the situation is not a perspective but the objective correlate of the 'inexistence' of a Universe.

183 Badiou 2005a, p.193; Badiou 2003b, p.21. It is Bergson's alternative view that even the least organised occurrences – randomness, chance, and luck – are perceptions mediated by our own ego's interests. See Bergson 1977, Chapter Two. In *The Clamor of Being* (Badiou 2000, p.76) Badiou contrasts his theory of the rarity of events with Deleuze's assemblage of numerous events into One Event via their conceptualisations of chance, the former again seeing it as rare, the latter as frequent. See also Brassier 2000.

184 Badiou himself has no place for either recognition or misrecognition: see Badiou 2005f, p.249.

185 Badiou's earlier *Théorie du sujet* tied novelty to destruction. In *Being and Event*, novelty is 'a supplementation by truth'. Badiou 2005a, p.408: terms can be *disqualified* though – what seemed particular may now appear general, or vice versa, what was first is now last, and so on. In *Logiques des mondes* destruction returns, only in an ancillary fashion as it regards existence and not being.

186 Badiou 2005a p.355: being is not one with truth as Heidegger claims, for truth is evental and so is not being (i.e., it is process). Yet 'there is still a *being of the truth*, which is *not* the truth; precisely it is the latter's being'.

187 Badiou 'One Divides into Two', p.7: the 'key question' of our century is that of the new, Badiou writes, 'what is the new?' And his concept of the new is processual: 'I am convinced that the new can only be thought as process. There certainly is novelty in the event's upsurge, but this novelty is always evanescent' (Badiou 2005f, p.253). See also Brassier and Toscano 2004, p.17: 'the commitment to the new ... is simply non-negotiable', and they cite Badiou saying 'the new is the just'. The new is *for* the universal as it irrupts out of there *being* no universe, no given whole (p.19). But is the new just to all, to every single thing? And if so, so what?

188 Indeed, even representation itself, the very nemesis of immanence, is inherently self-referential too, precisely in virtue of it distorting its 'object' when observing it: *its observation is a part of the whole that it observes.* That is why representations are productive, they reproduce rather than produce: the re-presentation is a presentation, or rather, re-presentation as pure repetition does not exist.

CHAPTER 4: FROM PHILOSOPHY TO NON-PHILOSOPHY: FRANÇOIS LARUELLE

1 Laruelle 1995b, p.63.

2 Badiou 2004a, p.xv; Badiou 2003d, p.131.

3 Ironically, for Badiou, 'without mathematics, we are blind': Badiou 1998, p.92.

4 If it seems unfair to Badiou to conflate axiomatics with dogmatics as I've tended to

here, we are not alone: Jason Barker concludes his analysis of *Being and Event* by asking whether its position is not 'in the end a bit too *dogmatic?*' He answers, with Badiou, that the spirit of dogmatism is the only proper mode of progress in the history of philosophy (Barker 2002, p.110).

5 Bergson 1946, pp.48–49.

6 Deleuze 1991a, pp.96, 93.

7 Deleuze 1994, p.86; Deleuze 1999, p.54.

8 Badiou 2004a, pp.111, 55 (we will discuss concepts that are really non-concepts or quasi-concepts in the next chapter). Oliver Feltham (Feltham 2005, p.xx) cites Deleuze's accusation that Badiou is guilty of analogical thinking in that it is circular, finding the structures in mathematics that he needs for his philosophy (a point made by Laruelle against all philosophy): but Feltham's counter-charge is that the accusation of imperialism (i.e. analogy as totalising) is itself analogical, mixing philosophy with politics. And if Badiou's were a metaphorical reading of set theory as ontology then he would be vulnerable to the charge of analogical thinking. But Badiou does not *interpret* mathematics as ontology, he identifies it as such. However, Feltham is incorrect, for the 'imperialism' here is solely logical, an accusation of circularity, not land-acquisition. And it can still be asked whether Badiou's identification is only an interpretation or is his *the* voice of Truth? The answer to this may have to be in the affirmative, as we'll see.

9 The view of François Wahl is that the 'philosophical operation is itself an event' (Wahl 1992, p.44). See also Brassier and Toscano 2004, p.8, though they add that the absence of any theory of the evental decision in Badiou's own philosophy may only appear as a flaw if the event is seen to ground rather than merely explain the book's opening decision to adopt an axiomatic approach.

10 Badiou 2004a, p.55.

11 See Ayer 1971.

12 See Brassier and Toscano 2004, p.3.

13 David-Menard 2002, p.21, my translation.

14 Badiou 2003a, p.33.

15 Badiou 2003a, p.49.

16 Badiou 2005a, pp.355–356.

17 Feltham 2005, p.xxvii

18 Badiou 2001, p.86: Badiou is speaking here of ontology, that is, of mathematics, of course, but it is arguable whether we can apply the same incompleteness theorem of Gödel to meta-ontology (that is, to Badiou): I am assuming, or deciding, or feeling, that we can.

19 Badiou 1999, p.37.

20 Badiou 1999, pp.126, 38, 39; Badiou 2005b, pp.14, 15. Badiou can describe compossibility as simply the temporal summation of the truths of one period, a 'measuring [of] our time' (Badiou 'Being by Numbers'). This might put one in mind of a *Zeitgeist*. The specifics of this summation is not explored in detail – it is simply an 'act' that 'displays them together'. Might this make philosophy the *Zeitraum* instead?

21 Indeed, Badiou adds that philosophy is *declarative* of there being truths – a naming.

So is its compossibility a wager, a 'dice throw' on an unpredictable future (Badiou 1999, p.138)? If so, it is because the nature of compossibility must mutate, and with it philosophy. For more on the lack of foundation for any logic of compossibility in Badiou, see Brassier and Toscano 2004, pp.7, 21.

22 Badiou 2005a, p.345 'A structure of torsion may be recognized here: *once* the general will is constituted, it so happens that it is precisely *its* being which is presupposed in such constitution'; p.360 '... what is at stake here is a torsion which is constitutive of the subject: the law of a fidelity is not faithfully discernible'; see also Badiou 1998, pp.77–78. For the diagonal, see Badiou 2005a, p.392.

23 Badiou 1999, p.126; Badiou 2006, p.15/Badiou 2005g, p.23; Badiou 'What is Love?', p.38. The notion of a point of truth is related to the 'point of being of infinity' (Badiou 2005a, pp.71, 73) already encountered, and also to the Lacanian 'punctual differentiation' and 'point of the real': see Badiou 2003d, p.120.

24 Badiou 2003a, 192. See also Badiou 'What is Love?', p.42, on the 'humanity function' that 'knots' the four types of subject, militant, scientific, amorous and artistic: hence humanity is to subjectivity what philosophy is to truth. Love is deemed the place where paradox is treated and made truth (p.43), and love is this philosophical knotting (p.51).

25 Brassier 2003b, p.24.

26 See Badiou 'What is Love?'; Badiou 2004a, pp.157–159 (also in Badiou 2005c); and Badiou 2003b, p.5. The truth procedures have 'different numericalities', but they are all of number, that is what they have in common.

27 Yet in this same interview ('Being by Numbers') he later observes that there is a 'matheme of each of the procedures' the provision of which is a task to be fulfilled.

28 Badiou 2005a, pp.355–356. See Fries 1828–1831, most notably discussed by Karl Popper in *The Logic of Scientific Discovery* (Popper 2002, pp.75ff).

29 See also Deleuze and Guattari 1984, pp.20–21 on names and circles in Klossowski's reading of Nietzsche.

30 Merleau-Ponty 1996, p.39.

31 Laruelle 1989, pp.11, 179–212, 201–203.

32 Aguilar 1995, pp.45, 39; Laruelle 1996, pp.125, 31, 57.

33 Laruelle 1996, p.253. See Kieffer 2003 and Schmid 2003.

34 See del Bufalo 2003, p.46.

35 Deleuze 1990, p.261; see also Deleuze 1995, p.156. Deleuze credits Claude Lévi-Strauss with the formulation of this dichotomy. Deleuze 1994, p.76, phrases it as follows: '*Difference lies between two repetitions*. Is this not also to say, conversely, that repetition lies between two differences ... ?'

36 Laruelle 1989, pp.7, 8, 104, 9; Laruelle 1996, p.2; Laruelle 2000, p.178.

37 Laruelle 1996, pp.3–5, 6.

38 Brassier 2003b, p.33. Laruelle 1995b, p.60: Non-philosophy is the limit [*restreinte*] of philosophy.

39 Laruelle 1998, pp.171, 172; Laruelle 'A New Presentation of Non-Philosophy', p.7.

40 Laruelle 2003, p.183; del Bufalo 2003, p.30; Laruelle 2000, p.174. See also Laruelle

2003, pp.178, 179 on the 'theoreticist idealism of philosophy'; yet non-philosophy's practice is theoretical and is not opposed to theory.

41 Laruelle 1996, p.22; Laruelle 1999b, p.147.

42 Laruelle 1989, pp.8, 99ff; Laruelle 1991, p.247.

43 Laruelle 2003, p.184.

44 Laruelle 1996, pp.v, 11, 12; on metaphilosophy, see Laruelle 1998, p.95; del Bufalo 2003, p.47.

45 del Bufalo 2003, p.42: It is a '*science première*' because, estranged from philosophy, it is 'the essence (of) the science of science'.

46 Laruelle 1996, p.22; Laruelle 1989, p.213ff.

47 Laruelle 1989, p.14; del Bufalo 2003, p.26; Laruelle 1991, p.246; Laruelle 1999b, p.144; Laruelle 1996, pp.10–11.

48 Brassier 2003a, p.170; del Bufalo 2003, p.14; Brassier 2003b, pp.29, 30. See also Choplin 2000, p.43. The unfalsifiable circularity of this is worth noting – if philosophy resists then non-philosophy is right; if it doesn't, then it is not philosophy.

49 Laruelle 1995b, p.50.

50 Choplin 1997, p.95. For comparison (especially of where they come closest to each other, Henry's auto-affection and Laruelle's Ego-in-Ego), see pp.155–158.

51 Choplin 1997 pp.96–97.

52 Kant 1929, A261-292/B316-348; del Bufalo 2003, pp.7, 51.

53 See Schmid 2003.

54 Laruelle 1999b, p.139; Laruelle 2003, pp.182, 185.

55 Laruelle 1998, p.96. This begs the question as to what the difference is between what Laruelle says of philosophy and what Kant says of metaphysics. In Laruelle 1996, p.viii, Laruelle does suggest that his method is a form of Kantian critique. And in Laruelle 1991, pp.172–174, the 'neighbours' of the non-philosophical project (version II) are said to include the Vienna Circle, Marx, Husserl, Deconstruction *and* Kant. But Kant's philosophy needs to be generalised from a critique of metaphysics to one of philosophy as such: as it currently stands it is only a 'half-psychology' and 'half-metaphysics', in other words, a *mixte* itself (Laruelle 1996, p.90).

56 Brassier 2003b, p.26.

57 Laruelle 1998, p.158; Brassier 2003b, p.32.

58 Laruelle 1998, pp.39, 158; Laruelle 1996, pp.124, 136–138, 140. Choplin 1997, p.165: Henry is still too much a philosopher for Laruelle: he remains an idealist because his 'Life still remains constitutively determined by thought'.

59 Laruelle 1995b, pp.62–63; Laruelle 1998, p.82; Laruelle 1999b, p.141.

60 Hallward 2003b, pp.17–18; Valdinoci 2001, pp.232n, 267. See also del Bufalo 2003, p.35, and Brassier 2003b, p.26.

61 Laruelle 1986, p.99.

62 For the following see Laruelle 1995b, pp.51, 53, 63, 65, 66, 72, 76.

63 Laruelle 1995b, p.66.

64 del Bufalo 2003, pp.37–38, 26.

65 Badiou 2005d, p.228n.

66 See Laruelle 1988.

67 See Laruelle 1988; Laruelle 1996, p.349. To say that thought is a thing is not yet to say that it is the Real, however, but to suggest that it is aligned to the Real in a non-representational way. As Laruelle cautions us: 'the One is not in reality "non-philosophy", this would be an ultimate philosophical decision of a neo-platonic type; it is absolutely indifferent to philosophy as much as to science, a real and not transcendental indifference'.

68 Laruelle 1999b, p.138; Laruelle 1995b, p.64.

69 Laruelle 1999b, p.141. See also Badiou 'A New Presentation of Non-Philosophy', pp.15–16: '. . . non-philosophy knows – dare I say it – the miracle, but one that has been mathematized, shorn of its theological transcendence'.

70 Laruelle 2003, p.174: 'Non-philosophy is founded in another experience of identity.'

71 Laruelle 2000, p.188. Laruelle 2003, pp.175–176: identity is not found by abstraction, it is not a symbol, though it and its effects are articulated in a 'play of symbols'. It is abstract without an operation of abstraction.

72 del Bufalo 2003, p.28.

73 Laruelle 1989, pp.61–64.

74 Laruelle 1996, p.44; Laruelle 1989, p.7; Laruelle 2003, p.177. Such is this performativity that, hand in hand with its universal ambition, the constative/performance dualism is undone, though again, should the question of the subject arise, it is a performed without performance: see Laruelle 1998, p.157. See also Laruelle 2000, pp.188–189: 'In virtue of its nature as a radical identity, it is more of the order of a kind of performative, or more exactly, a Performed-without-Performance.'

75 Laruelle 1996, p.38.

76 Choplin 2000, p.72; Laruelle 1996, p.55; del Bufalo 2003, p.40; Laruelle 1999b, pp.139–140. Laruelle 2000, p.182: 'Non-philosophy does not invert the vector of philosophy, transcendence, but substitutes the Real, the real presupposition, which is to say radical immanence, for the event's transcendent construction as part-ideal, part-real. The real presupposition is identity as such, that which is not predicated of the entity, of being, of the Other, or even of itself: an Identity of immanence, one which is non-consistent. The radical One does not consist within itself.'

77 Laruelle 1998, p.72; Laruelle 1996, pp.55, 230.

78 Laruelle 1998, p.60.

79 Laruelle 2003, p.185. The term 'determination-in-the-last-instance' is actually of Marxist-Althusserian provenance.

80 del Bufalo 2003, p.29; Laruelle 1998, pp.48, 49, 50; Laruelle 2003, p.181: 'non-philosophy is entirely oriented towards the future and, more fundamentally, it is entirely oriented towards a utopia of the real'.

81 Laruelle 2000, p.187. But such force is not to be likened to energy – it has less to do with Deleuzian forces or Henry's *idée force*, but is closer to Badiou's adventist forcing of the event, being a construction of the Real, a force-thought.

82 Laruelle 1989, p.170; del Bufalo 2003, p.38.

83 Laruelle 2000, pp.183–184.

84 Laruelle 1996, p.75.

85 Laruelle 2003, p.182; Laruelle 1995b, p.77; Laruelle 1996, pp.51, 48, 54, 21, 61; Laruelle 1998, p.83.

86 This analogy with psychotherapy has many resonances, not least with the Lacanian roots of non-philosophy, notions such as 'projection', or 'resistance' having a bearing going back to Freud. Note also Didier Moulinier's *De la psychanalyse à la non-philosophie: Lacan et Laruelle* (Moulinier 1998) and the third chapter of Laruelle's *Théorie des Étrangers* (Laruelle 1995a) on unifying philosophy and psychoanalysis as non-psychoanalysis.

87 See Badiou 2000, p.17; Deleuze and Parnet 2002, pp.1–35.

88 Badiou 'A New Presentation of Non-Philosophy', p.4; Laruelle 1988; Laruelle 1996, p.10; Laruelle 1998, p.125; Laruelle 2003, p.177; del Bufalo 2003, p.28; Brassier 2003b, p.25.

89 Conversely, perhaps non-philosophers will never understand philosophers' attempts to understand non-philosophy. Perhaps philosophy's so-called resistance is actually a projection by non-philosophy, a transference (that may also lead to counter-transference). Such re-mirroring could be interminable.

90 Laruelle 1996, p.64.

91 Choplin 2000, p.74. The One is not opposed in itself to a language in itself: there is a 'vision-in-One as matrix of thought', a 'speaking/thinking – *according to* – the One'. See also Laruelle 1999b, p.140; del Bufalo 2003, p.17.

92 Laruelle 1996, pp.77, 81; Lacan 1999, pp.118–119.

93 See Quine 1976, pp.5, 7, 12.

94 See Laruelle 1988, where Laruelle counters Derrida's '*retortion*' when the latter interpreted the former as still making classical philosophical gestures: but this is illegitimate (to non-philosophy) – it just *seems* that it too is following philosophical moves.

95 Laruelle 2000, p.179: 'more rigorous and less circular'; Laruelle 1991, p.75: philosophy is the endless proliferation 'of vicious circles, mixtes, doublets and melanges'. Laruelle 1996, p.30: 'this thought is itself, but in-the-last-instance, "in-One" or pertains to the One on its mode, immanent and non-reflective or noncircular: this is the force (of) thought'.

96 Laruelle 1971, pp.75–76. See also p.83: '*the flexuous line, which is not only the essence of nature but of the philosophical act … expresses … the movement itself of Being in its act of manifestation*'.

97 Laruelle 1971, p.91. Non-philosophy has gone through three stages, 'non-philosophy I' being co-extensive with all Laruelle's works from 1971 to 1981 (their inadequacy being that they concerned difference too philosophically). 'Non-philosophy II' (but really non-philosophy proper) begins with *Le Principe de Minorité* in 1981 and extends to *Théorie des Étrangers* in 1995, when 'non-philosophy III' appears. The transition from II to III is marked by replacing the empirical scientism of II with the true democracy of III wherein science *and* philosophy are both unified according to the Real.

98 Dominique Janicaud agrees: Bergson virtualises Ravaisson erroneously – the flexuous line is not 'behind' the visible in some ideal topology (Janicaud 1969, p.54). Whether this is fair to Bergson's reading of Ravaisson is another matter we cannot tackle here.

99 Laruelle 1971, pp. 89, 88–89, 80.

100 Laruelle 1971, pp.89, 75–77, 87, 84, 93. See also p.93: The noumenon can only manifest itself in 'a movement that twists [*se tord*] on itself'.

101 Laruelle 1971, pp.90, 92 (my italics), 247.

102 Valdinoci refers to the zigzag of non-philosophy, or '*zigzague*' of '*First Science*', at Valdinoci 2001, p.343. See also p.338. See Bergson 1946, p.110: 'Of these departures toward affirmation and these returns to the primary intuition are constituted the zigzaggings of a doctrine which "develops", that is to say which loses itself, finds itself again, and endlessly corrects itself.'

103 Laruelle 1995b, p.71; Badiou 'A New Presentation of Non-Philosophy', p.11; del Bufalo 2003, p.21.

104 Lacan 1999, pp.118–119.

105 See Badiou 'What is Love?', pp.52, 53 on woman's knotting and man's metamorphosising of four types of truth. See also Badiou 'The Scene of Two', pp.9–10.

CHAPTER 5: THINKING IN DIAGRAMS

1 Badiou 2005c, p.118.

2 See Protevi 2003, p.184.

3 Derrida 1976, pp.19, 65.

4 See Derrida 1978, p.114, where he does refer to the 'indefinite', but still thinks of it negatively.

5 I'm referring here, of course, to Derrida's further musings on drawing and self-portraiture in *Memoirs of the Blind* (Derrida 1993b). Derrida here sees drawing as a withdrawal into trace and trait. The hand that draws itself is always blinded to itself. But can't this negativity be seen as a complexity, its own constant re-drawing rather than its withdrawal? If the trace is an absence that defines a presence, a past that was never present, a blind memoir, or, in other words, a virtual memory, then this virtual too can be actualised as a memory *engramme*, a diagrammatic outline, an actual percept that is always partially (in view to) *some* perspective, never the blind spot to every *frame* of reference. Point of view is not blindness but the complex opacity that comes from being made up of *other* points of view.

6 Derrida's attraction to the negative, and ultimately to death, has been a mark of his work, as he himself explains in *H.C. for Life, That is to Say …* (Derrida 2006).

7 Bergson 1988 p.270. For the proximity of Derridian *espacement* to Bergsonian spatialisation, see Jay 1993, pp.207–208, 498.

8 See Derrida 1987, especially pp.23ff. Badiou's own artistic truth procedures clearly warrant a similar treatment as regards his figurative use of the term 'edge' in artistic evental sites being on the 'edge of the void'. Is the concept of edge doubled-edged?

9 See Newman 1994, p.219; McNeill 1999. Of course, this glimpse is also Derrida's reworking of Husserl's momentary present, a blink of an eye that is now given its own duration – see Derrida 1973, pp.49, 59 and 65. See also Derrida 1993b, p. 48.

10 The same defence would have to be made against a Wittgensteinian critique of ostensive signs, for instance at *Philosophical Investigations* §454 on the arrow (Wittgenstein 1967, p.132) – namely that the critique relies on too strong a dissociation between the

embodied action of making the drawing of the sign and the sign itself as a dead letter (that would need 'forms of life' or *différance* to disseminate it).

11 See Knoespel 2000, p.xvi, on the drawing and redrawing of figures tied to the Greek meaning of 'diagram'.

12 Kojève 1969, pp.105, 119.

13 See Mitchell 1981.

14 Dipert 1997, p.329: 'the concrete world is a single, large structure induced by a single, two-place, symmetric relation, and thus best analyzed as a certain sort of graph'; Châtelet 2000; Peirce 1933.

15 See Le Doeuff 1989.

16 For some surveys of work in this area, see: Bertin 1983; Tufte 1990; and Lynch 1991.

17 Larkin and Simon 1987, p.98. Diagrams may also be central to the mental imagery debate and possibly even Fodor's 'language of thought' thesis, both of which indicate massive problems for Sartre's position that images are not *in* the mind but are precisely what transcend the world by negating it – the 'illusion of immanence' argument – but none of these *psychologies* are relevant here: we are not interested in the question of the immanence of the diagram *to* the mind but in the diagram as immanence in itself (or not) – the immanent being of the diagram – and so its adequacy for expressing a philosophy of immanence.

18 See Latour 1987 and Châtelet 2000. See also Knoespel 2000, the introduction to Châtelet's work, on Châtelet's relation to diagrammatology, the discipline Knoespel describes as 'the phenomenological analysis of diagrams and diagrammatic practice in science' (p.ix). We think this is already a biased description, however.

19 These examples are taken from Microsoft PowerPoint: on the manner in which this format stifles the mind rather than extending it, see Tufte 2003.

20 Mark Johnson, especially, refers our spatial language back to the body (see Johnson 1987). But there is no need to privilege either the organised or dis-organ-ised body (following Deleuze). The diagram is an embodied language, only not grounded on either one actual organised (human) body, nor on the virtual, disorganised, Body without Organs. Brian Massumi, for example, typically puts the emphasis on the virtual body, or 'bio-gram'. For him (Massumi 2002, pp.189, 190) biograms are 'peripersonal' and emerge from a 'collective darkness'. For Manuel DeLanda (DeLanda 1999), we must look to 'the one and the same' topology that guides the 'morphogenesis' of different geometrical forms (p.34). And a virtual topology does not look like the geometry at all. But this forgets that there are types of actual body as numerous in levels of organisation as there are types of diagram. D'Arcy Thompson's work, for example, goes a long way to rehabilitate actual 'laws of form' in the biological sphere, work that has more lately influenced James H. Bunn in aesthetics: see his *Wave Forms: A Natural Syntax for Rhythmic Language* (Bunn 2002).

21 See Badiou 1992, pp.111, 113. This is no surprise given the spatialised unconscious present in Mallarmé's work: see Conley 1992.

22 Badiou 'What is Love?', p.52; Badiou 1982, p.243.

23 Introduced in Seminar XIX, … *ou pire*, in February 1972. See Nobius 2003, p.63. See also Lafont 2004.

24 See Lacan 1999, p.119.

25 In 'Subject and Infinity' (Badiou 1992, pp.287–305), Badiou engages with Lacan's mathematicism in *Encore* and ... *ou pire*, but only its numericity, 1, 2, and especially infinity, which he critiques as intuitionist and pre-Cantorian.

26 See Badiou 2006, p.333; Badiou 2004a, pp.173, 174.

27 Badiou 2004a, pp.175, 186, 185. The inventors of category theory, Samuel Eilenberg and Saunders Mac Lane, borrowed the concept of category explicitly from Kant and Aristotle in their paper, 'General Theory of Natural Equivalences' (Eilenberg and Mac Lane 1945).

28 Badiou 2006, p.70.

29 See Book V of *Logiques des mondes*, pp.375ff on the four forms of change: modifications, facts, weak singularities and strong singularities (or events).

30 Badiou does say that this work places 'philosophy under condition of *topos* theory' at Badiou 1998, p.125.

31 Badiou 2006, p.330. Here we have a situation initially sketched with the progressivist type of subject connected with it. A second rendering also incorporates a reactive subject (pp.331–332). The incident was the confrontation between the Mohawk Indians, the Quebec Provincial Police, and the Canadian Armed Forces near Oka, Quebec between March and September 1990, after the Oka Town Council agreed to enlarge a golf course into Mohawk sacred land. Despite many arrests and some brutal policing of the situation, the Mohawks were successful in repelling the developers.

32 See Badiou 2001, pp.136–138.

33 Badiou 1998, p.117; Badiou 2004a, p.187; Hallward 2003a, p.308.

34 Badiou 2006, pp.129, 613; Brassier and Toscano 2004, p.10; Hallward 2003a, pp.304, 297.

35 Berkeley looks within to phenomena, Category Theory looks to *topoi*. Ironically, Keith Ansell Pearson likens Badiou's treatment of the virtual in Deleuze to that of Berkeley on substance: see Ansell Pearson 2001, p.231.

36 Badiou 2006, pp.131, 140.

37 Badiou 2004a, p.110.

38 Badiou 2004a, p.110. The text that uses the pincers image, 'The (Re)turn to Philosophy Itself', was composed in the early 1990s, around the same time as the article from *Conditions* that uses the gamma diagram, 'On Subtraction'.

39 Badiou 'Being by Numbers'. See also Badiou 1999, p.124: the space of thought is also the *time* of thought – the eternal – and renouncing the eternal amounts to sophism in philosophy.

40 Hegel 1942, p.11.

41 See the section 'Diagrammes' in *Logiques des mondes*, pp.343–362, for some, but not much, theorisation on this.

42 This is a reproduction of a diagram presented at a talk by Badiou on 'Art's Imperative: Speaking the Unspeakable' at New York City, 8 March 2006.

43 Lyotard 1971, p.338.

44 Deleuze 1993a, p.81.

45 Clemens 2003, p.89. See Badiou 2006, p.577 for Badiou's reference to this excellent article.

46 Clemens 2003, p.91.

47 Badiou 2005b, p.34. Clemens uses Peter Hallward's slightly different translation from the original French at Hallward 2003a, p.369n52.

48 Clemens 2003, pp.93–94.

49 Henry 1988, pp.91, 96, 83, 85, 86, 89, 102, 120, 155, 147, 156–157, 175.

50 Deleuze 2003, p.192n. See also Deleuze and Guattari 1994, p.218.

51 Deleuze and Guattari 1987, pp.141, 142, 183.

52 Knoespel 2001: see pp.153–154 on the difference between the English and original French versions of the diagram of the Baroque house (Deleuze, *Le Pli: Leibniz et le Baroque*, Editions de Minuit, 1988, pp.7, 22). In the French they are hand-drawn by Deleuze, a significant fact given his own fascination with drawing.

53 Deleuze 2003, pp.102, 110.

54 Deleuze 2003, pp.66–67, 76–78, 85–86, 46. In *Foucault* (Deleuze 1988a, p.37), Deleuze describes how 'the diagram acts as a non-unifying immanent cause which is coextensive with the whole social field: the abstract machine is like the cause of the concrete assemblages that execute its relations; and these relations take place "not above" but within the very tissue of the assemblages they produce'. This 'within' is another subtraction, perhaps one bordering a little perilously on an essence.

55 Deleuze 1994, p.132. Deleuze will also call for a 'new image of thought', of course (e.g. Deleuze 2004, p.139), but then the issue becomes how it is *possible* that there is something wrong with the old image and something valuable about the new image.

56 Knoespel 2001, p.156.

57 Though Badiou also looks to a purported conceptual content as well as the rhetoric and thus, despite his anti-hermeneutical stance, ends up interpreting his chosen subject-matter.

58 See Perec 1969/1994.

59 See Mullarkey 2000.

60 Thanks to Alan Hook for his great work at Design, Technology and ICT, in the Institute of Education, Manchester Metropolitan University.

61 W.J.T. Mitchell (Mitchell 1987, pp.69–70) sees the diagram as partly digital, partly analogical, but then adds that 'differences in color of ink, thickness of line, shade, or texture of paper, do not count as differences in meaning. Only the position of the coordinates matters.' But the *metaphilosophical* diagram is not so Cartesian. See Pia Ednie-Brown (Ednie-Brown 2000, p.79): 'diagramming practices realise an overturning of the homogeneity of Cartesian space, perhaps this can be seen as akin to a kind of knowledge that all smooth surfaces attain texture with certain modes and levels of attention and proximity'.

62 Ednie-Brown 2000, p.78

63 Knoespel 2001, pp.150, 160–161.

64 See Michaud 2004.

65 Deleuze and Guattari 1984, p.282; Deleuze 1993a, p.125. The cone is also applied to the universe in *Bergsonism* (Deleuze 1991a, p.100).

66 Lacan 1994, p.95.

67 Merleau-Ponty 1968, p.125. In addition to the fact that Merleau-Ponty mentions only Bergson's name on this page, the reference to 'coincidence' and 'pure memory' make it clear that this is an allusion to Bergson. However, in *Matter and Memory* Bergson talks only of the 'object O' and not an 'O-point'. Merleau-Ponty may have been conflating his reference to Bergson with one to Husserl who does refer to a point 'O' in some of his famous time-diagrams from *On the Phenomenology of the Consciousness of Internal Time* (Husserl 1991), for instance, on p.98.

68 See Derrida 1978, p.151, 320n90.

69 See Ansell Pearson 2002; Lawlor 2002a; Mullarkey 2000.

70 Bergson 1988, p.116.

71 'It will be seen that the progress of attention results in creating anew not only the object perceived, but also the ever widening systems with which it may be bound up; so that in the measure in which the circles B, C, D represent a higher expansion of memory, their reflexion attains in B', C', D' *deeper strata of reality*' (Bergson 1988, p.105, my italics). This quotation seems to leave most of the work of creating depth to the subject, but it is clear that it is a process that implicates subject and object equally. As Bergson says: 'We maintain, on the contrary, that reflective perception is a *circuit*, in which all the elements, including the perceived object itself, hold each other in a state of mutual tension as in an electric circuit, so that no disturbance *starting from the object* can stop on its way and remain in the depths of the mind: it must always find its way back to the object whence it proceeds' (Bergson 1988, p.104, second italics mine).

72 In 'The Actual and the Virtual' (Deleuze and Parnet 2002, p.149), Deleuze, alluding to this very circuit-diagram of the virtual and actual, attempts to see it as a depiction of how 'the actual object becomes itself virtual', which is something of a last-gasp attempt to keep the virtual in the ascendancy. He also tries to virtualise it at Deleuze 1989, p.289n3.

73 The *object O* is certainly not the '*objet petit a*'! Analogues for this diagram can be found in other works of Bergson beyond *Matter and Memory*, in the fan-wise movement of the law of two-fold frenzy in *The Two Sources of Morality and Religion*, but also in the *élan vital*'s own enlarging concentric waves, sheafs, or steam-pressure movements of ascent and fall in *Creative Evolution*, or the zigzag movement of 'Philosophical Intuition' (in Bergson 1946).

74 See Roy 2006.

75 See Carbone 2004.

CONCLUSION

1 See Deleuze 1994, pp.33–35; Deleuze 2003, pp.111–121.

2 Deleuze 1990, p.36. It is notable that whenever Deleuze mentions Badiou, Henry, or Laruelle in his work, it is mostly to affirm their projects, no matter the differences: see for example Deleuze and Guattari 1994, pp.151–153, 218.

3 The diagram is growing, but it is not all-encompassing – its extent can only be taken in so much, and its future shape is also beyond our vision.

4 See Kundera 1985, p.8. By contrast, the 'heaviest' burden of Nietzsche's eternal return, where life's events do take on immortal significance, reflect a filling in of the sketch, a circle whose inner density comes from being eternally redrawn in the same place. For us, it has been the reason why we dissociated Deleuze's *Aion* from his process thought.

5 Henry 1988, pp.94–95.

6 Bergson 1946, p.118.

7 Alongside Laruelle and Bergson (see Bergson 1911, pp.202–203 on how 'action breaks' the 'circle of the given'), the allusion here is also to Isabelle Stengers' work (see Stengers 1997) on the recalcitrance of scientific evidence (such as of the arrow of time) to the principle of sufficient reason: Kepler himself let nature's own ellipses break the astronomic circles of Greek antiquity, whose self-evident rationality seemed impervious beforehand.

8 I'm using a special twist on the meaning of the phrase, 'turning of experience', which is the title of Renaud Barbaras' study of Merleau-Ponty, *Le tournant de l'experience* (Barbaras 1998), but also an idea Barbaras takes from Bergson's *Matter and Memory* concerning the locus of philosophy (Bergson 1988, p.185) as well as Badiou's essay 'The (Re)turn of Philosophy *Itself*' (Badiou 1999, pp.113–138).

Bibliography of Works Cited

WORKS BY DELEUZE

Proust and Signs, trans. Richard Howard, Allen Lane, 1973.

Nietzsche and Philosophy, trans. Hugh Tomlinson, Athlone, 1983.

Cinema 1: The Movement-Image, trans. Hugh Tomlinson and Barbara Habberjam, Athlone, 1986.

Foucault, trans. Seán Hand, Athlone, 1988a.

Spinoza: Practical Philosophy, trans. Robert Hurley, City Lights Books, 1988b.

Cinema 2: The Time-Image, trans. Hugh Tomlinson and Robert Galeta, Athlone, 1989.

The Logic of Sense, trans. Mark Lester with Charles Stivale, ed. Constantin V. Boundas, Columbia University Press, 1990.

Bergsonism, trans. Hugh Tomlinson and Barbara Habberjam, Zone Books, 1991a.

Empiricism and Subjectivity: An Essay on Hume's Theory of Nature, trans. Constantin V. Boundas, Columbia University Press, 1991b.

Expressionism in Philosophy: Spinoza, trans. Martin Joughin, Zone Books, 1992.

The Fold: Leibniz and the Baroque, foreword and trans. Tom Conley, Athlone Press, 1993a.

Difference and Repetition, trans. Paul Patton, Athlone Press, 1994.

Negotiations, 1972–1990, trans. Martin Joughin, Columbia University Press, 1995.

Francis Bacon: Logic of Sensation, trans. Daniel W. Smith, Continuum, 2003.

Desert Islands and other texts 1953–1974, ed., David Lapoujade; trans. Michael Taormina, Semiotext(e), 2004.

and Félix Guattari, *Anti-Oedipus*, trans. Robert Hurley, Mark Seem and Helen R. Lane, Athlone, 1984.

and Félix Guattari, *Kafka: Toward a Minor Literature*, trans. Dana Polan, University of Minnesota Press, 1986.

and Félix Guattari, *A Thousand Plateaus*, trans. Brian Massumi, Athlone Press, 1987.

and Félix Guattari, *What is Philosophy?*, trans. Hugh Tomlinson and Graham Burchell, Verso, 1994.

and Claire Parnet, *Dialogues*, trans. Hugh Tomlinson and Barbara Habberjam, Athlone Press, 1987.

and Claire Parnet, *Dialogues II*, trans. Hugh Tomlinson and Barbara Habberjam, Continuum, 2002.

Articles by Deleuze

'Letter-Preface', in Jean Clet-Martin, *Variations – La philosophie de Gilles Deleuze*, Payot & Rivages, 1993b.

'Immanence: A Life . . .', trans. Nick Millet, in *Theory, Culture, and Society*, Vol. 14 (1997), pp. 3–7.

'To Have Done with Judgement', in *Essays Critical and Clinical*, trans. Daniel Smith and Michael A. Greco, Verso Press, 1998a, pp. 126–135.

'Boulez, Proust, and Time: "Occupying without Counting"', trans. Timothy S. Murphy, in *Angelaki*, Vol. 3, no. 2 (August 1998b), pp. 69–74.

'Bergson's Conception of Difference', trans. Melissa McMahon, in John Mullarkey, ed., *The New Bergson*, Manchester University Press, 1999, pp. 42–65.

Internet Archive

Anti-Oedipe et Mille Plateaus: Cours Vincennes: Dualism, Monism and Multiplicities 26/03/1973, at http://www.webdeleuze.com/php/texte.php?cle=167&groupe=Anti%20Oedipe%20et%20Mille%20Plateaux&langue=2

WORKS BY HENRY

The Essence of Manifestation, trans. Girard Etzkorn, Nijhoff, 1973.

Philosophy and Phenomenology of the Body, trans. Girard Etzkorn, Kluwer, 1975.

Marx: A Philosophy of Human Reality, trans. Kathleen McLaughlin, Indiana University Press, 1983.

La Barbarie, Grasset, 1987.

Voir l'invisible: Sur Kandinsky, Éditions Bourin-Julliard, 1988.

Phénoménologie Matérielle, Presses Universitaires de France, 1990.

The Genealogy of Psychoanalysis, trans. Douglas Brick, Stanford University Press, 1993.

I am the Truth: Toward a Philosophy of Christianity, trans. Susan Emanuel, Stanford University Press, 2003a.

Le Bonheur de Spinoza, suivi de 'Étude sur le spinozisme' de Michel Henry, Presses Universitaires de France, 2004.

Articles by Henry

'Speech and Religion: The Word of God', trans. Bernard G. Prusak, in *Phenomenology and the 'Theological Turn'*, ed. Dominique Janicaud, Fordham University Press, 2000, pp. 217–241.

'Phenomenology of Life', trans. Nick Hanlon, in *Angelaki*, Vol. 8, no. 2 (2003b), pp.100–110.

WORKS BY BADIOU

Théorie du sujet, Seuil, 1982.

Number and Numbers, part transl. Robin Mackay of *Le Nombre et les nombres*, Seuil, 1990, at http://blog.urbanomic.com/dread/archives/badiou-numbers.pdf

Conditions, Seuil, 1992.

Court traité d'ontologie transitoire, Éditions du Seuil, 1998.

Manifesto for Philosophy, trans. Norman Madarasz, State University of New York Press, 1999.

Deleuze: The Clamor of Being, trans. Louise Burchill, Minnesota Press, 2000.

Ethics: An Essay on the Understanding of Evil, trans. Peter Hallward, Verso, 2001.

Infinite Thought: Truth and the Return to Philosophy, ed. and trans. Oliver Feltham and Justin Clemens, Continuum, 2003a.

On Beckett, ed. Alberto Toscano and Nina Power, Clinamen Press, 2003b.

Saint Paul: The Foundation of Universalism, trans. Ray Brassier, Stanford University Press, 2003c.

Theoretical Writings: Alan Badiou, ed. and trans. Ray Brassier and Alberto Toscano, Continuum, 2004a.

Being and Event, trans. Oliver Feltham, Continuum, 2005a.

Handbook of Inaesthetics, trans. Alberto Toscano, Stanford University Press, 2005b.

Metapolitics, trans. Jason Barker, Verso, 2005c.

Le Siècle, Seuil, 2005d.

Logiques des mondes, Seuil, 2006.

Articles and Interviews by Badiou

'L'Être, l'événement, la militance', interview with Nicole-Édith Thévenin, in *Futur anterieur* 8 (1991), at http://multitudes.samizdat.net/article.php3?id_article=620

'Being by Numbers', in *Artforum* (October 1994), at http://www.findarticles.com/p/articles/mi_m0268/is_n2_v33/ai_16315394

'Review of Gilles Deleuze, *The Fold: Leibniz and the Baroque*', in *Gilles Deleuze and the Theatre of Philosophy*, ed. Constantin V. Boundas and Dorothea Olkowski, Routledge, 1994, pp.51–69.

'What is Love?', trans. from *Conditions* pp.253–274, Justin Clemens, in *Umbr(a)*, (1996), pp.37–53.

'Beyond Formalisation: An Interview', in *Angelaki*, Vol. 8, no. 2 (2003d), pp.115–136.

'Afterword', in Hallward, ed., *Think Again: Alain Badiou and the Future of Philosophy*, Continuum, 2004b, pp.232–237.

'The Adventure of French Philosophy', *New Left Review*, 35, Sept–Oct 2005e, pp.67–77.

'Can Change be Thought? A Dialogue with Alain Badiou', in *Alain Badiou: Philosophy and Its Conditions*, ed. and intro. by Gabriel Riera, State University of New York Press, 2005f, pp.237–261.

'Democratic Materialism and the Materialist Dialectic', in *Radical Philosophy* 130, 2005g, pp.20–24, trans. of Section 1 from the preface to *Logiques des mondes*, pp.10–17.

'The Scene of Two', trans. from *De L'Amour* by Barbara P. Fulks, at http://www.lacan.com/frameXXI3.htm

'One Divides into Two', trans. from *Le Siècle* by Alberto Toscano, at http://www.lacan.com/divide.htm#Note%201

Unpublished Papers by Badiou

'Art's Imperative: Speaking the Unspeakable', talk at New York City, 8 March 2006.

WORKS BY LARUELLE

Phénomène et différence: Essai sur l'ontologie de Ravaisson, Klincksieck, 1971.

Le Principe de Minorité, Aubier, 1981.

Les philosophies de la différence: Introduction critique, Presses Universitaires de France, 1986.

Philosophie et non-philosophie, Mardaga, 1989.

En Tant Qu'Un: La non-philosophie expliquée au philosophes, Aubier, 1991.

Théorie des Étrangers: Science des hommes, démocratie, non-psychanalyse, Kimé, 1995a.

Principes de la Non-Philosophie, Presses Universitaires de France, 1996.

Théorie des identités, Presses Universitaires de France, 1999a.

with collaborators, *Dictionnaire de la non-philosophie*, Kimé, 1998.

Articles by Laruelle

'Controverse sur la Possibilité d'une Science de la Philosophie', in *La Décision Philosophique*, ed. François Laruelle, No.5 (1988), Osiris, pp.63–76.

'Réponse à Deleuze', in Non-Philosophie, Le Collectiv, ed., *La Non-Philosophie des Contemporains,* Kimé, 1995b, pp.49–78.

'A Summary of Non-Philosophy', trans. Ray Brassier, in *Pli: The Warwick Journal of Philosophy*, Vol. 8 (1999b), pp.138–148.

'Identity and Event', trans. Ray Brassier, in *Pli: The Warwick Journal of Philosophy*, Vol. 9 (2000), pp.174–189.

'What Can Non-Philosophy Do?', trans. Ray Brassier, in *Angelaki*, Vol. 8, no. 2 (2003), pp.173–189.

'A New Presentation of Non-Philosophy', at http://www.onphi.com

OTHER WORKS CITED

Agamben, Giorgio, *Potentialities: Collected Essays in Philosophy*, trans. Daniel Heller-Roazen, Stanford University Press, 1999.

Aguilar, Tristan, 'Badiou et la non-philosophie: un parallèle', in Non-Philosophie, Le Collectiv, ed., *La Non-Philosophie des Contemporains*, Kimé, 1995, p.37–46.

Alliez, Eric, *De l'impossibilité de Phénoménologie*, Vrin, 1995.

—— *The Signature of the World: What is Deleuze and Guattari's Philosophy?*, trans. Eliot Ross Albert and Alberto Toscano, Continuum, 2005.

Ansell Pearson, Keith, *Germinal Life: The Difference and Repetition of Deleuze*, Routledge, 1999.

—— 'The Simple Virtual', in *Pli: The Warwick Journal of Philosophy*, Vol. 11 (2001), pp.230–252.

—— *Philosophy and the Adventure of the Virtual*, Routledge, 2002.

Ayer, A.J., *Language, Truth and Logic*, Penguin, 1971.

Babich, Babette E., *Continental and Postmodern Perspectives in the Philosophy of Science*, Avebury, 1995.

Balibar, Etienne, 'The History of Truth: Alain Badiou in French Philosophy', in Peter Hallward, ed., *Think Again: Alain Badiou and the Future of Philosophy*, Continuum, 2004, pp.21–38.

Barbaras, Renaud, *Le tournant de l'expérience: Recherches sur la philosophie de Merleau-Ponty*, Vrin, 1998.

Barker, Jason, *Alain Badiou: A Critical Introduction*, Pluto Press, 2002.

Barwise, Jon, and John Perry, *Situations and Attitudes*, MIT Press, 1983.

—— 'Semantic Innocence and Uncompromising Situations', in A.P. Martinich, *Philosophy of Language*, second edn, Oxford University Press, 1990, pp.392–404.

Bateson, Gregory, *Steps to an Ecology of Mind: Collected Essays in Anthropology, Psychiatry, Evolution and Epistemology*, Ballantine Books, 1972.

Baugh, Bruce, 'Deleuze and Empiricism', in *Journal for the British Society for Phenomenology*, Vol. 24 (1993), pp.15–31.

—— *French Hegel: From Surrealism to Postmodernism*, Routledge, 2003.

Bensaïd, Daniel, 'Alain Badiou and the Miracle of the Event', in Peter Hallward, ed., *Think Again: Alain Badiou and the Future of Philosophy*, Continuum, 2004, pp.94–105.

Bergson, Henri, *Time and Free Will: An Essay on the Immediate Data of Consciousness*, trans. F.L. Pogson, George Allen and Unwin, 1910.

—— *Creative Evolution*, trans. Arthur Mitchell, Macmillan, 1911.

—— *The Creative Mind: An Introduction to Metaphysics*, trans. Mabelle L. Andison, Philosophical Library, 1946.

——*Mind-Energy: Lectures and Essays*, trans. H. Wildon Carr, Greenwood Press, 1975.

—— *The Two Sources of Morality and Religion*, trans. R. Ashley Audra and Cloudesley Brereton, with the assistance of W. Horsfall Carter, Notre Dame Press, 1977.

—— *Matter and Memory*, trans. Nancy Margaret Paul and W. Scott Palmer, Zone Books, 1988.

Bernet, Rudolf, 'Christianity and Philosophy', in *Continental Philosophy Review*, Vol. 32 (1999), pp.325–342.

Bertin, Jacques, *Semiology of Graphics*, University of Wisconsin Press, 1983.

Biletzki, Anat, 'Introduction: Bridging the Analytic–Continental Divide', in *International Journal of Philosophical Studies*, Vol. 9, no. 3 (2001), pp.291–294.

Bogue, Ronald, *Deleuze and Guattari*, Routledge, 1989.

Bosteels, Bruno, 'On the Subject of the Dialectic', in Peter Hallward, ed., *Think Again: Alain Badiou and the Future of Philosophy*, Continuum, 2004, pp.150–164.

Braidotti, Rosi 'Discontinuous Becomings: Deleuze on the Becoming-Woman of Philosophy', in *Journal for the British Society for Phenomenology*, Vol. 24 (1993), pp.44–55.

Brassier, Ray, 'Stellar Void or Cosmic Animal? Badiou and Deleuze on the Dice-Throw', in *Pli: The Warwick Journal of Philosophy*, Vol. 10 (2000), pp.200–216.

—— 'Translator's Introduction', in *Angelaki*, Vol. 8, no. 2 (2003a), pp.169–172.

—— 'Axiomatic Heresy: The Non-Philosophy of François Laruelle', in *Radical Philosophy* 121 (Sep/Oct 2003b), pp.24–35.

—— and Alberto Toscano, 'Aleatory Rationalism', editors' postface to *Theoretical Writings: Alain Badiou*, 2004.

Brouwer, L.E.J., 'Consciousness, Philosophy and Mathematics', in *Collected Works: Volume One: Philosophy and Foundations of Mathematics*, ed. A. Heyting, North-Holland, 1975, pp.480–494.

Buchanan, Ian, and Claire Colebrook, eds., *Deleuze and Feminist Theory*, Edinburgh University Press, 2000.

Bunn, James H., *Wave Forms: A Natural Syntax for Rhythmic Language*, Stanford University Press, 2002.

Čapek, Milič, *Bergson and Modern Physics: A Reinterpretation and Re-evaluation*, D. Reidel, 1971.

Carbone, Mauro, *The Thinking of the Sensible: Merleau-Ponty's A-Philosophy*, Northwestern University Press, 2004.

Châtelet, Gilles, *Figuring Space: Philosophy, Mathematics, and Physics*, trans. Robert Shore and Muriel Zagha, Kluwer, 2000.

Choplin, Hugues, *De la Phénoménologie à la Non-Philosophie. Levinas et Laruelle*, Kimé, 1997.

—— *La Non-philosophie de François Laruelle*, Kimé, 2000.

Clemens, Justin, 'Letters as the Condition of Conditions for Alain Badiou', in *Communication & Cognition*, Vol. 36, no. 1–2 (2003), pp.73–102.

Colebrook, Claire, 'Postmodernism is a Humanism: Deleuze and Equivocity', in *Women: A Cultural Review*, Vol. 15, no. 3 (November 2004), pp.283–307.

Conley, Tom, *The Graphic Unconscious in Early Modern French Writing*, Cambridge University Press, 1992.

Critchley, Simon, *The Ethics of Deconstruction: Derrida and Levinas*, Blackwell, 1992.

—— '"Fault Lines": Simon Critchley in Discussion on Alain Badiou', in Matthew Wilkens, ed., *Polygraph*, Vol. 17 (2005), pp.295–307.

Damasio, Antonio, *The Feeling of What Happens: Body and Emotion in the Making of Consciousness*, Heinemann, 2000.

David-Menard, Monique, 'Être et existence dans la pensée d'Alain Badiou', in Charles Ramond, ed., *Alain Badiou, Penser le multiple*, L'Harmattan, 2002, pp.21–38.

Davidson, Donald, *Essays on Actions and Events*, Clarendon, 1980.

de Beistegui, Miguel, *Time and Genesis*, Indiana University Press, 2004.

—— 'The Vertigo of Immanence: Deleuze's Spinozism', in *Research in Phenomenology*, Vol. 35 (2005), pp.77–100.

Dehaene, Stanislas, *The Number Sense: How the Mind Creates Mathematics*, Oxford University Press, 1997.

DeLanda, Manuel, 'Deleuze, Diagrams, and the Open-Ended Becoming of the World', in Elizabeth Grosz, ed., *Becomings: Explorations in Time, Memory, and Futures*, Cornell University Press, 1999, pp.29–41.

—— *Intensive Science and Virtual Philosophy*, Continuum, 2002.

del Bufalo, Erik, *Deleuze et Laruelle: de la Schizo-analyse à la non-philosophie*, Kimé, 2003.

Depraz, Natalie, Francesco Varela, and Pierre Vermesch, eds., *On Becoming Aware: A Pragmatics of Experiencing*, John Benjamins, 2003.

Depraz, Natalie, and Dan Zahavi, eds., *Alterity and Facticity: New Perpectives on Husserl*, Kluwer, 1998.

Derrida, Jacques, *Speech and Phenomena, And Other Essays on Husserl's Theory of Signs*, trans. David B. Allison, Northwestern University Press, 1973.

—— *Of Grammatology*, trans. Gayatri Chakavorty Spivak, Johns Hopkins University Press, 1976.

—— *Writing and Difference*, trans. with an introduction and notes Alan Bass, Routledge, 1978.

—— 'Signature, Event, Context', in Jacques Derrida, *Margins of Philosophy*, trans. Alan Bass, Harvester Press, 1982, pp.307–330.

—— *The Truth in Painting*, trans. Geoff Bennington and Ian McLeod, University of Chicago Press, 1987.

—— *Glas*, trans. John P. Leavey and Richard Rand, Nebraska University Press, 1990.

—— *The Other Heading: Reflections on Today's Europe*, trans. Pascale-Anne Brault and Michael B. Naas, Indiana University Press, 1992.

—— *Aporias*, trans. Thomas Dutoit, Stanford University Press, 1993a.

—— *Memoirs of the Blind*, trans. Pascale-Anne Brault and Michael Naas, University of Chicago Press, 1993b.

—— *On Touching: Jean-Luc Nancy*, Stanford University Press, 2005.

—— *H.C. for Life, That is to Say …*, trans. Laurent Milesi and Stefan Herbrechter, Stanford University Press, 2006.

Descombes, Vincent, *Modern French Philosophy*, trans. L. Scott-Fox and J.M. Harding, Cambridge University Press, 1980.

Dipert, Randall, 'The Mathematical Structure of the World: The World as Graph', in *Journal of Philosophy* XCIV, no. 7 (July 1997), pp. 329–358.

Dummett, Michael, *Elements of Intuitionism*, Clarendon Press, 1977.

Düttmann, Alexander Garcia, 'What Remains of Fidelity After Serious Thought?', in Peter Hallward, ed., *Think Again: Alain Badiou and the Future of Philosophy*, Continuum, 2004, pp. 202–207.

Ednie-Brown, Pia, 'The Texture of Diagrams', *Daidalos; Diagrammania* 74 (2000), pp. 72–79.

Eilenberg, Samuel, and Saunders Mac Lane, 'General Theory of Natural Equivalences', *Transactions of the American Mathematical Society*, Vol. 58 (1945), pp. 231–244.

Feltham, Oliver, 'Translator's Preface', in Alain Badiou, *Being and Event*, Continuum, 2005, pp. xvii–xxxiii.

—— and Justin Clemens, 'An Introduction to Alain Badiou's Philosophy', in *Infinite Thought: Truth and the Return to Philosophy*, ed. and trans. Oliver Feltham and Justin Clemens, Continuum, 2003, pp. 1–38.

Forthomme, Bernard, 'L'Epreuve affective de l'autre selon Emmanuel Levinas et Michel Henry', in *Revue de Métaphysique et de Morale* (1986), pp. 90–114.

Foucault, Michel, *Dits et Écrits*, tome III, Gallimard, 1994.

Fries, Jakob Friedrich, *Neue oder anthropologische Kritik der Vernunft*, second edition, 1828–1831.

Grene, Marjorie, *Philosophy In and Out of Europe*, University of California Press, 1976.

Grosz, Elizabeth, 'A Thousand Tiny Sexes: Feminism and Rhizomatics', in *Gilles Deleuze and the Theatre of Philosophy*, ed. Constantin V. Boundas and Dorothea Olkowski, Routledge, 1994, pp. 187–210.

Guattari, Félix, *Molecular Revolution: Psychiatry and Politics*, trans. R. Sheed, Penguin, 1984.

Guillmard, Patrice, 'L'Autre et l'immanence: Étude comparée sur les ontologies de Michel Henry et Emmanuel Levinas', in *Revue de Métaphysique et de Morale* (1999), pp. 251–272.

Gunter, P.A.Y., 'Review of Keith Ansell Pearson, *Philosophy and the Adventure of the Virtual: Bergson and the Time of Life,*' forthcoming in *Philosophia* (Israel), Vol. 34, no. 2 (2007).

Hallward, Peter, 'Ethics without Others: A Reply to Critchley on Badiou's Ethics', in *Radical Philosophy* 102 (July/August 2000), pp. 27–30.

—— *Badiou: A Subject to Truth*, University of Minnesota Press, 2003a.

—— ed., *The One or the Other: French Philosophy Today: Special Issue of Angelaki*, Vol. 8, no. 2 (2003).

—— 'Editorial Introduction', in Peter Hallward, ed., *Angelaki*, Vol. 8, no. 2 (2003b), pp. 1–32.

—— ed., *Think Again: Alain Badiou and the Future of Philosophy*, Continuum, 2004.

—— 'Introduction: Consequences of Abstraction', in Peter Hallward, ed., *Think Again: Alain Badiou and the Future of Philosophy*, Continuum, 2004, pp.1–20.

Hass, Lawrence and Dorothea Olkowski, eds., *Resituating Merleau-Ponty: Essays Across the Analytic-Continental Divide*, Prometheus Press, 2000.

Hegel, G.W.F., *The Philosophy of Right*, trans. T.M. Know, Clarendon Press, 1942.

Heidegger, Martin, 'The End of Philosophy and the Task of Thinking', in *Basic Writings*, ed. D.F. Krell, second edn, Routledge, 1993, pp.431–449.

—— *Being and Time*, trans. Joan Stambaugh, State University of New York Press, 1996.

Hume, David, *Enquiries Concerning Human Understanding and Concerning the Principles of Morals*, Selby-Bigge edn, Clarendon Press, 1975.

Husserl, Edmund, *On the Phenomenology of the Consciousness of Internal Time*, trans. John Barnett Brough, Kluwer Academical Press, 1991.

Irigaray, Luce, *This Sex Which Is Not One*, trans. Catherine Porter with Carolyn Burke, Cornell University Press, 1985.

Janicaud, Dominique, *Une Genealogie Du Spiritualisme Français*, Nijhoff, 1969.

—— *Phenomenology and the 'Theological Turn': The French Debate*, trans. Bernard G. Prusak, Fordham University Press, 2000.

—— *Heidegger en France*, Vols. I et II, Albin Michel, 2001.

Jay, Martin, *Downcast Eyes: The Denigration of Vision in Twentieth-Century French Thought*, University of California Press, 1993.

Johnson, Mark, *The Body in the Mind: The Bodily Basis of Meaning, Imagination, and Reason*, University of Chicago Press, 1987.

Kant, Immanuel, *Critique of Pure Reason*, trans. Norman Kemp Smith, Macmillan, 1929.

Kelly, Michael, 'Dispossession: On the Untenability of Michel Henry's Theory of Self-Awareness', in *Journal for the British Society for Phenomenology* 35 (2004), pp.261–282.

Kerslake, Christian, 'The Vertigo of Philosophy: Deleuze and the Problem of Immanence', in *Radical Philosophy* 113 (2002), pp.10–23.

Kieffer, Gilbert, 'Le postulat premier de la non-esthétique future', paper given at 'Non-philosophy Now' conference, Middlesex, November 2003. http://www.onphi.com

Kierkegaard, Søren, *Concluding Unscientific Postscript to Philosophical Fragments*, two volumes, ed. and trans. Howard V. Hong and Edna H. Hong, Princeton, 1992.

Knoespel, J. Kenneth, 'Diagrammatic Writing and the Configuration of Space', introduction to Gilles Châtelet, *Figuring Space: Philosophy, Mathematics, and Physics*, trans. Robert Shore and Muriel Zagha, Kluwer, 2000, pp.ix–xxiii.

—— 'Diagrams as Piloting Devices in the Philosophy of Gilles Deleuze', in *Deleuze-chantier*, special edition of *Théorie – Littérature – Enseignment*, no. 19 (2001), pp.145–165.

Kojève, Alexandre, *Introduction to the Reading of Hegel*, trans. James H. Nichols, Jr., Cornell University Press, 1969.

Kundera, Milan, *The Unbearable Lightness of Being*, trans. Michael Henry Heim, Faber and Faber, 1985.

Lacan, Jacques, *The Four Fundamental Concepts of Psycho-analysis*, ed. Jacques-Alain Miller, trans. Alan Sheridan, Penguin, 1994.

—— *Encore: The Seminar of Jacques Lacan Book XX*, trans. Bruce Fink, Norton, 1999.

Lafont, Jeanne, 'Topology and Efficiency', in *Lacan: Topologically Speaking*, ed. Ellie Ragland and Dragan Milovanovic, Other Press, 2004, pp. 3–27.

Lambert, Gregg, 'What the Earth Thinks', in Ian Buchanan and Gregg Lambert, eds., *Deleuze and Space*, Edinburgh University Press, 2005, pp. 220–239.

Larkin, J., and H. A. Simon, 'Why a Diagram is (Sometimes) Worth Ten Thousand Words', in *Cognitive Science*, Vol. 11 (1987), pp. 65–99.

Latour, Bruno, *Science in Action*, Harvard University Press, 1987.

Lawlor, Leonard, 'The End of Ontology: Interrogation in Merleau-Ponty and Deleuze', in *Chiasmi International*, Vol. 1, Vrin/Mimesis/University of Memphis, (1999), pp. 233–251.

—— *The Challenge of Bergson*, Continuum, 2002a.

—— *Derrida and Husserl: The Basic Problem of Phenomenology*, Indiana University Press, 2002b.

—— *Thinking Through French Philosophy: The Being of the Question*, Indiana University Press, 2003.

—— 'What Immanence? What Transcendence? The Prioritization of Intuition over Language in Bergson', in *Journal for the British Society for Phenomenology*, Vol. 35, no. 1 (2004), pp. 24–41.

Lazzarato, Maurizio, 'Immaterial Labour', in Michael Hardt and Paolo Virno, eds., *Radical Thought in Italy: A Potential Politics*, University of Minnesota Press, 1996, pp. 133–147.

Lecercle, Jean Jacques, 'Cantor, Lacan, Mao, Beckett, *même* combat', in *Radical Philosophy* 93 (Jan 1999), pp. 6–13.

Leclercq, Stéfan, *Gilles Deleuze: Immanence, Univocité et Transcendental*, Les Éditions Sils Maria, 2003.

Le Doeuff, Michèle, *The Philosophical Imaginary*, trans. Colin Gordon, Athlone Press, 1989.

Levinas, Emmanuel, *Otherwise Than Being or Beyond Essence*, trans. Alphonso Lingis, Nijhoff, 1981.

Llewelyn, John, *The Middle Voice of Ecological Conscience: A Chiasmic Reading of Responsibility in the Neighbourhood of Levinas, Heidegger and others*, Macmillan, 1991.

Longneaux, Jean-Michel, 'Étude sur le spinozisme de Michel Henry', in Michel Henry, *Le Bonheur de Spinoza, suivi de 'Étude sur le spinozisme' de Michel Henry*, Presses Universitaires de France, 2004.

Lynch, Michael, 'Pictures of Nothing? Visual Construals in Social Theory', in *Sociological Theory*, Vol. 9, no. 1 (1991), pp. 1–21.

Lyotard, Jean-François, *Discours, figure*, Klincksieck, 1971.

—— 'Alain Badiou, *L'Être et l'événement*', in *Le Cahiers du Collège Internationale de Philosophie*, Vol. 8 (1989), pp.227–245.

Madarasz, Norman, 'Translator's Introduction', in Alain Badiou, *Manifesto for Philosophy*, trans. Norman Madarasz, State University of New York Press, 1999, pp.3–23.

Margolis, Joseph, 'A Sense of "Rapprochement" Between Analytic and Continental Philosophy', in *History of Philosophy Quarterly*, Vol. II (1985), pp.217–231.

Massumi, Brian, *A User's Guide to Capitalism and Schizophrenia: Deviations from Deleuze and Guattari*, MIT Press, 1992.

—— *Parables for the Virtual*, Duke University Press, 2002.

Matte Blanco, Ignacio, *The Unconscious as Infinite Sets: An Essay in Bi-Logic*, Duckworth, 1975.

May, Todd, 'The Politics of Life in the Thought of Gilles Deleuze', in *SubStance*, Vol. 66 (1991), pp.24–35.

—— 'Difference and Unity in Gilles Deleuze', in Constantin V. Boundas and Dorothea Olkowski, eds., *Gilles Deleuze and the Theatre of Philosophy*, Routledge, 1994, pp.33–50.

—— 'Badiou and Deleuze on the One and the Many', in Hallward, ed., *Think Again: Alain Badiou and the Future of Philosophy*, Continuum, 2004, pp.67–76.

McNeill, William, *The Glance of the Eye: Heidegger, Aristotle, and the Ends of Theory*, State University of New York Press, 1999.

Meillassoux, 'Nouveauté et évenément', in Charles Ramond, ed., *Alain Badiou, Penser le multiple*, L'Harmattan, 2002, pp.39–64.

Merleau-Ponty, Maurice, *Phenomenology of Perception*, trans. Colin Smith, Routledge & Kegan Paul, 1962.

—— *The Structure of Behaviour*, trans. Alden L. Fisher, Beacon Press, 1963.

—— 'The Primacy of Perception and its Philosophical Consequences', trans. James M. Edie, in Maurice Merleau-Ponty, *The Primacy of Perception*, Northwestern University Press, 1964, pp.12–42.

—— *The Visible and the Invisible: Followed by Working Notes*, trans. Alphonso Lingis, Northwestern University Press, 1968.

—— *Notes de Cours 1959–1961*, Gallimard, 1996.

Michaud, Philippe-Alain, *Aby Warburg and the Image in Motion*, trans. Sophie Hawkes, Zone Books, 2004.

Mitchell, W.J.T, 'Diagrammatology', in *Critical Inquiry* 7:2 (Spring 1981), pp.622–633.

—— *Iconology: Image, Text, Ideology*, University of Chicago Press, 1987.

Moulinier, Didier, *De la psychanalyse à la non-philosophie: Lacan et Laruelle*, Kimé, 1998.

Morris, David, *The Sense of Space*, State University of New York Press, 2004.

Mullarkey, John, 'Deleuze and Materialism: One or Several Matters?', in *A Deleuzian Century?*, ed. Ian Buchanan, Duke University Press, 1999, pp.59–83.

—— *Bergson and Philosophy*, Notre Dame University Press, 2000.

—— 'Creative Metaphysics and the Metaphysics of Creativity', in *Bergson Now*, special issue of the *Journal of the British Society for Phenomenology*, ed. John Mullarkey and Stephen Linstead, Vol. 35, no. 1 (January 2004), pp.68–81.

—— 'Forget the Virtual: Bergson, Actualism, and the Refraction of Reality', in *Continental Philosophy Review*, Vol. 37 (2005), pp.469–493.

—— 'The Gift of Movement: Film, Philosophy, and the Fabulation of Life', forthcoming in *Theory, Culture, and Society*, 2007.

Mulligan, K., 'Post-Continental Philosophy: Nosological Notes', *Stanford French Review* 17 (1993), pp.133–150.

Nagel, Thomas, 'What is it Like to be a Bat?' (1974), in Thomas Nagel, *Mortal Questions*, Cambridge University Press, 1979, pp.165–180.

Newman, Michael, 'Derrida and the Scene of Drawing', in *Research in Phenomenology*, Vol. 24 (Fall 1994), pp.218–234.

Nietzsche, Friedrich, *Gay Science*, trans. Walter Kaufmann, Vintage, 1974.

Nobius, Dany, 'Lacan's Science of the Subject: Between Linguistics and Topology', in Jean-Michel Rabaté, ed., *The Cambridge Companion to Lacan*, Cambridge University Press, 2003, pp.50–68.

Owens, Joseph, 'Analytic and Continental Philosophy in Overall Perspective', in *Modern Schoolman*, Vol. LXX (1993), pp.131–142.

Papineau, David, *Philosophical Naturalism*, Blackwell, 1993.

Parr, Adrian, ed., *The Deleuze Dictionary*, Edinburgh University Press, 2005.

Patton, Paul, ed., *Deleuze: A Critical Reader*, Blackwell, 1996.

Peirce, C.S, *Collected Papers*, Harvard University Press, 1933.

Perec, Georges, *La Disparition*, Denoël, 1969; trans. Gilbert Adair as *A Void*, Harvill, 1994.

Petitot, J. et al, *Naturalizing Phenomenology*, Stanford University Press, 1999.

Popper, Karl, *The Logic of Scientific Discovery*, Routledge 2002.

Protevi, John, *Political Physics*, Continuum, 2001.

—— 'Love', in Paul Patton and John Protevi, eds., *Between Deleuze and Derrida*, Continuum 2003, pp.183–194.

Prusak, Bernard G., 'Translator's Introduction', in Dominique Janicaud, *Phenomenology and the 'Theological Turn': The French Debate*, trans. Bernard G. Prusak, Fordham University Press, 2000, pp.3–15.

Quine, W.V.O., *The Ways of Paradox and Other Essays*, Harvard University Press, 1976.

Radcliffe, Matthew, 'Husserl and Nagel on Subjectivity and the Limits of Physical Objectivity', in *Continental Philosophy Review*, Vol. 35, no. 4 (2002), pp.353–377.

Ravaisson, Félix, *L'art et les mystères grecs*, Éditons de L'herne, 1985.

Reichenbach, Hans, *The Rise of Scientific Philosophy*, University of California Press, 1959.

Rockmore, Tom, *Heidegger and French Philosophy: Humanism, Antihumanism, and Being*, Routledge, 1995.

Roy, Tony, 'What's So Bad with Infinite Regress?', 2006, draft article at http://cal.csusb.edu/Faculty/Philosophy/roy/regress-pap.pdf

Sartre, Jean-Paul, *Imagination: A Psychological Critique*, trans. Forrest Williams, University of Michigan, 1962.

Sasso, Robert, and Arnaud Villani, eds., *Le Vocabulaire de Gilles Deleuze*, no. 3 in series *Le Cahier de Noesis*, Vrim, 2003.

Schmid, Anne-Françoise, 'The Hypothesis of a Non-Epistemology', paper given at 'Non-philosophy Now' Conference, Middlesex, November 2003, at http://www.onphi.com

Sellars, John, 'The Point of View of the Cosmos: Deleuze, Romanticism, Stoicism', in *Pli: The Warwick Journal of Philosophy*, Vol. 8 (1999), pp. 1–24.

Shaviro, Steven, *The Cinematic Body*, University of Minnesota Press, 1993.

Sherry, David M., 'Zeno's Metrical Paradox Revisited', in *Philosophy of Science*, Vol. 55 (1988), pp. 58–73.

Smith, Dan, 'Badiou and Deleuze on the Ontology of Mathematics', in Hallward, ed., *Think Again: Alain Badiou and the Future of Philosophy*, Continuum, 2004, pp. 77–93.

Smith, Quentin, 'The Infinite Regress of Temporal Attributions', in L. Nathan Oaklander and Quentin Smith, eds., *The New Theory of Time*, Yale University Press, 1994, pp. 180–194.

Sokal, Alan and Jean Bricmont, *Intellectual Impostures*, Profile Books, 1998.

Spinoza, Baruch, *Ethics*, ed. and trans. Samuel Shirley, Hackett, 1992.

Stengers, Isabelle, 'Breaking the Circle of Sufficient Reason', in Isabelle Stengers, *Power and Invention: Situating Science*, trans. Paul Bains, University of Minnesota Press, 1997, pp. 21–30.

Tarby, Fabien, *Matérialismes d'aujourd'hui: de Deleuze à Badiou*, L'Harmattan, 2005.

Terada, Rei, *Feeling in Theory: Emotion after the 'Death of the Subject'*, Harvard University Press, 2001.

Tillette, Xavier, 'Une Nouvelle monadologie: le philosophie de Michel Henry', in *Gregorianum*, Vol. 61 (1980), pp. 633–651.

Toscano, Alberto, 'To Have Done with the End of Philosophy', in *Pli: The Warwick Journal of Philosophy*, Vol. 9 (2000), pp. 220–238.

Tranoy, Eric K., 'Contemporary Philosophy – Analytic and Continental', in *Philosophy Today*, Vol. VIII (1964), pp. 155–168.

Tufte, Edward R., *Envisioning Information*, Graphics Press, 1990.

—— *The Cognitive Style of PowerPoint*, Graphics Press, 2003.

Tye, Michael, 'The Subjective Qualities of Experience', in *Mind*, Vol. XCV (1986), pp. 1–17.

Valdinoci, Serge, *L'Europanalyse et les structures d'une autre vie*, L'Harmattan, 2001.

Vieillard-Baron, Jean-Louis, *Bergson*, Presses Universitaires de France, 1993.

Wahl, François, 'Le Soustractif', preface to Alain Badiou, *Conditions*, Seuil, 1992, pp. 9–54.

Whitehead, Alfred North, *The Concept of Nature*, Cambridge University Press, 1920.

—— *Process and Reality*, corrected edn, David Ray Griffin and Donald W. Sherburne, eds., Free Press, 1978.

Williams, James, *Gilles Deleuze's* Difference and Repetition: *A Critique and Commentary*, Edinburgh University Press, 2003.

——*The Transversal Thought of Gilles Deleuze: Encounters and Influences*, Clinamen Press, 2005.

Winograd, Terry and Fernando Flores, *Understanding Computers and Cognition*, Ablex, 1986.

Wittgenstein, Ludwig, *Tractatus Logico-Philosophicus*, trans. D.F. Pears and B.F. McGuinness, Routledge & Kegan Paul, 1961.

—— *Philosophical Investigations*, trans. G.E.M. Anscombe and R. Rhees, Blackwell, 1967.

—— 'Philosophy', in Paul Moser and Dwayne Mulder, eds., *Contemporary Approaches to Philosophy*, Macmillan, 1994, pp.125–140.

Wood, David, *The Deconstruction of Time*, Humanities Press, 1989.

Worms, Frédéric, ed., *Le Vocabulaire de Bergson*, Ellipses, 2000.

—— ed., *Le moment 1900 en philosophie*, Presses Universitaires du Septentrion, 2004.

Yamagata, Yorihiro, 'Cosmos and Life, According to Henry and Bergson', in *Continental Philosophy Review*, Vol. 32 (1999), pp.241–253.

—— 'L'Immanence et le mouvement subjectif', in Alain David and Jean Greish, eds., *Michel Henry, L'Épreuve de la Vie*, Cerf, 2000, pp.129–140.

Zahavi, Dan, 'Michel Henry and the Phenomenology of the Invisible', in *Continental Philosophy Review*, vol.32, (1999), pp.223–240.

Zaner, Richard, M., *The Problem of Embodiment: Some Contributions to a Phenomenology of the Body*, Martinus Nijhoff, 1971.

Žižek, Slavoj, *The Ticklish Subject: The Absent Centre of Political Ontology*, Verso, 2000.

—— *Did Somebody Say Totalitarianism? Four Interventions in the (Mis)use of a Notion*, Verso, 2001.

—— 'The Matrix: Or, the Two Sides of Perversion', in *The 'Matrix' and Philosophy: Welcome to the Desert of the Real*, Open Court Publishing 2002, pp.240–266.

—— *Organs Without Bodies: On Deleuze and Consequences*, Routledge, 2003.

——'An Interview with Slavoj Žižek: 'On Divine Self-Limitation and Revolutionary Love', in *Journal of Philosophy & Scripture* (Spring 2004), at http://www.lacan.com/zizekscripture.htm

Zourabichvili, François, *Deleuze: Une philosophie de l'événement*, Presses Universitaires de France, 1994.

—— 'Deleuze et le possible, de l'involuntarisme en politique', in Alliez, Eric, ed., *Gilles Deleuze: Une vie philosophique*, Institute Synthélabo, 1998, pp.335–357.

Index